Breaking the Thread of Life

Breaking the Thread of Life

ON RATIONAL SUICIDE

Robert L. Barry

Transaction Publishers
New Brunswick (U.S.A.) and London (U.K.)

Library of Congress Catalog Number: 93-36053
ISBN: 1-56000-142-9
Printed in the United States of America

Library of Congress Cataloging-in-Publication Data

Barry, Robert Laurence.
Breaking the thread of life: on rational suicide/Robert Barry.
p. cm.
Includes bibliographical references and index.
ISBN 1-56000-142-9 (cloth)
1. Right to die. 2. Suicide—Moral and ethical aspects. 3. Suicide—Religious aspects—Catholic Church. 4. Catholic Church—Doctrines. 5. Assisted suicide. I. Title.
R726.B288 1994
241'.697—dc20 93-36053
CIP

Contents

Preface

With the emergence of the AIDS epidemic, *de facto* legalization of widespread assisted suicide in Holland and the introduction and defeat of "aid-in-dying" referenda introduced by the Hemlock Society in California, Washington, Oregon, and then again in California, controversy has grown over legally, morally, and socially endorsing rational suicide.[1] Increasingly, many people, including AIDS patients, are questioning whether suicide should be considered a morally legitimate option as they confront their death. In both Europe and America, debates about the morality of permitting voluntary euthanasia, or assisted suicide, are developing because of new perspectives on patient autonomy, the care and treatment of patients, and because of the increasing cost of providing high quality health care. The sharpness of these debates has also grown with the emergence of an international right-to-die movement and with increasing concerns over the economic efficiency of the international health care system. Voluntary suicide is the first choice of the international euthanasia movement as there are fewer legal, familial, or social obstacles than to involuntary euthanasia and it is easier to gain public endorsement of it. In response to this "right-to-die" rhetoric and demands for compassion, the morality and rationality of suicide has become quite popular, and in many circles, both in the popular and academic press, suicide has gained favor and broad appeal.

This book arose from concern over the mounting campaign not only in our nation, but also throughout the world, to give legal endorsement to suicide. As my understanding of the issue grew I not only learned how immensely difficult and complex the topic was, but also how much the traditional Catholic faith had contributed to the control of suicide in Western society. As my research broadened and deepened, I came to realize that the Catholic church probably did more than any other institution throughout Western history to curb suicide. At the present time, the traditional teachings and practice of the Catholic church on this issue is under sharp and, in many instances, unfair assault and my purpose is to trace their development and show their validity. In contrast to what these emerging trends in our society and in the world are asserting, the classical Catholic teachings have argued consistently and vigorously against allowing rational suicide. The Catholic church's condemnation of suicide has prompted accusations that these teachings lack both rationality and compassion, and it has been accused of standing against the traditions of our free society by holding that people can be forced to continue living against their wills and without their consent. It is charged with mistaking legitimate acts of privacy, free choice, autonomy, and self-determination with morally objectionable actions.

A great deal of gratitude is in order to many people. I must thank the Campus Honors Program and the Program for the Study of Religion of the University of Illinois for their support while writing this book. And the students and staff of the Newman Foundation also deserve much gratitude for the help, comfort, and support during this long project.

Acknowledgments

I would like to express my appreciation and gratitude to the editors and publishers of those journals who so willingly gave me permission to reprint within the covers of this book material that had originally appeared in their publications: chapter 7, "Indirectly Intended Analgesic Suicide: Clarifying the Issues," was reprinted with appropriate changes by permission of the publisher, *Issues in Law and Medicine*, vol. 6, no. 2, Fall 1990. Copyright © 1990 by the National Legal Center for the Medically Dependant and Disabled, Inc. I originally wrote this article and it was reviewed by Dr. James Maher, M.D. and initially entitled "Indirectly Intended Life-Shortening Analgesia: Clarifying the Principles."

Introduction: The New Face of Suicide

In 1987, Louise Orr was recuperating in a nursing home from a stroke. She and her husband, Richard, had been married for fifty-six years, and Richard came to see her every day while she was in the hospital. On 22 February 1987, he came to see her, and no one in the hospital thought there was anything peculiar about his visit. However, that morning, Mr. Orr shot Louise, apparently at her request.[1] Their son Robert said it came as a total shock, and he was totally unaware of the loneliness and despair from which they were suffering.

On 27 April 1987, police in Tucson, Arizona found former University of Illinois assistant football coach John Tarwain and his wife Amelia dead in their home, their deaths apparently resulting from a suicide pact.[2] Both in their eighties, they had consumed a prescription sedative and alcohol before putting plastic bags over their heads. Shortly before they died, John wrote a letter to the Arizona *Daily Star* urging legalization of voluntary mercy killing.[3] In recent years, they had become increasingly debilitated, as he suffered from heart disease and bladder cancer and she developed worsening Alzheimer's disease. The Tarwains had been longtime associates of Derek Humphry of the Hemlock Society, who had referred to their deaths as "self-deliverance."

In Princeton, New Jersey, seventy-five-year-old Rutgers University professor Richard Schlatter shot and killed himself to spare his family the pain and suffering of seeing him die from cancer.[4] And in Sun City, Arizona, seventy-two-year-old postman Joseph Wiseman shot himself and his wife, apparently for the same reasons.[5] Almost identical cases have been reported in a number of cities across the country, and suicide rates among the elderly are significantly higher than among the young. There have been many predictions by experts that suicide rates among the elderly will increase dramatically in the near future.[6]

"Mary Jane" wrote in *USA Today* that she and her husband have talked seriously between themselves and with their children of hiring an assassin to end their lives if they should become seriously ill or suffer from a grave debilitating disease.[7] They said they had heard of so many people who suffered from severe and prolonged pain in their latter years, or who found themselves living in a state of mental or emotional exhaustion, that they decided that they would not want to continue living in such a condition. Being killed quickly, painlessly, and without warning seemed almost kind to them.

In Underwood, Minnesota, seventy-one-year-old Walter Lund applied for permission to establish a resort where the elderly, terminally ill, and dying could come to commit suicide and "die in a dignified manner." Calling his spa "The Last Resort," Lund believed that it would be a "dignified place to die" and it would provide legal services, including facilities for the survivors who come there to remember those who suicided there.[8] A house legal officer would take care of last-minute legal affairs, and arrangements could be made for funerals, coffins, ministers, and music. However, this proposal was turned down by the town council and Minnesota courts persisted in holding that assisting a suicide carried at least a seven-year jail term and a $14,000 fine. And while the "Last Resort" proposal failed, it is quite possible that something similar to it might succeed in the future.

In 1985, twenty-nine-year-old Elizabeth Bouvia petitioned a California court to allow her to be given a massive dose of painkillers while being denied nutrition and fluids so that she could end what she perceived to be a useless and painful life. Mrs. Bouvia suffered from multiple sclerosis, which caused her much pain. She considered her almost totally paralyzed body to be a useless and painful trap, and she wished to be freed from it by death. She showed that increasing numbers of patients who suffer from painful and long-standing diseases are asking themselves why they have to suffer as they do and why they cannot be permitted to end their lives in a "rational and painless" manner.

In June 1990, fifty-four-year-old Janet Adkins committed suicide in Holly, Michigan by being connected to a "suicide machine" created by a retired pathologist, Dr. Jack Kevorkian.[9] Mrs. Adkins was suffering from Alzheimer's disease and she persuaded him that her decision was rational and the result of long and careful reflection. She flew from Portland, Oregon to Michigan and had dinner with Dr. Kevorkian who then took her to a Volkswagen van parked in a local park and connected her to his machine. The machine first dripped saline solution into her veins and when she pressed the button, the saline stopped and the machine dripped thiopental into her, which caused her to lapse into unconsciousness. Then, after a minute, the machine switched solutions and dripped potassium chloride into her, which caused cardiac arrest.[10]

Although ordered by a court not to employ his suicide machine again, Dr. Kevorkian assisted in the suicides of two other women in late October 1991. On 9 May 1992, he was again taken into custody after accompanying Susan Williams, fifty-two years old, who committed suicide in his presence. Reportedly, she died after taking a "self-administered" dose of carbon monoxide. Dr. Kevorkian apparently connected her to a canister of this gas and allowed her to switch it on to kill herself.[11] On 23 November 1992, Kevorkian was present when a forty-six-year-old female cancer patient committed suicide by turning on a device that allowed her to inhale carbon monoxide.[12] Kevorkian claimed that "she had no hope of a normal life, where her every day was filled with pain, where she could not sleep because of her condition." This was his sixth episode of assisting suicide, and because three previous attempts to convict him had failed, prosecutors decided not to indict him. Kevorkian has had his medical license suspended in Michigan and California and has been the object of extensive criticism both within the medical profession and in other circles. This has not stopped his deadly deeds, however, for on 15 December 1992 he helped two more women commit suicide.[13] And by the end of November 1993, Kevorkian had assisted in twenty suicides.

Dr. Timothy Quill added fire to the debate in March 1991, when he reported participating in the suicide of one of his female patients.[14] Diagnosed with leukemia, she rejected chemotherapy and discussed suicide with Dr. Quill who agreed to give her a dose of life-ending barbiturates. Quill is not alone in the medical profession in supporting assisted suicide, for in recent months, more and more physicians have joined him in calling for legalization of medical assistance for those who wish to deliberately end their lives.

One of the most dramatic of recent suicides was that of Ann Wickett, second wife of Derek Humphry, and co-founder with him of the Hemlock Society. She wrote *Double Exit* which described the double suicides of her parents and with Derek they authored *Jean's Way* describing how Derek helped his first wife commit suicide when she was diagnosed with cancer, and *The Right to Die*, a defense of assisted suicide.[15] Diagnosed with breast cancer in 1989, she was divorced by Derek shortly before she began chemotherapy. She said in her suicide note:

> Derek: There. You got what you wanted. Ever since I was diagnosed as having cancer, you have done everything conceivable to precipitate my death. I was not alone in recognizing what you were doing. What you did – desertion and abandonment and subsequent harassment of a dying woman – is so unspeakable that there are no words to describe the horror of it.[16]

Assisted suicide opponents have protested that it is very difficult to control and that deadly acts of compassion can easily degenerate into simple deadly acts. Ann's last letter to her personal friend but ideological opponent, Rita Marker, is powerful testimony to the truth of that claim. In this note, Ann was claiming that Derek Humphry's claims that he merely assisted in the suicide of his first wife, Jean Humphry, in his book *Jean's Way* were false and that he in fact murdered her. But even though she seems to have been aware that compassionate killing could easily degenerate into simple killing, that did not sway her from ending her own life.

> Rita: My final words to Derek. He is a killer. I *know*. Jean actually died of suffocation. I could never say it until now: who would believe me? Do the best you can – Ann."[17]

In 1991, Humphry wrote a book *Final Exit*, which described methods that could be employed to commit suicide.[18] This book recommended that terminally ill people who wished to end their lives rely on asphyxiation and use the "self-deliverance via the plastic bag" method along with various drugs to eliminate any pain they might experience from asphyxiation. In November, 1993 research showed that this book had a "noticeable effect" on the methods used by people committing suicide.[19] Between March 1991 and March 1992 researchers found in New York city that suicides by asphyxiation rose from 8 to 33 and that almost of a third of those who killed themselves by this method were influenced by this book. This was a disturbing finding for psychiatrist Peter Marzuk at Cornell University Medical Center because most suicide attempts are "half-hearted, impulsive and later regretted" and the use of a plastic bag is a very lethal means of suicide. But Sidney Rosoff, president of the Hemlock Society, considered the use of plastic bags a positive development because it was an easier method of self-deliverance. But Dr. Marzuk persisted in his objections by noting that of the 33 people who used plastic bags to kill themselves only two had terminal illnesses and six had no medical illnesses at all.

Dr. Stephen Yarnell was a physician who contracted AIDS and saw in his future a long and painful death with accompanying loss of dignity and control over his life.[20] He campaigned for legalization of euthanasia in the face of a painful death, but rather than killing himself, Dr. Yarnell died a natural death in 1988. Some AIDS patients find dying by their own hand to be a more private, rational, and sensible action than ultimately succumbing to the disease; they have even vigorously campaigned for legalized suicide in some instances. Such patients do not wish to force this kind of dying on others, but they do not want anyone else to impose their style of dying on them either. They validate their views by claiming that just as procreating and giving life should be private matters, so also should one's dying; they have found some support from many Americans looking at the prospects of financial ruin as a result of a catastrophic illness. They see their suffering and pain as truly useless, and the savings that would result from allowing suicide and assisted suicide to be permitted as substantial. Hence, they do not view the consequences of legalized suicide as causing any great harm.

There is growing support throughout the world for euthanasia and assisted suicide. The results of a survey published in *Medical Times* in February 1988 indicated that 46.7 percent of all physicians believed that "[U]nder certain very specific conditions" a physician should be given the right to "perform" euthanasia.[21] A survey conducted by the Dutch Voluntary Euthanasia Society in April 1989 indicated that 80 percent of the Dutch population thought that patients suffering without hope of recovery should have the right to ask doctors to end their lives. Two out of three Dutch patients thought there should be laws regulating voluntary suicide so that doctors who practiced it could not be prosecuted as long as they met the prescribed conditions.[22] The submission of this initiative forces us to ask this most important question: would the legalization of suicide be beneficial or harmful to society?

On 11 December 1987, the American Association Against Human Suffering, the political arm of the Hemlock Society, introduced a referendum in California that would have granted physicians the legal power to give lethal injections to terminally ill patients on request.[23] Hemlock was in search of 450,000 signatures for its ratification in 1987, and the Roper Organization polled Californians finding substantial support for the measure.[24] Nearly 60 percent of those polled endorsed this measure, and the California Bar Association voted in favor of it also.[25] However, the Roman Catholic hierarchy of California, the American Medical Association and the California

Medical Association joined together to work against this proposal, and it was ultimately defeated.[26] Since then, Hemlock has moved to Oregon where it attempted to gain ratification for another proposal. And in the fall of 1992, California voters were again presented with an "assistance-in-dying" initiative that was supposedly more refined and discriminate than was the previous California initiative.[25] But the California Medical Association, pro-life groups, evangelical churches, and the Catholic bishops of California waged a vigorous campaign against the initiative and it failed by a narrow margin.

By a margin of 54 to 46 percent, voters in the state of Washington rejected Hemlock's Initiative 119, which would have legalized physician-assisted suicide. This was an extraordinary proposal because it did not require that patients be terminally ill to be assisted in their suicides, but allowed those who would die within six months to request assistance in suicide, and it did not require persistent and explicit requests for aid in suiciding. But had it not been for the following events, it is quite likely that this referendum would have passed. First, the Washington State Medical Association and the Roman Catholic church of Washington coordinated efforts to stop this. Second, in the weeks prior to this vote, Dr. Kevorkian used his suicide machine again and his abrasive style apparently deterred at least some from supporting the measure. Third, Ann Wickett committed suicide shortly before the vote; and finally, the Remmelink commission in Holland revealed in its report that nearly 1000 suicides were assisted in 1991 without the consent of the victim.[26] The narrow margin by which this measure was defeated after all of these events argues powerfully that there is deep and widespread support for legalized suicide in this country.

Many will assert that these suicides are rational, but there is a menacing character to suicide that needs to be brought to light. The suicidal person is trapped in a dark, churning realm of despair with seemingly little or no chance of escape or relief. Usually this person self-destructs in a panicky moment of sharp, bitter grief and pain that he or she claims cannot be understood by anyone but himself or herself, even though the great and vast majority of individuals are sorely tempted to commit suicide at one time or another. This is important, for it suggests that it is often, if not always, a sense of aloneness and isolation that drives a person to the ultimate self-destructive act.

Suicide has been and is becoming a very serious problem for our society because it is becoming more and more trivialized. A recent report indicated that suicide is the second leading cause of death among older teenagers and it is becoming more and more common among children.[27] Depression and substance abuse are the two leading factors that induce more than a half-million young people to attempt suicide every year.[28] Suicide rates among young children and teenagers have tripled in the past three decades. In the past decade, many professional organizations and the media have come to be active promoters of suicide, and to do this they have romanticized death and suicide. This is unfortunate because many will be seduced by this campaign and do their final deed in a superficial and thoughtless manner.

What makes suicide such a threat is that it seems to be utterly rational and intelligent in some instances. But determining if this is actually so is difficult, for if it were an utterly irrational action, there would be little debate about it. It is precisely because many philosophers, theologians, dramatists, poets, and writers throughout the centuries have accepted it as rational and intelligent in at least some instances that evaluating it is so difficult. But to say that suicide can be rational may not resolve the important moral issues surrounding it, for there are many acts that are rational but are nonetheless utterly reprehensible. Many actions have a reasonableness to them, like exterminating one's political foes, but they remain despicable and morally intolerable in spite of their rational coherence.

Suicide seems rational in many instances because it appears to banish suffering and misery swiftly and certainly; and often the only deterrents to it are the pain of death and uncertainty about whether anything follows death. But modern analgesia has overcome even this barrier because there are few sorts of pain that cannot be controlled, which makes arguments for assisted suicide unpersuasive. Those who espouse the rationality and acceptability of suicide must reflect long and hard about the consequences of social endorsement of this act and about the alternatives available to suicide. They must also think hard about whether there is some hidden meaning, value, or significance in suffering and particularly in suffering that ends in death. And they must also think hard about the freedom of the suicidal and whether they can give valid consent to their actions.

In the Roman Catholic traditions, death has been regarded as an evil that is to be avoided because it is the enemy of the Lord Jesus, who sought to bring about the destruction of his ministry of salvation and redemption. This is not to say that death is an absolute evil, for only sin is absolutely evil, but rather that death is never to be welcomed as a friend because it is the great enemy of Christ himself, who is our true friend and brother. In a suicidal action, one embraces that which sought to impede our Savior's redemptive mission, and because suicide embraces death, it is alien to genuine Christian life.

The purpose of this book is to examine rationality, morality, voluntariness, and social aspects of suicide from the perspective of the classical Catholic view. From the Roman Catholic perspective suicide is not compassionate, just, rational, or of social merit because it does not protect the weak and vulnerable from self-inflicted harm. On a step-by-step basis, this work will argue against the various objections to the traditional Catholic condemnation of suicide and argue for the validity of the Catholic church's traditional position.

Chapter 1 will critically summarize various recent definitions of suicide and propose a more accurate and comprehensive definition of suicide from the classical Catholic perspective. Doing this is important, for if suicide is defined too narrowly, many objectionable forms of self-execution would be excluded from moral condemnation. This chapter will propose a definition of suicide that is not only in accord with Catholic teachings, but which also distinguishes the various kinds of suicide from martyrdom or self-sacrifice. Chapter 2 will study the practice of suicide in the ancient Greco-Roman world and the response of Latin Christianity to this phenomenon. This chapter will assert that medieval Church and society were able to bring suicide to a virtual halt because of its moral teachings, theology, civil and canon law, sacramental life, preaching, and doctrine of the *imago Dei*.

Chapter 3 will discuss the development of suicidal practices from the Middle Ages to contemporary times. It will outline the collapse of the medieval Christian opposition to suicide because of the onslaught of rationalism and romanticism. Chapter 4 will summarize traditional Catholic teachings against suicide and their theological and scriptural foundations. Contrary to the claims of critics, it will contend that the Catholic tradition finds moral condemnations of suicide in the Bible, that fidelity to the mainstream Catholic moral tradition requires rejection of suicide, and that these teachings are internally coherent and consistent.

Chapter 5 will question claims that suicide can be rational, and it will examine the proposals of various ethicists, physicians, suicidologists, and commentators who support the rationality of suicide. It will highlight the deficiencies of their views of rationality and it will espouse the view that the real-world situations in which suicide could be construed as a rational action are so few as to be insignificant. Chapter 6 will challenge the claim that suicide is rational by arguing that it is "subvoluntary" and does not meet the minimal requirements for freedom and voluntariness necessary for it to be accepted as a free and voluntary act. It has been widely held that many suicidal persons are not competent when they make their suicidal decision. This chapter will endorse that view that there are so many subtle psychological and social factors impinging on the freedom of suicidal individuals that their decision is not fully free but is "subvoluntary" and is not truly a rational act.

Chapter 7 will directly confront the claim that pain can be a morally justifying cause for suicide by arguing that there have been such remarkable advances in pain relief in recent years that there are hardly any types of pain that cannot be controlled today, which eliminates all medical reasons for giving patients lethal doses of analgesia to relieve their pain. Chapter 8 will assert that suicide should not be legally endorsed because of the profoundly harmful impact such a policy would have on society and public policy. Endorsing a liberal suicide policy would create serious social problems not only for individuals, but also for institutions and society as a whole, and this should not be allowed. Chapter 9 will reflect on some contemporary theological doctrines supporting the morality of rational suicide. A recent report by a task force of the Dutch Reformed Evangelical church urged pastoral ministers to give support to those who make a suicidal decision, and this chapter will argue that pastoral, professional, and ethical responsibility requires pastoral ministers to not support suicidal desires or aims. It will be asserted that such actions are contrary to Catholic spirituality and understanding of the relation of Catholic moral life to spiritual growth.

Notes

1. "AIDS Patients' Silent Companion is Often Suicide, or Thoughts of It," *New York Times*, A1, A30.

1. "Elderly Couple Who Want to Die Together," *The San Francisco Chronicle,* 5 April 1987: A7.

2. "Couple's Suicide Spur 'Right-to-Die' Debate," *The Champaign News Gazette,* 16 June 1987: A1, A12.

3. Ibid., A1.

4. "A Scholar's Suicide: Trying to Spare a Family Anguish," *The New York Times,* 26 October 1987, B1, A12.

5. "After Years of Decline, Suicide Rate Rising among Elderly in U.S.," *The Wall Street Journal,* 30 July 1986, A1, A16.

6. Ibid. Also see "Increase in 'Rational Suicide' among Elderly Patients Foreseen," *Family Practice News,* 17, 22, 3, 49.
7. "We've Talked of Hiring a Hit Man," *USA Today,* 15 May 1985, 8A.
8. "'Last Resort' Proposed for the Dying," *Daily Journal,* Fergus Falls, MN, 21 November 1987, A2.
9. "Doctor Tells of First Death Using His Suicide Device," *New York Times,* 6 June 1990, A1, B6.
10. Ibid., B6.
11. "Michigan Woman Commits Suicide with Gas Provided by Kevorkian," *The New York Times,* national edition, 17 May 1992, A1.
12. "Kevorkian Assists in Another Suicide," *Chicago Tribune,* 24 November 1992, A1.
13. "Doctor Assists 2 More Suicides in Michigan," *New York Times,* 16 December 1992, A21.
14. Quill, T., "Death and Dignity--a Case of Individualized Decision-Making," *New England Journal of Medicine,* Vol. 324, 1991, 691-94.
15. Wickett, A. *Double Exit,* (Eugene, Oregon: Hemlock Society, 1989) Humphry, D; and Wickett, A. *Jean's Way,* (New York: Harper & Row, 1986) and *The Right to Die.* (New York: Perennial Books, 1986)
16. Bole, W., "Ann Humphry's Final Exit," *Our Sunday Visitor,* 17 November 1991, 12.
17. Ibid., 13.
18. Humphry, D., *Final Exit,* (Eugene, OR: Hemlock, 1991).
19. "Methods Used in Suicides Follow Book: Study Finds an Increase in Self-Asphyxiations" *The New York Times,* 6 November 1993, A25-6.
20. Yarnell, S., "A Physician's Thoughts on Euthanasia," *The Hemlock Quarterly,* October 1987, 5.
21. "50.5 % Say Physicians Should Not be Given the Right to Perform Euthanasia," *Medical Times,* February 1988, 49.
22. *Newsletter for Participants of the International Courses in the Netherlands,* published by the Netherlands Organization for International Cooperation in Higher Education, P.O. Box 90734, 2509 LS, The Hague, 3. The notice also made mention of the fact that two-thirds of the Christian Democrats polled favored the legislation despite the fact that most of the objections came from Christian Democrat members of Parliament.
23. See "Right-to-Die Initiative Proposed," *The San Francisco Chronicle,* 11 December 1987, A1, A4. A similar proposal was introduced in Washington, Oregon and California in 1990. See "Minister Describes Group's Proposal as 'Assistance in Dying,'" *The Spokesman Review,* 5 January 1989, B2.
24. See "Most Americans Think There Should be a Right-to-Die," *The Hemlock Quarterly,* July 1986, 1.
25. See "Attorneys Back Law Permitting Right to Die," *The Hemlock Quarterly,* October 1987, 2.
26. "Catholics and Doctors' Group Oppose Change," ibid., 1.
25. "Euthanasia Opponents Prepare for Ballot Battle," *Our Sunday Visitor,* 31 May 1992, 17 .
26. "Dutch Euthanasia Program Called a Disaster," *Life at Risk,* September 1991, I, 3.
27. "Suicide Myths Cloud Efforts to Save Children," *The New York Times,* Tuesday, 16 June 1992, C1, Col. 1, C3.
28. Ibid.

1

Defining Suicide in the Catholic Context

Because of the increasing incidence of suicide in our society, philosophers, suicidologists, physicians, and ethicists have reflected more deeply on its nature, and as part of this reflection there has been much discussion of what actually constitutes true and authentic suicide and how one is to define it. Some philosophers and ethicists have become rather pessimistic about the possibility of developing an accurate and comprehensive definition of suicide because of the incredibly diverse views of it found in various cultures and traditions. My belief, however, is that these pessimistic appraisals are not entirely warranted and that one can accurately and adequately define it. In what follows, I will first review the various definitions of suicide and then suggest a more adequate definition that will bring a fuller understanding of it. Defining suicide accurately is an important issue for Catholic theology, for if suicide is defined too broadly and comprehensively, then Christ's death could be considered as a suicide. Because his passion, death, and resurrection are normative for Catholic theology, considering his death as suicidal would radically alter Catholicism itself, for if spiritual formation required us to imitate Christ, considering his death a suicide could make suicide morally normative for perfect imitation of Christ. Defining suicide too broadly could have even further harmful consequences for Catholic theology, as it could transform the deaths of the martyrs from self-sacrificial acts undertaken to realize a higher and more perfect good into egotistical and cowardly acts of escape or self-destruction. This would turn some of the most venerated of Christian saints into little more than religious fanatics and self-killers with a religious gloss.

Defining suicide too narrowly or broadly would not only be detrimental to Catholic theology, but it could be quite damaging for others as well; for if it were defined too narrowly, then many of the deaths people bring upon themselves from despair, emotional turmoil, or immaturity could be seen as permissible and morally upright. And excessively broad definitions of suicide would make some renunciations of ordinary and readily available life-sustaining measures suicidal, which would be false and damaging. Overly broad definitions of suicide pose serious problems as they could readily miscategorize some actions as suicidal when they are either accidents, unintended deaths, or acts of generous self-sacrifice.

From a social and legal standpoint, defining suicide accurately is also important. Suicide should be defined with a sufficient broadness that it can morally justify intervention to prevent irrational suicides but also with sufficient narrowness to permit morally legitimate acts of self-sacrifice. Defining suicide too narrowly could destroy moral justifications for preventive interventions and could place the emotionally unstable, despairing, depressed, and dying in danger of losing even minimal social protection. These unfortunates need to be protected from themselves, and an excessively restrictive understanding of suicide could jeopardize whatever security they might have.

In what follows, I will first consider various broad and narrow definitions of suicide and then propose a definition that is not only more accurate and precise, but also in harmony with mainstream Catholic thought. Following this discussion, certain problematic and complicated cases will be examined to determine if they are authentically suicidal or not.

Defining Suicide Broadly

A number of students of suicide have sought to define it in a very broad manner, primarily so that it could be studied in a more objective and nonjudgmental manner.

Robert Martin has noted that it is difficult to define suicide consistently because of the evaluational overtones associated with self-killing.[1] This is probably true, but it should not deter attempts to define it accurately merely because suicide is often associated with certain moral judgments. There are strong evaluational overtones to definitions of rape, child-abuse, or murder, but that does not deter attempts to accurately and truly define these. Martin seems to want to define suicide without these evaluational overtones precisely so that people will not react emotionally in the face of deliberate self-assassinations, but it is not fully evident that eliminating all evaluations involved in its definition would lead to a greater understanding of what it is.

Margaret Pabst Battin has urged abandoning the project of defining suicide and proposes that we

> avoid these disputes by describing our inquiry as one concerned with the issue of whether it is morally permissible for an individual to choose to die, to determine that he shall die, to acquiesce in death or to bring about his own death.[2]

But this suggestion is unsound because any inquiry about the permissibility of choosing death would have to ascertain what constitutes a choice for death and what does not. One cannot settle questions concerning the morality of death choices unless one first settles the dispute about the nature and definition of suicide, and to abandon attempts to distinguish these sorts of dying would be intellectually irresponsible.

Emile Durkheim advanced a very broad definition of suicide which held that suicide was any action that brought about one's own death.[3] He wrote that suicide was any "death resulting directly or indirectly from a positive or negative act of the victim himself, which he knows will produce this result."[4] This definition is inadequate because it cannot distinguish genuine acts of self-assassination from legitimate non-suicidal acts of allowing-to-die, martyrdom, and self-sacrifice for the good of another. Durkheim's definition has a certain simplicity and conceptual clarity to it, but it is unable to distinguish various kinds of self-inflicted death because it does not encompass questions of the intentionality of the action or agent. Durkheim's definition is noteworthy because it stresses that a suicide involves a choice of either a reflexive lethal performance or forbearance to be authentic. If a reflexive killing is to be authentically suicidal, the agent must know that the consequence of this performance or omission will be the loss of life.

Durkheim studied self-killing from an empirical and social-scientific standpoint, and to do this he had to exclude consideration of the intentional, emotive, and motivational states of the agent. Thus, he sought to concentrate only on what was open to empirical examination, the material aspects of acts. But in defining suicide empirically, he eliminated the possibility of obtaining not only a more precise understanding of suicide, but also such an understanding of the inner intentional, motivational, mental, and emotional states of those who kill themselves.

Durkheim's definition does not take into sufficient account those actions that bring about death knowingly but unintentionally, for a knowing but unintended suicide is different from one done intentionally. A woman who runs into the path of an oncoming car while fleeing an attacker kills herself by that action and dies knowingly but unintentionally, and her action is quite different from one where a woman deliberately throws herself in front of a car. Durkheim seemed to presume that an action done with adequate knowledge was intentional, but this confused one's knowing the nature and effects of an action with directly intending the action, and according to Durkheim, this woman's action would be a true and authentic suicide. To understand what constitutes an authentic suicide, one must attend not only to the agent's knowledge, but also to the agent's intentional aims.

Richard Brandt studied the morality of suicide in a very open and forthright fashion, and he proposed as comprehensive and value-free a definition as possible. He considers a suicidal act or omission to be

> doing something which results in one's death, either from the intention of ending one's life or the intention to bring about some other state of affairs (such as relief from pain) which one thinks is certain or highly probable can be achieved only by means of death or [an act that] will produce death.[5]

Brandt's conditions for defining a true suicide are looser than Durkheim's, for he only requires that there be a belief that death will probably occur, while Durkheim demands that the agent know that the action will effect death.[6] But there are also difficulties with this definition, for it would hold that a woman who ran in front of a train to escape a rapist, believing that death would probably occur, would be committing suicide. But that does not necessarily mean that she would be killing herself intentionally in the same way that a woman who hanged herself would be suiciding. Brandt's definition is inadequate because it ignores the crucial role of the agent's intentionality in self-killing. An authentic suicide occurs when a person intends and aims at his or her own death as an end or a means through a deliberate, knowing, and consented performance or forbearance. Performing a reflexive death-dealing deed with the belief that death will result does not necessarily mean that the action is truly suicidal, for these beliefs can be false, and the action can be the product of external forces or internal compulsions beyond the control of the agent.

R. G. Frey offers the broadest definition of suicide possible, for he simply considers it to be "killing oneself."[7] He wishes to include in his definition actions in which one manipulates others into killing themselves, and he justifies his claim by invoking Kolber's assertion that 25 percent of all homicides were provoked by their victims.[8] While this might be a good legal definition of homicide, it is not a fully adequate moral account of suicide, and its weakness is that it could confuse the clear responsibilities of those who actually perform lethal acts against others. If provoking a homicidal act is suicidal, does that mean those who lead others to suicide are free of responsibility? And what of actions in which the killing is not actually provoked, but in which the risk or probability of death is increased? If provoking another to kill oneself is suicidal, then drunken driving on expressways that resulted in death could constitute self-killing because such acts significantly increase the risk of death. Slipping on a banana peel carelessly dropped on a stairway could also probably be suicidal, for one would be materially causing one's death by such an action, and self-sacrificial deaths of fire fighters trying to save others will also be true suicides according to this definition. Given Frey's claim that provoking suicide is equivalent to suicide, it is hard to see how acts that significantly increase the risk of death or suicide would not also be suicidal.

The next section will examine narrower definitions of suicide. These narrower definitions also present serious difficulties because they can facilitate granting moral permission to actions that are in fact culpable suicides.

Narrow Definitions of Suicide

Joseph Margolis claims that there is a great deal of cultural relativity in definitions and evaluations of suicide, and he expresses concern over our ability to move beyond understandings of suicide that are significantly conditioned by our culture.[9] He believes it is obvious that people should be allowed to kill themselves to instrumentally realize their fundamental interests, and this sort of self-killing should count as authentic suicide. However, he believes that suicide should only include those actions that aim explicitly and deliberately at death and seek nothing more than death itself. Thus, he would regard the vast majority of suicides as morally irrelevant because most people kill themselves in order to achieve some objective other than their own death. But this would exclude the great majority of suicides, for most who self-assassinate do so for purposes other than to simply make themselves dead.

Margolis is more concerned with the rationality of suicide than with its morality, and he considers suicide to be "the deliberate taking of one's life simply in order to end it, not instrumentally for any ulterior purpose."[10] But in ordinary circumstances, people kill themselves to escape loneliness, debt, suffering, loss of dignity, or humiliation. Few do this only to end their lives, and those who do are often in a doubtfully competent state. Yet Margolis wants to consider these to be normative suicides, and they would be his only candidates for rational suicide. Margolis's definition would exclude suicides for the purpose of preserving honor or escaping what he regards as senseless suffering, which is contrary to our basic belief about what constitutes a true suicide.

This is an excessively narrow definition of suicide as it would rule out most self-killings not only to escape suffering, but also for other reasons. It fails to see that true self-assassinations are done simply to destroy oneself. Just as few murders are committed simply to see another dead, so also few suicides are committed only to bring death on oneself. Authentic murders occur not only when one kills another to make the other person dead, but also to solve problems, eliminate frustrations, gain a fortune, eliminate competition, destroy a nuisance, or eliminate a competing lover, for example. These killings are no less murderous just because they are not done solely to make another person dead. As is the case with murders, so also suicides can occur when they are ends in themselves, but also when they are means to other ends as well. Suicides are done to escape pain and suffering or to preserve dignity, and these are true and authentic self-killings. Because of this, it is true that authentic suicides occur when people kill themselves to achieve other ends, just as people murder others in order to accomplish an end other than the death of the victim.

Glenn Graber faults Margolis's definition of suicide and claims that

> suicide is defined as doing something that results in one's death in the way that was planned, either from the intention of ending one's life or the intention to bring about some other state of affairs (such as relief from pain) that one thinks it certain or highly probable can be achieved only by means of death.[11]

Graber argues that Margolis's definition does not make room for the person who remains silent while being tortured to death to prevent revealing state secrets; he believes this is an authentic suicide and not a homicide.[12] Graber believes that a foreseen death is a kind of suicide, which is why he believes the above mentioned spy commits suicide.

The difficulty with Graber's definition is that it fails to explain how individuals can commit suicide in some instances when they neither do nor intend anything to bring death on themselves, and when the actions of other agents are the causes of their deaths. One can commit suicide by omitting life-protective actions after having begun a lethal act, but that is different from what the captured spy does. For example, one can point one's car toward a cliff, gun the engine, and "commit" suicide by not doing anything to prevent the car from hurling over the cliff. One can commit suicide by neglecting to repair his car, knowing that its failure will sooner or later become lethal. Unless we consider omissions to be "doings" in some fashion, one who rejects basic medical treatment, or who stops eating, commits suicide by not acting to sustain their life. There are such things as suicides by omission and Margolis's definition is so narrow that it would exclude them.

Tom Beauchamp presents a definition of suicide that is also quite narrow, but nonetheless encompasses many different kinds of self-killing:

> [A]n act is a suicide if a person intentionally brings about his or her own death in circumstances where others do not coerce him or her to the action, except in those cases where death is caused by conditions not specifically arranged for the purpose of bringing about his or her own death.[13]

Beauchamp is correct in asserting that a true suicide results when there is an intentional and planned action or omission to bring death upon oneself. He also affirms that suicide requires the absence of coercion, fraud, or force used to effect the death of the person.[14] His definition leaves the status of more than a few types of reflexive death-dealing action in doubt, however. His approach eliminates some choices to not accept treatment for terminal pathological conditions from authentically suicidal actions, but it includes those positively lethal acts. The means-ends relationship in a suicidal action is not clear in this understanding, and self-killing to preserve another's life might not be suicide for Beauchamp. It is not clear whether or not killing to spare one's family disgrace and dishonor would be suicide for Beauchamp.

Beauchamp definitionally excludes medicalized self-killing through the omission of morally required care and treatment from the class of suicidal actions. This is unfortunate because one of the most common forms of suicide in the foreseeable future could well be self-killing by rejection of clinically beneficial, inexpensive, and painless medical treatment, and his definition is unduly narrow because it does not hold that refusing these life-sustaining measures is suicidal. He does not understand that the nature of the treatments rejected by individuals has a role in determining if the action is suicidal or not. For example, a 25-year-old diabetic who refuses insulin when it would keep him medically stable and who would die shortly as a consequence of its removal would be committing suicide. But a cancer patient who was expected to die within a few weeks and who needs a cardiac bypass would not be committing suicide by refusing to have it done. His definition is attractive because of its simplicity, but it is incapable of determining what would be culpable self-killing in some complex and subtle situations.

Peter Windt presents a definition of suicide that is even narrower than Beauchamp's. Windt's understanding is based on Wittgenstein's principles, and he argues that suicide is "reflexive" killing, and any definition of suicide would have to meet the following criteria:

1. the death was caused by the actions or behavior of the deceased;
2. the deceased wanted, desired, or wished death;
3. the deceased intended, chose, decided, or willed to die;
4. the deceased knew that death would result from the behavior;
5. the deceased was responsible for his death.[15]

This definition is sound in many ways, but it does not consider the freedom of the agent to refrain from the suicidal choice. In true suicides, the person is responsible for, intends, and acts to bring about death, and is also free to refuse to do the deed. But in his view it is not clear that the individual has the freedom to not choose suicide, for the agent might be under significant duress. The issue of an agent's freedom to refrain from suicidal choices will be discussed more fully in chapter 6 where the voluntariness of suicide in general will be discussed at greater length.

These narrower definitions of suicide have distinct advantages over the broader definitions, but they do not adequately perceive the difference between killings that are truly deliberate, willful, and intentional either by omission or commission and those that are death-dealing deeds lacking adequate consent, knowledge, or freedom and do not truly flow from the choice of the agent. Many of the broader definitions of suicide would exclude suicidal acts when the person omits medically ordinary and readily providable forms of care and treatment, where the person aims at ending suffering, but not explicitly at ending life, and they do not give adequate consideration to the freedom of the agent. These kinds of actions are true suicides, and it is not clear that they would be included in their narrow definitions of suicide.

Because of these problems, I would like to propose a more accurate definition of suicide, one that identifies more precisely culpable self-killings, and does not consider as suicides what are in fact legitimate martyrdoms or omissions of life-sustaining measures when one merely lets another die without causing their demise in any way.

A More Adequate Definition of Suicide

A fully adequate definition would have to be able to differentiate between performances or omissions that are true self-killings and those where death results from an action or omission performed by the agent, but is unplanned and unconsented. It would have to take into consideration the freedom of the agent to refrain from the suicidal choice, and distinguish intentional self-killings by omission from omissions that are not the fundamental and underlying cause of death.

An accurate and comprehensive definition of suicide must be able to determine when death would result from a deliberate, free, and consented choice of the agent on the one hand, and from another intrinsic or extrinsic underlying cause on the other. It must be able to distinguish acts of martyrdom and self-sacrifice from authentic self-killings and distinguish morally tolerable omissions that merely permit another to die from deliberate acts of self-assassination. A legitimate definition of self-killing has to be able to distinguish accidental deaths, for which the agent would be the material but not formal cause, from deaths in which the agent wishes to bring death upon himself or herself. It should be able to distinguish deaths resulting from the rejection of a life-sustaining procedure that was not morally required from those deaths brought about by rejection of an obligatory life-saving measure. Authentic suicides occur in some cases when people seek relief from suffering or loss of dignity, and a definition of suicide must be open enough to allow for those who use death instrumentally for such ulterior purposes. And it should be able to distinguish true suicides from the provoked homicides done by others.

In light of these requirements, I would propose the following as a definition of a true, culpable, and authentic suicide:

> *A suicide is a deliberate and voluntary performance or omission, done with adequate freedom and knowledge, that aims at the destruction of one's life. It is a planned, chosen, intended, and consented action to bring death as either a means or an end in itself. It is a choice made where death is reasonably expected to result from the specified performance or omission in common circumstances and situations.*

The following points should clarify this definition.

1. This definition excludes actions from being truly suicidal that bring death either as a means or as an end but that are not planned for this purpose. Thus, a woman who runs on to a highway to escape attack does not commit suicide because ending her life by flight was not part of the plan of her performance or omission. If, however, the woman used the occasion to end her life by running onto the highway and deliberately omitted taking routine precautions, her flight would be suicidal. If a man slips on a banana peel and dies while on his way to a suicide attempt, his death would not be an authentic suicide because he did not plan to end his life in this way.

2. In a suicidal action, the person chooses a performance or omission either for the explicit purpose of ending life and bringing death or to accomplish some other end for which death is a necessary and sufficient condition for the realization of that objective.[16] This definition excludes actions where death results from causes not fundamentally originating from the agent's free and uncoerced choice, intentional action, plan, or performance.[17] Thus, a man who accidentally drops a loaded pistol, which then discharges and kills him does not commit suicide because the death did not result from a choice or plan to self-execute. But if he dropped the gun hoping it would go off and kill him, the death would be suicidal because it resulted from a choice, plan, performance, or omission of an action, that the agent could freely reject.

3. According to this definition, a true suicide would be a deliberate performance or omission that brings about death in and of itself. An act is authentically suicidal when one performs a reflexively lethal act that is deliberate, resulting from a decision made with adequate presumptions, beliefs, and knowledge about the nature and consequences of the action, and flows from the will of the agent who

intends the act, consents to and agrees with the act, and is done for a conscious purpose.[18]

4. This definition would affirm that suicide is the result of a choice, and it would not count as suicides any actions forced by others upon agents, but not selected by them.[19] It would also exclude killings done from desperation in the face of suffering, pain, and death where these factors become the primary and fundamental cause of the action. In these instances, the freedom of the individual would be radically limited, and the self-destructive act would not be authentically suicidal. Those killings that are associated with, but do not flow from deception or force, would not be true self-killings, and whether they could be regarded as fully rational is controversial. They would be reflexive death-dealing events, but they would not be suicides in the strict sense because they do not exhibit the freedom necessary for an authentic suicide.

5. This definition asserts that an authentic suicide only occurs when one has adequate presumptions, beliefs, and knowledge of what is being done.[20] One philosopher suggested that this requirement would eliminate any suicidal action from being a fully culpable act because death, which is consented to in a suicidal action, is nonexistence and cannot be adequately known.[21] Because one cannot experience death, it is impossible for there to be true and adequate knowledge of it, and choosing death could not be a voluntary act.

Ignorance of the nature, moral character, or effects of an action can limit or destroy the freedom, voluntariness, or deliberateness of an action; and reflexively lethal acts done when these qualifying conditions are present are not true suicides.[22] But when ignorance, inadequate presumptions and beliefs are willed by an agent, the act remains free, voluntary, and deliberate. Unintended and intractable ignorance, however, destroys the freedom, voluntariness, and culpability of a suicide because only willed and known acts are truly voluntary. Other forms of involuntary and unintentional ignorance such as error, forgetfulness, inadvertence, or lack of attention can diminish the freedom of a suicide and disqualify an action as verifiably suicidal.[23]

6. According to this definition, a suicidal action would be one in which death would be chosen or planned as either a means to an end, or as an end of the act itself, and this plan could be brought about either by means of actions or omissions. A person who rejects an effective, nonpainful, and inexpensive medical treatment to avoid pain and suffering would be committing suicide because the medical

treatment would be a morally ordinary form of treatment.[24] An adequate definition of suicide would demand that rejection of these sorts of life-sustaining measures be considered as true and authentic suicides.

This definition implies that a person who commits suicide after being deliberately provoked by another to bring about his or her death would not so much commit suicide as facilitate the murderous deed of another. It also implies that when a patient plans his or her death by rejecting nonpainful, effective, and inexpensive medical treatments and chooses death to end suffering, he or she would be performing suicide because this choice aims at bringing death. Even further, it would be suicidal if a person's death was a part of a strategy to preserve dignity or avoid suffering.

7. This definition demands that the agent give adequate consent to the suicidal decision, which requires an evaluation of the quality of the agent's consent, even though this can be extraordinarily difficult in many instances. If a suicidal person claimed that he would not suicide if he had freedom to do otherwise, his consent would probably be inadequate for a fully voluntary suicide. But if he still killed himself even if free not to, he would be giving valid consent to his death. If a concentration camp guard was free to do things other than order women and children into gas chambers and did not do so, one could conclude that he was fully consenting to his duties. Hence, if a suicidal person would choose and plan for death even in the event of other options, then he or she would probably be consenting to the suicide. If one would not choose the deadly deed in the face of other options, then their death-dealing deed is probably a consented action.

This definition of suicide implies that when one reluctantly consents to death and plans for or intends it, the action is a true self-execution.[25] Consent may be given by degree, just as can resistance to an action or omission, and this mitigates subjective responsibility for suicide in some cases.[26] It is true that *full* consent would not have to be given; that would be too strict a standard for determining this issue. This definition holds that the agent consents to the means and intends death as the end in an authentic suicide. And when a person consents to a means that causes death, but does not intend the death itself, then the act would not be authentically suicidal. Thus, when a woman flees an attacker and runs in front of an onrushing car, she consents to the means, but does not intend death, and her action is not to be considered suicidal. But when one gives consent to death as a means to another objective, a suicidal action occurs.

8. A true and authentic suicide derives from a plan or intention to embrace death, and the loss of life resulting from a suicide is perceived as either neutral or good in the given circumstance and situation, and not as an evil to be avoided. The motivation behind an authentic suicide would be the perception that innocent human life itself is not something that is always to be protected from deliberate and intentional killing, but only retains its value in proportion to its capacity to serve one's projects, plans, and concerns. Unlike the basic values of justice or truth, which most would say are never to be deliberately violated or attacked, innocent human life acquires a conditional character and becomes an entity that can be disposed of at will because it no longer serves one's private purposes.

9. This definition of suicide holds that an authentic suicide is not coerced, compelled, or done on account of undue, excessive, or extreme psychological pressure but is freely and voluntarily performed.[27] Its voluntariness depends on whether the agent had sufficient freedom at the time of choice to abstain from the action. If freedom of this kind is present, there would be a true suicide, but if not, the self-killing would not be authentically suicidal. A suicide would be genuine in a limited sense if it was chosen with a certain reluctance, but it would be fully authentic if it was chosen for its own sake or as a means to another objective.

10. This understanding of suicide would acknowledge that fear can sometimes be a factor that not only compromises the voluntariness of a suicidal choice, but also may completely destroy it in some instances.[28] The impact of fear on a suicidal action will be discussed at length later, but it is sufficient to hold that if fear is the fundamental cause of a suicidal decision the action would not be authentically suicidal. If a soldier became so paralyzed by fear that he could not make reasoned judgments and fled from battle, his flight would not be voluntary, consented, or free. But, if, however, the fear would only diminish but not destroy his ability to judge the action, the act would be authentically voluntary.

11. A critical problem in defining suicide is that of distinguishing authentic suicide from self-sacrifice for the sake of others. The classical case of this was that of Captain Oates who walked away from his camp in Antarctica to save the lives of his comrades. His action was probably suicidal for the reason that he chose death and undertook means to bring it about to do good to others and also because there were other things he could have done to save their lives. His was probably a benevolent suicide because he sought to do good to others by undertaking measures that would certainly end his

life when he was free to refrain from them and he had adequate knowledge of what he was doing. Oates could have remained with the party and refused his share of rations for the sake of others, and by doing this he would not have imposed any more burden on his comrades than he did by totally abandoning the shelter of his camp. And if he had remained in their company, he would not have made his death certain, and he would have increased his chances of rescue or reaching safety together. Oates was the immediate cause of his own death and even though it was motivated by benevolence, it was still an authentic suicide because he had sufficient freedom to refrain from the action. In contrast to this case, a soldier who jumped on a live grenade to save his comrades probably would not have committed suicide but would have sacrificed himself for their sake because there was little or nothing else he could have done to save them. His action would have been suicidal if he pulled the pin on one of his own grenades, but if he was trying to smother a grenade thrown by an enemy, his action would be one of self-sacrifice. Unlike Oates's action, his would not be suicidal because there was no other means available to him to save the lives of his comrades, and if there was, he presumably would have taken that action.

This proposed definition is much more discriminating and precise than the alternatives discussed here and it is more capable of differentiating the various kinds of self-killing from one another. Not all reflexive death-dealing acts are true suicides, and this definition can distinguish them from true suicides as well as from true acts of self-sacrifice. On the other hand, it excludes those that do not flow from such choices. This definition does not construe suicide so narrowly that only those deaths in which the self-killer wants death and nothing else are regarded as authentic suicides because authentic self-killers often seek other things than just death through their self-assassination.

In the next section, we will briefly consider what difficult sorts of reflexive killing count as true and authentic suicides.

What Counts as a Suicide?

In light of this definition of suicide, one must ask what sorts of reflexively lethal events would be authentic suicides.

1. It would be suicidal to refuse readily available, clinically effective, and nonpainful medical treatments irrespective of one's medical condition. If one rejects means that are not expensive or painful and are effective in remedying, controlling, or palliating a

clinical condition, one would be committing suicide. But if one rejects treatments that are extremely costly, questionably effective, or which cause radical and extreme pain in and of themselves, one would not be suiciding in most instances.

This definition would also hold that a death would be authentically suicidal if one refused to receive ordinarily available and effective life-sustaining measures to promote, protect, and preserve life. A person would also be truly suiciding if he or she died after deliberately exposing himself or herself to the elements when shelter would be easily available. One who deliberately neglects ordinary sanitary care would be performing a suicidal act if this was done to bring on a lethal disease. Or one who declined to take inoculations when there was a clear and present danger of malaria would also be committing suicide, unless there was some dominating moral reason for declining this treatment.

If a medically stable, but permanently comatose person were to order removal of all life-sustaining, readily providable, and inexpensive nutrition and fluids when competent, he or she would be suiciding, since death would be an obvious consequence of such an action. In this case, one would be choosing death by rejecting a futile, painful, expensive, and burdensome medical treatment. Some would claim that such a person would not be planning death, but would only be rejecting futile treatments. However, this is questionable because there would be so little harm or risk associated with the treatment. It is difficult to see how its rejection could not involve a plan to bring death. But it would not necessarily be a suicidal action to refuse food and water after lapsing into a coma with death imminent because the measures would ultimately be futile.

Even further, a person who receives a certainly lethal dose of analgesics to deliberately bring on his or her death as a means or an end would be committing suicide. This would not merely be a therapeutic act to end suffering, but intentional killing for this purpose. Death is part of this individual's plan, intention, choice, and proposal and is not merely an extrinsic effect of some other choice or plan. Those who freely and knowingly take positive actions to end their lives to escape suffering and despair are not merely engaging in an act of flight, but are positively choosing to end life.

Such individuals might give reluctant consent to their deaths but they would nonetheless be committing a genuine suicide because we often give reluctant consent to acts which remain authentic choices despite our reluctance. Children take medicine in spite of their aversion, and yet they give valid consent to taking it. Adults often go to work reluctantly, and yet the consent they give to their tasks is valid. Resistance to an act or its effects may at least diminish consent, but it is not evident that mere reluctance to perform an act or omission destroys it. Nazi death camp guards frequently performed their duties reluctantly, yet they consented to the acts, and only those who clearly refused to do the deeds can be certainly said to have withheld consent.

According to this definition, some actions commonly thought to be suicides would not be genuine acts of self-assassination. For example, a spy who refused to give information to his enemy and was killed by his tormenters would not be committing suicide by this decision since the proximate and immediate cause of his death would be the actions of his tormenters. Even further, one who accedes to execution rather than renounce their religious beliefs would not be committing suicide because death would not be part of the plan to uphold their beliefs, even though they realize that death would be the result of their action. The person is merely consistently professing religious beliefs in even the most trying of situations.

What of a person who kills himself because he is being so horribly tortured by others that he cannot bear it any longer and he sees suicide as the only escape? Did prisoners of Nazi concentration camps commit true suicide when they threw themselves on electric fences because of the suffering inflicted by their tormenters? Such individuals did not commit authentic suicide, for their fear, pain, humiliation, despair, and depression so radically limited their freedom and voluntariness that they could not be considered fully responsible for their actions.

Conclusion

This chapter has dealt with the important issue of how one defines an authentic suicide, and it has been argued that an accurate definition of suicide must be neither too broad nor excessively narrow. The value of the definition of suicide proposed in this chapter is that it neither condemns morally legitimate acts of self-sacrifice nor morally permits suicidal acts of despair and irrationality. Making this precise sort of definition is necessary to understand not only the morality of suicide, but also to understand the Catholic response to claims that some suicides can be truly called "rational" self-killings.

Notes

1. Martin, R. M., "Suicide and Self-Sacrifice," in Battin, M., and Mayo, D., Eds. *Suicide: The Philosophical Issues* (New York: St. Martin's Press, 1980), 48-56. Martin goes on to argue that the principle of double effect is able to distinguish true suicides from other forms of self-killing, but he rejects this principle as being of little practical use for ethics and morality.
2. Battin, M. P., *Ethical Issues in Suicide*, (Englewood Cliffs, NJ: Prentice-Hall, 1982), 21-22.
3. See Durkheim, E., *Suicide,* Tr. Spaulding J. A., and Simpson G., (New York: Free Press, 1951), 44.
4. Ibid.
5. Perlin, S., Ed., *Handbook for the Study of Suicide*, (New York: Oxford University Press, 1974), 117.
6. Durkheim, E., *Suicide,* 44.
7. Frey, R. G., "Suicide and Self-Inflicted Death," *Philosophy*, 56 (1981): 193-202.
8. Kobler, A., "Suicide: Right and Reason," *Bioethics Quarterly*, 2 (1980): 49.
9. Margolis, J., *Negativities: The Limits of Life*, (Columbus, OH: Charles E. Merrill, 1975), 21-36.
10. Ibid.
11. Graber, G., "The Rationality of Suicide," *Suicide and Euthanasia: The Rights of Personhood,* Ed. Wallace S. E., and Eser A., (Knoxville: University of Tennessee Press, 1981), 57-58.
12. See Mayo, D., and Battin, M., Eds., "Contemporary Philosophical Literature on Suicide: A Review," *Suicide and Ethics*, (New York: Human Sciences Press, 1983), 317.
13. Beauchamp, T., "Suicide?" in *Matters of Life and Death,* Ed. Regan, T., (Philadelphia: Temple University Press, 1980), 77.
14. Ibid., 67-108. Also see Childress, J., and Beauchamp, T., *Principles of Biomedical Ethics*, (New York: Oxford University Press, 1979), and "What is Suicide?" in Beauchamp, T., and Perlin, S., Eds. *Ethical Issues in death and Dying*, (Englewood Cliffs: Prentice Hall, 1978), 97-102.
15. Windt, P., "The Concept of Suicide," in Battin, M., and Mayo, D. *Suicide: The Philosophical Issues*, Ed. Battin, M., and Mayo, D., (New York: St. Martin's, 1980), 41.
16. See McHugh, J., and Callan, C., *Moral Theology: A Complete Course,* vol. 1 (New York: Joseph Wagner, 1929), 6-17.
17. Suicide can only be attributed to an agent who is fundamentally and essentially responsible for the action, and this can be interpreted so broadly to mean that it could be imputed to a person who manipulated another person into killing them. See McHugh, J., and Callan, C., *Moral Theology,* vol. 1, 16-7.
18. O'Donnell, T., *Medicine and Christian Morality*, (New York: Alba House, 1975), 22.
19. Ashley, B., and O'Rourke, K., *Health Care Ethics: A Theological Analysis*, (St. Louis: Catholic Health Association, 1982), 58.
20. O'Donnell, T., *Medicine,* 25.
21. Devine, P., "On Choosing Death," in *Suicide: The Philosophical Issues,* Ed. Battin, M., and Mayo, D., 138-42. Unlike other "goods" or "values" that one might choose, Devine argues that there is a certain "opaqueness" about death that precludes a rational choice of it.
22. O'Donnell, T., *Medicine,* 22-27.

23. Ibid., 25.
24. Ashley, B., and O'Rourke, K., *Health Care Ethics,* 383.
25. Aquinas, T., *Summa Theologica,* I-II, q. 74, a. 7.
26. McHugh, J., and Callan, C., *Moral Theology,* 16. They claim that the voluntary can be both direct and indirect, but in both of these instances, actions are voluntary if they are made reluctantly.
27. O'Donnell, T., *Medicine,* 26.
28. Fear impedes the judgment of the mind, and it can become so great that a person can lose his capacity to judge. These are only extreme situations, however, for in most instances, fear accompanies informed and competent judgments. Actions done with fear, but not out of them, are relatively voluntary. But if they are done through fear, they are involuntary in a limited way. In most instances, fear only inhibits our freedom but does not destroy it. See McHugh, J., and Callan, C., *Moral Theology,* 17-18.

2

The Changing Face of Despair: The Catholic Response to Ancient Suicide

The French positivist philosopher Auguste Comte claimed that the eternal glory of Catholicism was that it did not permit suicide for any reason.[1] This is quite true, for the only other world religion that protests suicide as vigorously and effectively as Catholicism is Islam, and most historians of suicide admit that the only time that suicide was successfully curbed in Western society was in medieval Europe where the moral teachings of the Catholic church on suicide ruled.

In virtually all societies, some sorts of religious or therapeutic suicides were permitted, and almost all of these societies had very serious difficulties in curbing suicides. The most widely cited historian of suicide, Henry Fedden, acknowledged the pervasiveness of suicide and argued that it was the most efficient and satisfactory way to cope with suffering, failure, and pain for some.[2] Catholicism recognized the powerful lure of suicide and it argued for uncompromising prohibitions of it, for in the traditional Catholic perspective, suicide was a sinful act of despair. The classical Catholic ban on suicide was more effective during the Middle Ages than that of any other Christian religion, and even critics of this position admit that suicide was virtually unheard of among orthodox Catholics then.

There are a number of reasons why Catholicism was able to curb suicide so effectively. First, it created a profound and comprehensive sacramental, theological, and moral system that supported its prohibitions of self-killing. This belief system made the ban on suicide logically coherent and more persuasive for orthodox Catholics. Second, the Catholic church did not permit any "institutional suicide" to promote institutional goals of the Church. Heterodox Christians such as the Cathari, Donatists or Circumcellions allowed this, but the orthodox Catholic community never gave this official approval. The Catholic church prohibited this form of suicide because it understood that allowing any kind of institutional and deliberate self-killing would make it more difficult, if not impossible, to prohibit other forms of undesirable self-killing. Catholicism freed itself from this problem by simply prohibiting all forms of deliberate self-killing. Classical Catholic teachings insisted on prohibiting suicide not only because it was deliberate killing of the innocent and a violation of the principle of the sanctity of life, but also because it recognized through its nearly 2,000-year history of dealing with suicide in all kinds of societies and civilizations that only an absolute prohibition could effectively control it. Classical Catholicism regarded suicide as not only immoral killing but also as a serious threat to the poor, despairing, oppressed, and abandoned, and it saw an absolute ban on it as the best means of protecting them.

A common feature of the religions that were more permissive of suicide than Catholicism was that they either had a less powerful and comprehensive notion of the value of the person or no such concept at all. Their policies on suicide were a direct result of their evaluation of human life and the human person, and throughout history, the intensity of prohibitions of suicide rose or fell in relation to the estimations they made of it. But relative to other religions, Christian denominations, and moral systems, Catholicism presented some of the highest evaluations of human life in history and it proposed very rigid bans on self-killing because of these evaluations. Like Catholicism, Islam absolutely banned suicide, while mainstream Hinduism rejected it for all but the Brahmin nobility. But this ban has been associated with a terrible problem of suicides among not only the upper castes, but the lower as well. Traditional Catholicism rejected this class-specific ban because it believed that allowing it for any class would increase the vulnerability of other classes to suicide, and it parted company with many proponents of rational suicide. It recognized that the irrational are more prone to suicide than advocates of rational suicide would admit and that only a thoroughgoing prohibition would give them the protection they need.

The comprehensive Catholic prohibition of suicide was based on its doctrines of the Incarnation and creation of human life in the image of God. The doctrine of the Incarnation held that human nature was sufficiently good to warrant being assumed by the Word of God into the Hypostatic Union in spite of any afflictions or disabilities it might suffer. Because human nature retained this goodness, it was worthy of preservation, and it should never be deliberately turned against or destroyed. Fundamental to Catholicism's Incarnational teaching was the doctrine that human nature was not fundamentally corrupted by Original Sin, but retained sufficient goodness to be able to receive the divine nature. The immediate ethical consequence of the latter was that any deliberate attack on a person was seen as a remote attack on God himself.

In what follows, I will survey the history of suicide to show that the classical Catholic ban was almost unique in history, was extremely effective in preventing suicide, and should not be demeaned as immoral and irrational. I will show that suicide plagued the ancient world and that ancient Latin Christianity did a great service by establishing this ban.

Suicide in Preliterate Society

In his comprehensive history in support of rational suicide, Henry Fedden argued that a "suicide-horror", an irrational terror and fear of self-inflicted death in preliterate cultures made it a taboo, and he implied that any modern comprehensive prohibition of suicide was little more than an intellectualized and rationalized modern expression of "suicide-horror."[3] Fedden considered this horror to be irrational, and would not agree that there could be any sound reason for this banning of certain types of suicide. But such a reaction may not be irrational in many instances, for all suicides are tragic because an innocent person loses his or her life and, as we well know today, one suicide can lead to an uncontrollable epidemic of reflexive killing.

Many now believe that two kinds of suicide were common in preliterate societies: personal suicide to escape shame, pain, and suffering; and institutional suicide to promote a given institutional value. But in reality, our knowledge of the suicidal practices of preliterate societies is spotty and uncertain, for while we have a good number of reports of personal suicides in preliterate societies, we can assume it must have been rather widely practiced, even though it was condemned in many of these societies.[4] In some instances it provoked a strongly negative response because of the harm it did to its victims and others, while in other instances it was treated quite casually.

It is probably true that institutional suicides were less frequent than personal suicides in preliterate societies, but nonetheless, they were still widely found.[5] These involved the suicides of the wives or attendants of kings, enforced suicides as punishments for offenders, the voluntary deaths of widows, and suicides of the aged and infirm. In addition, Moslems forbade self-killing but permitted the killing of others, particularly if they were of another religious faith.[6] Alfred Alvarez claims that Tasmanian Aborigines committed suicide when the Europeans came by refusing to procreate.[7] Among the

Massegetae, a tribe of Scythians mentioned by Herodotus, it was customary to eat one's friends when they grew old.[8] And among certain Central American Indians and Melanesians, a man's wife would be buried alive with him when he died.[9] The Crestoneans allowed deadly struggles among the wives of a man who died for the right to share his grave.[10] Celtic kings often had hundreds of servants who vowed to commit suicide at their death and, having made this vow, they received a share in his worldly wealth and power.[11] The servants of the king of Benin would leap into his grave and vie with one another to be the first to die after him.[12] And while many preliterate societies deeply despised suicide, others extolled it. North European worshipers of Odin believed that only those who died by the sword would enter eternal bliss, and thus, many would commit suicide when they fell sick, as this would win paradise for them and relieve them of their suffering and disgrace.[13]

It was not uncommon in preliterate societies to commit suicide as a means to gain revenge, or express anger or jealousy. Some tribes, such as the Todas, would even prescribe a precise ritual for an anger-revenge suicide.[14] In Southern India, a woman who was insulted by another woman would kill herself by smashing her head against the door of the offender to force her to do the same.[15] The woman who gave the insult would then have to commit suicide or else a ghost would haunt her, her house would be burned and her cattle would be carried off. And if these misfortunes did not befall her, tribal laws would require retaliation to force her to suicide.[16]

Military defeat was often a motive for suicide in preliterate society, probably because suicides were allowed for so many other reasons as well. Montaigne tells how a king of Malucca suicided when it became clear to him that the Portuguese would be victorious over his forces.[17] It is by no means certain, but it is quite possible that many of the Oceanic tribes similarly disappeared in the face of European conquerors between 1550 and 1900 because of mass suicides.

Epidemics of diseases were also known to cause waves of suicide in preliterate societies. A traveler among the Mandan Indians in the 1830s wrote:

> When they saw all of their relations buried, and the pestilence still raging with unabated fury among the remainder of their countrymen, life became a burden to them, and they put an end to their wretched existence, either with their knives and muskets or by precipitating themselves from the summit of the rock near their settlements.[18]

Among the native North American Indians, suicide was quite common and the Kwakiutl, Sikanni, Carrier tribes, and the Tasmanians practiced a form of *suttee* in which widows would either lie upon their husband's funeral pyre or allow themselves to be pushed into it.[19] In Melanesia, a similar form of *suttee* was practiced in which the wife of a deceased husband let herself be strangled shortly after his death.[20] In the New Hebrides, this custom was followed, but the woman was buried alive instead of being strangled.[21]

It is difficult to know how widely suicide was practiced in pre-Columbian America, but there is good reason to believe that it was quite common because of the waves of suicides of natives following the Spanish conquest.[22] The Seri Indians of southern California and northern Mexico were virtually extinguished because of suicide.[23] Seeing that they could not recover their former life, they consciously and deliberately sought to end their lives by suicide.[24] Historian Girolamo Benzoni claimed that of 2,000,000 native Haitians, only 150,000 survived the European invasion because of slaughter and suicide.[25] The Taino population on the island of Hispaniola shrank from millions to thousands and eventually became extinct because of mass suicides.[26] He added that 4,000 men and women committed suicide in order to avoid living under Spanish domination.[27] But it is unlikely that the conquest alone would have precipitated these mass suicides, for these tribes were probably predisposed to this by previously tolerated ritualistic, personal, political, and military suicides. The Natchez and Maiori Indians strangled the wives of husbands who died,[28] and the Iroquois and Mohawks were quite violent, practicing cannibalism and torture, which suggests that suicide was probably not uncommon among them.[29]

Prescott, in his *History of the Conquest of Peru,* claimed that concubines of Peruvian kings were immolated on the king's tomb after his death.[30] The Aztecs allowed the practice of offering human sacrifices to the gods, which often assumed a voluntary character. Each spring a young man was chosen a year in advance to be sacrificed to the god Tezcatlipoca.[31] He was honored as a god during that year and was able to choose the time and place of his death. They also sacrificed attendants or wives when chiefs died, but it is not clear if these were voluntary deaths. And there is reason to believe that personal suicide was commonly permitted by other Central American tribes.[32]

Suicide for personal motives was common in preliterate societies, especially in Malaysia among the Bontoc Igorots[33] and in the Philippines among the Bukiddnon.[34] In Africa, personal suicide was found among all of the tribes except the Bushmen and Hottentots.[35] The Ibos, Egba, Yoruba, and Tshi allowed suicide as a means of gaining revenge on others.[36] Suicide among black slaves in the English colonies was also rather common.[37] Their suicides appeared unique, for their aim was not only to escape their terrible lot, but also to find life after death by returning in death to their native homeland.

Suicide was probably common in a number of preliterate societies, and therefore a threat, because many of these societies did not have an adequate concept of the transcendence and sanctity of human life. This denied them a foundation for a comprehensive prohibition of self-killing, and, as a result, desperate social and ritualistic measures were taken because many of these societies understood the threat of suicide. They faced virtually the same problems we face today, and they opted for these extreme social and ritualistic measures to curb it, precisely because they had no other means available to stop it. Extreme and often bizarre methods were sometimes used in preliterate society to curb suicide because many preliterates suicided for much slighter reasons than people do today.[38] The intensity of these antisuicide measures and their bizarreness suggest that preliterate people saw suicide as a serious threat, and they were often willing to go to extreme measures to curb it. They were probably aware that suicide epidemics could start easily and were quite difficult to control once begun; thus they took extreme measures to deter their outbreak.

One study claimed that in China there were 500,000 suicides per year, amounting to a rate of 1 suicide for every 800 citizens, an extraordinarily high figure.[39] Some consider these figures inflated, but in defense of them, it is known that in the eighteenth century boats circulated around the Foochow bridge to rescue those who flung themselves into the river.[40] These extreme measures were warranted also by the large number of suicides in preliterate cultures. Some tribes (including Hellenic tribes later on) would cut off the hands of those who self-executed while others floated their bodies down rivers to drive out the spirits that caused the suicide.[41] The Wajagga of East Africa sacrificed a goat in the place where someone committed suicide to mollify the spirit that caused the suicide.[42] Others also took steps to purify themselves of the unclean spirits that caused the suicide and to protect themselves from its malevolence.

What seem to be mere taboos to us may have been partially effective social, ritualistic, and moral measures undertaken to curb outbreaks of suicide grounded on their deficient understanding of the transcendence of human life. Some preliterate societies may well have understood better than do contemporary proponents of rational suicide that permitting suicide for one reason or in one circumstance commits one to permitting it in others, and that could well be the reason for the taboos and rituals. Suicide advocates believe that they can both allow certain suicides that they desire and be free to prohibit all others, but I would suggest that preliterates recognized that one must ban all suicides and one cannot selectively proscribe only some of them, and in holding this, they may have been wiser than contemporary advocates of self-killing.

Hellenistic Suicide: A Schizophrenic Approach

The Hellenistic suicidal practices were typical of those of many ancient peoples, for on the one hand there were pre-Homeric elements that strongly and bitterly opposed suicide and that developed moral condemnations and antisuicide rituals to stop it. But on the other hand, there were elements in Hellenistic society that became increasingly tolerant of various sorts of suicide. Realizing that it could not be curbed in all instances, these post-Homeric elements came to countenance it more and more.

Suicide was probably rather common in Hellenic society, despite the fact that some undertook extreme measures to curb it. Some educated Greeks raised strong moral objections to suicide, but we know of only a few who protested with much vigor. Suicides to escape disease were a later development, even though the Egyptian pharaoh, Ramses the Great, killed himself to put an end to his chronic illness in 1250 B.C.[43] In Homeric times, suicide was often an act of revenge, much as was the case in preliterate society. But suicide often occurred for less vindictive reasons. The Sidonians and Tyrians burned themselves and their cities when besieged by Artaxerxes Ochus.[44] Calanus traveled with Alexander the Great, and suicided after his excesses blinded him, and he went to his death by leaping into a flaming pyre in front of the entire Macedonian army.[45]

Many early Greeks seemed to have accepted some suicides to preserve "honor" as perfectly legitimate and they extolled these suicides in Greek mythology. The mythical figure Aigeus flung himself into the sea when he mistakenly believed his son had been killed by the Minotaur.[46] Ajax committed suicide and may have done so partly out of revenge.[47] When Jocasta discovered she was living with her son, she hung herself, which was probably accepted as a proper response to the situation.[48] Frazer recalled that Erigone committed suicide and that many Athenian girls almost immediately followed suit.[49] To put an end to this, the custom was developed of hanging a doll on a tree to commemorate this episode and to deter further suicides.

Post-Homeric Greek society became quite tolerant of suicide and in many places actually encouraged it, particularly for sickness, egregious crimes, military defeat or political catastrophes. On the island of Ceos, a supply of poison was stored to enable those over 60 to self-execute,[50] and it seems that the Athenians did this also.[51] In the Greek colony of Marseilles, magistrates kept a supply of poison for those who had adequate reasons for suiciding. The law governing its use was clear:

> Whoever no longer wishes to live shall state his reasons to the Senate, and after having received permission shall abandon life. If your existence is hateful to you, die; if you are overwhelmed by fate, drink the hemlock. If you are bowed with grief, abandon life. Let the unhappy man recount his misfortune, let the magistrate supply him with the remedy, and his wretchedness will come to an end.[52]

But as tolerance of suicide developed, so also did a more abusive and degrading view of the value of human life. Athenaeus tells us that the Thracians would play a game of hanging and would

> fix a round noose to some high place, exactly beneath which they place a stone. . . then they cast lots, and he who draws the lot, holding a sickle in his hand, stands upon the stone, and puts his neck into the halter. Another person then moves the stone from under him, and if he cannot cut the rope in time with his sickle, he is hung; and the rest laugh, thinking his death good sport.[53]

This episode typifies the contempt for life and low value placed on human life by many Greeks and it explains why those of more sensitive conscience welcomed the higher valuation of life offered by the Christians. The senselessness of many of these suicides also suggests that it would be difficult, if not impossible, to go back to the easy tolerance of suicide shown in antiquity that is now being espoused by many advocates of rational suicide without also reviving the frivolous and contemptuous attitudes toward human life that were so common then.

At certain times individuals were required to commit suicide.[54] The most famous of these was Themistocles who offered his services to the Persians after being banished from Athens. When the Persians experienced difficulties defeating the Greek navies, they called on him, but rather than subduing his own country, he supposedly drank bull's blood.[55] The custom developed that it was dishonorable to fall into the hands of one's enemies, and the possibility of such a disgrace warranted suicide.[56] Isocrates, for example, starved himself to death to keep from falling into the hands of Philip of Macedon.[57] Sometimes, there was such pressure to commit suicide that the sole survivor of the battle of Thermopylae killed himself for no other reason than that fate would allow him to survive the battle.[58] Charondas of Catana supposedly forbade anyone to enter the assembly armed, but when he forgot to remove his sword and inadvertently broke his own law, he allegedly committed suicide.[59] Codrus, the last Athenian king, killed himself by sneaking into the enemy camp and provoking a fight, and his death roused the Athenians to victory.[60] It appears that the women of Miletus killed themselves in large numbers when their husbands were called to war.[61] The horrible story is told of the town of Abydos, which suffered an epidemic of suicides when Philip of Macedon's army approached.[62] He withdrew to prevent the suicides, but when he returned he found all its inhabitants dead.

On occasion, the Greeks viewed suicide quite harshly. Because he died by suicide, Ajax was buried and not cremated, which was considered a gross desecration of his remains, and even Plato allowed those who suicided for insufficient reason to be buried apart from all others in nameless tombs.[63] The Thebans and Spartans were the most severe in punishing suicide, and Plutarch says that citizens of Miletos stopped a wave of suicides among young girls by threatening to drag their unclad bodies through the market place to the cemeteries with the rope they used to hang themselves.[64] But other communities viewed suicide more permissively. Many Greek city-states frequently declined to punish those who starved themselves to death, possibly because they considered them to be performing a considered and thoughtful action. It might also be that these were seen as similar to the *suttee* of the Brahmins of India and were regarded as quasi-religious acts of abandonment of the world that would be morally tolerable.

Greek philosophy and religion were generally critical of suicide, but they did allow it for certain reasons. Pythagoras forbade men to "depart from their guard or station in life without the order of their commander, that is, of God."[65] The Orphic cult objected to suicide and considered it a deliberate mutilation of the property of the gods.[66] Apuleius said that "the wise man never throws off his body except by the will of God".[67] In the *Laws,* Plato generally opposed suicide except when one had been struck down with calamity or poverty.[68] But in the *Phaedo,* he became much less tolerant of it.[69] Plotinus admitted that there could be cases of "stern necessity" when suicide would be legitimate, but he was even less tolerant of suicide than Plato.[70] Cleombrotus supposedly read Plato's argument that the soul was immortal and then threw himself out of a window to find a life better than this one.[71] Diogenes seems to have agreed, for he handed a knife to his pupil Antisthenes when he was in great pain.[72] Socrates was not deterred from suiciding, even though he considered the person to be the property of the gods, and yet when he suspected that Porphyry wanted to commit suicide, he went out of his way to convince him not to do so. He also considered the person to be the soldier of the gods, and he believed suicide should be allowed for only the most serious reasons.[73] Aristotle considered suicide unjust to the state, and he also believed it to be an act contrary to courage, but he nonetheless permitted it in some situations.[74] While post-Homeric society considered suicide compassionate, liberal, and even just in some cases, beneath it lay a subtle contempt for the value and sanctity of human life. Despite these objections, there was some philosophical support for suicide, for Democritus is said to have died by suicide,[75] and this claim was also made about Thrasymachus.[76] Hellenistic tolerance for suicide is presently being extolled as a moral model, but such a perception leaves out the fact that this society was plagued by tragic and frivolous suicides, which in many respects it desperately sought to curb. Suicide may have brought relief to some, but this has been bought at a high price by this society.

Roman Suicide: Libertinism and the Trivialization of Human Life

The Romans acquired at least some of their views about the value of life from the Greeks, but they gave suicide a scope, dimension, and intensity not seen in the Hellenistic world.[77] They committed suicide to preserve honor, avoid the ignominy of old age and disease, honor a loved one in the hope they would be together after life, advance the empire, a cause, faction or family, or avoid falling into the hands of an enemy. But they also did it for exhibitionist reasons, to avoid slavery, or to escape poverty. The Roman intelligentsia and aristocracy suicided to preserve honor and escape shame, to prove one's patriotism, and to show fidelity, but they also suicided for frivolous reasons in far greater numbers than did the Greeks, and they developed a propensity for suicide that was unseen before.[78]

Fedden claims that suicide among the upper classes of Roman society was common, but not in the lower classes.[79] This view is difficult to accept for two reasons. First, it ignores the fact that suicide was so common in the Roman world that it was known as "Roman death," and it would not have acquired this infamy if it was restricted to the aristocracy.[80] And second, the poor of Rome suffered hardship, poverty, servitude, cruelty, and ignorance so far beyond that experienced by the upper classes that they would have had far stronger reason for reflexive killing than did wealthy and powerful Romans. Whatever reasons aristocratic Romans may have had for suiciding were insignificant in comparison to those of the Roman slaves or lower classes. At slave auctions, sellers frequently had to verify that a given slave did not have epilepsy or chronic ill health, and was not prone to theft or suicide.[81] And when defeated enemy soldiers were taken back to Rome to be sold, they had to be watched closely because so many prisoners of war committed suicide.[82] And if these classes along with the upper classes were suiciding frequently, it is quite likely that the lower classes did so as well.

Suicide seems to have been less common in the republic than in the empire. The suicides of Cato, Seneca, Marc Anthony, Brutus, and Cleopatra are the most famous of the republican era, which suggests that it was widely practiced among the upper classes even during the republic, and it is well known that many nobles committed suicide to escape humiliation or for political reasons. Lucretia was also famous for her suicide, and a wave of these suicides broke out shortly after her death.[83] Roman soldiers who were forced by Tarquinius to dig ditches considered their tasks so demeaning that they threw themselves from the Capitoline hill to avoid what they considered a disgrace.[84]

There were a number of "patriotic suicides" in the empire. Hadrian's physician supposedly took the hemlock with the emperor's permission when he refused to comply with one of Hadrian's demands.[85] The story was famous through Rome of Marcus Curtius who threw himself into a fissure in the earth, which opened in the forum as a result of an earthquake. An oracle said that a gift of Rome's most precious possession would close the rift, and he claimed that a brave citizen was that gift. Cornelia killed herself after the defeat and death of Crassus, and Arria suicided after being discovered in plot against Claudius.[86] The emperor Otho suicided in 69 A.D. after he retreated from a battle to prevent sacrificing more Roman soldiers in a civil war,[87] and many of his soldiers were so moved by it that they killed themselves as well.

The Romans suicided not only for serious reasons, but also for utterly trivial ones as well. Pliny the Elder allowed those who were so ill that their color or countenance changed to commit suicide.[88] Echoing the Greek customs, suicide was also frequently forced on individuals as a punishment, which Nero did with Seneca.[89] Suicides for purely "entertainment" purposes seemed to have become rather common in the republic and even more so in the empire. Fedden claimed that it was easy to recruit individuals at the time of the Punic wars who would offer themselves to be executed for rather small amounts of money, which would be given to their heirs.[90] And for a higher price, others could be found to be slowly beaten and mangled to death, which created an even greater spectacle. These unfortunates were beheaded or cudgeled to death simply for the entertainment of the spectators, and as Fedden asserts, their real deaths were fare for the theater-going public.[91]

The casual attitude of even the early Romans toward the death of those in the lower classes was typified by Symmachus. He wanted to bring twenty-nine slaves to the public games he was giving in honor of his sons, but all twenty-nine rebelled before the games and committed suicide. He was furious that "impious" hands had deprived Rome "of her sport," which is startling because he was considered one of the finest of the Roman aristocrats, embodying its highest values and integrity.[92] This also suggests that suicide was quite common among the lower classes who were treated very badly by the aristocracy and were seen merely as resources for their sport and profit.

Like some Greeks, Romans also suicided for exhibitionistic reasons. Peregrinus traveled through the empire preaching contempt for death and claiming that he would commit suicide as a sign of his disdain.[93] He finally did this with great fanfare by throwing himself on a flaming pyre at the start of the Olympic games.[94] The cynic Diogenes Laertes supposedly killed himself by holding his breath.[95] Both Greeks and Romans imitated Indian Brahmins who sought to speed their rise to immortality by ending their lives; Empedocles, for example, jumped into a volcano in a vain attempt to show that he had gone to the gods.[96] Sardanapalus is reported to have set 150 gold couches and tables on a vast pyre in a room and collected 10 million talents of gold. He summoned his wife and concubines and committed suicide by ordering his slaves to set it on fire with him in the middle of it.[97] Heliogalbus purchased a rope of purple and gold and a golden sword, and ordered a pavement of jewels to be built between two towers from which he was going to leap after stabbing himself. Unfortunately (from his perspective), he was murdered by his guards before he could do this.[98]

With the spread of humanistic ideas in the empire, philosophical or analgesic suicides became more common. Suicide as a sign of devotion and love increased also, as is seen in the case of Paulina and Portia who tried suicide to be with Seneca and Brutus in death.[99] Antony's suicide was unique in the Roman world because it was the first one motivated by love. There is not much by way of evidence of suicide among the poor to escape poverty, but it was probably common because many destitute freemen were sold into slavery.

Suicidal practices reached their peak intensity after Stoic and Epicurean philosophy gained dominance in the empire. Seneca permitted suicide, but he admitted that he had to curb the passion for suicide among some of his followers.[100] He wrote:

> As I choose the ship in which I will sail, and the house I will inhabit, so I will choose the death by which I will leave life. . . . The lot of man is happy because no one continues wretched but by his own fault.[101]

Seneca believed it was braver to face death than one's troubles, and he asserted that he would not relinquish

> old age if it leaves my better part intact. But if it begins to shake my mind, if it destroys its faculties one by one, if it leaves me not life but breath, I will depart from the putrid or tottering edifice. I will not escape by death from disease so long as it may be healed, and leaves my mind unimpaired. I will not raise my hand against myself on account of my pain, for so to die is to be conquered. But if I know that I must suffer without hope of relief, I will depart, not through fear of pain itself, but because it prevents all for which I would live.[102]

Stoics, Epicureans, and Cynics urged suicide as a rational way of preserving dignity and honor, and even as a duty in some instances.[103] Epicurus urged men "to weigh carefully whether they would prefer death to come to them, or would themselves go to death."[104] His student, the poet Lucretius, was supposed to have suicided, as was Atticus[105] and Cassius Longinus.[106] Epictetus said that

> [a]bove all things, remember that the door is open. Be not more timid than boys at play. As they, when they cease to take pleasure in their games declare that they will no longer play, so do you, when all things begin to pall upon you, retire; but if you stay, do not complain.[107]

Musonius claimed that

> [j]ust as a landlord who has not received his rent, pulls down the doors, removes the rafters, and fills up the well, so I seem to be driven out of this little body, when nature, which has let it to me, takes away one by one, eyes and ears, hands and feet. I will not therefore delay any longer, but will cheerfully depart as from a banquet.[108]

Some of these suicides were permitted for the most trivial of reasons and life was often treated with great ridicule and contempt. Zeno, the founder of the Stoics, supposedly committed suicide after having put a toe out of joint.[109] The Stoics believed it was brave and honorable to face the knife, for none of the beasts could die in such a way. Attalus advised Marcellinus, who was contemplating suicide,

> Be not tormented, my Marcellinus, as if you were deliberating of any great matter. Life is a thing of no dignity or importance. Your very slaves, your animals, possess it in common with yourself: but it is a great thing to die honorably, prudently, bravely. Think how long you have been engaged in the same dull course: eating, sleeping and indulging your appetites. This has been the circle. Not only a prudent, brave or a wretched man may wish to die, but even a fastidious one.[110]

Marcellinus took his advice and starved himself to death.[111]

A fuller expression of their contempt for human life was seen in the writings of Hegesias. He extolled self-starvation and claimed that the pleasures of life were so worthless that death was the only wise alternative.[112] Ptolemy was forced to take action and when his follower began to preach these ideas, he was forced to leave

Alexandria because of the threat he posed.[113] Stoicism continued to grow in the Roman world and suicide from despair became more common as the Stoics took a much more grim view of the possibility of happiness.[114] Lecky gave a credible account of why this happened:

> Stoicism taught men to hope for little, but to fear nothing. It did not array death in brilliant colors as the path to positive felicity, but it endeavored to divest it, as the end of suffering, of every great terror. Life lost much of its bitterness when men had found a refuge from the storms of fate, a speedy deliverance from dotage and pain. Death ceased to be terrible when it was regarded rather as a remedy than as a sentence. Life and death in the Stoical system were attuned to the same key.[115]

The Stoics and Epicureans looked on suicide as a purely personal affair that was permitted under any circumstance and certainly desirable when there were issues of dishonor, old age, or illness at stake. The Epicureans allowed it when one's pain overcame the pleasure to be found in one's life, and the Epicureans were not far behind the Stoics in their disregard for the value of human life. Lucretius the Epicurean poet wrote:

> If one day, as well may happen, life grows wearisome, there only remains to pour a libation to death and oblivion. A drop of subtle poison will gently close your eyes to the sun, and waft you smiling into the eternal night whence everything comes and to which everything returns.[116]

In this perspective, there is no concept of a life after death, and terminal suffering is regarded as a human experience that is of no value. The Epicureans, nonetheless, suicided in ways very different from the Stoics, who ended their lives while contemplating philosophical problems and truths. The Roman Epicurean Petronius, who was appointed by Nero as the *arbiter elegantarium,* was a man of exquisite taste and manners and he committed suicide at a banquet by opening and closing his veins at his leisure.[117] And rather than contemplating the nature of human life and the soul, he spent his final hours in humor, conversation, and discussion of the affairs of the day. Fedden contends that suiciding in the face of the cruel and inhumane conditions of the empire was an act of courage and bravery. But self-execution for this reason was questionably courageous, and it probably hurt the plight of the suffering masses of the empire more than it helped them. Had the lower classes stood up to protest their atrocious conditions and not killed themselves, others might have taken their claims more seriously and their plight may have been improved. In contrast to this practice, the Christians protested vigorously against many of the cruelties that led others to suicide, but they did not commit suicide in protest, and these objectionable practices often vanished almost immediately after Christians were given legal authority. When Christian religious values appeared that did give an adequate valuation of life, these practices were rather swiftly abolished.

Disrespect for the value of human life prevailed at all levels of Roman life, and even the best Romans had a feeble concept of the sanctity of human life and little esteem for it. This was due in large part to the failure of Roman and Greek religions to offer an adequate concept of the value of life or clearly articulate its purpose and meaning. There was not only the studied contempt of human life seen in Cato, but also the thoughtless and passionate contempt of it in Marc Antony. The suicides of these luminaries were tragic, not only because valuable assets were lost to Rome, but also because life was senselessly destroyed. Cato's suicide was held as the model of Roman Republican virtue and it showed not only a contempt and lack of love for human life, but also a lack of love for his friends, for on the night of his suicide, they pleaded passionately with him not to end his life, but he turned a deaf ear. His was an act of despair that was due in part to the failure of Roman religion, law, and the republic to foster any higher virtues than those that served its immediate needs.

Suicide was probably widespread in Roman society because it was caught up in the institutionalized violence of the republic and empire, which manifested an astonishing ferocity to sustain itself. In the empire, the most violent won power and wealth, even though this violence made no one secure. Many peoples attacked by the Romans desperately feared enslavement and would do virtually anything to escape their cruelty and violence, for the viciousness of the Romans toward many of their enemies was extreme even by ancient standards. For many Romans, life itself seemed to have had no value and was to be used to advance imperial or personal interests. The only institutions that might have stopped this devaluation of human life were the Greek and Roman religions, but they were so superficial, unreflective, and devoid of moral insight that they could not meet this challenge. There was so little serious theological reflection in Roman religion and such a web of superstition and myth that it was unable to overcome the critical power of the philosophers, Stoics, Cynics, and Epicureans and challenge their ethic of suicide, so that when critical minds turned to these religions, they found no opposition to suicide for a great number of reasons.

There were some protests against suicide but these were generally few and far between. In Roman literature, Virgil expressed a horror of suicide that may have won sympathy in some circles, but his was probably a minority view.[118] As was the case with the Greeks, Roman law only punished suicide attempts of soldiers or slaves because such attempts would violate their duties to society or debts to others.[119] Roman imperial law (as seen in Justinian's *Digest*) imposed virtually no prohibitions on suicides by free men, and only criminals, slaves, and soldiers were penalized for attempting it.[120] It was unable to stop the spread of suicide because it penalized only its harmful effects, and it did not see suicide as a legally punishable action if done by free men.[121] This suggests that it regarded the person only as an entity of monetary or utilitarian value, and that it protested suicide only because of the loss of power or value it entailed for others. But the Romans had no other laws to prohibit it, which showed that they had virtually no concept of the value of human life.

Christianity entered the Roman empire with its absolute condemnation of suicide, and this condemnation may account in part for the speed of its growth. Many conscientious individuals may have been so disgusted with the prevailing disrespect for human life in the empire that they embraced Christianity. As many were repelled by the luxury and indulgence of the Roman aristocracy, so also many might have been repulsed by the cruel Roman disregard of human life that prevailed in the latter empire.

The Judeo-Christian Response to Ancient Suicide

One of the remarkable features of ancient, medieval, and modern Judaism is the nearly total absence of suicide throughout these times. About the only recorded instances of large numbers of Jewish suicides were at Massada when the Romans finally breached their defenses, and in the Middle Ages when they were made the victims of pogroms.[122] A tradition developed in ancient and medieval Judaism that regarded suicide as sacrilegious; as a result, there were very few instances of it, so few that even at the height of the Holocaust, relatively few Jews committed suicide.[123]

Suicide in Early Christianity

The orthodox Christians entered the Roman Empire with a theological and moral perspective grounded in Judaism that strongly opposed suicide. Human life was regarded as a treasure of such great value that even God took it to himself in the Incarnation.[124] Human nature was weakened and corrupted by the sin of Adam, but it was not so deeply corrupted that it was unable to receive the divine nature. The orthodox Christians neither despised life and embraced death nor did they make sport of it as did the Romans.[125] They did not fear death, *pace* Fedden; but they did treasure life, unlike the Stoics and Romans who demeaned it. Christians acknowledged the sufferings of this life but these did not warrant them fleeing the world as the Brahmins did by suiciding, and the early Christians believed that even suffering could lead to God.

The orthodox Christian view of suicide of this time was grounded on its belief that the Incarnation so intimately related us to God that it imputed a radical value to human life. This doctrine gave the early Christians a theological structure that enabled them to see the value in human suffering, and it permitted them to both esteem this life and not fear death. For ancient philosophers, suffering was often seen as vain, senseless, and empty, particularly when it would end only in death. But the orthodox Christian understanding of the value of human life based on the Incarnation and *imago Dei* was able to give even the most problematic forms of suffering meaning and value, which was not possible for the ancient religions and philosophies.[126]

The early Christians saw the world as the place where charity was to be practiced not only to imitate and draw closer to Christ, but also to speed his return in the Parousia.[127] The pagans had little to say about charity while Christians spoke about it incessantly. Unlike their pagan adversaries, the early orthodox Christians were not as deeply troubled by the *ennui* of the world because of the centrality of charity for this life as it was revealed in the Incarnation, ministry, passion, death, and Resurrection of Jesus.

Alfred Alvarez and Henry Fedden claim that Christians provoked the Romans to persecute them, but the early orthodox Christians hardly had to provoke the Romans to violence, for it was almost second nature to them.[128] The difficulty with their claim is that many more orthodox Christians negotiated with or fled their persecutors than actively sought their own martyrdom.[129] Alvarez asserts that the early Christian martyrs provoked their killers by the thousands, but this view turns the Christians into Romans who used the weapons of the Romans against them. He also does not distinguish the orthodox Christians from those such as the Montanists, Circumcellions, and Donatists who did provoke the Romans in great numbers.[130] The Circumcellions actively sought death, but they were the enemies of the orthodox and could hardly be considered as representative of the orthodox Christian view of suicide. They pleaded for death as a sign of holiness, while the orthodox usually allowed it only when it was thrust on them.

The approach of the early orthodox Christians to martyrdom is best seen in their reverence for human life. Initially, they only considered those who died for the faith at other's hands as true saints, and those who did not suffer in this way were not regarded as authentic saints. The orthodox Christians accepted martyrdom but did not actively provoke their persecutors, and this distinguished them from the Donatists and Circumcellions.[131] But the notion of martyrdom as a necessary condition for sanctity was misunderstood by many, and this misunderstanding caused much confusion. Many of the Donatists and Circumcellions provoked their deaths in the belief that this would bring them sanctity and they would readily permit others to suicide in order to achieve this as well.[132] The orthodox community expanded its understanding of holiness to include the teachers of the faith, those who developed an extraordinary life of prayer or asceticism and those who served the Church in an exceptional way.

While there were early heterodox Christians who committed suicide in the name of the faith, the great portion of orthodox Christians who died at the hands of the Roman persecutors did not act to bring their deaths on themselves, and to call these deaths suicidal would be to misrepresent their actions, aims, and objectives. They did not cause or provoke their deaths as did the Circumcellions, and in many instances they contemplated fleeing their persecutors rather than being delivered into their hands. However, they did not flee death when it was thrust upon them as the only alternative to betraying their fidelity to Christ. They saw the death they *accepted* as one that would win them union with Christ because it was a vicarious sharing in the death he *accepted* for our sins. It is even more unfair to compare their deaths with those Romans who had themselves killed to provide monetary compensation for their families or simply for sport. The deaths of the early Christian martyrs, accepted as a sign of fidelity to Christ, are of a different order than those who killed themselves for the pleasure of the crowds, to escape shameful situations or to flee pain, suffering, ridicule or abuse.

For the early orthodox Christians, the Roman persecutors were only intermittently lenient and tolerant, and most often they were persecutors who demanded that the Christians betray their loyalty to Christ and adore what the Christians regarded as false gods. The Romans were quite difficult in their dealings with the early Christians, often treating them quite badly and persecuting them sporadically.[133] They acted violently toward the Christians, not only because they saw them as posing a real threat, but also because the superior Christian moral codes and more advanced theological doctrines threatened Roman claims to moral preeminence.[134] There is little reason to claim that Christians who were not associated with the Circumcellions, Montanists or Donatists actively sought out martyrdom in significant numbers.[135] Many of these orthodox Christians were martyred by Nero, Domition, Marcus Aurelius, and certainly Diocletian, and they did not die because they searched for martyrdom, but because the empire violently lashed out against the Christians in a vain attempt to suppress a very real threat to its power.

As examples of the abusive way the Romans treated the Christians, Trajan objected not only to Christian religious practices, which he considered bizarre and possibly dangerous, but also to the tenacity with which they clung to their faith and their refusal to adore the emperor.[136] An entire congregation of Christians was burned alive in Phrygia by a mob, more the result of the fanaticism of the *ruditores* who were quite accustomed to resolving difficult political, social, and religious difference with fire and the sword than to any Christian provocation.[137] Decius came to a Christian church to see the people, but was turned away by Babylas, and one of the Christians justified this inhospitality by saying that the wolf should not enter the fold, a remark that cost him his life.[138] This hostility of the Romans came fully out into the open under Diocletian who prohibited all Christian worship in the hope of destroying them,[139] and he was so driven that he even required his daughter and wife to offer sacrifice.[140]

The early orthodox Christians disregarded Diocletian's edict, which banned the Christian religion and required sacrifice to the Roman gods, just as it would be disregarded today if similar laws were to be promulgated, and they could not be considered fanatics for so doing.[141] Some would charge that this constituted a provocation, but had these Christians acceded to his demands, they would probably have been considered religious frauds and charlatans, and just because they would not acquiesce to these demands does not mean they were suicidal fanatics. The Romans were not reluctant persecutors, for it would have been easy for them to let the Christians worship as they saw fit. This had been done with other religions, and it is not clear why it could not have been done with Christianity. We would not consider Jews or Buddhists who refused to worship the Christian God under penalty of death as suicidal fanatics, but would consider their killers to be zealots who kill those who do not share their beliefs. We would not consider Jews who spat on rather than kissed the Nazi flag to be suicidal fanatics, and Christians who desecrated altars they were ordered to venerate under penalty of death should not be considered as religious and suicidal maniacs.

Some critics argue that the early Christians killed themselves to gain heaven, which is true of the Circumcellions. But generally, the early Christians did not self-assassinate to flee this life, but allowed themselves to be killed by others to show fidelity, loyalty, and love of Christ.[142] Their deaths were quite different from the "noble" suicides of Cato, Seneca, and Antony who killed themselves not to witness to the truth of Roman religion or to show loyalty and fidelity to the gods, but primarily from the motives of escaping shame, disgrace, and loss.

The Christians of the third century developed a respect for martyrdom as a full expression of the devotion to the faith, but the Circumcellions and Donatists turned this desire into an active pursuit of self-inflicted death as a sign of holiness.[143] Possibly because of this, the early orthodox Christians were regarded with such misunderstanding and suspicion in the Roman world that they did not have to actively provoke the authorities or seek out suicide and martyrdom to become the objects of imperial violence.[144] The Romans seemed quite eager to treat the Christians violently, for they perceived them as an alien and threatening presence that justified treating them as Romans usually did their adversaries.[145] And many in the early community such as the Apologists, Justin Martyr, and Athenagoras bent over backwards to show the Romans that they were not a threat to Roman power.[146]

And contrary to Fedden's claim, the early orthodox Christians did not have a horror of this world.[147] Rather than regarding the world as filled with evil and hostile spirits, they saw it as renewed and restored through the salvific work of Christ.[148] The early Christians believed they were to recreate the world in the image of Christ and were not to flee it by means of suicide, for Christ was to return to assert his dominion over it. They believed Christ had overcome all of the powers that could cause horror of this world. It was their firmly held belief that Christ had made peace between God and man, and this peace had neutralized the powers of the world over us. No longer fearing the world, because God had destroyed the "powers, thrones, dominations, and principalities" (Eph. 6:12), they feared only being separated from Christ by sin, and they considered the sin of suicide to be one of the most certain ways of separating oneself from him.

The basis of the early Christian objections to suicide was not primarily economic, for this was of little concern to Christian leaders, and there were no significant Christian arguments against suicide in the first five centuries for this reason. Orthodox Christianity did not object to suicide because of an irrational, primitive or savage horror of blood, but from a principled theological perspective. The early Christians did not have a horror of blood, but they did have a profound fear of deliberately killing the innocent because Christ was an innocent one who was sacrificed to save from sin. Their real horror of killing the innocent was based on the belief that this act destroyed the Spirit's life in the Christian.[149] These Christians did not have a horror of death, for its power had been conquered by Christ, but they had a horror of culpable killing, which made them allies with death and alienated them from Christ.[150]

Most of the early orthodox Christians permitted killing when the requirements of justice demanded it, and the Church did not believe all forms of killing or bloodletting were sinful.[151] They had a horror of killing the innocent since this was unjust to them.[152] Fear of becoming involved in this kind of killing moved many Christians to abstain from military service, and early Christian pacifism diminished as a more acute awareness of the morality of war grew.[153] Orthodox Christians practiced asceticism, not to deliberately bring death on themselves, but to grow in charity and protect themselves from the despair and *ennui* that were such threats to ancient Romans and Greeks.[154] Many early Christians practiced chastity and pacifism to gain the moral strength to withstand the violence and indulgence of the pagans.[155] Unlike many of the early heretics, such as the Montanists, Gnostics, or Circumcellions, the early Christians did not wish to flee this life to meet the Lord in the next, for he was already personally present to them through faith in the Eucharist.[156] The early Christians believed the Spirit dwelt among them in this life, spurring them to proclaim and live the Gospel of Jesus, to find the Lord in new ways in this life through prayer, charity, and worship.[157] They saw their task as waiting for, praying to, and serving the Lord in this life, and they did not presume they could expedite his coming by suiciding.

The early Christians would have agreed with Plutarch that suicide was contrary to human dignity, but they would have done this because we were created in the image of God.[158] They would also criticize Plutarch's concept of human dignity as inadequate because he did not understand the way in which Jesus' Incarnation elevated human dignity. These Christians would also concur with Aristotle that suicide was wrong because man did not belong to himself but was made the adopted child of God by Christ.[159] They would bolster their objections to suicide by claiming with St. Paul that the Christian belonged to Christ, and having been freed from Original Sin by Baptism they became servants of Christ. The early Christians rejected suicide and saw life as a treasure gained at the price of Christ's blood, which made its deliberate destruction a sacrilege. For these Christians, suicide was not so much a desertion of one's post in wartime as it was an abandonment to death and a betrayal of Christ who gave his life so that we would not suffer eternal death.

The early orthodox Christian church issued few official moral condemnations of suicide, or of any action for that matter, even though the great proportion of early Christian writers condemned deliberate self-killing vigorously.[160] And just because there were no "official" condemnations of suicide does not mean that the early Church countenanced suicide. The early Church produced many theological and moral writings against suicide, and these views later came to be expressed in conciliar and juridical documents after Constantine granted legal status to the Church.

The Fathers objected to suicide because, unlike some killings in war, they did not see that suicide could ever be done to protect the innocent or promote justice in the community.[161] Clement of Alexandria condemned voluntary suicide.[162] Tertullian advocated acceptance of martyrdom in some instances, but this was only when it was thrust upon someone by a persecutor.[163] It is true that he and other Montanists argued that to flee persecutors and not accept martyrdom was wrong, but saying this would be different from saying, as did the Circumcellions, that one should suicide to find salvation. And even though Christian writers from the second to the fifth centuries did not call for penalties for suicide, that should not be understood as condoning self-killing. The early Fathers condemned suicide because it implied an absolute rejection of divine forgiveness and the efficacy of grace. As the orthodox Christians came to understand the scope of divine mercy more fully, they recognized that there were no unforgivable sins if one truly repented. They condemned suicide as the one act from which one could not repent because suicide was only completed in death and it was morally impossible for there to be authentic repentance *inter gladium et jugulum.*[164]

In the first three centuries of Christianity, many fled to the desert of Egypt in an attempt to live their Christian lives more perfectly by more intense asceticism, self-denial, and prayer.[165] They hoped that doing this would bring them greater freedom from the forces and temptations of the world. It is a known fact that some of these early monks died as a result of their self-imposed rigors, and some committed suicide because they imposed deprivations on themselves beyond their abilities. Some of these early Christians were driven to madness by their mortifications but their deaths could hardly be called deliberate. Some of these monks certainly died from their austerities and deprivations, but it is not clear that their deaths were deliberate or intentional, and it would not be fair to compare their deaths to those who suicided to escape shame or suffering.

There was the famous episode in St. Jerome's time of Blesilla who entered a convent after her husband died.[166] She adopted such rigorous ascetical practices that she eventually died, and the spectacle of her mother's grief at her death caused a riot, but Jerome defended this unintended death.[167] If there was any malice in most of these deaths, it would be negligible because they were not directly seeking death but only tolerated it as an unintended side effect of their self-perfecting actions. Many Christian leaders in the early Church were aware that the rigors and sufferings of primitive monastic life increased temptations to despair and suicide and they cautioned against excesses.[168] Because many seemed to have succumbed to these temptations, early Christian councils and writers warned the weak against adopting such a rigorous life.[169] Their deaths were neither "egotistical" nor "altruistic," but rather unintended deaths; and because they were not condemned as strongly as deliberate self-killings, one should not think they were endorsed.

The early Christian community pressed a very forceful new moral code on the Roman world, and that is why it provoked pagan adversaries to such resistance. The Christian ideals of chastity lodged one of the most effective protests against the debaucheries of the empire that it had seen in its history. The Christians' evaluation of the value of virginity was unparalleled in the history of the empire, and Clement of Alexandria, for example, called the virgins "the elect of the elect."[170] Cyprian called them "the more splendid part of Christ's flock, the flower of Mother Church."[171] And, as Gibbon said, Rome could only with the greatest of difficulty support six virgins while the relatively small Christian church produced them by the thousands.[172] So strong was the devotion of many of these virgins that they would rather die freely and voluntarily than suffer its loss. Such a commitment to virginity and the virtue of chastity was rare in the empire and it points to the profound moral challenge Christianity posed. Christian apologists thus argued that the large number of virgins showed the moral superiority of Christianity over paganism.[173]

With the collapse of the empire, opinion became more critical of suicide, and St. Augustine was reluctant to condone suicides for any reason. His thought and medieval thought, which sprang from it, will be reviewed in detail in chapter 4 where the Catholic teachings on suicide will be summarized.

Suicide in Medieval Christianity

What is striking about the history of suicide in the Middle Ages is that there were few notable suicides between 400 and 1400 A.D. among orthodox Catholics.[174] Catholic doctrines had so permeated society during this era that individuals did not find suicide to be an efficient means of resolving personal, financial or political issues. Medieval Catholicism had given such emphasis to repentance, confession, and penance that suicide to escape shame virtually disappeared. In antiquity, suicide on account of poverty was not uncommon, but medieval society removed the stigma of poverty far more than most other societies, and, as a result, there were an insignificant number of suicides.[175] Catholicism's stress on the value of the life of poverty and simplicity destroyed the grounds of suicide to escape the shame of poverty.

The Christians abolished the practice of forcing others to commit suicide as did the Greeks and Romans, and the Greek custom of the state holding stores of poison for those who wished to end their lives was also eliminated. Roman exhibitionist suicide vanished, and there is little evidence of medievals suiciding to avoid slavery or serfdom as was often the case in antiquity. The uniquely Roman types of suicide found in the coliseums, palaces, and slave camps ended quickly. The Roman practice of generals or political leaders killing themselves to avoid disgrace virtually vanished. The custom of nobles killing themselves to avoid disgrace evaporated.[176] In light of all the pagan cruelties abolished by the medieval Christians, the claim that the medievals did not have respect for this life dissolves into fantasy.[177]

Medieval Christianity did not allow suicide to escape suffering, and it did this because it believed it had a better way of dealing with suffering than self-execution. It regarded self-execution as an inane and unintelligent way of coping with suffering in comparison to facing suffering in a spirit of Christian faith, hope, and charity. Medieval Christians asked why one should self-execute to escape suffering when acceptance of suffering could lead to eternal life. These Christians were not being insensitive to the needs of the suffering, but were objecting to what they saw as the profitlessness of suicide. And the old Roman practice of philosophical, political, and military suicide almost totally vanished in medieval Christian Europe.[178]

Heterodox Christians, however, seemed to have suicided with much greater frequency than did the orthodox, for they were more isolated and were less influenced than the orthodox by the Christian teachings concerning suicide. The Albigensians were disposed to this sort of killing, as many killed themselves by starvation in what they called the *endura* after receiving the *consolatum*.[179] Many of these heretics were also close to being social and political revolutionaries who called for the total overthrow of the social, political, and ecclesiastical structure, and their suicides were striking because they were the first in this era who suicided in ways similar to the ancients. Those who were condemned for witchcraft and the abandoned concubines of priests frequently committed suicide because they had little protection, and they seemed to have been the only class in medieval society who practiced suicide frequently.[180]

What was it about medieval Christianity and society that enabled it to virtually abolish suicide? What perspective prevailed in this era that so totally destroyed a practice that was so pervasive in antiquity? The answer seems to be the combination of theological developments, effective moral teaching, superior preaching, and advances in medieval civil and canon law. First, the fundamental preaching themes of this era were quite effective against suicide for a number of reasons. In addition to the doctrine of *imago Dei,* Christian preaching esteemed life because it was valued highly enough by God to receive the divine nature in Jesus Christ. This was the most important reason why Latin Christianity so effectively deterred and prohibited suicide. This was as high a valuation of human life as was possible in the Christian scheme, and the absence of this high valuation both before and after the medieval era is the primary reason why suicide was so common then. Second, because of its sacramental approach to grace, Christian preaching was able to provide the kind of substantial hope that classical religion and ancient philosophy could not. Medieval theology also succeeded in mediating the active and salvific divine presence and enforce moral prohibitions of killing more effectively than the pagan religions were able to, which resulted in a decline in suicides. While many of the ancients believed that some kinds of suicide were condoned by the gods, medieval Eucharistic theologians developed doctrines that encouraged a spirit of hope and reinforced prohibitions of killing. Third, because of its emphasis on development of the moral virtues and ascetical practices, medieval Christianity was able to stave off the influences of the *taedium vitae* that so afflicted the ancient world. Suicide was condemned by these theologians, and there was hardly any discussion of suicide among the scholastics because they simply presumed it could not be a morally good act. And because of its emphasis on asceticism, medieval Christian society did not look on material poverty as a curse or misfortune, for possession of property entailed duties to the poor and riches were seen as a trust for them to be used for their benefit. Fourth, medieval theology and society presumed the absolute inviolability of innocent human life from direct lethal attack, which won it the sympathy of the lower classes who were easily brutalized by the rich and powerful. And finally, much medieval theology argued that the Church and state were to cooperate, for the well-being and protection of all in society was a major advance over what was possible in pagan society. As a result of this preaching, medieval society clung to its revulsion of direct killing and it transmitted this revulsion across cultural and national boundaries.

The canonical and ecclesiastical punishments of suicide became stronger through the centuries, and these worked to limit the practice of suicide. The Council of Nimes refused to grant those who suicided a Christian burial.[181] The Council of Orleans in 533 forbade burial of all suicides who were accused of crimes,[182] and the Council of Braga in 563 similarly forbade Christian burial to all suicides.[183] This was affirmed by the Council of Auxerre fifteen years later,[184] and the Council of Arles forbade families to commit suicide.[185] In 590 the Council of Antisidor held that no one could make offerings to expiate their suicide,[186] but in 878, the Council of Tryoes permitted the burial of those who committed suicide, and, later on, Pope Nicholas I (d. 867) required the burial of all suicides.[187] Early canon law was as severe in condemning suicide as were the decrees of councils; the *Decretals* of Gratian condemned suicide,[188] and the great medieval canonists Burchard of Worms, Ivo of Chartres, and Gratian all upheld this condemnation.[189]

In addition to developing canons on this issue, the Church urged secular rulers to take measures against suicide, and their cooperation created more effective curbs on suicide than had ever been seen in European history. Medieval laws against suicide initially imposed few penalties, probably because suicide was so uncommon, but also because the preaching of the time was so effective against it. But over time, the kings and rulers of Europe imposed penalties, fines, and punishments on suicides, and by the High Middle Ages, virtually all European kingdoms imposed some sort of penalty or forfeiture on those who attempted or committed suicide, even though the civil law of most of these kingdoms made concessions to those who attempted suicide because of insanity or extreme duress.[190] Various social customs emerged to deter potential suicides from committing suicide, even though few of these can be countenanced today.[191] The custom of humiliating the corpse to deter future possible suicides developed at this time and the bodies of those who suicided were beaten, hung out in public, or sent down rivers in barrels, and the inheritances of the families of suicides were confiscated.[192]

Conclusion

Alfred Alvarez claims that in the Middle Ages this earthly life was devalued, and because of this, suicide became rather common.[193] But quite the opposite was true, for the promise of eternal life gave a higher value to this life than it had ever received in the ancient world, which may explain in part the virtual elimination of suicide during this era. Medieval Christianity was able to curb suicide, not because it despised this life as some of its critics contend, but because its Incarnational theology led it to highly esteem and respect human life and it did not wish to see it frivolously destroyed. Medieval orthodox Christianity never condemned suicide as an heretical action because its most authoritative dogmatic pronouncements did not focus on purely moral issues such as suicide. The canonical penalties imposed on those who attempted suicide varied in intensity during the medieval era in order to show the seriousness of suicide. When life was highly esteemed and suicides declined, penalties for attempting it relaxed, but when the value of life was lost sight of, penalties were increased to illustrate the seriousness of self-killing. There is little reason to hold that Latin Christianity believed that everyone was entitled to their opinion concerning the morality of suicide, for it was considered a gravely immoral action that significantly harmed the community. In matters of such moral gravity the medieval Latin church did not allow dissent from these sorts of teachings, just as it did not allow dissent from its teachings on the immorality of murder, lying or adultery because they were such gravely evil acts. Medieval Christianity was successful in curbing suicide to a degree matched only by medieval and modern Islam, and its success should be the object of study of those who are serious today about seeking to deter people from attempting it. This is not to say that we should simplistically return to its theological, social, and cultural forms, but it is to say that we should study the medievals critically and objectively to learn how they became so successful in dealing with this important issue.

Notes

1. Comte, A., *A System of Positive Polity,* vol. 3 (New York: Burt Franklin, 1876), 381.
2. Fedden, H., *Suicide: A Social and Historical Study* (New York: Benjamin Blom, 1972), 10. The vast part of the material in this chapter comes from Henry Fedden's history of suicide. This is the only comprehensive work on this issue, and, unfortunately, he has not noted in detail the sources of many of his claims. I found the vast portion of his sources, and they indicate that he did not always preserve them in utter faithfulness. In particular, he claimed that many committed suicide who may have only attempted it unsuccessfully or were only recorded as having done so in unreliable legends. A comprehensive history of suicide is beyond the scope of this work, and this chapter will only argue that suicide has been most effectively curbed by the monotheistic religions: Latin and Greek Christianity, classical Judaism, and Islam.
3. Ibid., chap. 1.
4. Ruth Cavan claims that personal suicide was probably rather common in preliterate culture, but she then goes on to say that suicide was probably rather infrequent because preliterate society was highly organized and there was little opportunity for personal disorganization. She does claim that there were some opportunities when the social structures failed, but when they were operative, suicide would be difficult. I would object and hold that it was probably rather common, which would account for the frequent strong measures taken by many preliterate societies to curb it. See Ruth Cavan, R., *Suicide,* (New York: Russell & Russell, 1965) 68.
5. Fedden would consider Eastern civilizations as primitive because they have the same static character of primitive tribes.
6. Cavan, R., *Suicide,* 65. Also see Gilmore, E., "The Amok of Malay," *Journal of Mental Science,* 34: 331.
7. Alvarez, A.. "The Background," in *Suicide: The Philosophical Issues*, (New York: St. Martin's Press, 1980), 17.
8. Herodotus, *The Complete and Unabridged History of Herodotus*, (New York: Random House, 1942), Book 1.
9. Fedden, *Suicide,* 19.
10. Ibid., 124-25.
11. Ibid., 21. Here Fedden is quoting Athenaeus from Nicholas of Damascus.
12. Ibid., 21.

13. See Frazer, J. G., *The Golden Bough,* abridged ed. (New York: Limited Editions 1959), 467; Moore, C., *A Full Enquiry into the Subject of Suicide,* 2 vols. (London: J.F. & C. Rivington, 1790), 144-50.
14. Fedden, *Suicide,* 46.
15. Ibid., 46.
16. Ibid., 46.
17. Montaigne, Michael, de, *Essays*, (Stanford: Stanford U. Press, 1976) Ch. III. Also see Moore, C., *A Full Enquiry*, I, 81
18. Thwaites, R. G., Ed., *Early Western Travels, 1748-1854,* vol. 22, part 1 of *Maximillian, Prince of Weid's Travels in the Interior of North America, 1832-34,* (New York: AMS Press, 1966), 34-35.
19. MacLeod, W. C., "Certain Mortuary Aspects of Northwest Coast Culture," *American Anthropologist*, Vol. 27, 122ff.
20. Williams, T., *Fiji and the Fijians,* vol. 1, (New York: Appleton, 1859), 123.
21. Codrington, R. H., *The Melanesians*, (Oxford: Clarendon, 1891), 288-89. This practice was also found among the Tonga and Maoris. See Tregear, E., *The Maori Race*, (New York: AMS, 1975), 390.
22. See Alvarez, A., *The Savage God*, (New York: Random House, 1970), 57; Donne, John. *Biathanatos,* Ed. Battin, M. and Rudick, M., (New York: Garland, 1982), 68-69. These peoples were probably predisposed to suicide and the collapse of their societies before the Europeans provided the occasion for the self-executions.
23. Fedden, H., *Suicide,* 292.
24. Ibid., 293.
25. Wise, J., *Selbstmord und Todesgurcht bei den Naturvolkern*, (New Haven: Human Area Relations Files, 1976), 207-8.
26. Alvarez, A., *The Savage God,* 57.
27. Ibid.
28. See Moore, C., *A Full Enquiry*, 126.
29. Ibid.
30. Prescott, W. H., *A History of the Conquest of Peru,* vol. 1 (Philadelphia: Mackay, 1892), 60.
31. Bernardino de Sahagun, *Historia General de los Cosas de Nueva Espana,* vol. 1, Ed. by Carlos Maria de Bustamente (Nashville: Fisk University Press, 1932), 56.
32. Yarrow, H. C., "Study of the Mortuary Customs of the North American Indians," *First Annual Report, Bureau of American Ethnology*, (Washington, D.C., 1891), 190.
33. See Jenks, A. E., *The Bontoc Igorot*, (Manila: Bureau of Public Printing, 1909), 74.
34. Cavan, R., *Suicide,* 57.
35. Ibid., 60.
36. Frazer, J. G., "The Dying God," in *The Golden Bough,* (New York: Criterion, 1959), 41; Ellis, A. B., *Tshi-Speaking People of the Gold Coast of West Africa,* (London, 1887), 302.
37. Fedden, H., *Suicide,* 198.
38. Fedden asserts that a strong condemnation is found only in primitive societies, but is absent in more advanced ones such as in Rome or Greece, and thus prejudices assessment of this position. Even though he admits that primitives suicided for many more reasons than we do today in a more enlightened society, he will not consider the possibility that the frequency and frivolity of many suicides in primitive society provoked their taboos. See ibid., 41.
39. Ibid., 48. There is a strong tradition of suicide in China, however. At the end of the rebellion of Hung Hsiu-ch-uan, nearly 100,000 of his soldiers committed suicide after he killed himself.

40. Ibid., 48.
41. Ibid., 37.
42. Ibid., 41.
43. Herodotus, *History* ii, 102-11. Diodorus, *The Antiquities of Asia: A Translation of Book I of the Library of History of Diodorus Sicilus*, Tr. by Murphy, G., (New Brunswick: Transaction, 1990), i, 5359; Strabo, *Geographia*, Tr. by Godolphon, F. (Paris: Belles Lettres, 1966), xv, 686.
44. Diodorus, *The Antiquities*, xiv, 40-52. Later, when attacked by the Persians, the Sidonians burned their boats so no one could escape and as many as 40,000 committed suicide. Bengstrom, R., *The Greeks and the Persians: The Sixth to the Ninth Centuries*, (New York: Dell, 1965), 407-8.
45. Plutarch, *The Invasion of India by Alexander the Great*, (Westminster: Constable, 1896), 69; Strabo, *Geographia*, xv. 686.
46. Grote, G., *History of Greece*, vol. 1, (New York: George, 1854), 281.
47. Sophocles. *Ajax*, Tr. and ed. by Stanford, W., (New York: Arno, 1979), 42, 277, 852.
48. Sophocles, *Oedipus Tyrranus*, Tr. & ed. by Brunner, T., (New York: Norton, 1970), 447, 713, 731, 774.
49. Cited in Fedden, H., *Suicide*, 41.
50. See Durkheim, E., *Suicide*, trans. Spaulding, J. A., and Gibson G., (Glencoe: Free Press, 1951), 55, 59, quoting Libianus.
51. Valerian Maximus, *Factorum ac Dictorum Memorabilium, Libri Novi*, (Venice: Berlini, 1753), ii, 6, 7. A similar law was instituted during the Reign of Terror. See Carlyle, T., *The French Revolution*, Ed. by Hartley, T., (New York: Modern Library), book 5, chapter ii, and Moore, *A Full Enquiry*, 238.
52. Libianus, quoted in Durkheim, E., *Suicide*, 330.
53. Fedden, E., *Suicide*, 83-84.
54. See Lecky, W., *A History of European Morals*, vol. 1 (New York: Appleton, 1869), 228.
55. Fedden, H., *Suicide*, 59-60.
56. Johnstone, H. W., *The Private Life of the Romans* (Salem, NH: Ayer, 1987), 105.
57. Hammond, N. and Scullard, H., *The Oxford Classical Dictionary*, 2nd Ed. (Oxford: Clarendon, 1992), 555.
58. Fedden, H., *Suicide*, 26.
59. Valerius Maximus, *Factorum*, vi, 5.
60. *Ibid*., vol. 6.
61. Lecky, W., *European Morals*, vol. 1, 227.
62. Fedden, H., *Suicide*, 90.
63. Plato, *Laws*, Tr. and ed. by Bury, R., (Oxford: Clarendon, 1983), IX, 873C-D.
64. See Moore, C., *A Full Enquiry*, 242; Donne, J., *Biathanatos*, 235. This claim is based on the authority of Plutarch and may not be fully reliable.
65. Cicero, *De Senectute*, Tr. and ed. by Allen, J., W., and Greenough, J., (Boston: Ginn, 1886), xx.
66. See Freeman, K., *Presocratic Philosophers*, (Oxford: Basil Blackwell, 1949), 14; Fedden, H., *Suicide*, 71-72.
67. Apuleius, *De Philos*. Plato, *Laws*, Book 1.
68. Plato, *Laws*, Book 9.
69. Plato, *Phaedo*, 61b-63a.
70. Plotinus, *Enneads* Tr. by O'Brien, E., *The Essential Plotinus*, (New York: New American Library, 1964), I, ix. He was less tolerant of it probably because he saw it causing a disturbance to the soul. See Lecky, W., *European Morals*, vol. 1, 351.
71. Cicero, *Tusc. Disp.*, 1, 34, 84.

72. Diogenes Laertes, *Lives of Eminent Philosophers*, Tr. by Hicks, R. D., (Cambridge: Harvard, 1970), Book 6, 18-19.
73. Plato, *Phaedo*, 61a-63b.
74. Aristotle, *Nicomachean Ethics*, Tr. by McKeon, R., (New York: Random House, 1941), 1116, a, 13.
75. This claim was made by Lucretius and it is not clear that it is true. See Freeman, K., *Presocratic Philosophers*, 293.
76. Ibid., 375.
77. Fedden and Albert Bayet, upon whom Fedden depends for much of his moral analysis of suicide, demean this "suicide horror," but in doing this they trivialize the scope and intensity of suicide in the Roman world in particular. See Bayet, A., *Le Suicide et le Morale*, (Paris: Felix Alcan, 1922). One of the first projects of the post-Constantinian Christians was to curb ancient suicide, which was one of its greatest contributions to not only Western civilization, but also to world civilization. See Lecky, W., *European Morals,* vol. 2, 47-65.

Alvarez holds that the Roman law concerning suicide was simply practical with little spirit of revenge or vindictiveness. But he mentions only the philosophical suicides and says little of the desperate suicides of slaves, prisoners of war, the impoverished, the lovelorn, weak, or immature. Alvarez, A., "The Background," 223. His views are self-contradictory because in *The Savage God* he laments the deaths of so many artists, poets, and writers, and yet when virtually the same phenomenon occurred in Rome, he lauded it as a superb example of liberty and toleration.
78. Concerning suicide in the Roman world, the historian of European morality, Lecky, said the following:

> A general approval of it floated down through most of the schools of philosophy, and even to those who condemned it, it never seems to have assumed its present aspect of extreme enormity. This was in the first instance due to the ancient notion of death; and we have also to remember, that when a society once learns to tolerate suicide, the deed, in ceasing to be disgraceful, loses much of its actual criminality, for those who are most firmly convinced that the stigma and suffering it now brings upon the family of the deceased do not constitute his entire guilt, will readily acknowledge that they greatly aggravate it. *European Morals*, Vol. 1, 226.

Even further he writes about Roman suicide:

> From an early period, self-immolation, like that of Curtius or Decius, had been esteemed in some circumstances a religious rite, being as has been well suggested, probably a lingering remnant of human sacrifices, and towards the closing day of paganism many influences conspired in the same direction. Lecky, W., *European Morals*, 228.

79. Fedden, W., *Suicide,* 65.
80. Moore, C., *A Full Enquiry*, vol. 1, 245.
81. Johnstone, H. W., *Private Life,* 105.
82. Ibid.
83. Ovid, *Fasti*, (Cambridge: Harvard, 1959), II. 721ff.
84. See Donne, J., *Biathanatos,* 235.
85. Dion Cassius, *Roman Histories*, (New York: Macmillan, 1914), lxix, 8.
86. Pliny, *Epistles*, (Boston: Bibliophile Society, 1925), iii, 16; Dio. Cass. *Roman Histories*, lx, 16. Also see Moore, *A Full Enquiry*, 258.
87. Hammond, N. and Scullard, H., *Classical Dictionary*, P. 763.
88. Pliny, *Historia Naturalis*, (Venice: Lugdune, 1483), ii, 5.
89. Hammond, N. and Scullard, H., *Classical Dictionary*, P. 976.

90. Quoted in Fedden, H., *Suicide,* 84. Also see Alvarez, A., *The Savage God,* 67.
91. Fedden, H., *Suicide,* 84.
92. Symmachus, *Epistolae,* (Paris: Belle Lettres, 1972), ii, 40.
93. Hammond, N. & Scullard, H., *Classical Dictionary,* 799.
94. Ibid.
95. Diog. Laert., *Lives,* viii, 67, 69, 70, 71.
96. See Lecky, W., *European Morals,* 223-24.
97. Diodorus, *Antiquities,* ii, 23-27.
98. Smith, W., *Dictionary of Greek & Roman Biography and Myth* (London: Little-Brown, 1916), 2, 6.
99. Tacitus, *Annals,* Tr. by Martin, R. H., (Chico CA: Scholars Press, 1985), xv, 63-64; Val. Max. *Factorum,* I. 1, V. 6 & XII, 2. Also see Moore, C., *A Full Enquiry,* 186.
100. Seneca, *Epistolae,* Tr. by Costa, C., (Warminster: Aris & Philips, 1987), xxiv.
101. Ibid., lxx.
102. Ibid., xviii.
103. See Lecky, W., *European Morals,* 222-33.
104. Seneca, *Epistola,* xxvi.
105. Cornelius Nepos, Tr. by Hornfall, N., *A Selection Including the Lives of Cato and Atticus,* (New York: Clarendon, 1989).
106. Hammond, N. and Scullard, H., *Classical Dictionary,* 212.
107. *The Discourses as Reported by Arianus,* Tr. by Matheson, P., (New York: Heritage, 1968), 1, 24.
108. Cited in Fedden, H., *Suicide,* 78.
109. See Moore, C., *A Full Inquiry,* 170; Lactantius, *Institutones Divinae,* Tr. by Divine, P., (Paris: Cerf, 1978), iii, 18. This is a doubtful claim as are many others about the early Greek philosophers.
110. Fedden, H., *Suicide,* 79-80.
111. Alvarez, A., "The Background," 22.
112. Aulus Gellius, *Noctes Atticae,* Tr. by Rolfe, J. W., (New York: Putnam, 1927), xv, 10. His writings became so widely endorsed that an epidemic of suicides resulted.
113. Hammond, N. and Scullard, H., *Classical Dictionary,* 492.
114. Lecky, W., *European Morals,* vol. 1, 227.
115. Ibid., 234-35.
116. Fedden, H., *Suicide,* 81.
117. Hammond, N. and Scullard, H., *Classical Dictionary,* 807.
118. Virgil, *Aeneid,* Tr. by Harrison, S. J., (Oxford, Clarendon, 1991), vi. 434-37.
119. See Lecky, W., *European Morals,* 230-31.
120. Johnstone, H. W., *Private Life,* 104-5.
121. See Silving, A., "Suicide and Law," in *Clues to Suicide,* Ed. Shneidman, E. and Farberow, N., (New York: Blackinston Division, 1957), 80-81.
122. For a detailed account of the siege and fall of Massada, see Josephus, Flavius, *The Wars of the Jews,* (New York: Dutton, 1928), vol. 2, 408, 433. Lecky claims that a "multitude" committed suicide in France in 1095 to avoid torture and that 500 killed themselves in York and another 500 in 1320 when besieged by the Shepherds. Lecky, W., *European Morals,* vol. 2, 53.
123. Johnson, P., *A History of the Jews,* (New York: Harper, 1987), 155.
124. See Clement of Alexandria, *Stromata,* Tr. by Stahlin, O., (London: SPCK, 1930), Bk. IV, ch. xxvi:

> Those who run down created existence and vilify the body are wrong; not considering that the frame of man was formed erect for the contemplation of heaven, and that the organization of the senses tends to knowledge; and that the

members and parts are arranged for good, not for pleasure. Whence this abode becomes receptive of the soul which is most precious to God; and is dignified with the Holy Spirit thorough the sanctification of soul and body, perfected with the perfection of the Savior.

125. Fedden claims that the basis for the Christian objections to suicide were its horror of the world and its doctrine of salvation. Fedden, H., *Suicide,* 109.

126. See Augustine, "On the Morals of the Catholic Church," in *Later Nicene and Post-Nicene Fathers*, Tr. by Southest, R., (Grand Rapids: Eerdmans, 1956), chap. xxii:

> Then there is the great struggle with pain. But there is nothing, though of iron hardness, which the fire of love cannot subdue. And when the mind is carried up to God in this love, it will soar above all torture free and glorious, with wings beauteous and unhurt, on which chaste love rises to the embrace of God. . . . And yet even here we may see with what force the mind presses on with unflagging energy, in spite of all alarms, towards what it loves; and we learn that we should bear all things rather than forsake God, since those men bear so much in order to forsake Him.

127. See *Letter of St. Clement to the Corinthians*, Tr. by Clark, R., (London: SPCK, 1937), chaps. 23, 35, 38, 49.

128. Alvarez, A., *The Savage God,* 67. This is seen best in his apparent ignorance of the different phases in the life of Tertullian. He cites the later Tertullian, apparently not knowing that he had passed from the orthodox community at that stage of his life, to the Montanists. Like others, Fedden fails to see any difference between the orthodox Christians and the heterodox and schismatics such as the Circumcellions and Donatists in their views of suicide. It is peculiar that Fedden makes this claim that the Christian martyrs had a passionate disregard for life because they ordinarily "did" nothing to destroy their lives. In contrast, those who deliberately suicided, like the Epicureans, Cynics and Stoics were not charged with disregarding life, but with having no fear of death. They were the ones who complained so bitterly about the emptiness, monotony and meaninglessness of life and took measures to escape it. Yet the Christians were accused of showing no respect for life even though they did nothing to imitate these and other ancient self-killers. Fedden, *Suicide,* 122. Paul Johnson wonders why the Christians tolerated the weird megalomaniac system of the Romans and did not seek to overthrow the empire. *A History of Christianity* (New York: Athenaeum, 1985), 69. Tertullian argued in his time that Christians were numerous enough to overthrow the empire if they desired, but they were generally docile before the Romans (ibid., 70).

129. See Jedin, H., Ed., *History of the Church,* vol. 1 (New York: Crossroads, 1990), 219.

130. Alvarez, A., "The Background," 26-27.

131. See Ignatius of Antioch, *Epistle to the Romans,* Tr. by Srawley, J., (London: SPCK, 1935) iv:

> I am writing to all the Churches and state emphatically to all that I die willingly for God, provided you do not interfere. I beg you, do not show me unseasonable kindness. Suffer me to be the food of wild beasts, which are the means of my making my way to God. God's wheat I am, and by the teeth of wild beasts I am to be ground that I may prove Christ's pure bread. Better still, coax the wild beasts to become my tomb and to leave no part of my person behind: once I have fallen asleep, I do not wish to be a burden to anyone. Then only shall I be the genuine disciple of Jesus Christ, when the world will not see even my body.

132. Jedin, H., *History,* vol. 2, 139.

133. Ibid., vol. 1, 217-28.

134. Jedin claims that Diocletian may have felt quite insecure with so many Christians in the army and so many refusing to offer homage to the emperor, which may have been one of the primary causes of his persecution. Ibid., vol. 1, 397-99. For the impact that the early Christians had on the pagans, see Walzer, J., *Galen on Jews and Christians,* (New York: Oxford, 1949).

135. Jedin, H., *History*, vol. 2, 138-40, 146-47, 158-59. Gibbon and Alvarez would like to claim otherwise, but there is little historical evidence to support this opinion.

136. See Pliny the Younger, *Epistles: A Critical Edition*, Tr. by Stout, S., (Bloomington, Ind: University of Indiana Press, 1962), 10, 96, 97.

137. Eusebius, *The Ecclesiastical Histories*, Tr. by Cruse, C., (R. Davis: Philadelphia, 1833), 8, 12, 8-10.

138. Ibid., 6, 41, 14-23; 6, 42, 1-4.

139. Jedin attributes the outbreak of the persecution to Diocletian's view that Christianity was the last obstacle to his plans to reconstruct the empire. Regaining financial security, reorganizing the army and government, Diocletian sought to restore the old religion, which he saw as the foundation of Roman greatness. Jedin, H., *History,* vol. 1, 397.

140. Ibid., 399.

141. See Lactantius, *De Mortibus Persecutorum*, Tr. by Creed, J. K., (Oxford: Clarendon, 1984), 15, 2-4; Eusebius, *Hist. Eccl.* 8, 6, 6.

142. Ignatius of Antioch:

> I would rather die and come to Jesus Christ than be king over the entire earth. Him I seek who died for us; Him I love who rose again because of us. The birth pangs are upon us. Forgive me, brethren; do not wish me to die; do not make a gift to the world of one who wants to be God's. Beware of seducing me with matter; suffer me to receive pure light. Once arrived there, I shall be a man. Permit me to be an imitator of my suffering God. If anyone holds Him in his heart, let him understand what I am aspiring to; and then let him sympathize with me; knowing in what distress I am.
>
> The Prince of this world is resolved to abduct me, and to corrupt my Godward aspirations. Let none of you, therefore, assist him.

Letter to the Romans, Tr. by Srawley, T., (London: SPCK, 1935), vi-vii.

143. See Jedin, H., *History*, vol. 2, 292-95.

144. In defense of the early Christians, see Anon., *Letter to Diognetus*, Tr. by Radford, L. B., (London: SPCK, 1908), v, vi. Septimus Severus believed that the Christian religion was as dangerous to the state as was the radical opposition of the Monatanists. Jedin, H., *History,* vol. 1, 218.

145. Eusebius was so impressed with the violence of the persecution of Christians by Septimus Severus that he believed it was the coming of the Antichrist. Eusebius, *Hist. Ecc.*, 6, 7.

146. See Jedin, H., *History,* vol. 1, 178 174-77.

147. Fedden, H., *Suicide,* 109.

148. Clement of Alexandria, *Strom*. Bk. IV, ch. xxvi.

149. Suicide was regarded as a most serious sin, and as such it could destroy the life of the Spirit within the Christian. See Clement of Rome, *Letter to the Corinthians*, Tr. by Roberts, A., Donaldson, J, and Crombie, F., vol. 1, (London: Ante-Nicene Christian Fathers, 1870) Ch. xxxv.

150. This is best seen in the "Didache" or "Teachings of the Twelve Apostles," which rejects many forms of deliberate forms of killing of the innocent. *Didache,* Tr. by Lightfoot, J. B. and Harmer, J. R., (London: Apostolic Fathers, 1893), Ch. ii.

151. Tertullian sternly rebuked those who volunteered for service in the Roman army in *De Corona Militis*, Tr. by Dodgson, C., (Oxford: Library of the Fathers, 1842) which testifies in a left-handed way to the growing acceptance of the early Christians increasing the legitimacy of military service (ibid., XI). Gelarius sought to weed the Christians out of the forces in 303-4, A.D. and they were the first to bear the brunt of his persecution. Christians probably constituted less than 10 percent of the army, however, for few rulers would want to deprive themselves of such a portion of their army. See Cadoux, C. J., *The Early Church and the World* (Edinburgh: T & T Clark, 1925), 580.

152. Tertullian, *Apology*, Tr. by Waltzing, J. P., (Paris: Cerf, 1921), XXXVII; Minucius Felix, *Octavius*, Tr. by Freese, J. P., (London: SPCK, 1919), XXX, 6; Cyprian, *To the Donatists*, Tr. by Donaldson, R., (Edinburgh, T & T Clark, 1866), VI. 10; Arnobius, *Nationes*, Tr. by McCracken, G. E., (Westminster: Newman, 1949), I, 6; Lactantius, *Inst.*, VI, 20.

153. They would join military service, but had objections to such service if it would involve giving adoration to pagan idols or deliberate killing of the innocent. Bainton claims that there is no evidence of Christians in the Roman army from the beginning of the Apostolic to 170-180 A.D., which may be because it was either assumed or abstention taken for granted, Bainton, R., *Christian Attitudes Toward War and Peace*, (Nashville: Abingdon, 1960), 667-8. In 211, A. D. Tertullian rebuked those who joined the army, which suggests that large numbers of Christians had entered its ranks, *De Corona Militis*, XI.

154. Clement of Alexandria, *Strom.*, Bk. VI, Ch. ix.

155. See Ignatius of Antioch, *Ep. ad Rom.*, v.

156. See *Didache*, VI, ix.

157. Clement of Rome, *Letter to the Corinthians*, chaps. xxx-xxxv.

158. Clement of Alexandria, *Strom.*, Bk. II, Ch. ii.

159. *Ep. ad Diognetus*, ix.

160. Basil, *Letter*, 4, Tr. by Deferarri, R., (Cambridge: Leob, 1950), 188; Clement of Alexandria, *Strom.*, IV, x; Jerome, *To Eustochium*, Tr. Wright, F., (Cambridge: Leob, 1973), 13; *In Amos,* Adriaen, M., (Paris: Corpus Christianorum, Latinae, 1963), II, 5; Cassian, *De Institutis Coenobiorum*, Tr. by Gibson, F., (New York: Library of Nicene and post-Nicene Fathers, 1894), IX, 9; Bayet, A., *Le Suicide et la Morale*, 322.

161. This view is best expressed by Augustine in his tract on suicide:

> For it is clear that if no one has a private right to kill even a guilty man (and no law allows this); then certainly anyone who kills himself is a murderer, and is the more guilty in killing himself the more innocent he is of the charge on which he has condemned himself to death.

Augustine, *City of God*, Tr. by Knowles, D., (New York: Penguin, 1972), I, 17.

162. Clement of Alexandria, *Strom.*, Bk. vii, ch. xi. "Such a one consequently withstands all fear of everything terrible, not only of death, but also poverty and disease and ignominy, and things akin to these." Also see *Strom.* IV, 4, (II, 256) Clement claims that the true Gnostic faces these and does not despair by suiciding, but bears with them through the power of the Holy Spirit in his soul.

163. Tertullian, *On Martyrdom*, Tr. by Dodgson, C., (London: Library of the Fathers, 1892), IV. i.

164. Ibid., Bk. I, Ch. 27.

165. See Jedin, H., *History,* 295-96.

166. Jerome, *Epistle*, Tr. by Quasten, J., (Westminster: Ancient Christian Writers, 1946), xxiii.

167. Ibid., xxxviii.

168. See Tertullian, *On Virginity,* Tr. by Thelwell, S., (Edinburgh: Ante-Nicene Christian Library, 1876), *Passim.*, Cyprian, *On the Dress of Virgins*, Tr. by Thornton, C., (Oxford: Library of the Fathers, 1839), *Passim*; Methodius, *Symposium*, Tr. by Clark, W., (Edinburgh, Ante-Nicene Library, 1866), 4, 5; 7, 2.

169. See Jedin, H., *History,* vol. 1, 297-98; Lecky, W., *European Morals,* 55-56. Lecky also notes that the monasteries, by providing shelter for the despairing and hopeless, probably prevented more suicides than they caused.

170. Clement of Alexandria, *Who is the Rich Man that is Saved?*, Tr. by Wilson, W., (Edinburgh, Ante-Nicene Library, 1871), 36.

171. Cyprian, *On the Dress of Virgins*, 3.

172. Gibbon, E., *History of the Decline and Fall of the Roman Empire*, Ed. by Bury, J., 7 vols. (London: Metheun, 1909-14), 117.

173. Justin, *Apology*, in *Ante-Nicene Fathers*, Tr. by Coxe, C., (Edinburgh, T & T Clark, 1885), 15, 29; Athenagoras, *Supplication for the Christians*, Tr. by Pratten, B., *Ante-Nicene Library*, (Edinburgh, T & T Clark, 1870); 33; Minucius Felix, *Octavius*, 31.

174. See Lecky, W., *European Morals,* vol. 2, 56.

175. Fedden, hardly a friend of medieval Catholicism, writes the following:

> Poverty carried no moral stigma; you were not bad or stupid, or undesirable, simply because you were poor. In the capaciousness of an all-comprehensive Church, and at his particular post within the feudal hierarchy (that state of life to which God had called him), the poor man could feel a certain equality and sense of fellowship with the rich. He was acknowledged to be part of the whole. Property involved duties first and foremost; it was primarily a trust rather than a source of income. Poverty, on the other hand had acquired, from religious associations, a certain mystical importance and glamour. . . . For these reasons, poverty rarely seemed a sufficient cause for suicide.

Fedden, H., *Suicide,* 200.

176. Lecky, W., *European Morals,* vol. 2, 57.

177. Ibid., 52.

> Direct and deliberate suicide, which occupies so prominent a place in the moral history of antiquity, almost absolutely disappeared within the Church; but beyond its pale, the Circumcellions, in the fourth century, constituted themselves as the apostles of death, and not only carried to the highest point the custom of provoking martyrdom, by challenging and insulting the assemblies of the Pagans, but even killed themselves in great numbers, imagining, it would seem, that this was a form of martyrdom, and would secure for them eternal salvation.

178. O'Dea, J. J., *Suicide: Studies in its Philosophy*, (New York: Prentice-Hall, 1970), 85. "Deliberate suicide seems to have ceased almost entirely with the establishment of Christianity, and to have continued in abeyance until the reign of philosophical skepticism." This is a judgment few philosophers or historians would disagree. Also see Lecky, W., *European Morals,* vol. 2, 52. Alvarez notes that John Donne in his *Biathanatos* was the first Renaissance thinker to challenge the Christian teachings on suicide in a thousand years, which is a backhanded compliment on the power of the medieval prohibitions of suicide. He admits that the medieval Christian was brutal in condemning suicide, but this probably came from a concern for the soul of the suicidal person.

179. Lecky, W., *European Morals,* vol. 2, 52-53. The *endura* was a penitential rite which freed the spirit of the *perfecti* from the shackles of matter, and the *consolatum* was the sect's central rite of baptism by imposition of hands in which one became a true Christian.

180. Jedin, H., *History,* vol. 3, 365-66; Lea, M., *History of Sacerdotal Celibacy* (Hyde Park, N.Y, University Books: 1966), 248.
181. Mansi, J., *Sacrorum Conciliorum Nova et Amplissima Collectio,* (Graz: Akademische, 1960), XXIV, 546.
182. Alvarez, A., "The Background," 27-28.
183. Mansi, J., *Collectio*, XVI, IX, 779.
184. Mansi, J., *Collectio*, XVII, IX, c. 913.
185. Mansi, J., *Collectio*, LII, VII, 884,
186. Fedden, H., *Suicide,* 134.
187. See Mansi, J., *Collectio*, XV, 401; Also see Bayet, A., *Le Suicide,* 409. This relaxation did not continue, however, probably because an increase in suicides resulted from this relaxation of strictures.
188. See van Howe, A., *Commentarium Lovaniense in Codicem Iuris Canonici,* tom. 1 2nd Ed. (Rome: Meuchlin, 1945), X, 4.
189. See Fournier, P., *Un Tournant dans l'Histoire du Droit,* (Paris: Recueil-Sirey, 1917), 129.
190. Lecky, W., *European Morals,* vol. 2, 53-65.
191. King St. Louis (1214-1276) ordered confiscation of the property of suicides. The Council at Braga forbade interring suicides in consecrated ground, and in some countries, removing a suicide from a house through the door was not permitted, and they could only be removed by making a hole in the wall. Elsewhere, suicides were dragged through the streets, thrown into sewers, or transfixed on a stake along public highways. Ibid., 53.
192. A credible account of the measures taken by civil authorities in the Middle Ages is given by Bayet, A., *Le Suicide,* 437-39. Fedden, who is hardly sympathetic to the medieval approach to suicide admits that it was civil authorities and not ecclesiastical authorities who called for punishments as a deterrent to suicide.
193. Alvarez, A., "The Background," 217.

3

The Emergence of Modern Suicide

The Catholic church has not only had to confront the suicidal practices of antiquity but those of the modern world as well, and to adequately grasp its position on this issue, one should also be familiar with the history of suicide during this time. In this chapter, I will trace not only the development of modern suicide in the Western world, but also some of its history in the Orient to the extent that this has a bearing on Western suicidal practices. The two Oriental nations most frequently connected with suicidal practices are Japan and India, even though it is quite probable that other Oriental nations have also endorsed or promoted suicidal practices as they have. And while we do not know a great deal of the history, moral, philosophical, and religious foundations of Japanese and Indian suicidal practices, we know more of them than of suicidal practices in other Oriental nations. Promoters of rational suicide in the West often invoke the Japanese and Indian suicidal practices to demonstrate its moral and social legitimacy, but it is not entirely clear that they understand how harmful these practices are or the deep social changes that Western society would have to adopt to implement similar suicide policies.

Suicide in Japan

Shinto, the traditional religions of Japan, had little or no concept of the sanctity of human life as this idea is understood in Western Christianity, in spite of its profound respect for its various gods and deities, and it permitted withdrawal from this life through suicide for a wide variety of reasons. Shinto permitted suicide for various religious motives as well as for purely personal reasons; personal suicides have remained at a high level. Shinto required a profound respect for elders and the innocent, but it did not translate this into a doctrine of the sanctity and inviolability of human life that would ban suicide. And in the Shinto traditions, there was little hesitation about allowing suicide for higher moral values such as honor or religion. But this was not the only sort of suicide allowed, for Shinto history is replete with suicides for patriotism, philosophy, romance, and despair. The history of suicide in the Shinto traditions reads very much like that of the Romans, except that Shinto tradition did not allow exhibitionist suicide.

The form of suicide most commonly associated with Japan and Shinto was *hara kiri*, which was a highly formalized rite throughout most of its history. The individual would perform *hara-kiri* after he or she had done some action or became involved in some event that brought shame, disgrace, or dishonor on himself, his family, or associates. Often the formalities were dispensed with when this rite was performed in a military setting, but if possible, the person would invite those he offended to witness the ritual. When done with full formality, the individual would strip to the waist, reverently embrace the dagger, and then plunge it into the left side of his abdomen, draw it all the way across his stomach, and then turn the blade upwards. He would withdraw the dagger, make a minor cut in his throat, after which his retainer would then decapitate him. It was to be done in a way that the individual would show no sign of pain and at the end of the gory affair he was to fall forward.[1] The purpose of *hara-kiri* was to demonstrate the purity and honorableness of the individual.[2] Much like the ancient Greeks and Hebrews, medieval Japanese saw the seat of the human soul or spirit in the bowels, and *hara-kiri* was seen as a means to escape shame or dishonor, and as such, it has never been punished to any significant degree. In the practice of *hara-kiri,* they symbolically opened their soul to the world to show that it was pure and unpolluted.[3] To be able to withstand this agony with undisturbed countenance was a sign of the integrity of one's soul and being.

The medieval Japanese romanticized not so much suicide itself, as the instruments of death. They created fabulously carved swords and daggers, which were given positions of prominence in their homes and were treated with the utmost reverence. But in modern times, death itself was romanticized for the Kamikaze pilots who were told not to fear death but to regard their death as the "falling of petals from flowers." During the Second World War, suicide rather than surrender was expected of Japanese soldiers, and thousands killed themselves when faced with the prospect of capture. In the early phases of the war, it was not uncommon for Allied armies to capture only one Japanese soldier alive in the midst of a thousand dead.[4] And many Japanese soldiers committed virtual suicide in reckless *banzai* charges against impregnable allied defenses. The psychological reasons for these suicides were most complex, for they were undertaken not only to preserve honor, but also to avoid the guilt and shame of being perceived by others as disloyal to the emperor or Japan.

Honor and guilt played an important role in Japanese suicide. The first recorded episode of *hara-kiri* took place in 1170 A.D. when the chief Minamoto Tametomo disemboweled himself after failed attempts to fashion a principality for himself in eastern Japan.[5] There were sporadic attempts at suicide thereafter, and the most famous mass suicide in Japanese history took place after the battle of Dan-no-ura on 25 April 1185 when virtually the entire Taira clan threw themselves into the sea after they were trapped by the Minamoto.[6] 270 of the followers of the chiefs Yasumura and Mitsumura committed *hara-kiri* in 1247,[7] and their clans were eventually eliminated and all of their land expropriated. In the 1430s there were a number of episodes of military suicide as various feudal lords struggled among themselves.[8] A similar mass suicide took place in 1555 when hundreds of samurai killed themselves by drowning or *hara-kiri*.[9] The last of the great samurai deaths was in 1877 when the leader of the Satsuma rebellion Saigo Takamori had a retainer put an end to his life after his revolt failed.[10] One of the most pitiful recorded episodes of suicide involved a warrior who wrote this pathetic message at the end of a day of fighting. "Would you please send me a cask of sake? I will share it with Mananaga, then will commit *hara-kiri* together."[11]

Few modern Japanese perform *hara-kiri* suicides, which were most famous before World War II, and present-day suicides ordinarily seem to be undertaken to adjust to fear and hostility, because "relatively few modern Japanese believe in, or are concerned with, life beyond death."[12] Modern Japanese culture has transformed the honor suicide of medieval and early modern Japan into purely personal suicide. A consequence of the absence of religious opposition to suicide has been that personal suicide is now quite common in Japan. Suicide is now done less frequently to escape shame or dishonor, and public officials aggressively intervene to prevent virtually all suicides. Today, most Japanese who slay themselves do so by quicker and less painful methods than *hara-kiri,* such as drowning, jumping, shooting, or hanging.[13]

Despite the fact that Japan's contemporary suicide rate is 2.5 times that of the next highest country, there has been little formal and systematic study of suicide in Japan.[14] A contemporary suicidologist holds that among the contributing factors to this high level of

Japanese suicide is a great deal of emotional and task dependency, self-inflation, insecurity, and explosiveness.[15] Among those Japanese youth who suicide, there is often a deep sense of guilt, which is more related to a failure to fulfill maternal expectations than anything else.[16] There is a rather strong sense of despair among the Japanese, and an early study suggested that nearly two-thirds of the population suffer from this.[17] In contrast to Western countries, there seems to be a higher prevalence of female suicide in Japan, for in the West there are generally three male suicides for every female suicide, while in Japan, the ratio is only two to one.[18]

The most common form of suicide in contemporary Japan is not the traditional *hara-kiri* or *seppuku,* but the romantic love suicide of *shengu*. In a *shengu* suicide, lovers bind themselves together and throw themselves from cliffs, tall office buildings, or under trains so that they can live together through seven reincarnations.[19] So many lovers throw themselves under trains that ceremonies are often held with railway executives in attendance on railroad platforms to memorialize them after their deaths.[20] Suicide season in Japan runs from May through July, and private citizens and public agencies put signs at the edge of cliffs and on high office buildings urging potential suicides to rethink their decision and not kill themselves. And during this season, the owners of high office buildings will post guards to prevent suicides.[21] Rewards are also given for those who prevent suicides, and because parents now regularly watch for their children, it has become harder and harder for lovers to commit *shengu*. But, lovers often accomplish their objective by agreeing through written notes to commit suicide at the same time.[22]

One of the most tragic developments in Japanese suicide in recent years has been the emergence of suicides among children and suicides in response to business failures. The intense pressure on children in grade school and high school for exceptional performance has proven to be too much for many children, and the increase of child suicide has been almost without precedent. And business suicide has increased in proportion to the scope and success of Japanese corporate and industrial influence. The emergence of these new and utterly untraditional forms of self-killing shows how intensely difficult it is to control this practice. Despite the long tradition of allowing suicide only for the most grave and serious reasons, suicide is now being resorted to more and more for trivial reasons. Those who hold that Japanese suicide should be used as a model for Western suicide fail to see that the collapse of strict controls on suicide for purposes of retaining honor has caused its degeneration into romantic or erotic suicide, which is very difficult to control.

Suicide in India

It is difficult for Westerners to understand suicide in India primarily because there are few reliable witnesses to Indian suicidal practices prior to the modern era, and contemporary works on Indian suicide have been of uneven and undependable quality.[23] Despite these limitations, a number of points can be made about Indian and Hindu suicidal practices. In the Indian traditions, the real and authentic self is revealed through ascetical self-purgation, self-emptying abandonment of the world, and self-denial. Suicide is seen as more of an act of self-purification to recover the true self than it is one of self-killing.[24] Rather than being an action of "self-slaying," suicide is an act by which the true "self" is discovered. Suicide destroys the false self, the empty image we create, and it empowers us to truly accept, control, and advance ourselves.[25]

In the perspective of the Indian religious traditions, one can only find peace and rest by escaping the sufferings of this world and entering the state of Nirvana, a condition where desire and striving have been overcome. The world is alien to the divine presence, and peace and happiness can only be found by escaping it. Indian traditions believe that nothing in this life is permanent and everything inevitably disappears, often with great pain. Reality is intrinsically empty, which makes all striving ultimately futile, and the goals of human destiny can only be realized by escaping this emptiness through asceticism or fleeing life altogether.

The Indian traditions do not directly and generally devalue human life or any other form of life, but they do so indirectly and specifically by esteeming the life of Nirvana to such an extraordinary degree that they are quite tolerant of the use of a wide variety of reflexively lethal measures to attain it. This tolerance of self-killing is somewhat paradoxical, not only because of Hinduism's traditional respect for the sanctity of all life, but also because of its support for family values, which suicide undermines. From the Catholic perspective, Hinduism developed a far greater respect for animal life than human life, and has traditionally been aghast at the slaughter of certain animals, but has accepted suicide for a great number of reasons. Despite its intense efforts to promote the value and integrity of the family, Hinduism has been quite tolerant of suiciding to escape the suffering and emptiness of this life, in spite of the pain and anguish this would cause their families.

In the classical Catholic perspective, this tolerance of suicide is also paradoxical because the Indian traditions promote asceticism in a way that is seemingly in conflict with their tolerance of suicide. In the mainstream Catholic approach, ascetical practices are and were endorsed to strengthen one against suffering and despair, and those religions that encouraged asceticism have usually discouraged acts of despair such as suicide. The Indian traditions believe that this existence could be a source of holiness and spiritual growth, but these states are only substantially realized by escaping this life. This is paradoxical because it shows an awareness of the sacredness of the worldly life of impersonal animals but denies it in free, intelligent, moral, and (most importantly) suffering human beings.

Traditional Indian religion and mythology have little esteem for this existence in this world and allow those who wish to escape to do so for "sufficient reasons," which could be as varied as weariness, poverty, disgrace, loss of a loved one, dishonor, or political tyranny. Existence in this world is only one of many that the restless wanderer experiences in his journey to his final resting place, and one can only escape the cycles of death and rebirth by abandoning all striving, seeking, and desiring. The most persistent type of striving is for life itself, and suicide is seen as tolerable because it is a sign of one's victory over the most intense form of striving.[26]

There has been a long tradition in the Indian history of *suttee* in which widows throw themselves onto the funeral pyres of their deceased husbands. This was a sign of proper devotion to one's spouse and was either highly recommended or even demanded at various times.[27] Hinduism's tolerance of religious suicide finally came to an end under Christian influence and the British *raj,* but the practice of *suttee* was quite common even during the early years of their rule; as late as 1803, 200 wives voluntarily killed themselves at their husband's death.[28] And in 1821 there were more than 2000 deaths of this sort in all of India.[29]

Throughout history, Brahmins commonly self-executed by starvation in order to flee this world and achieve Nirvana. Not only was this was an acceptable reason for suiciding, but killing oneself to express a dislike of this world or to escape shame or disgrace was also tolerated.[30] Suiciding by holding one's breath was seen as one of the most acceptable ways of ending one's life and self-starvation is still rather widely practiced in India. Many believed sickness and disease were shameful, and to commit death by self-immolation was considered preferable to living with illness.[31] There was also a tradition of exhibitionist suicide among the Brahmins, and it is probably true that many came to Rome to commit their grand and ostentatious suicides before the emperors and aristocrats in the Coliseum.[32] And there was also something akin to institutional or political suicide in some places. For example, the king of Calicut in Malabar would hold a grand banquet after twelve years of reign and commit suicide in front of the guests at the end of the banquet.[33]

The leniency of Indian upper classes toward self-execution for various reasons makes it quite probable that suicide among the lower castes was indirectly tolerated or promoted. As the Brahmins allowed the upper classes to "leave this life" for a better world, it is hard to believe they would object to similar actions by the lower castes, for they had an intense contempt for these castes. The difficulty with allowing these religious suicides for the lower castes was that they could have appeared to be suiciding for religious reasons but could in reality have been doing it for less worthy motives such as revenge, despair, or escape from poverty, and it would have been difficult if not impossible to distinguish these motives. The pressures on the lower castes to choose suicide to escape shame and degradation must have been (and probably still are) tremendous. Their degraded and impoverished condition brought great shame on them in the eyes of many, and the pious lower castes yearned for the life of the monk, which many regarded as the most perfect form of life in this world. The temptation to suicide had to have been overwhelming for many of these people because it would be the most expeditious method of escaping suffering, increasing one's chances for a higher existence, and attaining Nirvana.

In contrast to Hinduism's tolerance of suicide, Jainism was very hostile toward self-execution, even when done for religious reasons. Avoidance of killing and doing harm were the fundamental rules of Jainism, and they ground all other moral prescriptions. Jainism required that five vows (*anu-vratas*) be observed: do not willfully destroy any kind of life, do not tell a lie, do not use another's property without consent, remain chaste, and limit one's necessities of life such that one does not kill living things unnecessarily.[34] Pious Jains would tread lightly on the ground, so as not to kill even the smallest insects.[35] For the Jain, life thrived on life, and noninjury was possible only if the soul was in perfect condition and had freed itself from matter.[36] This principle required that life not be destroyed unless so doing was necessary to support higher life, and this principle limited harming to the absolute minimum. Even the rules governing trade, social behavior, food, drink, and civil and criminal wrongs were governed by this basic principle.

Christianity would agree with Indian religions that existence is permeated with trials and suffering, but it would balance this view with the view that we are open to the presence of divine life and power of God through the Holy Spirit. The Holy Spirit, given through the salvific work of Christ, provides the believer the means of living a life of holiness in spite of these trials and difficulties. It discourages suicide because it counts the sufferings of this life as little in comparison to the glories to come and believes them to be quite worth the price to be paid for such a reward. It is surprising that Buddhism and Hinduism have not become more intolerant of suicide by demeaning the suffering and emptiness of this life in comparison to that of the next life and by encouraging patient toleration of suffering.

Many Western proponents of suicide call for attitudes toward self-slaying similar to those of Hinduism, but this would not be wise. In these societies there is neither the sympathy for the poor and distressed seen in the United States, for example, nor is there the confident belief that their lot can be improved in this world. In contemporary American culture, there is great sympathy and compassion for the disadvantaged and extensive private and public programs were founded in the twentieth century to alleviate the plight of the poor. Poverty is not considered a mark of shame or disgrace in our society, and yet significant elements of our national community look with suspicion on the wealthy and privileged. Despite that and the fact that most American Christian religions show little tolerance and give few incentives to suicide, the suicide rate among our poor remains significantly higher than that of the wealthy. In a culture such as that of India where poverty is often seen as a mark of religious inferiority and where suicide is accepted as a valid means of escaping one's suffering and plight, the destitute must be sorely tempted to attempt it throughout the duration of their lives.[37] Hinduism's tolerance of suicide should not be imitated in American society not only because it allows some unethical suicides, but also because it may result in profound social and cultural alterations and transformations that could have a harmful effect on our society.

Renaissance Suicide and the Age of Melancholy

The first major breach in the barrier against suicide constructed by Latin Christianity was made not by the Reformers, for they were generally supportive of the ban, but by Enlightenment philosophers.[38] Martin Luther (1483-1546) mistrusted the cynicism and disbelief of the new humanists and he knew their teachings could not enable one sorely tempted to suicide to resist for long.[39] But the division the Reformers fostered in Western Christianity created an opportunity for the humanists to neutralize Catholicism's traditional opposition to suicide. Even Lecky and Fedden noted that an increase of rationalism in the Renaissance led to an increase of self-destruction.[40] The first attack on the medieval reverence for life came with Pico della Mirandola (1463-1494) and his *Oration on the Dignity of Man,* which made suicide a mark of human dignity.[41] The Renaissance shattered the high valuation medieval Christianity gave to the life of poverty, and it initiated the age of commercialism, which gave more emphasis to the economic worth of the individual than to other aspects. This was the era when melancholy was regarded as the mark of genius, and William Shakespeare (1564-1616), perhaps the most melancholic of all Renaissance figures, forced classical Stoic views of suicide into an Elizabethan mold. He made use of suicide repeatedly in his plays and he reestablished suicidal themes in drama, which had been largely absent from medieval art and literature. In these plays only one of his suicides received ecclesiastical disapproval. Antony dies claiming "I am Antony still," and in eight tragedies there are an average of nearly two suicides in each play. In many of his plays, those who opposed suicide were presented as churlish and insensitive, and even good Catholics sometimes approved it.[42]

Dramatists after Shakespeare did not make suicide an obligatory or central part of their productions, even though Dryden (1631-1700) and Otway (1652-1685) both constructed some of their plays around suicides. Dryden's *All for Love* established the principle that lovers should not survive one another. Cervantes (1547-1616), Robert Burton (1577-1640), and John Donne (1573-1631) also drank at the wells of this new melancholy, and Samuel Johnson (1709-1784) would claim that it is not how a man dies, but how he lives that makes a difference.[43]

Many of the strongest writings favoring suicide came from France. The Jansenist Abbe' of St. Cyran, Verger de Hauranne (1581-1643), presented a interesting justification for suicide.[44] He claimed that the Decalogue prohibited the killing of others, even though it allowed self-killing in some circumstances. Just as one could deliberately kill others for the common good, so also could one kill oneself for the same reason, and he considered suicide for the well-being of one's prince, one's country, or one's family as morally legitimate. And suicide motivated by charity was morally permissible and not different from martyrdom.

Renaissance thinkers revived many of the old pagan views of the world and philosophical principles in support of suicide, and they turned the light of critical reason on Christian teachings and doctrines on suicide. Donne wrote the first principled defense of the morality of suicide in his *Biathanatos,* which was published against his wishes by his son after his death and there were few responses to it.[45] He was prone to suicide (some commentators believed he was obsessed with it), and he approached it very personally and quite differently from the Stoics who made it merely an object of deliberation, debate, and reflection. The ancient Stoic committed suicide when he was certain that life had no more value, but Donne allowed suicide when the mood of the person judged life to have lost value, and even when objective evidence was to the contrary. He did not consider suicide rational or good, but only necessary when people found life intolerable, and he believed sympathy demanded it be allowed in those instances. Renaissance thinkers posed new practical arguments against suicide, and a few raised again the older social, theological, and moral arguments against it, but these objections had lost their persuasiveness in the face of arguments made by those such as Donne.

Bourgeois suicides for practical reasons emerged with much greater frequency during the Renaissance, and Montaigne (1533-1592) illustrated best of all the spirit of these suicides:

> All comes to one period, whether man make an end of himself, or whether he endure it; whether he run before his day, or whether he expect it: whence soever it come, it is even his owne, where ever the threed be broken, it is all there, it's the end of the web.[46]

He also cast a more pragmatic and less principled light on death:

> Death is a remedy against all evils: It is a most assured haven, never to be feared, and often to be sought. All comes to one period, whether man make an end of himself, or whether he

> endure it; whether he run before his day, or whether he expect it; whence soever it come, it is ever his owne, where ever the thread be broken, it is all there, its the end of the web. The voluntarist death is the fairest. Life dependeth on the will of others, death on ours.[47]

Critics of suicide argued, however, that it was harmful to the person, family, and society, but these claims were not terribly effective.

Laws concerning suicide began to relax at the end of the Renaissance, and the traditional Latin Christian prohibitions of Christian burial were relaxed or abolished in many places.[48] Confiscation of the property of suicides came to be gradually limited or totally prohibited, primarily because some would try to obtain the estates of suicides by unscrupulous means. Both Protestant and Catholic rulers continued to oppose suicide during this era and call for strong civil penalties for suicide. Antisuicide arguments in this era became more pragmatic, philosophical, and persuasive while medical arguments were developed to add force to traditional moral and theological arguments against suicide. Hey received an award from Oxford for his comprehensive antisuicide work, *Dissertation on Suicide,*[49] and later he wrote a highly rationalist work, *Traite' du Suicide,* which condemned suicide as a violation of the virtue of prudence.[50] Hutcheson (1694-1746), an early utilitarian opponent of suicide, argued against suicide for theoretical reasons in his *System of Moral Philosophy* and also because it created exceptionally harmful consequences for others.[51]

The incidence of suicide apparently increased during this era because of diminished hope and increased skepticism engendered by the antireligious rhetoric of the Renaissance. Life was no longer seen as either a pilgrimage from an alien spiritual land to a paradise or as a journey up the mountain of the Lord, but was limited to the existence that only this world could offer. The increasing secularization of society broke down the barriers erected by Latin Christianity against self-killing, and because the Renaissance lost its grasp of the transcendent dimensions of human life, transcendent hope was destroyed and suicide became more reasonable, attractive, and widespread. Renaissance thinkers could promise only a frail and fleeting hope devoid of the salvific grace of God, and anything more substantial was not taken seriously. The medieval Christian was able to look forward to an eternal participation in divine life and love, and suicide became more prevalent because Renaissance secularism, rationalism, and cynicism could equal the promise offered by medieval

Christianity. The Renaissance drove the divine presence from the physical and spiritual world, and in so doing, it inadvertently promoted suicide by emptying out the cosmos and giving more substance to a spirit of despair. By driving out the divine, humanity was left disconnected, isolated, and alone in an alien, cold, and hostile universe that made escape through suicide much easier. Forcing the divine presence from the world intensified early modern obsessions with death and the spirit of melancholy replaced the macabre spirit of the late Middle Ages.[52]

The Enlightenment and the Reemergence of Suicide

Eighteenth-century philosophers demeaned the value of human life in relation to other values in a way that had not been seen since the Roman Empire. They developed a tolerance of idealistic suicide, and in the early part of the century, there was a notable increase in literary and philosophical suicide, as many of the English and French scholars ended their academic careers by this means.

Christian moral and theological arguments lost their persuasive power in the Renaissance, and only social and emotional objections to suicide retained any force. Rational arguments too had lost their persuasiveness, and yet many seemed to be searching for reasons to justify their emotional reaction against suicide. The classical, medieval, scholastic, philosophical, and theological antisuicide arguments were given little heed by the beginning of the nineteenth century, and the only forceful objections to suicide were made at the emotional level. Proponents of suicide showed little imagination in arguing for it and most opponents merely argued that it was contrary to nature. Some attempts were made to show the practical and psychological value of suffering that were destroyed by suicide, but these did not meet with much success. During the eighteenth century, suicide for purely economic reasons increased, as the growth of capitalism forced many people unexpectedly and undeservedly into poverty. And when theological objections to suicide deteriorated at the end of this century, the nineteenth century treated it as a medical or legal phenomenon and came to see it as either a crime or an act of insanity.

David Hume (1711-1776) exemplified the spirit of many English intellectuals of this time and claimed that most suicide prohibitions were ridiculous. Viewed cosmically, the life of an individual was of no more significance than that of an oyster, which made one's suicide insignificant.[53] In his view, the obligations of individuals to society ceased when they no longer derived benefits from their fulfillment, and suicide was justified when existence became a burden, for one was not obliged "to prolong a miserable existence, because of some frivolous advantage which the public may perhaps receive."[54] But in making this claim, he did not directly deal with assertions that one often had obligations to one's friends, wife, or children, for these relationships were often most effective in deterring one from suiciding.

Hume made the mainstay of his argument the claim that suicide was not contrary to nature:

> Were the disposal of human life so much reserved as the peculiar province of the Almighty that it were an encroachment on his right, for men to dispose of their own lives; it would be equally criminal to act for the preservation of life as for its destruction. If I turn aside a stone which is falling upon my head, I disturb the course of nature, and I invade the peculiar province of the Almighty by lengthening out my life beyond the period which by the general laws of matter and motion he had assigned it.
>
> A hair, a fly, an insect is able to destroy this mighty being whose life is of such importance. Is it an absurdity to suppose that human prudence may dispose of what depends on such insignificant causes? It would be no crime in me to divert the *Nile* or the *Danube* from its course, were I able to effect such purposes. Where then is the crime in turning a few ounces of blood from their natural channel? . . .
>
> 'Tis impious, says the old Roman superstition, to divert rivers from their course, or invade the prerogatives of nature. 'Tis impious, says the French superstition, to inoculate for small pox, or usurp the business of providence, by voluntarily producing distempers and maladies. 'Tis impious, says the modern *European* superstition, to put a period to our own life, and thereby rebel against our creator; and why not impious, say I, to build houses, cultivate the ground, or sail upon the ocean? In all these actions we employ our powers of mind and body, to produce some innovation in the course of our nature; and in none of them do we any more. They are all of them therefore equally innocent, or equally criminal.[55]

Notice that he attacked the argument that suicide is impermissible by claiming it is not against nature, but he did not attack the assertion made initially by Augustine that it was immoral because it was direct killing of innocent human life. Few proponents of suicide, including Hume, directly confronted this argument for the simple reason that assailing it would bring down the whole moral edifice that protects the innocent from direct and willful killing. Justifying suicide, not because nature allowed it, but because it is legitimate to kill the innocent, would legitimize all sorts of violence against the undeserving, and Hume probably knew he could not make a persuasive argument for suicide on those grounds. He did not wish to attack Augustine's argument because he would not be able to categorize it as taboo or superstition, and attacking it would show that there was a solid and rational basis for morally opposing self-killing.

In his nine-volume panegyric on death, *Night Thoughts,* the English poet Edward Young (1683-1765) deprived death of its negative and macabre character and made it a more positive reality.[56] For him, the grave became the gate to paradise and was to be loved rather than feared. He displayed a deep desire for death and a concomitant passionate melancholy that was only compensated for by his Christian faith. During Young's time, an anonymous libertine author argued that suicide was the sweet cure of all ills, and this poem was important because it argued that Stoicism, Epicureanism, and Cynicism historically led to libertinism on the issue of self-murder.[57]

With the philosophical critique of traditional Christian approaches to suicide complete, legal restraints quickly began to collapse.[58] It was under the influence of the libertinism, rationalism, and secularism of this era that the religious prohibitions of self-killing were broken. Beccaria (1738-1794) challenged the medieval laws demanding abuse of the corpse of a suicide and confiscation of property,[59] and he also and claimed that suicide should be placed entirely beyond the scope of the law, denying any moral or religious dimensions to it.[60] He asserted that antisuicide laws unduly punished innocent victims by expropriating the estates of suicides, punishing their families, or degrading their corpses, and these criticisms were well received in many quarters. Baron D'Holbach (1723-1789) challenged the notion that human life had an extraordinary value by claiming that death was the remedy given by nature to despair.[61] Like Hume, he set forth the framework of the secular, humanist arguments for suicide by arguing that it was neither against nature nor antisocial. For D'Holbach, nature did not object to one ending an unhappy life, and one's duties to society were based only on the social contract. But if society could not prevent intolerable misery, it would not be wrong to commit suicide as an act of last resort.[62] Voltaire (1694-1778) approached suicide in a very pragmatic manner, for he rejected any religious or romantic reasons for self-killing and argued that circumstances should determine when suicide should be allowed.[63] He considered the confiscation of the property of a suicide mere brigandage, and he became a symbol of growing popular sentiment against punitive measures to prevent suicide.[64] He permitted certain forms of "rational" suicide, but he had no sympathy for the romantic suicides that were often associated with his cause. He complained that this was not the era of noble suicide of ancient Rome and Greece, but of the bourgeois suicide.[65] Madame DeStael echoed this theme in her *Reflexions sur Suicide,* and claimed that the most common reasons for suicide during this time were dishonor and poverty.[66] Rousseau (1712-1778) was tolerant of suicide in many different situations, and he gave best expression to the idealistic and romantic attitude of the age. The twenty-first letter in his *Nouvelle Heloise* argued vigorously for the moral legitimacy of romantic suicide and he felt that only a madman would endure what he could escape.[67] He believed one could leave life when it no longer seemed good, and reason dictated that death should be seen as a remedy to a sad life. Montesquieu (1689-1755) also favored suicide when life did not give pleasure, for the prince could not expect one to remain a subject when he gained no benefit from servitude.[68] Diderot (1713-1784) initially condemned suicide, but showed sympathy for Donne's *Biathanatos* and finally agreed that it should not be considered criminal when the person who suicided was insane.[69] And even though intellectuals supported suicide, the law and popular opinion at this time were still strongly set against it, and there was much writing against suicide.

The French Revolution revived virtually all of the forms of suicide that prevailed in ancient Greece and Rome: political, philosophical, military, romantic, anesthetic, exhibitionistic, and egotistical suicide to preserve honor. The incidence of suicide increased markedly as revolutionaries attacked not only the Catholic church and its prohibitions of suicide, but also the secular laws banning it. Life became much cheaper than it had been in previous centuries and suicide became quite common, as Dumas wrote in 1773: "Suicide is becoming. . . common throughout all parts of the Christian world."[70] Some, such as Madame DeStael, tried to resist this growing trend and claimed that suicide was contrary to the moral dignity of the human person and was impermissible for any reason.[71] And she confronted the common argument that suicide preserves human dignity by arguing that self-killing is contrary to the moral dignity of the person.[72]

This was the era of the guillotine, the first appearance of national armies, and mass suicides by both aristocrats and revolutionaries. With the prevalence of political executions, civil rebellion, and international warfare, many killed themselves for a wide variety of reasons. Political suicide returned with the French Revolution and many revolutionaries ended their lives in this way. Wolfe Tone committed suicide in prison after the failure of the rebellion in Ireland in 1798.[73] The elder Robbespierre did so and the younger one attempted it,[74] and Lebas the younger tried to kill himself but failed.[75] Some believed that Couthon committed suicide, but the historical evidence for this is ambiguous.[76] This pattern continued through the Restoration, and Gracchus Babeuf tried to imitate the Decii of ancient Rome by stabbing himself before his judges to protest the tyranny of the Directory.[77] And his son, Camille, imitated him by throwing himself from the top of the column in the Place Vendome to mark the entrance of the allies into Paris.[78] Along with these suicides, there also occurred the more common suicides about which the ordinary man seemed to be quite apathetic.

So many aristocrats and revolutionaries died by their own hand that suicide became commonplace and banal, and the only suicides that provoked any sort of reaction were the patriotic suicides of the republicans, harkening back to the ancient Roman suicides. Petion suicided, as did Roland, Buzot, and Clavie'res, and like the suicide of DuFrieche-Valez, their deaths caused little commotion.[79] Military suicide also reappeared with the suicide of General Beaurepaire after the battle of Verdun.[80] Even Napoleon carried a dose of opium with him and used it on 12 April 1814 after being driven from Paris, even though it was not strong enough to end his life.[81]

In England, late eighteenth-century suicide became an act of aristocratic boredom and people usually committed suicide for money rather than love, finding greater shame in impoverishment than was usually the case in the Middle Ages.[82] It was during this time that the suicide statistics appeared, suggesting a significant increase in suicide in the eighteenth century, and if these records are accurate, London experienced a higher *per capita* rate of suicide at that time than it does today.[83]

In the nineteenth century, more conservative forces reemerged and sought to curb suicide by legal measures. Stringent measures were enacted in France to stop suicide because of the excesses of the revolutionaries, and many of the traditional prohibitions that existed prior to the revolution were restored. The wave of revolutionary suicides slowed with the utopianism of Saint-Simon (1760-1825) and Owen (1771-1858), who channeled much of this revolutionary energy into social reform. But their reforms were temporary, and when it was clear they would fail, Saint-Simon shot himself. By the middle of the century, legal penalties for suicide, amended during the revolution, were reestablished, and the Church denied Christian burial to suicides.[84] This succeeded in curbing many suicides, but it also promoted concealment of acts of self-murder. The extent to which the Catholic church lost influence on this issue in this era is the extent to which suicides increased, and in the 1880s the government punished those who denied suicides burial, whether for civil or religious reasons.

Romantic Suicide: The New Circumcellions

One cannot understand the development of modern suicide unless one sees its historical roots in Romanticism. In the Renaissance and Enlightenment, the force of the Christian objections to suicide was broken, which resulted in the emergence of romanticized suicide. It was the Romantics, in the figures of Chatterton and Werther, who made suicide not only acceptable, but a mark of honor, genius, and cultivation. By the middle of the nineteenth century, the view that suicide was permissible for at least some reasons gained widespread social acceptance, and most agreed that all suicides had to be judged on their own merits.

The Romantic era of suicide began when the English poet English Thomas Chatterton (1752-1770) suicided because he was unable to support himself financially, and his death became a model for Romantic self-destruction. He was a gifted poet who was thrust into poverty as a child because of his father's death. He wrote his own poetry, claiming to have discovered it in a medieval church and attributed it to a fictitious medieval poet, Thomas Rowley. Chatterton's reputation spread, and even though he published widely, he was never given proper recognition or remuneration for his work. He struggled to avoid financial ruin and finally failing, he was driven to madness and suicide. Ensuing generations canonized Chatterton and transformed his suicide into a martyrdom and model for Romantic suicide, and they regarded him as the epitome of the Romantic genius who was persecuted, misunderstood, impoverished, and ultimately driven to despair and death because of his gifts. Chatterton was the new saint-genius of the Romantics, not only possessing all of the virtues they revered, remarkable insight, creativity, and imagination, but also suffering all the horrors they condemned, poverty and persecution by a pedestrian aristocracy and the bourgeoisie. He was the perfect Romantic poet who emerged briefly from nowhere to enlighten the darkness of the world and then disappeared in self-inflicted death. The new Romantic secular saint-genius was a playwright, actor, poet, scholar, or artist who was driven by forces and powers not shared by others. Alone and misunderstood, he suffered poverty, alienation, and destitution precisely because of his gifts. The Rationalists of the previous century had given suicide a moral legitimacy, but the Romantics saw suicide as a mark of the new secular holiness. The Rationalists were the moral reformers who destroyed the credibility of the old arguments against suicide, but it was the Romantics who became the saints of the new movement. For, as Alfred Alvarez says, the Romantic stance was suicidal.[85] With the destruction of traditional religion by the Rationalists, Romantic artists became the new secular saints and spiritual leaders who served as beacons along the way significantly darkened by the destruction of religious belief and proscriptions of suicide. Charity, devotion to God, selflessness, and holiness were devalued by the Rationalists, and the Romantics made passionate, erotic infatuation its secular counterpart that consumed its truest worshipers, and those who suicided in the midst of its storms were their new holy and venerated ones. Those slaying themselves in service of this love became its new martyrs, not unlike the Donatists of old, and their burial grounds became the new Romantic shrines.

The Romantics made death infinitely sweeter by glossing over its more hideous aspects, and the worthiest death two lovers could hope for would be to plunge over a cliff arm in arm. Death became a friend or confidant and was no longer an alien or source of terror, and as the movement progressed, French Romanticism gave death a darker, more haunting, and mysterious character.[86] When a young man was accused of pushing his pregnant wife into the Seine, he defended himself by claiming that it was the age of suicide.[87] To die by one's hand was the road to fame, and suicides were reported in newspapers in great detail.

In the world of opera, suicide was pervasive. Verdi seemed unable to write an opera without a suicide. Leonora poisoned herself in *Il Trovatore,* Aida concealed herself in her lover's vault, Otello stabbed himself, and Ernani stabbed himself in *Ernani* to fulfill a pledge to die when his enemy sounded his horn. Cio-Cio-San committed *hara-kiri* in Puccini's *Madama Butterfly,* Tosca leapt to her death, and Sister Angelica poisoned herself in *Sour Angelica.* Dido in Purcell's *Dido and Aneas* stabbed herself as she mounted her funeral pyre, and Gioconda took the knife in Ponchielli's *La Gioconda.* Brunhilde rode her horse onto Siegfried's funeral pyre in Wagner's *Gotterdammerung,* and Gwendoline stabbed herself in Chabrier's *Gwendoline.* In Massanet's *Herodaide,* Salome stabbed herself when she learned of the death of John the Baptist. Mascagni's Iris threw herself into a river in *Iris,* and Marfa and Andrea threw themselves with others onto a funeral pyre in Mussorgski's *Kovanchina.* Katerina Ismailova drowned herself in Shostakovich's *Lady Macbeth of Mzensk,* and Lakme poisoned herself in Delibes's *Lakme.* Edgardo stabbed himself in Donizetti's *Lucia di Lammermoor,* and Liu stabbed herself in Puccini's *Turandot.* Fenella drowned herself in Auber's *Masaniello,* Pollione killed himself in Bellini's *Norma,* and Herman stabbed himself in Tchaikovsky's *Pique Dame.* Mizguir in Rimsky-Korsakov's *The Snow Maiden* drowned himself, and Werther shot himself in Massanet's *Werther.*

In the writings of the era, suicide became the keystone of the Romantic edifice, and it often stood as the culmination of their dramas. Virtually all of the great Romantic figures ended their writing careers at a young age, either by suicide or by other equally destructive means. The Romantics believed that life was unequal to the demands of passion, love, and romance, and to be true to the new passionate love they espoused, suicide was the properly courageous way to exit this troubled existence. Byron (1788-1824), Keats (1795-1821), and Shelley (1792-1822) all died as young men, and even though Coleridge (1772-1834) lived into his sixties, he committed *litterateuricide,* admitting that his latter years were virtually posthumous existence and utterly unproductive. They all subscribed to the view that the middle years of one's life were hostile to the passionate and erotic spirit of Romantic poetry. Along with Goethe (1749-1832) they accepted suicide as legitimate and permissible for the common man, and the characters in their poems were models for real-life people. Keats saw suicide as the happiest and surest escape from the troubles of life, and Byron saw death in *Don Juan* as "the lurking bias. . . to the unknown." Certainly for them, death became an object of love, and it seems that most of the great artists and literary figures of this age toyed with suicide.

Gustave Flaubert (1821-1880) claimed that he dreamed of suicide, and he and his friends

> lived in a strange world, I assure you; we swung between madness and suicide; some of them killed themselves. . . another strangled himself with his tie, several died of debauchery in order to escape boredom; it was beautiful.[88]

In the plays of Alfred de Musset, suicide played a prominent role, and it was often trivialized.[89] Alvarez maintained that Gerhard de Nerval strangled himself with a cord that he believed to be the girdle of Madame de Maintenon,[90] but this is disputed by other literary critics who are not sure if his death was deliberate or accidental.[91] There was another side to Romantic suicide that involved frustrated love, *ennui*, and the boredom of youth, and is epitomized in George Sand's (1804-1876) *Indiana*.[92] Indiana was a woman who was ruined by a man for whom she sacrificed everything, and she was rescued by her devoted cousin Ralph. Sand wanted the two of them to commit suicide by throwing themselves from a cliff, but ultimately they did not do this. For Sand, lovers such as Indiana and Ralph could legitimately commit suicide because of a general malaise from which they suffered on account of their love and misfortune.

In Villiers de l'Isle' Adam's *Axel,* the main character spent his life searching for the perfect woman, and when he found her they committed suicide together.[93] Suicide was no longer Romantic or principled, but rather an escape from bored youth. Nothing was more intolerable to them than living to middle age when their gifts would perish, and their youthful suicides showed their true Romantic faith. Romantic suicides had to have a certain creativity to them, and if this was present, it guaranteed the perpetrators the status of heroes. Romantic poets became their characters, were hounded as are contemporary movie stars, and suicide became the price to be paid for their poetic genius.[94]

Even though Goethe was skeptical of the whole suicide craze, his *Trials of Young Werther* gave a particularly Romantic tinge to this sort of death.[95] Rather than suiciding because of poverty, boredom, or passionate love, he broke the thread of life because of his failed love for Lotte.[96] Werther transformed Chatterton into a Romantic figure who was driven to suicide, not by poverty and rejection, but by passion, love, and his genius to self-assassinate. Werther became the saint-figure for the Romantics, and not only did young men dress in his blue and yellow clothes, but they mimicked his own self-killing. He typified the ideal Romantic who was the young man whose genius and inspiration showed brightly in youth, only to vanish quickly. Suicide, much like Werther's blue coat and yellow waistcoat, enhanced the personality of the poet, and *Werther*'s progress was measured in the number of bodies counted. It is estimated that suicides in France doubled between 1820 and 1840, and this is primarily due to the influences of these Romantics.[97]

Like the Circumcellions of old, the Romantics made suicide mandatory and a litmus test for secular canonization, and what these people did in their lives was less important than what they did in their dying. The Circumcellions could believe almost anything they wanted, just as long as they died a bloody death, and the Romantic poets did not necessarily have to display any artistic gifts or creativity, just as long as they posed as geniuses and ended their lives by suicide. The secularization of society was complete.

Absurdity, Dada, and Suicide

As Romanticism degenerated in the nineteenth century so also did its view of death, and objections to suicide weakened as the secularization of society in this century progressed. As the glamour of Romantic suicide wore off, the average bourgeois committed suicide more from a general malaise than from Romantic passion. Suicide in the post-Romantic era ceased to be the result of desperate passion, but of boredom, and suicide from *taedium vitae* became more common than even during the Renaissance when this sort of self-killing was quite frequent.[98] Suicide in this era was judged tolerable if it promoted happiness and intolerable if it destroyed the possibility of happiness. It was no longer regarded as a sinful or immoral act, and the worst that was said of it was that it was a betrayal of one's family and caused disgrace. It soon lost its criminal character as well, and the primary argument against suicide in this era was that it harmed one's family and brought shame and malicious gossip.[99] Suicide was believed to run in families, and it could radically impair one's social standing. It was seen as so corruptive and poisoning that often extraordinary efforts were often made to cover it up. This era marked the end to virtually all prohibitions of Christian burial, and in England in the 1820s suicides were allowed to be buried on consecrated ground, although this had to be done at night.[100] Suicide was removed from the legal category of homicide, and the penalty for attempted suicide was reduced to two years imprisonment, but assisting suicide carried a penalty of mandatory life imprisonment. Coroners were still reluctant to bring a verdict of *felo de se* because of the penalties it would still bring to family members.

The pessimist philosopher Arthur Schopenhauer (1788-1860) initially gave strong support to suicide as a fundamental human right, but he would only allow it as an expression of human freedom because it alone definitively overcame the will to live.[101] But in the end, he found the desire for death to be merely an expression of the will to live and became more critical of it. Bonser, in his work *The Right to Die,* argued that retiring from life was not always and everywhere selfish and was commendable in some cases.[102]

Fedden claims that the French writer Jules Lafourges and his wife (the daughter of Karl Marx) both committed suicide in their old age and left behind a note that harkens back to the Stoics:

> before pitiless old age (which is taking from me one by one the pleasures and joys of existence), paralyses my energy, breaks my life, and makes me a burden to myself and others. Years ago I promised myself I would not live beyond seventy.[103]

However, the common opinion among his commentators is that he died of tuberculosis and that his wife died a few months later also of natural causes.[104] Suicide could benefit others and be a great act of heroism, and he denied that there was any condition under which others could justifiably intervene to prevent a suicide.

The Rationalists destroyed the arguments against suicide and claimed that these arguments were merely superstitions, taboos, and falsehoods. They regarded suicide as not only a fact but also as a part of life and saw the arguments raised against it as simply absurd. But Dostoyevsky argued vigorously against accepting suicide, and he believed it was imperative to reject suicide to be able to look beyond the absurdity of the world to see a coherent cosmology and anthropology. He was diametrically opposed to the Rationalists and saw that suicide was not a "part of life" but was its end, and he concluded that the arguments for it were ultimately absurd. To accept the rationality of suicide was to accept the absurd, and this was a factor in his return to Christianity. In Dostoyevsky's *The Possessed,* Kirilov committed what is called "logical suicide," which Dostoyevsky regarded as nothing but a logical absurdity. Dostoyevsky understood that regarding suicide as rational and logical made our existence absurd and only marginally above the cattle. This was irrational, for it insulted us by imputing meaninglessness to our lives and for Dostoyevsky, it forced him to believe in God to make sense of our existence. With the weakened power of religion, the power of suicide grew, and Mersault, the hero of Camus's *The Stranger,* found death without afterlife.[105] Camus transformed Kirilov's suicide into a twentieth-century style suicide, and called it a metaphysical suicide. Dostoyevsky and Camus argued persuasively that if the Rationalists were correct and suicide was rational, then reality and life were also absurd and irrational. And for both, Kirilov's suicide captured the spirit of post-Rationalist and post-Romantic suicide, for Kirilov was serious, irritable, obsessed, methodical, energetic, and tender in his self-killing. In Kirilov, one almost captures the heart of reflexive killing in our century, and all that is missing is the element of technological romanticism.

Kirilov could endorse suicide because he was a literary figure who lacked flesh and blood, but Dostoyevsky was a real and existing person who found existence more rational than death, which for him was the terminal zero. He saw that if there is no God to condemn suicide, then man is a god, not as Nietzsche saw the *ubermensch,* but straightforwardly and baldly. If God did not exist, we were divine and we had to kill ourselves to be the lord of the living and the dead, which in itself is illogical. Hence, suicide was absurd for Dostoyevsky, and its logic was an expression of an absurdity that Kirilov unleashes. Kirilov acted out this logic in a dramatic fashion and Camus gave it the title of "absurd": there is no order in the world, and it merely exists in all of its contradictoriness and confusion. Suicide was logical if death was merely tomorrow's zero with nothing standing beyond it. This is the kernel of the rationalist argument for suicide, but Dostoyevsky saw this reduction of death to the final zero point of life as making life absurd and illogical. He sided with the rationality and coherence of life and existence itself and concluded that the argument for suicide, "logical suicide" is itself illogical.

Philosophers, poets, and then artists all accepted self-destruction as legitimate by the end of the nineteenth century. T. S. Eliot's *Wasteland* expressed not only this exterior chaos of the world during World War I, but also the inner chaos of the person brought about by Rationalist and Romantic endorsements of the absurd. Wittgenstein understood the absurd logic of suicide quite well:

> If suicide is allowed then everything is allowed.
> If anything is not allowed then suicide is not allowed.
> This throws a light on the nature of ethics, for suicide is, so to speak, the elementary sin.
> And when one investigates it, it is like investigating mercury vapors in order to comprehend the nature of vapors.
> Or is even suicide in itself neither good nor evil?[106]

Rationalists argued persuasively (but not well) that suicide was morally permissible, and the Romantics carried this further and claimed that suicide was the best testimony one could give to the passionate way in which one lived one's life as an artist. It was the Dadaists, however, who carried out with brutal logic the arguments of the Rationalists and Romantics. They concluded that if life is absurd, and it could not support even foolish romantic love, then suicide would be the only intelligent and responsible choice. Suicide fit the Dadaist movement well because it espoused destructive agitation against everything. Dada ridiculed the absurdity of existence, which Dostoyevsky affirmed, and it believed that sustaining this ridicule was more important than art or even existence itself. Dada bludgeoned existence and asserted the meaninglessness of its values. Dada was anti-art, anti-everything, and ultimately anti-itself. It was suicide in its most complete form and it treated everything, even itself, as worthless, absurd, and the object of ridicule.

Dadaists treated life itself as worthless, and they ridiculed it as much as they did art. But Dada did not consider the valuelessness and ridiculousness of existence tragic and sorrowful, and it stripped away the despair surrounding the absurdity of existence by making a joke of existence. The Romantics needed to justify suicide because of the inability of life to sustain passionate love, but the Dadaists needed no such reasons, for merely the patent absurdity and senselessness of life justified suicide. The Romantics treated life as worthless in the face of passionate love, but Dada saw even this love as worthless. Life was so trivial and meaningless that they did not even try to justify suicide and they even required it for admission into their artistic avant-garde. Jacques Vache was the Dadaist *par excellence,* and as a cruel joke he ended his life by a lethal overdose of opium, which he also administered to two of his friends without their knowledge. Jacques Rigaut was called an "empty suitcase" by a friend, implying that beneath the shell of his exterior existence there was nothing but emptiness and absurdity. Arthur Cravan believed suicide should be a work of art, and he disappeared from a boat in the Gulf of Mexico. His wife sought him out in South American jails, but was unable to locate him and justifiably concluded that he committed suicide. Rigaut considered suicide a vocation, and his own suicide ended the Dadaist period.

While accepting the legitimacy of suicide for Romantic reasons, the Romantics rejected the Rationalist arguments in favor of suicide, and they made suicide part of life for everyone. The Dadaists, however, made suicide to be life itself. To a greater or lesser extent,

Rationalists, Romantics, and Dadaists rejected the notion of the sacredness of human life, and the Dadaists went the furthest by treating human life and existence not only as worthless but as a bad joke. Unlike suicide advocates who went before, the best death for them was not one of reason, romance, sanctity, or passion, but was a farce and a bad joke. While the Rationalists challenged the notion that human life must always and everywhere be protected, the Dadaists regarded life as something so absurd, farcical, and empty that it was always and everywhere legitimate to destroy it. Life was so riddled with insanity, foolishness, and iniquity that it was never wrong to terminate it.

Dadaists rejected moral prohibitions of suicide, as well as the belief that suicide was a sign of mental instability. While modern suicide advocates consider it eminently rational, Dada saw it as the best action possible to express the irrationality of life. Postenlightenment thought rejected theological condemnations of suicide, but Dada made suicide an artistic and moral value. In many respects Dada was thoroughly modern, for it glorified destructiveness and saw it as the greatest of human accomplishments. Dadaists made death part of their art, just as did the Romantics, but their art was to be anti-art and ultimately anti-everything.

Modern Suicide: The New Dilemma

The Dadaist movement showed that the modern era brought a return of suicidal practices unseen since ancient Rome, including many of its more ridiculous forms. Besides the mocking, derisive, and ridiculing deaths of the leading Dadaists, there were further examples of absurd suicides. One Englishman decided he was too tired to get dressed in the morning and committed suicide.[107] Two young men in Paris balked at the idea of paying for a lavish dinner they had the night before, and they committed suicide.[108] But in a more serious vein, modern poets, artists, and literary figures followed the lead of the Romantics and Dadaists and carried on the theme that serious and committed artists had to pay for their gifts with blood and death. As eighteenth-century thought condoning suicide in some instances grew, more and more literary figures gave it qualified support. In previous centuries, artists who suicided were rare, but in this century, the greater artists were more vulnerable to suicide than ever before. Besides the Dadaist suicides, Van Gogh, Virginia Woolf, Hart Crane, Delmore Schwartz, Joe Orton, Sylvia Plath, Mark Rothko, Cesare Pavese, Mayakovsky, Paul Celan, Esenin, Modigliani, Arshile Gorki,

Tsvetayeva, Jackson Pollack, and Mark Gertler all ended their lives. Dylan Thomas and Brendan Behan drank themselves to death and Strindberg went insane. Berlioz and Poe nearly died from overdoses of opium after unhappy affairs, and Rimbaud stopped writing in his twenties in a kind of slow suicide.

What is it about the life of the modern artist and writer that attracts such unstable figures to it? To explain this, Alfred Alvarez argued that modern consciousness has suffered from what Robert Jay Lifton calls psychic numbing.[109] They claim the root cause of the increase in suicides was that the world moved toward more and more threatening and disastrous conditions that have anesthetized our sensitivity to the destruction of innocent life. Awareness that death can come swiftly and without warning to both the just and unjust brings about this numbing and increases vulnerability to suicide. But rather than blaming this on nonmoral, extrinsic, cosmic, social, or political factors, a more plausible explanation for this increase in suicide is that secularizing post-Rationalist and post-Romantic society has significantly weakened the force of moral and religious arguments against suicide. European intellectuals and artists discredited and denied the sanctity of human life, challenged the immunity of innocent life to deliberate attack, and rejected moral arguments against self-killing. The intellectuals and artists of the modern era were the first to understand this, and they paid the heaviest price in blood to give testimony to this new moral order. This movement not only weakened barriers against suicide, but it also inhibited efforts to use moral arguments to dissuade people from impermissible suicides. To have argued, for example, that the suicides of Rigaut or Vache were immoral would have only brought mockery and ridicule because of the weakened state of antisuicide moral arguments in this era.

The most notable development concerning suicide in the modern era, however, was not Dadaist philosophy of suicide of the absurd, but the growth of the field of suicidology and the professional, scientific study of suicide. From this movement came the new and authentic saints in the history of suicide: the suicidologists and health care professionals who tried to understand, save, and rehabilitate the suicidal. Approaching suicide as a medical and scientific problem, contemporary suicidology made it clear that depressive and psychiatric illnesses were critical in the suicidal decision. Its most striking finding was that more than 93 percent of those who died by suicide manifested major psychiatric illnesses, usually a depressive illness or alcoholism, prior to their suicide.[110] And of those with these symptoms, more than half had never seen a mental health professional, and the large portion of them had made a suicide attempt before. The depressive illness that precipitates suicide is temporary, fleeting, and eminently treatable; the period of lethality is ordinarily very brief, and if the individual can be brought through that period, they can usually be saved.[111] These symptoms include pervasive sadness, irritability, difficulties with sleep and appetite, weight changes, loss of interest, hopelessness, and loss of insight. Suicidal persons are usually the last to recognize these symptoms, will ordinarily resist attempts at intervention, and will usually deny these symptoms when questioned.[112]

It is known now that the depressed are frequently preoccupied with their physical well-being and health, and they often believe they are dying, even when solid medical evidence is to the contrary. It is not uncommon for the elderly to mistakenly believe they have cancer and kill themselves, and when the relatives and close friends of these suicides are interviewed, one discovers that they usually suffer from an eminently treatable psychiatric illness. In contrast to some proponents of the rationality of suicide, people commonly cling to life as long as they can. Suicidal wishes and desires are ordinarily serious symptoms resulting from temporary, treatable conditions. It is a widely held opinion of suicidologists that depression robs patients of their objectivity, freedom, and competence to make decisions, which renders the "autonomy" of suicidal decisions questionable.[113]

Even though modern suicidology has made very important advances, it also suffers from a serious weakness. It has shed much light on the etiology of suicide by laying bare the deep psychological roots that motivate it, and it has succeeded in restoring the psychological integrity of many who lapse into suicidal despair. Its dilemma is that the value-free, nonmoral methods it espouses of treating suicide are more humane and compassionate than those of previous centuries, but these new approaches are less able to deter those who resist them from suiciding. The traditional moral and social measures taken against suicide showed little mercy or compassion, and they were ineffective in healing the broken spirit of the suicidal person, but they were more effective in deterring suicide than are modern approaches. But the new methods of treating the suicidal have been hindered because few who are vulnerable to suicide actively seek help and a far greater number vigorously refuse efforts to help them.

Modern suicidology has been less effective in deterring potential suicides than was Christianity in the Middle Ages or contemporary Islam. These societies were able to prevent suicides by criticizing severely the morality of the suicidal action, which modern value-free suicidology simply will not do. Modern approaches are firmly set against either claiming a radical value for human life or using moral suasion to deter suicides, and in doing so, they might well be excluding a very effective means of deterring potential suicides. Traditional Christian theological anthropologies argued that the person is intimately related to the divine because of our creation in the image of God, and when coupled with strong arguments against killing the innocent, it can make effective arguments against suicide.

Modern suicidology's dilemma is quite difficult, for it is firmly committed to its nonreligious, value-free, empirical, and psychotherapeutic approach to the issue, even though this strategy has shown limited abilities to deter suicides in comparison to the medieval Catholic and religious approach. Even though it regards suicide as tragic and unfortunate, it does not feel any necessity to make moral judgments against self-killing or to argue for the transcendence of human life in attempts to deter it. It presumes that any moral argument against suicide would be ineffective and would only deter the suicidal person from obtaining needed help, and it rejects the use of moral censure as being inhumane and fruitless, but if its efforts against suicide are to be all-encompassing, it must find more effective means of deterring those who contemplate suicide.

Contemporary suicidology fails to see that it has a moral and ethical counterpart whose efforts to deter suicide would benefit from promoting the development of a strong and integrated moral character. Using well-formed moral arguments against self-killing can be effective in deterring some individuals against suiciding, for with many potential suicides, it is difficult to deter them from their decision by claiming that such decisions are the result of mental illness. But well-formed moral arguments might well be more effective precisely because guilt plays such an important role in many suicidal attempts. The suicidal patient struggles against not only psychological forces, such as depression, but also moral forces, such as guilt; and to gain moral strength and integrity the moral arguments of the pastor can often be as helpful as the psychological help of the therapist. To argue that a suicidal decision could set them against God or is an act of weak moral character could be more effective than other measures. An approach such as this was used by Catholics in the Middle Ages and may account partly for their success in deterring suicide. To effectively deter suicide, modern suicidology needs to develop its own contemporary doctrine of the sanctity and inviolability of human life as well as moral arguments that prohibit it, for this sort of doctrine is found in Judaism, Islam, and Catholicism and it may be partly why they were so effective in deterring suicide.

This crisis calls for a new relationship between formers of moral opinion, theologians, social scientists, suicidologists, and psychotherapists, for none of them alone can both deter and heal the suicidal person. A more balanced approach, including not only medical and psychological aspects, but also the moral dimensions of self-killing, would be more effective in deterring those prone to suicide because many suicides are undertaken to purge feelings of guilt. Many such suicidal persons believe their guilt to be rational and justified and seek a real and active escape from it by self-killing, and to be fully effective, one should not consider all of these feelings to be utterly irrational. To deter suicide, educational efforts by both mental health workers, moral educators, and social workers must stress that suicide is not only tragic because it solves no problems, but also that it is immoral.

The twentieth century has shown that the romantic suicides were neither secular saints nor martyrs, but were victims of their own guilt and mental disorders, and they deserved pity more than emulation. Many who would not otherwise be deterred from suiciding would be by this message. These twentieth-century developments have brought the modern history of suicide almost full circle, for at the beginning of this era, Christian anthropology and moral arguments against suicide were rejected almost *in toto* as useless and ineffective. But having jettisoned them rather hastily and with little reflection, it is becoming clearer that they might be one of the best means available for solving the one persistent problem now confronting contemporary antisuicide techniques: deterring the self-killer before he or she commits the final act of absurdity.

Notes

1. Nitobe, I., *Bushido: The Soul of Japan*, (New York: Putnam, 1905), 117-20. The original samurai deliberately made *hara kiri* as painful as possible to show their strength, but it was later modified, and being decapitated in the middle of the ritual was permitted. This is very different from modern suicide, which tries to make it as painless as possible. And modern suicide lacks this dimension of manifesting one's soul by one's dying. See Turnbull, S. R., *The Samurai,* (New York: MacMillan, 1977), 47.
2. While this was the ostensible purpose of this ritual, much contemporary thought would see it as an attempt to purge guilt and feelings of shame and not merely an act manifesting one's purity.
3. Nitobe, I., *Bushido,* 114.

4. In the battle of Iwo Jima, only 1083 Japanese soldiers were captured alive of the 21,000 trying to defend the island. See Wheeler, K., *The Second World War*, (Alexandria, VA: Time-Life Books, 1979), 41 & 56. Of 2,600 troops defending Betio island, only 17 surrendered alive. Sternberg, R., *Island Fighting*, (Alexandria, VA: Time-Life Books, 1978), 106,118. Of the 31,649 Japanese troops defending Saipan, some 29,000 were counted dead, and these did not include the hundreds of Japanese civilians who plunged to their deaths from the island's cliffs at the conclusion of the battle. Ibid., 167, 171. Eventually, the Japanese high command put an end to this tactic, and at the battles of Okinawa and Iwo Jima, suicidal charges were forbidden.
5. Murdoch, J., *A History of Japan*, vol. 1, (London: Kegan, Paul, 1910), 311-13. Turnbull noted that in 1156 when a group of soldiers were trapped in a burning building, they did not commit suicide because this tradition had not yet been established (*The Samurai*, p. 36).
6. Turnbull, S. R., *The Samurai*, 78-80.
7. Murdoch, J., *A History*, 470-71.
8. Murdoch, J., *A History*, 599-600.
9. Ibid., 133.
10. Ibid., 290.
11. Quoted in Turnbull, S. R., *The Samurai*, 117.
12. De Vos, G. and Wagatsuman, H., "Psycho-cultural Significance of Concern with Death and Illness among Rural Japanese," *International Journal of Social Psychiatry*. 5 (1959): 5-19. Durkheim reported that *hara kiri* was united with dueling occasionally, and he noted an episode in which two young men competed with one another in committing suicide. Durkheim, E., *Suicide*, trans. Spaulding, J. A., and Gibson G., (Glencoe: Free Press, 1951), 222.
13. Fedden, H., *Suicide: A Social and Historical Study*, (New York: Benjamin Blom, 1972), 48.
14. Iga, M., "Japanese Adolescent Suicide and Social Structure," in *Essays in Self-Destruction*, Ed. Shneidman, E., (New York: Science House, 1967), 224.
15. Ibid., 224-29.
16. DeVos, G. A., "The Relation of Guilt toward Parents to Achievement and Arranged Marriage among the Japanese," *Psychiatry*, 23 (1960): 287-301.
17. Stoetzel, J., *Without the Chrysanthemum and the Sword*, (New York: Columbia, 1955), 215, 219.
18. See Russell, O. D., "Suicide in Japan," *American Mercury*, 20 (1930): 341.
19. Ibid., 342.
20. Ibid., 343.
21. Ibid., 342.
22. Ibid., 344.
23. For example, see Paripurnanand, V., *Suicide in India and Abroad*, (Agra: Sihitya Bhawan, 1976); Veeraraghavan, V., *Suicides and Attempted Suicides in the Union Territory of Delhi*, (New Delhi: Concept, 1985). While these studies are comprehensive in some respects, they usually lack theoretical depth or sophistication, and their analysis of data is often somewhat flawed.
24. See Heard, G., "Buddha and Self-Destruction," in *Essays on Self-Destruction*, Ed. Shneidman, E., (New York: Science House, 1967), 88-89.
25. Ibid., 89.
26. What is not clear is why the *act* of suicide as self-inflicted death is not regarded as drawing one deeper into the cycle of dying rather than as a suppressing of the desire to live, which enables one to escape striving. I have not been able to discover

any Hindu religious or theological works that explain satisfactorily why this is not true.

27. Despite the pervasiveness of this practice, it is rather remarkable that there has been very little study of self-killing in India, for about the only studies done recently on this issue analyzed *suttee* by Indian women. These studies have focused on the sexist character of this action, but little study has been done on the prevalence of suicide among the lower castes. As will be explained later, there are good reasons to believe that it is quite common among these castes, as it would permit at least some to rise to higher states of life. See Paripurnanand, V., *Suicide in India and Abroad.*

28. Fedden, H., *Suicide*, 19.

29. Ibid., 19.

30. Ibid., 25.

31. Ibid., 25.

32. Ibid., 68. There is a good probability that this occurred because, as mentioned above, suicide was known throughout the ancient world as "Roman Death." It is quite likely that some or many Brahmins came to Rome knowing that their exhibitionist suicide would bring them fame and riches.

33. Ibid., 23.

34. Jagmanderlal, J., *Outlines of Jainism*, (Cambridge: Cambridge University Press, 1940), 69.

35. See Smart, N., *The World's Religions*, (Englewood Cliffs, NJ: Prentice Hall, 1989), 68.

36. Ibid., 71.

37. Classical Catholicism concurred that there are great evils and sufferings in this world but that the Holy Spirit present in the world as a result of the Incarnation, passion, death, and Resurrection of Christ enables us to transcend them. It believed that the sufferings of this life, terrible as they might be, are only transitory in comparison to the reward of life and glory given to those who place their faith in God.

38. See Lecky, W., *A History of European Morals,* vol. 1, (New York: Appleton, 1869), vol. 2, 57.

39. Fedden, H., *Suicide*, 157; Lecky, W., *European Morals*, vol. 2, 57.

40. See Lecky, W., *European Morals*, vol. 1, 228 and Fedden, H., *Suicide*, 77.

41. Pico della Mirandola, "De Hominis Dignitate," in *Pico Della Mirandola*, Ed. Garin, E., (Florence: Edizione Nationale dei Classici del Pensiero Italino, 1942), 58-68.

42. For an excellent study of suicide in Shakespeare, see Faber, M. D., "Shakespeare's Suicides: Some Historical, Dramatic, and Psychological Reflections," in *Essays in Self-Destruction,* Ed. Shneidman, E., (New York: Science House, 1967), 30-59. A unique aspect of his analysis is the insubstantial difference between the psychology of martyrdom and suicide, for they both derive from erotic, self-punitive, and aggressive urges that interact in different ways. See Menninger, K., *Man Against Himself* (New York: 1938), 142.

43. Burton is important because he was a Protestant pastor and scholar who suffered greatly from melancholy. Sorely tempted to suicide, he pitted Stoic arguments for suicide against the contentions of the Christians and argued vigorously against allowing self-killing. See Burton, R., *The Anatomy of Melancholy,* (New York: Farrar & Rinehart, 1927).

44. See Moore, C., *A Full Enquiry into the Subject of Suicide,* 2 vols., (London: J.F. & C. Rivington, 1790), vol. 2, 111-12.

45. See John Donne, *Biathanatos*, (New York: Garland, 1982), Introduction and Commentary by Rudick, M., and Battin, M. For examples of responses to his work, see Denny, W., *Pelicanicidium*, (London: for Thomas Hucklescott, 1653) and Sym, J., *Life's Preservative against Self-Killing*, (London: Flesher, 1637)
46. *The Essays of Michael Lord of Montaigne,* vol. 2, Tr. Florio J., (London, Allen Lane, 1991), 25.
47. Ibid.
48. Lecky, W., *European Morals*, 61. Laws against suicide were still defended by Hugo Grotius, but Beccaria and Montesquieu began to challenge them such that in France no laws against suicide existed by the end of the revolution.
49. Hey, R., *A Dissertation on Suicide*, (London: Cambridge, 1785).
50. Fedden, H., *Suicide*, 217.
51. Hutcheson, F., *A System of Moral Philosophy,* 2 vols., (New York: Kelley, 1968).
52. Fedden, H., *Suicide*, 168. Renaissance thinkers shattered the view that death was an evil never to be deliberately sought, just as injustice and lying were never to be deliberately done. Death was either a good or an evil depending on its circumstances, and having been cleansed of many of its evils, it became a matter of common and banal discussion. With the increased acceptance of the situationally dependent goodness of death, suicide also increased in comparison to levels found in the Middle Ages.
53. Hume, H., *Two Essays*, (London: Millar & Kindaid, 1778). Suicide, he argued, should be "free from any imputation of guilt or blame, according to the sentiments of all the ancient philosophers."
54. Ibid., 19.
55. Hume, D., *Essays Moral, Political and Literary,* vol. 2, (London: Routledge, 1894), 410, 411-12.
56. Young, E., *Night Thoughts*, (London, 1757), revised and corrected by the author.
57. Anonymous, *Suicide,* cited in Fedden, *Suicide*, 218.
58. Dueling was quite common during this era, and if the number of deaths from suicide were comparable to those from duelling, there must have been a great many suicides.
59. See Lecky, W., *European Morals*, vol. 2, 61.
60. Ibid., 54.
61. Baron D'Holbach, *A System of Nature,* vol. 1, (Boston: Mendun, 1869), chap. 14.
62. Topaizo, W. V., *D'Holbach's Moral Philosophy*, (Geneva: Institute et Musee Voltaire, 1956).
63. Ibid., 273.
64. Ibid., 224.
65. Fedden, H., *Suicide*, 218.
66. DeStael-Holstein, Anne, "Reflexions sur la Suicide," in *The Constitution of Man, Considered in Relation to External Objects*, (Columbus OH: Miller, 1881), 14. If this is true, it shows how far the Rationalist era migrated from the Middle Ages where poverty was not a mark of shame and where suicide did not protect but rather destroyed one's honor.
67. Rousseau, J. J., *Nouvelle Heloise*, (University Park: Pennsylvania State University Press, 1968), letter 21.
68. Montesquieu, *Lettres Persanes*, (Paris: Colin, 1961), letter 76. Also see his *Spirit of Laws,* (London: Bell, 1902) Book 29, ix.
69. Diderot, D., *Encyclopedie, Ouvres*, Ed. by Varloot, J., (Paris: Hermann, 1975), 20, 140-50.
70. Dumas, J., *Traite du suicide, ou du meurtre volontaire de soi-meme*, (Amsterdam, 1773), 2.

71. DeStael-Holstein, A., "Reflexions," 135.
72. Ibid., 135-58.
73. See Foster, R. F., *Modern Ireland 1600-1972*, (New York: Penguin, 1988), 280.
74. Scott, S. and Rothaus, B., *Historical Dictionary of the French Revolution*, vol. 2 (Westport, CT: Greenwood, 1985), 573.
75. Ibid., vol. 11, 49.
76. Fedden seems to assert that Couthon attempted suicide, but there is little clear evidence among most modern historians of the French Revolution to support this view. A. Lefevbre claims that Couthon was guillotined, and I could find no support for the view that he suicided. See Lefevbre, A., *The French Revolution*, vol. 1 (London: Routledge & Kegan, Paul, 1964), 176.
77. Scott, S. and Rothaus, B., *Historical Dictionary*, vol. 1, 17.
78. Fedden, H., *Suicide*, 273.
79. See Fedden, H., *Suicide*, 242; LaFevbre, A., *The French Revolution*, vol. 1, 176, and vol. 2, 70.
80. Fedden, H., *Suicide*, 244. His death was met with approval, for a parade was held in his honor, and he was buried in the Pantheon. His death set a pattern, for captains scuttled their ships and many officers blew themselves up in their last redoubt.
81. Johnson, P., *The Birth of the Modern*, (New York: Harper Collins, 1991), 76. Also see Herold, J., *The Age of Napoleon*, (New York, Houghton-Mifflin, 1963), 391.
82. Alvarez, A., *The Savage God*, (New York: Random House, 1970), 101.
83. Fedden, H., *Suicide*, 218.
84. See Lecky, W., *European Morals*, vol. 2, 62. Also see Fedden, H., *Suicide*, 264.
85. Alvarez, A., *The Savage God*, 209.
86. Fedden, H., *Suicide*, 276.
87. Alvarez, A., *The Savage God*, 212.
88. Flaubert, G., *Correspondence*, Tr. by Corlet, C., vol. 2, (Columbus: Ohio State University Press, 1968), 191, 58. L. S. Shanks in his biography of young Flaubert, *Flaubert's Youth*, (Baltimore: John's Hopkins, 1927), notes that he was highly neurotic, suffered a nervous breakdown, and was filled with pessimism in his youth. In Flaubert's *Dictionary of Platitudes*, (London: Rondale, 1954), he defined suicide as "Proof of Cowardice," 135.
89. In "Andre del Sarto," suicide is a sign of moral decay. See Sices, D., *Theater of Solitude: The Theater of Alfred de Musset*, (Hanover, NH: University of New England Press, 1974), 20.
90. See DuCamp, M., *Literary Reflections*, (Paris: Hackett, 1882)), vol. 1, 112; vol. 2, 68-99, 122, 159-86.
91. See Sowerby, B., *The Disinherited*, (New York: New York University Press, 1974), 160. While Nerval did mention suicide in his writings, Sowerby finds him to be too generous, selfless, and virtuous to suicide. According to him, Nerval wrote that suicide was the supreme act of egoism, implying a moral rejection of it (p. 160).
92. Sand, G., *Indiana*, (Paris: Calman-Levy, 1852).
93. Villers d'Lisle Adam, *Axel*, (Paris: Maison-Quanton, 1890).
94. In the romantic era, suicide was the price to be paid for possession of their gifts. Today, however, suicide may become the price paid for technological development and sophistication, just as it was the price paid for the genius of the romantics.
95. Goethe, J. W., *The Trials of Young Werther,* Tr. Hutter, C., (New York: Signet, 1962), 23-129.
96. The Romantics suicided in the belief that they would be present at their final dramatic and artistic act, which shows the schizophrenia and unreality of the movement.

97. Alvarez, A., *The Savage God,* 43.
98. Fedden, H., *Suicide*, 280.
99. See Joyce, J., *Ulysses*, (New York: Garland, 1975), vol. 1, 197.
100. See Fedden, H., *Suicide*, 261; Lecky, W., *European Morals*, vol. 2, 62.
101. Schopenhauer, F., "Studies in Pessimism," in *Studies in Pessimism,* Ed. T. Bailey Saunders (Lincoln: University of Nebraska Press, 1964), 151-58.
102. Bonser, T. O., *The Right to Die*, (London: Freethought Publishing Co, 1885), 85.
103. Fedden, H., *Suicide*, 268.
104. See Arkell, D., *Looking for Laforgue*, (Manchester: Carcanet, 1979), 223-39; Ramsey, W., *Essays on a Poet's Life and Work*, (Carbondale: Southern Illinois Press, 1964), xii-xiv.
105. Dostoyevsky, F., *The Possessed,* Tr. by Garnett C., (London: W. Heineman, n.d.).
106. Wittgenstein, L., *Notebooks, 1914-1916,* Ed. Anscombe, E., Rhees, T., and Von Wright, E., (New York: Oxford University Press, 1961), 91.
107. Ibid.
108. Fedden, H., *Suicide*, 303.
109. Alvarez, A., *The Savage God,* 243. Also see Lifton, R., *Death in Life: The Survivors of Hiroshima*, (New York: Basic Books, 1968), 479-541.
110. Clark, D., "Are Wishes to Implement a Rational Suicide Usually Justified and Usually Rational?" in *Exiting Gracefully: The Right to Die with Dignity*, (Palm Beach Gardens, FL: HCR Publications, 1992), Forthcoming, 2.
111. Clark, D., "Wishes," 3.
112. Ibid., 3.
113. Ibid., 4.

4

Catholicism and the Morality of Suicide

Margaret Battin, a leading contemporary advocate of rational suicide, argues that Christian teachings condemning direct suicide can be defeated and that there is nothing to be found in the Bible that directly condemns suicide.[1] Because Professor Battin is one of the nation's leading proponents of the moral acceptability of suicide, and because she has proposed the most wide-ranging defense of the morality of self-slaying to date, her claims deserve attention. In what follows, I will do five things. First, I will review contemporary arguments concerning the morality of suicide. Then, I will briefly summarize the classical Catholic approach to death. Third, I will show that the Bible is quite intolerant of suicide and that contrary views result from an inadequate understanding of its teachings. Fourth, the claim that the mainstream Catholic arguments against suicide do not succeed will be dealt with, and finally, the arguments against the Catholic moral arguments opposing suicide will be considered.

A Survey of Contemporary Literature

Virtually all proponents of rational suicide argue that there are many cases in which suicide is morally objectionable, but there are others where it is not.[2] They assert that suicide is neither inherently nor *a priori* wrong and that there are cases where self-inflicted death would not be immoral, but some commentators would reject suicide as unethical because of the dangers it poses to the vulnerable and to society as a whole. And most of these proponents of the morality of suicide would hold that only some acts of deliberate self-killing are morally wrong, even though many of them are quite legitimate and permissible.

Most who hold that suicide can be moral believe that one who is not terminally ill should have the right to request death as long as they understand what they are doing. For example, David Mayo points out that lurking beneath disputes about the morality of suicide is a controversy about whether suicidal actions are expressions of fundamental autonomy or whether they are symptoms of an underlying mental illness.[3] What Alan Sullivan calls "autoeuthanasia," the willful bringing of "good death" upon oneself, should be permitted.[4] This claim is contested by Leslie Pickering Francis who argues that the resulting situation would be quite chaotic.[5] She believes that the strongest objection one can raise against prohibiting suicide is that it inhibits other forms of permissible conduct. But this argument fails because it does not go to the deeper issue of determining the kinds of obligations the law ought to impose to protect innocent life. To justify proscribing suicide, it is not necessary to show that such a ban prevents other kinds of intolerable conduct, for it is sufficient merely to show that it is only needed to prohibit killing to protect innocent life.

The conviction that rational suicide should be permitted because of the requirements of autonomy is one of the strongest and most oft-heard claims for the morality of rational suicide, but despite this, one must ask why this autonomy exists and what it serves. Not everything can be justified by the principle of autonomy, and there are some expressions of autonomy that can be legitimately restricted. To simply argue that autonomy justifies suicide is too broad, for if autonomy would permit deliberate self-assassination, it would permit many other less dangerous and harmful actions too. Such a vague and ambiguous justification would undermine the possibility of prohibiting any action claimed to be an expression of autonomy with the possible exception of those that bring immediate, proximate, and obvious harm to others. And claims that self-assassination does no harm should be regarded cautiously, for the harm it causes might be neither subtle nor immediately obvious.

Mary Rose Barrington declares that objections to suicide are based primarily on fear of death, and she believes that suicide should be regarded as a proper and right way for a well-raised person in a civilized society to end life.[6] But if there is a right to suicide, fairness would demand that it should be universal and not limited to certain socioeconomic groups, and one must wonder what moral principle could justify limiting self-assassination only to well-raised people. One must wonder what socioeconomic status and cultural background have to do with the morality and justice of suicide. We can also ask whether we have that fear of death for good, sound, and ethical reasons. If anything is worthy of justifiable, reasonable, intelligent, and enlightened fear, it would be the fear of death. One can recover from loss of honor or financial ruin, but there is no recovery from death and this is the reason why we have an innate, powerful, and profound fear of death. The fear of death exists not only to preserve the species, but also to preserve ourselves as individuals, from the attacks of others as well as from our own lethal tendencies. Fear of death is a rational fear, just as a certain fear of heights or water is rational because there are real dangers involved in these, and this fear should not be simply dismissed as irrational. Fear of rape or enslavement are reasonable fears because they are truly evil, and a fear of death is similarly rational because death is not a true good for the human person. The issue of the morality of suicide here should not be whether moral objections to suicide are based on fear of death, but whether the fear of death is reasonable because it concerns something that is truly evil.

Barrington also claims that suicide is sometimes justified because it is a rational way of limiting the sum-total of suffering in a society.[7] But if this is true, suicide could be prohibited in some instances because it would limit the sum-total of suffering, and it could become mandatory if it would decrease suffering. If suicide is morally legitimate when it controls suffering in society, I would have to ask what other sorts of actions would be permissible to control suffering? Could not forced expropriations of excess wealth to end suffering be obligatory? Could not families be legally compelled to care for orphaned children in order to lessen the sum-total of societal suffering? Could not divorce be prohibited because of the harm it brings to the children of broken families? Could not moderate recreational drug use be permitted to lessen the sum-total of suffering? If suicide to limit suffering could be morally justified, it would seem that many other acts that are less harmful than suicide could also be regarded as morally upright.

Joel Feinberg argues in behalf of rational suicide by claiming that acting to end one's own life one is acting in behalf of one's right to life and is not contrary to it.[8] The inalienability of the right to life does not preclude suicide, and it can be overridden by the right to liberty, which permits an individual to be his or her own master.[9] Suicide can be a valid exercise of the right to life and he believes it is legitimate to use that right according to one's discretion and for one's good.[10] His claim that suicide is actually an exercise of the right to life is logically peculiar, and it confuses the right to life with a right to death. The right to life has been classically considered as a right to be free from deliberate lethal acts by oneself or another, and the right to death is a right to take deliberate lethal action against oneself. Feinberg attempts to use these definitions interchangeably and does not see any contradiction in so doing. Maintaining that the right to life can be exercised by suicide is logically analogous to demanding that extraordinary medical treatments be given when one is imminently dying as an exercise of the right to die. It is like saying that selling oneself into slavery is an exercise of one's liberty. He fails to see that the right to life exists to protect people from these occurrences and that it does not endorse or authorize them. Feinberg implicitly holds that this right makes suicide morally legitimate, but one must ask what it is about the right to liberty that gives it the power to override the right to life. Does the moral right to liberty give one the power to override the right to justice or truth as well? Can one deliberately, willfully, and intentionally defeat justice and violate the rights of others to exercise this right to liberty as well? Can one voluntarily transgress the requirements of truth to protect one's liberty where there would be no harm to others? I doubt it, and I think the burden of proof that this is not true rests on Feinberg's shoulders.

Thomas Szasz and Glanville Williams believe that suicide may be the only rational and only fully moral decision that many mentally incompetent and emotionally unstable people make, and therefore it should be seen as a moral act even for them.[11] This is a highly irresponsible statement coming from such prestigious scholars, for it could be employed to induce these people to think that they should self-execute because it would be the most ethical action they ever undertake. One must ask Szasz and Williams how these people, who are supposedly unable to do the small things in life in a rational and coherent manner, are able rise to do an action as complex and consequential as suicide with adequate rationality, freedom, and knowledge? Presumably lacking the ability to rationally order their day-to-day affairs, how is it that they become able to be rational about an action that baffles the greatest philosophers of our century? If it is truly the case that they can make a rational, free, and voluntary choice in this matter, then it would seem to be that they would be extraordinarily competent, rational, and free, given the difficult nature of their decision.

Some suicide advocates such as Karen Lebacqz and Tristam Engelhardt believe that suicide should not be permitted for those with outstanding obligations to society or family members, but this is hardly persuasive, for this view would morally endorse suicide for the lonely and abandoned but prohibit it for the well-connected.[12] If there is a true "right to die," it is not clear whether it should be restricted by these extrinsic forces; and to be fair to all involved, this liberty to die should be as great for those with obligations as for those without these extrinsic obligations. Prohibiting self-extermination for those with family or social duties while allowing it for those without would be "discriminatory," and they would ask why these extrinsic factors should be allowed to deny them this freedom. Could not Lebacqz's and Engelhardt's principle become a prescription for those with various sorts of problems to shirk their responsibilities and self-execute? It does not seem fair to prohibit an AIDS patient with a family from self-executing to avoid pain and suffering while permitting an unmarried patient in similar circumstances to do the same. Suppose that a young couple who has AIDS is given the children of relatives who were accidentally killed. It is not evident that they should have their "right to die" overridden because of their obligations to these children.[13] Lebacqz and Engelhardt do not see that once a right to suicide is granted, it is difficult if not impossible to fairly limit it on the basis of supposed responsibilities to others.

They also claim that suicide would not be permissible if it violated "covenant-fidelity" which means that it would violate duties of gratitude, promise-keeping or reparations, for example. As long as a person is rational, competent, and informed, there would be nothing morally objectionable about suicide if its performance would preserve fidelity to one's covenants. But when is a suicide against "covenant-fidelity"? Would a suicide to protest war or injustice violate "covenant-fidelity" to one's family and friends even though it upholds "covenant-fidelity" to society? Would suicides by parents who leave small children orphaned violate "covenant-fidelity" if the parents' choice was free, rational, and informed? Would the suicide of a criminal be a violation of "covenant-fidelity," or would the suicide of a mobster to keep investigators from acquiring evidence against other mobsters be a violation of covenant-fidelity? Would suicides of corporate tax evaders to prevent a company from being indicted and from having to pay large fines violate covenant-fidelity? This criterion is difficult to accept because, almost anything can be in accord "covenant-fidelity" at the speculative and hypothetical level. Lebacqz and Engelhardt affirm autonomy to be the fundamental right-making trait of individual, personal acts, and they believe suicide is permissible if it enhances their unique worth and gives the lives of persons meaning.[14] However, they conclude that only in a few circumstances would suicide be a responsible action because it would ordinarily break covenant-fidelity.[15]

Eliot Slater asserts that death is a natural cure for all suffering which is a highly doubtful claim because it would imply that slavery is the natural cure for all of the difficulties involved in properly using our liberty. Slater argues that the right to self-assassinate should be extended to the mentally ill, as they need it more than all others. He wonders if one can justify interfering with the privacy of hopelessly psychotic patients who might be debased and degraded by paternalistic interventions to prevent their deaths.[16] This is a highly questionable suggestion, for if one is not morally allowed to prevent an incompetent person from self-assassinating, what justification would there be for intervening to prevent a mentally disturbed and incompetent person from performing a less harmful action, such as self-mutilation, an intervention that most people would consider to be just and compassionate? If one would not be justified in preventing an insane person from suiciding, would one also be justified in intervening to lead such a person from their troubled existence to one more rational, stable, and fulfilling? The logical commitments involved in these principles pose an uncertain threat to the incompetent. This claim is analogous to asserting that selling oneself into slavery He claims that they might be able to do the most for their friends and for themselves by self-executing. Does this not, however, ignore the fact that generally the mentally ill need protection from themselves, and allowing them to kill themselves because they need escape from suffering does not truly give them any aid?[17]

It is also worthwhile to ask if it would be morally justifiable to intervene in order to prevent a rational person from accidentally or unwittingly suiciding. Most would say that intervention in such a case would be justified, despite the humiliation that the person might experience. But such a humiliation would be insignificant in comparison to the great act of saving one's life in the judgment of most observers. With an incompetent person, the same situation prevails, for when a truly incompetent person attempts self-execution he or she is probably not acting with adequate freedom and knowledge, and preventing them from self-killing is not significantly different from stopping a competent but ignorant person from accidentally self-executing. To say that we might not be justified in intervening to prevent an incompetent person from suiciding could, at a minimum, undermine our right to intervene to prevent competent persons from accidentally killing themselves because the two acts are so similar.

Some suicide proponents such as David Wood argue that suicide is no less natural than other forms of death because few if any deaths are "natural" in today's world of technology.[18] He claims that most deaths are predetermined and the result of human choice, and suicide is merely another form of planned and predetermined death. But he fails to see that there is a morally relevant difference between refraining to sustain human life that is quickly slipping away with medical treatments that are becoming clinically futile and taking lethal action against one who is not on an immediate trajectory toward death. And if it is true that few deaths are natural and that suicides are really no different from other kinds of deaths, then why is suicide a topic of such serious debate while removal of high technology life-support from the terminally ill is not? It is probably closer to the truth to say that there is a major difference between natural death and deliberately intended and willed death, and that deliberate self-execution cannot be put in the same category with death resulting from natural causes or the removal of high technology life-support.

Marshall Breger contends that contemporary prohibitions of suicide will soon become obsolete in the face of advancing technology, and he implies that our society will soon have to permit it.[19] This is a peculiar claim, for it is not clear why advances in technology necessitate endorsing the morality of suicide. Why do our increasing abilities to preserve life give better reasons for permitting people to destroy their lives? As technological capability increases, so also does the ability of medicine to limit suffering, and ordinarily, the cost of technology decreases over time while its capabilities increase, which should restrain the need for suicide. It is also not evident that technology is the driving force behind the movement to endorse suicide, for the actual impetus promoting suicide seems to be the increasing age of the population, higher medical costs, and more emphasis on patient control over treatment and care decisions.

Modern technology can already preserve many lives that could not have been saved many years ago; and in the future, it will probably be able to extend life even more. As an example of directions technology might take in the future, *Nature* magazine recently reported an experiment in which the Tithonin gene from the freshwater carp (*Cyprinus Carpa*) was implanted in a mouse to extend the life of the mouse and it appears that the experiment succeeded.[20] Researchers are now considering protocols in which this gene would be implanted in humans, and many are wondering about what to do if we could easily extend the human life span by another thirty to forty years. And already, the human genome project is discovering genes associated with various diseases and conditions such as colon cancer. And as our technology and therapy advance and this knowledge of the human genome increases, our abilities to extend the lives of those afflicted with these gene-based disorders increases.

The argument that technology increases the rationality and necessity for suicide can be reduced in essence to the following:

1. Advances in technology and therapy increase suffering without proportionate compensating benefits, which makes suicide more rational and necessary.

2. The application of technological advances is inherently unfair, which makes suicide more rational and imperative. Means of supporting advanced technology are being disproportionately expended on those who can benefit little from them, and those who could benefit from this technology often suffer deprivation as a result.

3. There is profound unfairness in contemporary advanced technology because it increases world population by extending the life span of many elders when we are trying to curb population growth. This will force younger generations to be unfairly burdened by the needs of the elderly and infirm.

4. Advanced technology, as it is now being applied and developed destroys human dignity in dying, which can only be recaptured by self-initiated death.

5. Advances in technology are increasingly prohibiting us from making our dying an expressive and meaningful act that draws our life to a close. Technological intervention into health care is coming to define our deaths more as a technological failure than as a human action and it is interfering with compassionate care for the dying. Increased use of technological and scientific means to stave off death deprive dying of its meaning and trivialize and secularize the event. The only means of escaping these forces is to grasp control of the dying event and shape one's own dying by one's own hand.

In what follows, I will present what I consider to be the mainstream response of Catholic morality to these claims.

1. Classical Catholic thought would not agree that advancing life-sustaining technology necessarily makes suicide more imperative or rational because it increases suffering. It would not allow technological interventions to be rejected because one believed they created a low quality of life or because one had lived too long, but merely because they cause excessive suffering or burden. If a life-saving technology was radically expensive, clinically ineffective, unproven,

the cause of radical pain, and/or burden to a patient, one could reject it, and the freedom to do this voids arguments that technological advances make suicide more rational or imperative. Only if such an intervention was inexpensive, effective, and minimally burdensome could a patient not be allowed to reject it, but if any of these were absent, the patient could escape suffering caused by the technological intervention.

2. Mainstream Catholic morality argues that technology does not strengthen the case for suicide because of anything inherently unjust in it. The classical Catholic interpretation of this principle focuses attention on the treatments themselves and what they do to the patient receiving them. If a life-preserving measure is considered to be too painful by the patient, clinically ineffective, or too costly, it can usually be rejected in good conscience. If it causes such problems for the person that they have to exercise heroic patience, fortitude, and perseverance, accepting the treatment is not required in justice for the person. It is true that advances in technology can sustain the lives of the seriously ill and save many who previously would have died. But this should not necessarily make suicide more rational or imperative, because as treatments lose their ability to sustain a higher quality of life, they become less obligatory, and the patient's right to refuse them grows stronger.

The claim that advancing technology makes suicide more rational and imperative because it involves expending disproportionate levels of resources for one class of persons at the expense of another is somewhat obscure. This claim might be reducible to a "social contribution" argument asserting that these resources are not being expended wisely because those who benefit from them do not contribute to society what is either adequate or in proportion to what others give them. Or it could also be a "demographic argument," which asserts that giving advanced technology to the elderly unjustifiably increases world population. Whatever is the case, there is a certain truth to these views, for the elderly and infirm do consume more medical resources and make much more use of advancing technology than do the young and healthy. But this is not the entire reason why the elderly and very sick consume so much of this advanced technology. They use it because they need it and gain substantial benefits from it. It would be foolish to provide these resources in equal amounts to others who might gain no benefit from them.

This claim raises the issue of allocating scarce medical resources. Gene Outka has argued that there are different grounds for allocating resources such as merit, randomness, need, ability to pay, similar treatment for similar cases, and social contribution, and there is good reason for invoking some of these principles to determine how to allocate resources.[21] We frequently allocate resources according to need, merit, social contribution, and randomness, for instance, but it is not entirely clear that this is always and everywhere fair. It is rather easy to give preferential treatment to some individuals such as national leaders on account of their social contribution, but it is difficult to accept this as a broader principle for allocation. Similarly, allocating care and treatment on the basis of randomness seems fair in some instances, but whether this is fair in a broader context is harder to accept.

The most radical proposal for allocating scarce medical resources comes from Daniel Callahan who argues that everyone has a "natural life span" that extends from the early seventies to the mid-eighties.[22] As the numbers of the old and very old increase and our resources for caring for them decrease, a fair way of treating them is to deny all care and medical treatment (with the exception of analgesia) to those who have lived beyond their "natural life span." This is fair according to Callahan because no one is deprived of their natural life span and no one is allowed to be a burden to others because of their desire to live beyond their naturally allotted life span. This view has gained some popularity in spite of the fact that it would deprive many people of additional years of life that could be bought at a small price. It has a certain attractiveness in American society because the birth rate of white Americans has fallen below zero in the past decade due primarily to abortion and contraception, and the notion of reducing the numbers of elderly Americans has the added benefit of balancing the age of the white American population. Eliminating medical care for the old and very old is also attractive to insurance carriers because the elderly consume the greatest amount of medical resources, and are their greatest liability. The question can be raised as to whether an age-based rationing scheme is fundamentally fair because under it some would be denied medical benefits solely on the basis of something about which they can do nothing: their age. Age can be a factor in deciding whether to provide care and treatments if the age of a patient would substantially reduce the benefits experienced from a treatment, but they would deny that the age of a person can be a sufficient condition to deny any and all forms of medical treatment. Age can be a reason to reduce the level of life-sustaining procedures because of the limited benefits that can often be expected from these treatments, but to deny all treatments because of age is discriminatory against the elderly.

The ordinary/extraordinary distinction is more in harmony with mainstream Catholic views of allocating resources because this principle expresses the traditional Catholic views of social justice.[23] This is a fair principle for allocation because it takes into consideration the ability of the community to provide the treatments, the capacity of the recipient to tolerate its burdens, as well as the therapeutic potency of the resources. In this perspective, the level of medical technology to be given or received by a patient should be proportionate to its clinical efficacy, the capacity of the health care providers to offer it, and the ability of the recipients to accept it. There are some treatments that individuals cannot freely renounce, however, because their rejection or withdrawal is morally equivalent to killing the patient. Rejection or withholding of relatively painless, inexpensive, and clinically effective treatments is suicide by omission because the only intention for such a decision could be an intention for death. The claim that suicide becomes more rational because these resources can be better expended elsewhere has some force, but it is not entirely persuasive, particularly in a society in which so many resources are expended so frivolously. It is hard to see why suicide is more necessary because resources to promote the development of medical technology are supposedly wasted when so many other resources are expended on in other ways that are either frivolous or malicious. At least this expenditure of resources extends or saves lives and promotes science, research, and therapy.

3. If advances in technology make suicide more rational and imperative because they indirectly increase world population, then the same arguments used against "demographic suicide" would apply to "technological suicide." Practically, suiciding to exercise restraint on the use of technology for demographic reasons would require millions of suicides to exert any influence and could impede growth in medicine and technology because they are all interrelated. There is something paradoxical about the claim that advancing technology promotes population growth because the societies experiencing the greatest increases in population are those with the lowest levels of technological development while those with the least growth in population have the highest levels of technology. It would seem that one would want to promote the growth and development of technology if one was serious about curbing population growth because, statistically speaking, it does more to suppress birth rates than does suicide.

4. The view that advancing technology compromises human dignity is certainly true in some instances because it often diverts attention from the plight, concerns, and needs of the dying person to the requirements of technological interventions supporting the patient. Patients commonly become the depersonalized objects of medical intervention, and when this happens it is time to terminate therapeutic intervention and provide more intensive counseling, pastoral care, and family intervention. The best response that can be given to this problem was that proposed by Arthur Dyck who argued that a dying patient can reach a point where it is less important to try to save their life and more important to preserve their dignity, and at this point it is more important to give the patient loving, attentive care and emotional support than medical therapy. When the application of life-preserving measures begins to interfere with the emotional, moral, and spiritual needs of the patient, it is more important to give personal care and attention to the patient than to try to cure his or her disease. Exceptionally aggressive care of some patients can inhibit attending to their more personal, spiritual, moral, and emotional needs.

Twentieth-century philosophers and theologians have persuasively argued that dying is not merely something that happens to us, but is an action we perform to express and complete our humanness. In our time, technology is being developed and applied in ways that make it increasingly difficult to shape our dying into a truly conscious, human, and spiritually fulfilling action. Dying is becoming more and more the last act of technology rather than the last act of the human person. Classical Catholic teachings have frequently urged that the spiritual, emotional, and moral needs of patients be considered along with or above their medical needs. The arguments that can be employed against this claim are identical to those used against claims that use of technology destroys the dignity of patients. In response to these problems, classical Catholic teachings have held that there can be no serious objections to withholding or withdrawing certain forms of medical technology when and where they become inimical to the spiritual, moral, and emotional well-being of the patient. For many persons, it is true that the time of dying is one to bring their lives to a close, be reconciled with God and others, and find peace in their lives. An unbalanced emphasis on the application of high technology therapy can overwhelm these legitimate concerns. Classical Catholic pastoral theology would hold that it is fully legitimate to withdraw life-sustaining measures when and where their provision would conflict with the spiritual and moral needs of the person. This does not mean that one could suicide in order to promote one's spiritual well-being, but it does mean that one could deliberately end one's life in order to promote these spiritual goods.

One of the most perplexing aspects of advancing technology is that it continues to make what were previously electable and burdensome measures nonburdensome, effective, and inexpensive, which morally requires patients to receive higher levels of treatment. But this does not in and of itself make suicide imperative, because patients can still reject almost all treatments judged to be too burdensome, and also because the technology, which lengthens our lives, does not necessarily make it harder or more burdensome. If one were not free to reject life-sustaining measures because of their burdensomeness, advances in medical technology would make suicide more necessary because some of these treatments would increase the pain and suffering of patients. But precisely because one can reject at least some treatments on account of their burden, advancing technology does not make this imperative.

The ordinary/extraordinary distinction, as a principle for allocating scarce resources, forces technology to become more efficient and effective and less burdensome before technological life-sustaining interventions can be made obligatory for patients, and this distinction implicitly holds that technology is only authentically successful when it reaches this stage of refinement. This principle permits recipients to exercise some control over technologists and experimenters, and does not inhibit advances in research and technology because it only protests imposing experimental and burdensome care and treatment on patients. It does not retard the development of inexpensive, effective, and nonburdensome treatments, but rather promotes them by requiring that researchers can only *impose* life-saving procedures on patients if they meet these criteria. It is true that these criteria would inhibit the development of medical technology to the extent that it prohibits researchers from speeding advances by imposing burdensome, expensive, and ineffective care and treatment on patients, but this is hardly an unjustifiable restraint on their research.

Advanced technology is no more conducive to suicide than primitive technology because the latter is less able to control pain and slow the progress of disease, which can make suicide attractive to many. Technology is merely a servant of the human will and mind, and depending on its use, it can either increase or decrease the rationality of and need for suicide. It is less a cause of degradation, or dignity, or meaning in itself than are the kinds of choices made to employ technology. Even further, claims that suicide is more necessary than when technology was less developed implies that technology is uncontrollable and that it becomes so tyrannical that one can only preserve rationality and dignity by ending one's life to escape its cruelty. There are situations in which there is no obligation to use some technologies, but advancing technology does not in itself make self-execution more rational.

Some hold that the evil of unnecessary suffering morally justifies suicide, but they do not see any significant difference between taking positive or active measures to end one's life, and ceasing measures designed to impede the course of pathological illnesses, measures that are in fact quite different. Joseph Fletcher, Thomas Beauchamp, and James Childress contend that suicide would be morally permissible if it maximized human well-being and did not impair the well-being of others.[24] But this is an extremely formal and abstract criterion for rational suicide, and it demands conclusive demonstration that it could promote a higher level of well-being, because when successful, it destroys human existence and all possibility of enjoying all values of human life. Destroying old, worn, or malfunctioning machines or instruments does not improve their quality or performance and destroying suffering persons does not maximize their well-being.

Some suicide advocates argue that the morality of suicide turns not merely on our concepts of self-determination, autonomy, or relief from suffering, but also our concepts of human worth.[25] They contend that any decision about suicide would involve conflicts of principle, particularly conflicts about the nature of human worth and the evil of unnecessary suffering. Principles of utility and autonomy would operate to provide justifications for self-executions in certain cases, but how these concepts of human worth could be administered in practice without discrimination is not clear. The absence of any practical specifications of this principle strongly suggests that it cannot meet this important demand.

Margaret Battin and David Mayo assert that when suicide is truly a human choice, struggling against it denies the individual's integrity.[26] But they do not specify what materially constitutes "integrity" or a "human choice," which is troublesome. There are many decisions and choices that are "human" in the sense that they are free, informed, and made with adequate knowledge, and yet these choices can often involve gross immorality. One must wonder if their principle that opposition to killing, which can involve true human choices, compromises the agents' integrity should be applied to other forms of killing as well. If actions that are true human choices are above reproach, it is not clear how one could protest other forms of killing. Drug-taking and self-mutilation can all be the result of true "human choices," and I doubt that they would agree that intervening to prevent them would be to deny the integrity of those performing them.

Joseph Fletcher strives to justify suicide by arguing that it must be judged in the situation in which the action takes place and not by abstract principles.[27] Because of this, he suggests that suicide is not merely ethically good, but also loving when it ends meaningless life, alleviates one's own suffering or the suffering of others, or maximizes human well-being. This could be true, but it is hard to say because of the ambiguous character of "love" and the uncertainty of its requirements in a given complex situation. But even if it were clear that love did require suicide in a given situation, one must ask why other important moral values such as justice, prudence, temperance, and fortitude, which might require other actions, should not be allowed to prevail in the situation. Fletcher gives no justification for allowing his rather ambiguously defined "love" to trump all other moral values, which is serious because this implicitly allows many other important values to be negated to bring about this vaguely defined condition of love. Most advocates of rational suicide admit that its right-making characteristics are neither self-evident nor unambiguous, and it cannot be adequately justified by merely asserting that it fosters a vaguely and formally defined "love."

Marvin Kohl rejects the claim that autonomy is a right-making trait of suicide, and he regards the right to life as only a *prima facie* right, meaning that it can be restricted and limited without doing injustice.[28] He believes the right to life should be grounded solely on utilitarian considerations, meaning that it could be overridden by the choice of a person to end one's life at the correct time and in the manner of one's choosing, thus making suicide permissible in some circumstances.[29] This is actually a rather revolutionary proposal, for it implicitly denies that the right to life is a fundamental and natural human right, and comes very close to declaring the right to suicide to be such a right. But if the right to life is only a *prima facie* right, then why are not the rights to justice, truth, and liberty *prima facie* rights too? If the right to life is *prima facie,* should not the right to die or the right to suicide also be *prima facie*? And if the right to life is a *prima facie* right, how would one balance its claims against the supposedly *prima facie* right to suicide or death? Classical morality and the common law tradition have not treated these rights as merely *prima facie,* and to be fully persuasive, Kohl should argue that the mainstream belief espousing this is wrong. If the right to life is *prima facie,* then the right to justice should also be a *prima facie* right, and if this is true, why could not a mob lynch an innocent man to protect peace? If liberty is only a *prima facie* value, why could not some people sell themselves into slavery for the benefit of others? Kohl fails to see what the popular mind has known since the *Magna Carta:* fundamental human values as justice, truth, life, liberty, and truth are natural, basic, and inalienable human rights and values that are not merely *prima facie.*

David Mayo and Margaret Battin object to Kohl's claims and point out that utilitarian justifications would make suicide obligatory in some instances, for if suicide promotes the greater good, then there would be an obligation to perform it in some circumstances.[30] When a great good would come about from a suicide and a great evil caused by not suiciding, it would then be obligatory according to their utilitarian calculus. They argue that suicide should be considered not merely as a liberty right, but as a fundamental human right on the same level with life, liberty, and the pursuit of happiness, which could not be made obligatory.[31] According to Battin, suicide should be permitted if it promotes the dignity of the person and she and Mayo believe that nonviolent suicides fulfill this requirement.[32]

There are a number of problems with this claim, however. First, it is not clear that there is such a thing as "nonviolent killing," because there is a certain kind of violence in all taking of human life. It is dangerous to hold that "nonviolent" forms of killing promote human dignity, for that would imply that quick and painless assassinations might promote human dignity.[33] Also, as Battin herself admits, it is not clear what constitutes human dignity, and how suicide would promote this ambiguous "dignity" is not at all evident. The concept of human dignity is so obscure and multifaceted that it is not possible to determine clearly and objectively if an action as complex as suicide would promote it. Battin argues that the right to suicide is a fundamental human right, and not a utilitarian right, because she wants to eliminate any obligation to self-assassinate that would be imposed if it was a utilitarian right. But even though she wants to deny an obligation to commit suicide, she presumably would hold that there is an obligation incumbent on others to permit "rational suicides." She would permit suicide when so doing would promote human dignity, and she argues that suicide would not be justified or obligatory even in cases where overall suffering would be diminished.[34] Battin rejects violent or malicious suicide and would only permit nonhateful or nonpunitive suicides, and would only allow suicide for morally upright intentions.[35] But if the "right" to self-execute is a fundamental human right, individuals would be under a strong moral duty to not only assist people in killing themselves, but also to defend their right to kill themselves. If suicide is a fundamental human right, one would be morally bound to not only defend those who wish to kill themselves, but also to kill those who sought to stop them if this was necessary to protect reflexive killers.

There were difficulties involved with Marvin Kohl's claim that the right to suicide was a *prima facie* right, but considering suicide a fundamental human right would also make attempts to stop others from exercising this "right" gravely wrong and immoral. If one considers the right to suicide a fundamental human right, that would probably force recategorization of the right to life as a *prima facie* right, which would have to yield to the right to suicide in many circumstances. But if this were done, there could well be substantial public policy and jurisprudential difficulties.[36] Margaret Battin wants to make the right to suicide as fundamental and powerful as the rights to justice, liberty, and truth, but it does not seem possible for such contradictory rights to be equally fundamental.

Battin also considers suicide to be morally licit if it is "in the fundamental interests" of the individual.[37] To support this, she claims that Captain Oates realized his fundamental interests by suiciding during his exploratory journey from the South Pole.[38] I am not so sure that he achieved his fundamental interests for one would have to also ask what his fundamental interests would have been if he had lived. If he had not suicided, he might have had an interest in promoting his accomplishments, celebrating his victory, advancing science, and learning through the study of his deeds. But these interests were not realized for the reason that he believed it was in his best interests to end his life. We cannot say, therefore, without qualification that his "interests" were promoted by self-assassination because we just do not know what all of them were. In addition, one can also ask why suicide gains its moral legitimacy by serving the needs and interests of only the individual who self-executes. Why should a suiciding person be allowed to self-exterminate when so doing might be detrimental to the interests of other interested parties? Why should not the interests of others, which might conceivably have some bearing on the morality of the proposed suicide, also be considered? Battin's principles require some balancing of interests that she apparently refuses to acknowledge.

Battin also insists that it is ethically acceptable and beneficial to one's dignity to self-execute for the sake of others. She claims that the ninety-three Jewish maidens who decided to commit suicide rather than be raped by members of the Hitler Youth enhanced their dignity, but this is by no means evident.[39] Their suicides raise the question of whether one can deliberately bring death to oneself to escape evil. If the maidens had resisted the rapists by force and were killed as a result, their dignity clearly would have been enhanced, but deliberately suiciding to escape the evil of rape is a greater moral evil than the rape itself and may not increase one's dignity. If it is true that suicide promoted their dignity, one must ask if Hitler increased his dignity by killing himself at the end of World War II to spare himself the evil of capture and a humiliating trial before his enemies. If suicide enhanced the dignity of the Jewish maidens because they killed themselves to preserve their dignity, then one should grant that Hitler enhanced his dignity by suiciding to protect the "dignity" of National Socialism. I say this not to support Nazism or Hitler, but to argue that dignity, when applied to suicide, is a very loose and woolly concept.

Lance Stell considers dueling under the aspect of the right to life and he concludes that dueling should be prohibited (as should suicide) because the right to life is an alienable property right that is violated by suicide.[40] The comparison between dueling or gunfighting and suicide is apt, for in both acts one is allowing self-killing, either by oneself or by proxy. And according to Stell, the only argument against dueling is that the dignity gained through a victorious gunfight would not be equal to the dignity lost by that death, which is not a strong argument against this practice.

It is doubtful that this is the only objection that could be made to suicide, and it is also doubtful that the right to life is basically a property right. The origin of property rights is quite different from that of the right to life, as property rights are ordinarily based on contracts involving the production of goods and services. Property rights can generally be readily disposed of at will, but this is not the case with one's own life. If the right to life is to be recategorized as a property right, one should ask about the status of other "natural rights" as well. Are the rights to truth, justice, or liberty also "property rights" that can be similarly disposed of by agents at will, and if not, why not? Like other claims about the moral validity of suicide, this one compromises important rights and values.

David Mayo and Margaret Battin point out that accepting suicide would benefit some but it would be purchased at a great cost,[41] and those who try to appraise the rationality of their lives but are unable to do so are most at risk from suicide.[42] And Battin claims that endorsing suicide would generally undermine our respect for the elderly, disabled, and debilitated, and she is also concerned that policies permitting suicide might become policies requiring it in some cases.[43] Nonetheless, she claims that if we accept some suicides as rational, which we must, we will also have to accept some manipulated suicides as well, which is also true.[44]

P. R. Baelz argues that Christian theology should *require* suicide in some cases.[45] But this claim could only be made by one who misunderstands the core and central Christian message of the Paschal Mystery. Taking death upon oneself is virtually equivalent to making it one's ally, an ally that sought the destruction of Christ who made no alliance with it because it was contrary to grace and divine life. Liberation from the effects of death through acceptance of suffering and death in faith is the central Christian message, but not in making it an instrument to achieve one's own objectives. The entire Christian economy of salvation aims at overcoming death, and death is not to be regarded as a mere instrument to be used at our convenience.

Mary Rose Barrington contends that there is very little that is natural about contemporary dying, and she promotes voluntary suicide for those who experience grave suffering by arguing that "natural death" is cruel and lacking in compassion.[46] She invokes David Wood's claim that most deaths in our world are the result of a human choice, and dying a natural death is no more "right" than dying as a result of a "planned death."[47] These assertions, however, miss the point, for the central issue is not whether a person dies a "natural death" or after extensive life-preserving measures have been withdrawn. Rather, the critical issue is whether the patient dies from the underlying pathological condition or from a deliberate commission or omission of morally required life-sustaining measures. The important moral issue is whether the person dies from the underlying pathological condition, from deliberate attempts to shorten the life of the patient, or from omissions of readily available, effective, and nonburdensome life-sustaining measures. Many do not die a "natural death," but that does not mean that they die as a result of deliberate choices by others to bring them to death.

Some suicide advocates reject the "wedge" argument which holds that any toleration of suicide acts like a wedge that logically commits one to tolerate other objectionable forms of killing, even though some suicide proponents such as Battin and Mayo take this argument seriously.[48] It is an argument that has been used not only against euthanasia, but also against contraception, abortion, infanticide, and capital punishment, and many have denied its validity when applied to these issues. But there does appear to be some truth in its assertion, for our society in the past twenty-five years has given widespread endorsement of contraception, abortion, and capital punishment, and it is now deciding whether to legalize mercy killing and suicide.[49] It is true that if one accepts principles allowing some forms of killing, one will be logically committed to accepting other forms of killing permitted by those principles.[50] Thus, permitting the direct killing of innocent unborn children when they are inconvenient logically commits one to allowing the killing of elderly, disabled, incompetent patients when they too are inconvenient. While there may not be a "slippery slope" in some of these moral arguments, it is rather clear that acceptance of certain moral principles commits one to certain conclusions that are often quite objectionable.

Margaret Battin holds that "manipulated suicides" should be morally accepted because refusing to allow this would require prohibiting rational suicide.[51] She believes this would be morally wrong because banning "rational" suicide would inflict intolerable suffering on some patients, and it would be better to accept the risk that some would be manipulated into suicide than to deny the freedom to escape suffering when this would be rational. This is an exceedingly dangerous policy, for it is extremely difficult to distinguish "manipulated" from "rational" suicides. Did Jim Jones "manipulate" his people into suicide or did they kill themselves with full or adequate knowledge and freedom? It would seem that those suicides should have been prohibited, even if they were not manipulated suicides; and if one wishes to be certain that all manipulated suicides are prohibited, one might well have to ban many other kinds of self-killing too. Once we hold that certain suicides can be allowed, it will be quite difficult to determine when a suicide truly fits the prohibited category, which is why it is so hard to ban only "manipulated" suicides. The great risk is that in permitting suicides, we might not be able to stop people such as Jim Jones from manipulating others into committing suicide.

Some advocates of rational suicide argue that abuses of suicide cannot be used to justify prohibiting it in all cases because of the principle *abusus non tollit usus*. Further, they assert that arguing from this principle is dangerous because it could be used to prohibit even legitimate killing in self-defense. They fail to see that if suicide is a morally good act, their claims would be valid, but it is not legitimate to apply this principle to an action whose morality is in dispute or certainly wrong. It is true that abuses of good actions should not prohibit them, but abuses of questionably moral or immoral actions give even further reason for prohibiting the action.

It would seem that immoral actions could be prohibited because the abuse is not compensated for by the good action. Rather than assuming that suicide is morally good, the burden of proof that it is permissible is on its advocates, and until that is done, the argument for abuse is weak.

Walter Steele and William Hill argue that suicide is morally good if the agent understands the situation.[52] This is a rather dangerous principle, for it would imply that dueling could be good if the combatants understood the situation. They do not state what procedures would be required to determine if authentic understanding has been obtained, and they do not define what level of understanding would be needed to change the moral character of a suicide. One would have to ask about the implications of this principle, for if understanding makes deliberate self-killing morally permissible, dueling and gunfighting would be moral because both parties understand what they are doing.

Samuel Wallace argues that only certain kinds of suicide should be permitted, those that are not "murderous," "masochistic," or "suicides by surrender." Justifiable suicides are those where "the survivors have been cared for; even goodbyes have often been said, although not always acknowledged."[53] This criterion is better than some alternatives because it recognizes that others besides the suiciding person have interests that should be considered, but it does have its flaws. What if a person is so embittered by his or her experiences, or so shattered by suffering, disease, failure, or betrayal that they are unable to perform anything but a "malicious" suicide or a "suicide by surrender"? I cannot see why they should be prohibited from suiciding, and it would seem that those who cannot suicide "gently" should have as much right to flee their sufferings as those who can do it with a light touch. Another problem with this standard is that men tend to kill themselves in more violent ways than women, and thus, this standard would be more tolerant of suicide by women than by men.

Wallace makes one's psychological state and motivation for suiciding a "right-making characteristic" of suicides, and it is not clear that this should be so. Does one who is truly "masochistic" have less right to self-execute than one who does not have such tendencies? If their masochism cannot be corrected, should they be denied the right to escape their suffering by self-execution? It is hard to see how Wallace could deny their request because they suffer from conditions over which they have no control. He appears to want to limit suicide to the "well-balanced and pleasant" who have control over their lives and emotions, but these sorts of people are seldom the ones who want to commit suicide. Wallace points out one of the intriguing paradoxes of those who espouse suicide: usually those who desire it most have the least control over their lives, while those who are most in control of their lives have the least interest in it.

One must also ask about the right-making characteristic of "goodbyes" in a suicide. What of people who could not make these farewells? Would their suicides be more reprehensible simply because they are emotionally incapable of this? What of the captured spy who suicides to avoid torture and betrayal of his country? What of the soldier who jumps on a grenade to save his friends and cannot say goodbye? Would that suicide be morally defective because he did not say his goodbyes? What if the dying person's family would find grave suffering imposed on them by the goodbyes? Should these painful farewells be forced on the family? And if well-intentioned and well-motivated goodbyes cause suffering for others, should they be required for a valid suicide? What if those to whom the suicidal person wants to say goodbye are malicious and spiteful and do not want any farewells? I doubt that Wallace would hold these sorts of farewells to be right-making traits, and that leads one to believe that he only considers suicide to be permissible when it is romantic or sentimental, which is difficult to accept.

A number of contemporary writers object to morally endorsing suicide. Erwin Ringel objects to suicide because doing this would entail failing to respect obligations to protect the vulnerable, which would undermine attempts to give psychiatric help to those who truly need it.[54] Ringel argues that libertarian proponents of suicide devalue life, which has the effect of inhibiting attempts to give needed psychiatric help to life-threatening individuals. James Bogen portrays the suicidal as lacking the virtue of fortitude.[55] Libertarian endorsement of suicide is also a more radical espousal of egotistical utilitarian ethics over and against other ethical viewpoints. This is a legitimate concern because it is becoming increasingly clear that individuals in clinical situations can be easily manipulated into not only receiving, but also rejecting medical care. The ease with which this can be done suggests that it would be easy for health care providers to persuade some patients to undertake suicidal actions in some instances. He objects to contemporary justifications of suicide by arguing that moral evaluations of suicide must include considerations of virtue. He calls for reviving the attention given by Plato, Aristotle, and the Stoics to suicide and he challenges the claim that suicide promotes the good life.[56] He is correct in arguing that voluntary suicide is contrary to the classical virtues of patience, fortitude, and perseverance, and this correctly identifies the essence of the moral malice of suicide. Courage, patience, and perseverance are clearly virtues, qualities, and powers that should be developed in persons. It is presumed that mature and competent persons have these qualities, and their absence is ordinarily considered to be a moral deficiency. Possession of these virtues does not mean that one may never reject painful and questionably effective medical treatments, but it does argue that, in the face of suffering and trials, it is wrong to self-execute.[57]

David Peretz asserts that the contemporary cultural climate romanticizes suicide and takes its sharp edge off, and he urges caution in doing this. Most importantly, he claims that altering the reality of suicide could lead to obligatory suicide:

> The creation of a climate of opinion in which suicide is labeled as "rational" has very serious consequences. To swing toward permissiveness opens the door to depriving people of their lives, and thus of any potential for future "rights." I can imagine agencies and institutions involved in social policy and political decisions arguing that individuals are irrationally clinging to life: the elderly, the feeble, defective, mentally ill, poor, etc,. when "rationality" (that is, scarcity) dictates that they "choose suicide."
>
> To idealize suicide is to incur several consequences: first, we send a message to individuals that we have given up on "caring"; second, we send the message that people *should* take their lives under certain circumstances; and third, we open the door to "ideals" becoming social attitudes, attitudes becoming legislation, and legislation leading to institutionalization. Picture a "brave new world" of "planned death" and "rational suicide," with its new bureaucracy, filled with idealism; its covey of social scientists who need to expand and justify their cost-effectiveness. Imagine who will serve as commissioners, federal or local. Picture their budget discussions; and the effects on their morale of a drop in the number of applicants for planned death. Imagine the search for untapped groups on whom to try the new, advanced, humane methods.[58]

Richard Hendin does not believe that suicidal acts are done with adequate freedom because probably less than 10 percent of all suicidal acts result in death.[59] He argues that there are so many profound compulsions and freedom-limiting factors operating in the suicidal person that they cannot be considered as adequately capable of free acts. He thus raises the question of whether suicide can be morally legitimate because it is a doubtfully free and voluntary act. Traditional morality has held that an act cannot be fully rational if it is not free, and if there is a great deal of compulsion, it cannot be free and, therefore, it cannot be voluntary.[60]

Some critics of "rational suicide" argue that self-killing is only permissible when the benefits accruing to others are from the action of the agent and not from the death of the agent.[61] Soldiers whose lives are saved by a comrade who jumps on a grenade benefit from the courageous deed and not from his death and for that reason, the self-killing is not immoral. But if a family profits from a member taking a lethal injection, they would benefit from his death and not from the injection. And a spy who kills himself to protect secrets is committing morally culpable suicide because the benefits result more from his death than from his action. However, if a spy is tortured to death and does not divulge secrets, his death is not morally objectionable because the benefit comes to others from his silence and not from his death.

A fundamental problem with arguments defending the moral goodness of suicide is that they are often based on an inadequately formulated notion of the relation of reason and morality. As has been argued by Philip Devine, the claim that rationality makes a suicide moral must be subjected to close scrutiny.[62] It is not rationality that makes suicide morally permissible, for rationality does not guarantee moral rectitude. Our century is quite familiar with the power of perverted rationality to justify human atrocities and with our astoundingly subtle and ingenious ability to make the most immoral acts appear rational and moral. What makes an action morally good is that it is in harmony with the virtues, or human excellence that lead to full humanness and flourishing. In what follows I will review the Roman Catholic view of the biblical teachings on suicide.

The Biblical Teachings on Suicide

Professor Battin claims that the Bible contains no explicit condemnations of suicide, but this view cannot go unchallenged as it manifests an indefensibly and unreflective understanding of biblical material.[63] This view fails to see that Scripture condemns or approves of actions in many different ways, sometimes by explicit legalistic condemnations, and other times by recounting actions or deeds that are held up by the Judeo-Christian community for condemnation.

The Old Testament saw death as a tragic condition because it condemned the person to the darkness of Sheol where they experienced mere existence and little else. This tradition interprets the Genesis creation story to mean that humanity was not created to die, but that death came as a result of the primeval offense of Adam and Eve, a view reaffirmed in Sir 25:24. There was a proper dread of death, which was not seen as trivial or frivolous, and Ps 49:16 expressed hope in Yahweh for delivery from it. Some expressed an extremely pessimistic view of death, such as Koheleth: "For the fate of the sons of men and the fate of the beasts is the same; as one dies so dies the other. They all have the same breath, and man has no advantage over the beasts; for all is vanity" (Eccl 3:19). Yet despite this bleak outlook, he still taught that "there is no work or thought or knowledge or wisdom in Sheol, to which you are going" (Eccl 9:10b), and holding that "a living dog is better than a dead lion" he reminds his readers that he who is living has "hope." Consciousness and our awareness of our dying is the basis of the majesty of the human person, and the nobility of the person who is dying is that they are aware they are dying. "For the living know that they will die, but the dead know nothing" (Eccl 9:5). The only desirable death was at the end of a long and happy life lived securely in Israel, which took place in the midst of one's family with the fullness of powers still intact (Gn 25:8). The opposite was a long and slow death after a long illness because it embittered the individual. (Jb 21:15)

In the New Testament, sin was seen as the cause of death (Rom 5:12ff). St. Paul explicitly held that all die in Adam but will rise in Christ, and death was the last adversary of Christ (1 Cor 15:22ff). Christ robbed death of its power, which made him Lord of life (2 Tm 1:10), and having risen from the dead, death was powerless over him (Rom 14:9). The Christian will experience victory over death by sharing in the death of Christ in this life, and in this the "old person" is crucified and the "new person" raised up with him (Rom 6:2ff). Faith in Christ does not protect from death in this life, but gives hope that one would not suffer death eternally (Jn 11:26).

Margaret Battin sought to show that the Bible not only tolerated self-killing but also positively encouraged it, but a close examination of suicide in the Bible does not confirm this view. That God commanded his faithful to kill themselves, even to show obedience to him is controversial, and only in a few instances was suicide anything but the lot of those who had abandoned or rebelled against God.

Despite Professor Battin's claims, a closer reading of the biblical materials strongly supports the prohibition of suicide rather than contradicts it.

Battin asserted that the prohibition of the Decalogue does not include suicide. But Genesis, chapter 9, verse 6, forbade the shedding of blood by anyone and did not explicitly exclude reflexively lethal acts: "He who sheds man's blood, shall have his blood shed by man, for in the image of God man was made." This prohibition was carried rather far by some in ancient Judaism for they would execute by stoning to avoid shedding blood. The fundamental reason for this was that innocent human life was not to be destroyed because it was made in the image of God, but Battin discounts this principle and fails to analyze the concept of *imago Dei*.[64] This injunction was purposely general, for it condemned the shedding of blood, be it one's own or that of another, and the only instance in which the Bible allowed killing was either for self-defense or for the purpose of punishing an individual for a clear and certain serious breach of the law.

Exodus, chapter 23, verse 7, condemned killing of the *innocent*, "The innocent and just person you shall not put to death," which Professor Battin regards as only applying to homicide. This law has usually been understood to mean that no one should be killed who does not deserve to die, including oneself. Relative to modern law and morality, the primitive Israelite law on killing was crude and inarticulate, and by itself, it could not stand as an adequate moral norm for us today.[65] Early Israelite laws held that guilt should be presumed if there was known enmity between the killer and victim.[66] Just as we would hold that its teaching that adulterers should be stoned is crude, cruel, and ineffective, so also would we regard its precepts on killing as not fully developed or articulated. The important point is that these laws were correct in condemning these actions as immoral, but the punishments to be meted out for them were unduly harsh because of the roughness and insensibility of the Israelites at the time. The Decalogue condemned willful killing of the innocent, but this judgment was not as refined as it should be. And even though the Decalogue clearly prohibited destroying innocent human life, it did not precisely define the object of the culpably lethal action.

To understand the Old Testament view of suicide, one should see that there were often rudimentary and not fully developed moral teachings on issues, and just because these teachings were not fully explicit, literal, and formal does not mean that the Old Testament expressed no moral judgments on issues. In the Old Testament, moral judgments were often shown by the kind of relation created by the action between the agent and God or one's neighbor. The biblical teachings on masturbation and sodomy would illustrate this. While sodomy was explicitly condemned by St. Paul (1 Cor 6:9-10), it was only implicitly condemned in the story of Sodom and Gomorrah (Gn 19:24). But both the explicit and implicit judgments assert that it is the sort of action that brings down divine wrath rather than favor. On the other hand, there are no unambiguous condemnations of masturbation in the Bible, and yet an implicit and rudimentary teaching against this action is in the episode of Onan (Gn 38:4-10). Rather than baldly condemning the action as wrong, the biblical writer condemns it by associating the action with a severe punishment. It is almost as if the biblical authors were so ashamed of the topic that they could not mention it, but when they did make mention of it, they spoke of it as contrary to the holiness of God.

There are two perspectives on suicide in the Old Testament. On the one hand, there were suicides that were condemned in various ways by the biblical writers. But on the other hand, some reflexively lethal acts were commanded or permitted by God, such as those of Samson (Jgs 13) and Razis (2 Mc 14:37-46) to preserve or promote obedience to God, and these deaths were analogous to Abraham's near-slaying of Isaac. These commanded acts of suicide demonstrated that those such as Abraham were models of fidelity and loyalty to God, for they would not allow even death to impede their duty to be faithful to God. Both Razis and Samson were examples of this sort of self-killing and their self-sacrifices illustrated their unswerving devotion to God.

The story of Samson (Jgs 16:25-31) is one of an amoral giant with uncontrollable anger and lust who wages a war of private revenge against the Philistines. He is a unique figure with little religious aura, and his feats reach extravagant proportions because he is the only one of his time who can give the Israelites hope when they are wholly dominated by the Philistines. Samson betrays Yahweh by falling into illicit relationships with Philistine women and this infidelity saps his strength. He dies in an attempt to avenge and punish the Philistines for their irreverence and oppression of the Israelites. But he is able to bring death on them because his strength is restored after he pledges his loyalty and obedience to Yahweh again.

Augustine and Aquinas argued that Samson's suicide is a morally valid killing done under a divine command, and this may have been true. Samson may have actually directly intended to kill the Philistines under a divine command and only indirectly killed himself. Samson's death has a double meaning, for it is a sign that Yahweh's favor and power had been restored through the destruction of his enemies and it also signifies Yahweh's punishment of Samson for his infidelity. The purpose of his death is not to show that suicide is justified in some instances, but that his self-sacrifice restored him to favor with Yahweh. The story shows that Yahweh would grant even physical strength to those who were loyal and obedient to him, and even one as violent and uncontrollable as Samson could still serve Israel and Yahweh.[67]

Later Judaism was more tolerant of heroic suicide in defense of the faith, as was illustrated by the story of Razis, the temple high priest (2 Mc 14). Nicanor the Greek sought to destroy Judaism and thought the capture of one as noble as Razis would demoralize the Jews. Razis was determined to frustrate this, and rather than suffering capture, he tried to impale himself on his sword, but he missed the stroke and then threw himself from a tower. Not yet dead, he tore out his entrails and threw them among the soldiers (2 Mc 14:42). All of these actions were but a sign of his unswerving fidelity to the Law and hatred for those who persecuted the Jews.

The attitude of the Bible here was mirrored by others of this era who felt that it was morally legitimate to bring death upon oneself when it became certain and imminent. This episode illustrates not so much the moral permissibility of suicide as it extols the heroic selflessness, devotion to God, and the resistance of this Jewish leader who would not permit the Gentiles to defile the Jews in any way. His death was tolerable, not because it was suicidal, but because it was seen as the last and only available means of protecting the faith from dishonor, and it was seen as a death virtually commanded by Yahweh, as was Samson's. The episode does not argue as much for the permissibility of suicide as it illustrates the sort of devotion to God the devout Jew should have.

It is instructive to examine episodes in the Old Testament where one was tempted to suicide, but refused. The story of Jonah is the best example of this, and it is strikingly similar to the Elijah cycle (1 Kgs 19). Jonah's story is one of a reluctant prophet who is called to preach repentance to Ninevah at a time when the Israelites detested them.[68] It tells of the universalism of divine mercy and forgiveness and of God's desire to give life and help to all. Rather than heeding Yahweh's call to preach repentance, Jonah boards a ship headed in the opposite direction, and when he is in danger of drowning, a giant fish is sent by Yahweh to save his life. When he finally makes it to Ninevah and preaches a message of repentance, the Ninevites bitterly disappoint him by repenting. Jonah then goes outside the city and sulks under a vine (Jon 4:9) hoping that the Ninevites will be punished, and he asks Yahweh for death.

This episode is strikingly similar to the story of Elijah who sulks under his broom tree and asks for death because Israel will not repent (1 Kgs 19:4). But rather than looking heroic, Jonah looks ridiculous. Elijah sulks because of infidelity of the people and the king, but Jonah because Yahweh is merciful to Israel's enemies and does not punish them. Elijah is in despair because the people will not listen to his message and he is given a vision of angels to bolster his spirits. Elijah is fed by the birds and Jonah is given a gourd plant to shade and comfort him, but when it dies he is bitter and calls on Yahweh to bring him death. Jonah flees the Lord, but Elijah seeks him in the wind, earthquake, and fire. Because Jonah asks for death for narrow-minded and selfish reasons, he is not given the comfort of revelations from Yahweh as is Elijah, but is challenged with questions from God. Jonah is in despair because Israel's enemy heeded Yahweh's command and Yahweh asks him the tantalizing question: "Are you right to be angry?" Elijah asks for death because of the obstinacy of Israel, and he is given encouragement and revelations by God. With the death of the vine, Jonah is given a taste of the treatment he asked Yahweh to give the Ninevites. From the perspective of the morality of suicide, Yahweh does not grant permission for suicide for any reason, neither for the altruistic reasons of Elijah nor the selfish and despondent reasons of Jonah. He does not want to bring death to Ninevah, Elijah, or Jonah, but wants all of them to live. He will even show this desire to give life to all by using nature to save them, for the crows feed Elijah and the whale saves Jonah. Jonah was like other Prophets of the Old Testament who wished for death: Moses (Nm 11:14), Tobit (Tb 3:6), and Job (Jb 6:9; 7:15). But Yahweh would not grant their wishes and he either questioned the rightness of their motives, or gave them encouragement, aid, or revelations to help them in their troubles.

A similar approach is found in the story of Tobit and Sarah. The aim of this story is to reassert the validity of faith and virtue at a time when God has apparently abandoned his people.[69] It also affirms the need for family support, charity, and religious integrity in times of persecution. Both Tobit and Sarah suffer deeply from the blind misfortune of the world, for Tobit is mysteriously blinded and Sarah becomes the victim of the cruel sport of heartless women who remind her of her failure as a mother (Tb 3:9-10). Disconsolate at their cruelty, Sarah goes to her room intending to hang herself, but instead offers a prayer to God (Tb 3:10-16). In her suicidal grief, Sarah declares her innocence, and like Tobit she asks God to let her die. This plea is similar to that of Job and Ezekiel, and, as was the case with them, Yahweh does not allow this to happen. Raphael brings Tobit's son Tobias to Sarah to marry her and he also gives Tobit a cure for his blindness. As is the case with Job, Yahweh does not permit suicide to escape the cruelty and misfortune of the world, but answers prayer, faith, and virtue with blessings and life. This prayer was answered by the angel Raphael ("God heals") who comes and vindicates his faithful ones. (Tb 5:4-28)

The other type of suicide in the Old Testament was performed by those who were utterly alienated from God, and these suicides were a sign not of devotion and loyalty to God, but of total alienation from him. These people suicided because they either rebelled against him or alienated themselves from divine favor by violating a grave religious duty. The Scriptures did not explicitly and formally declare suicide to be against the law of God, but they did portray those who deliberately killed themselves without his authority to be alienated from the life and holiness of God.

In a number of different situations, suicide was seen as alienating from the life of Yahweh, and the best example was that of Saul who violated his divine consecration and was punished for this by rebellion in his kingdom. Saul was specifically anointed by Yahweh to be the great king and unifier of the Chosen People, but he betrayed his mission by falling into sorcery, idolatry, and witchcraft (1 Sm 28). For this, he slowly became entangled in the snares of sin, infidelity, and death until he was so deeply enmeshed that he could not escape, and the depths of his involvement was confirmed by his self-killing. His life and actions were in sharp contrast to the Scriptural ideal of the God-fearing Israelite who lived out the full length of his days and saw his children's children down to the seventh generation.

The remarks of the famous Jesuit Scripture scholar, John McKenzie, on Saul's life and character are enlightening:

> The character of Saul is complex and tragic. Historians generally agree that he suffered from mental derangement. This was the 'evil spirit' from Yahweh which troubled him and it makes more intelligible his pathological jealousy and hatred of David, his murderous assaults on David and the priests of Nob and his neglect of his duty while he engaged in a vain pursuit of his adversary, the

alienation of even his children from him. These traits are not merely the result of a deliberate effort of the court historians of David to blacken his reputation; there is no evidence that they made this attempt, and the story was sufficient in itself. David himself in the opinion of almost all modern critics composed the tribute to Saul found in 2S 1:19-26, one of the great pieces of early Israelite poetry. He was solicitous for the family of Saul, although the family maintained a cordial hatred of David in some of its members. This may have been stimulated by David's yielding to the Gibeonites in their claim for blood revenge on the house of Saul; the episode which was responsible for this claim is not elsewhere recorded. The actions of Saul as they are reported in his later years appear to be the deeds of an abnormal mind. How much this inner weakness was aided by external events is difficult to say. The traditions contain allusions to the fact that Saul felt he was abandoned by Yahweh, as he felt that he was abandoned by his family and retainers in favor of David. One may suspect that Samuel's repudiation preyed upon his mind; in addition he had the Philistine threat. When he saw or thought he saw his own reign endangered by the rise of David, his mind gave way.[70]

Not only in the stories of Saul, but also in those of Judas Iscariot, Zimri, and Ahithophel, we find the theme of self-killing as a sign of utter alienation from God. Zimri was an officer of Elah, king of Israel, who assassinated Elah's entire family, but he only reigned for a single week before he was attacked by Omri and committed suicide in a palace fire (1 Kgs 16:9-20). His name, hurled at Jehu by Jezebel in scorn and condemnation, became an epithet for assassin (2 Kgs 9:31). Ahithophel was a member of David's council, but he advised Absolom to take possession of David's harem, which was a treasonable act. Then he recommended that he pursue David and kill him (2 Sm 17:23), and when this plan failed he hanged himself (2 Sm 17:28).[71]

The suicide of Judas Iscariot also illustrates the New Testament's critical view of this act, for he committed suicide in imitation of Ahithophel and apparently was his New Testament counterpart. By committing suicide just prior to the death of Jesus, Judas ironically proclaimed him to be in the line of the Davidic kingship, just as the suicide of Ahithophel ironically proclaimed the kingship of David.[72] Judas was chosen to be a member of the apostolic community by Jesus, and he was given privileged intimacy and knowledge of the Lord because of that call. But Judas rejected this call and betrayed

Jesus (Mt 10:4; Mk 3:19; Lk 6:16). Because of this he was not only denied knowledge of the Resurrected Lord, but he was also shunned by the community.[73] And the Christian tradition has long held that he was the only one certainly excluded from the kingdom because he did not repent of his suicide. (Jn 6:71)[74]

His betrayal and suicide gave new emphasis to the utter gravity of his abandonment of his apostolic call.[75] His suicide was a sign of the utter destruction of the life of God in him and his total immersion in death, and rather than being heralded as one of the cornerstones of the Church as were all of the other Apostles, Judas was reduced to shame. The frequency with which he was denounced and rejected signifies the horror with which early Christians regarded him. Judas was rejected by the people of his own town (Lk 4:28-29), the leaders of his own nation (Lk 11:53-54; 19:47-8; 20:1-19) and even by his own disciples (Lk 6:12-16). He was described as a "diabolos" in John's Gospel, which possibly meant that he was the adversary or "informer."[76] John also called him a "thief" and credited him with the ungracious and hypocritical remark at Bethany about the anointing of Mary Magdalene (Jn 12:4-6).

Judas was portrayed as being so perverse that the meaning of all his actions became twisted and perverted, and the sharing of the Bread with the Lord at the Last Supper became an act of division rather than communion (Mt 26:20-25; Mk 14:17-21; Lk 22:21-23). The Last Supper was the great prayer of the Christian people, and Judas could not bear being among them. Even then he could not enter in the Light of Christ but was driven by the powers of darkness to accomplish his act of betrayal. Taking the Last Supper with the Lord had no effect on him, for after that he still carried out his work of betrayal, an act that prompted the Apostles to ask who would do such a thing. Even the kiss of fellowship in Gethsemane (Lk 22:47-53) became a kiss of betrayal rather than one of friendship, and the act that epitomized friendship became the sign of infidelity. Rather than being a model of Christian life and discipleship, Judas was the paradigmatic treacherous apostate, and his suicide signified that despairing apostates such as he would be utterly cut off from salvation. His infidelity was contrasted to the loyalty of Jesus and Job who were able to maintain fidelity even in the midst of great suffering and trial, and rather than being a model of fidelity to God, he became the complete antithesis of obedience and devotion.

A good example of the New Testament perspective on suicide is seen in Paul's attempt to stop the jailer of Philippi in Acts from killing himself when he and Silas were freed from prison by an earthquake:

> Late that night Paul and Silas were praying and singing God's praises while the other prisoners listened. Suddenly there was an earthquake that shook the prison to its foundations. All the doors flew open and the chains fell from all the prisoners. When the goaler woke and saw the doors wide open he drew his sword and was about to commit suicide, presuming that the prisoners had escaped. But Paul shouted at the top of his voice, 'Don't do yourself any harm, we are all here.'
>
> The goaler called for lights, then rushed in, threw himself trembling at the feet of Paul and Silas, and escorted them out, saying, 'Sirs, what must I do to be saved?' They told him, 'Become a believer in the Lord Jesus, and you will be saved, and your household too.' Then they preached the word of the Lord to him and to all his family. (Acts 16: 25-34)

This passage clearly shows the falsehood of claims like Battin's that the New Testament does not condemn suicide. In a situation where some might justify suicide, the leading Christian apostle vigorously denounces it and instead calls for faith. This scene is important for Christian teaching on suicide because it shows that the Apostolic verdict was clearly against suicide. Standing second only to Peter, the Apostle of the Gentiles issued a thundering condemnation of self-killing and called for faith in the place of despair. In the very earliest years of the Christian community Paul makes the Christian view of suicide quite clear: faith in Christ delivers from death and suicide is not acceptable for anyone, even the non-Christian.

The Catholic Moral Arguments against Suicide

Margaret Battin claims that many, if not most, classical Catholic arguments against suicide are trivial and do not support its strong prohibition.[77] And even further, she claims that some traditional Catholic doctrines positively support self-murder in some cases. Her criticisms are not fully justified, however, because she does not confront Catholicism's strongest argument against suicide, which is that it is immoral because it is a direct attack on innocent human life. In what follows, I will show that her claims do not defeat the Catholic objections to self-slaying and that the Catholic claims are coherent and persuasive.

The traditional teachings of the Catholic church on suicide were well stated in the writings of St. Augustine and St. Thomas Aquinas. These teachings against suicide are based on the doctrine of the sanctity of human life, which is grounded on the biblical doctrine of the *imago Dei*. The doctrine of the sanctity of human life was founded on Gn 9:6, which holds that the blood of the innocent is not to be shed because it was made in the image of God: "He who sheds man's blood shall have his blood shed by man, for in the image of God man was made." While there has been much attention in the history of Christian reflection devoted to the *imago Dei* doctrine of Gn 1:27 there has been little consideration given to Gn 9:6. Most Christian studies of Gn 1:27 were anthropological or Trinitarian in nature and did not examine the moral dimensions of this principle. And there is very little evidence of attempts by either the ancient Fathers or the medievals to examine the link between the image of God and the prohibition of killing; and they usually commented on the teaching in order to expound upon the nature of man or our relation to God, but not on its implications for the morality of killing. Virtually all of the major Eastern Fathers who developed a serious theological anthropology claimed that the human person was made in the "image and likeness of God."[78] The fundamental difficulty with patristic and medieval discussions of the image of God was that they generally considered the concept of *imago Dei* for only two purposes: to show the uniqueness of the created person and to understand better our relationship to the Triune God. They showed how and why the human person is transcendent within the created order, but merely demonstrating this transcendence did not provide a clear moral reason for the wrongness of direct killing.

This doctrine stands at the foundation of both classical Christian theological anthropology and doctrines formulated about the special nature of the human person. But the doctrine of the divine image in man does not tell us why our creation in the image of God makes direct killing of the innocent immoral. Just because the human person in some fashion mirrors the divine nature in their being and is close to the Divine Being does not provide us a with moral reason for not killing human beings. There is little evidence of a belief in either the ancient or the medieval Church that human life possessed sanctity.

Lecky mentioned that early medieval moralists carried the doctrine of the sanctity of life to such an extent that they were able to resoundingly condemn all forms of direct suicide, but there was hardly any mention in medieval theology of the sanctity of human life.[79] Albert Schweitzer was the first to ascribe sanctity to life in his 1923 work *Kultur und Ethik* where he developed his philosophy of civilization and was harshly critical of Western ethics.[80] Schweitzer stated that not just human life, but all life possessed sanctity and that the destruction of any form of life, whether human or nonhuman, was unethical. Schweitzer's claim immediately set off a storm of controversy in Protestant theology because many objected to his view that the killing of any living being was wrong.

Another perspective on the sanctity of life during this time was provided by Pope Pius XI who reacted to the decision of the Anglican church at Lambeth in 1930 giving limited endorsement to artificial contraception by issuing his famous encyclical *Casti Conubii* in 1933.[81] Against Schweitzer, he claimed that only innocent human life was to be absolutely protected from direct killing. This was the first authoritative use of the precise phrase "sanctity of life" to refer to human life in contrast to Schweitzer who used it to refer more to the reverence that was due all living beings rather than to just human life.[82] Pius argued that it was not unjust to kill some human beings who were not innocent, but that the deliberate destruction of human beings who were not guilty of acts meriting death was always and every where immoral.

There are a number of general points of agreement in the classical teachings about the image of God in man. St. Athanasius argued, and it was generally agreed, that we were created in the image of God and that the aim of Christian life was to bring this image to perfection by growing in the likeness of Christ.[83] The physical body, almost universally rejected as the seat of the divine image, could only reflect the divine image in a vague and ambiguous manner, and the seat of the image was almost certainly in the spiritual part of the person.[84] Most Patristic authors agree that Christ is the perfect image of God because he is the perfect image of the Father.[85] Generally, the image of God within man was seen as dynamic because the perfection of the image was found in the process of sanctification and reconciliation with God.[86] There was some sympathy for the view that the image was found in human freedom, but this is almost totally absent in St. Augustine who was ancient Christianity's greatest exponent of *imago Dei*.[87] Either because of the perfection of the image or because of the perfection of the likeness of God within us, one achieves sanctification. Even though there was much agreement on the nature of being created *imago Dei,* there was also much diversity of opinion about what was meant.

Many of the Fathers considered immortality to be at least a vestige, if not the actual image of God itself, but this claim was not supported by either St. Augustine or St. Thomas. Gregory of Nyssa held that God was the source of immortality, which he shared only with men and the angels. Immortality was found in the body and was one of the gifts given at creation, which we received by being in the image of God.[88] He regarded immortality as a sign of the presence of the image of God, but this immortality was not the natural immortality of the Platonic soul, but was a gratuitous gift of God given to us at Creation.[89] According to Gregory, the true destiny of man is immortality and incorruptibility, and we were saved because we were given our "garment of skin," which provides us the means to reacquire immortality.[90]

Cyril of Alexandria affirmed our creation in and for incorruption and immortality, but he argued that these were lost by sin and then restored through the Spirit of Jesus.[91] Cyril gave up the search for the Trinitarian image in man as futile and he held that we remained human after receiving the Spirit, but we were made incomparably better for we reacquired immortality and were glorified as well.[92] According to Cyril, we were given divine filiation at creation, which raised us to the image of Christ, incorruptibility, and immortality. Origen followed Ireneus and considered immortality to be one of the fundamental gifts of creation.[93] St. Athanasius saw sin as covering over the image of God and causing us to lose immortality.[94] Christ, the perfect image of God, destroyed death and corruptibility and won for us a share of it.[95]

The most complete study of the image of God in man was St. Augustine's in *De Trinitate* where he thoroughly and carefully examined this concept.[96] He discovered a number of "vestiges" of the One and Triune God in man, and he concluded that the most perfect image of the Trinity was found in the *memoria, voluntas,* and *intelligentia* of the person.[97] Augustine's reflections about the *imago Dei* were influenced by ancient Platonism and he was hostile to any claim that the corporeal body could image God in any significant fashion. He found the most perfect image of the One God in the *mens* or the composite of spiritual and intellectual powers of the person. The *mens* had for him many of the features of a Plotinian soul, and he appears to have wanted to entirely separate the body from the image of God in the person.[98] Augustine was able to relate the operations of the inner soul (the *mens*) to the body only with great difficulty, and he believed that the body was only distantly involved in the image of God.[99] "[T]here is no doubt that man was made to the image of God that created him, not according to the body, nor according to any part of the soul, but according to the rational mind where the knowledge of God can exist."[100]

The *mens* was the highest part of the soul and it was the seat of reason and understanding.[101] The term *mens* had a multiplicity of meanings for Augustine, and it referred to *ratio, intellectus,* or *intelligentia.*[102] It could be identified with the *animus,* which is the principle of rational and intellectual life in man, but it is probably most accurate to identify the *mens* with the "inner man" of St. Paul's thought.[103] It encompassed all that was specifically human and rational in the person. Intelligible realities, including the divine being, were grasped by the *mens,* even though to Augustine's embarrassment the *mens* was found in close association with the body. The doctrine that human life was created in the image and likeness of God held that the very nature of God was communicated in some fashion at creation, and the communication of this nature elevated the human being above all creation, including the wholly spiritual creatures. Creation in *imago Dei* implied that the person was perfect from God's creating hand and that no human faults or errors could be imputed to the Creator.

Thomas Aquinas had the most well-developed understanding of the image of God of all medieval and ancient theologians, and even though he accepted many of the teachings of Augustine, he presented them in more of an Aristotelian form, and he gave them a precision not found in Augustine's works. Aquinas held that an image imitated the form of its exemplar, and manifested a likeness or an equality with the model. An image was a likeness to an exemplar, which was an express and proximate sign of the species of the exemplar:

> The nature of an image consists in imitation, from which its name is also taken. . . . Two things are to be considered about the nature of an imitation; that in which there is imitation and those things which imitate each other. But that in regard to which there is imitation is some quality, or a form understood in the manner of a quality. Whence likeness is of the nature of an image. Nor does this suffice, but it is necessary that there be some equivalence in that quality, either according to quality or according to proportion. . . . It is also required that this quality be the express and proximate sign of its nature and species.[104]

For Aquinas, an authentic image represented the paradigm with precision and clarity in comparison to a vestige of God that was a confused and imprecise image of the exemplar.[105] Because of this more perfect representation, one can gather something about the nature of the exemplar from an image, but not from a vestige. In his more mature thought, Aquinas held that an image was not only a likeness of the exemplar but also found its origin in the exemplar. An image proceeded "from another like to it in species or at least in specific sign," and a proportionate equality between the image and exemplar was all that was necessary for a perfect image of an exemplar.[106] In his later thought, Aquinas moved closer to Augustine and claimed that a proportional equality between the image and the exemplar was necessary for an image to perfectly mirror its model.[107]

But Thomas differed from Augustine in one respect and held that angels were created in the image of God because they possessed an intellectual nature, which is where the image was found.[108] The image was located in the *mens,* and by this term he implied not only the narrow sense of intellect alone, but also the wider sense of the seat of the spiritual powers of *memoria, voluntas,* and *intellectus.* There was an analogical likeness to God to be found in all creatures, and in the image of God in man, the analogical likeness of the person is in the intellect, which constitutes the very species of the person. This likeness is analogical because in God there are no species, and intellectuality (the highest grade of being and perfection proceeding from God) is only a sort of a "quasi-species." The human person was the most perfect image because it participated in the being, life, existence, and intellectuality of God. In the intellectual creature, the image conforms perfectly to this divine attribute. Augustine lacked the formal concept of analogy found in Aquinas and he held that there was an analogical likeness between the exemplar and image of God in man.

The immediate reason why the doctrine of the *imago Dei* prohibits direct killing of the innocent is the immortality with which persons are created. Simply put, willfully visiting death upon an innocent is wrong because they were created in the beginning for a future freed from death. Aquinas parted company with Augustine in his analysis of the *imago Dei* and held that the angels were created in the image of God because of their intellectual natures. In affirming this, Aquinas was implicitly teaching that both humans and the angels were created for immortality. Like the angels, the person was "created transcendence" and as a consequence was created for immortality, and only God, humans, and angels were spiritual and immortal either at creation or by nature. But because of Adam's sin, only man could suffer from death and thus be alienated from his natural and created immortality.[109] In this perspective, killing an innocent human person involves destroying a being destined at creation for eternal existence with God, and restoration of this capacity is the primary objective of the redemptive activities of Christ. This view would hold direct killing of the innocent immoral because it would deliberately destroy a being destined at creation to live immortally with God and would introduce death where there should be immortality. In this kind of killing, one comes as close as possible to striking a blow at our immortality and in the act one takes upon oneself the identity of a killer. The created immortality of the human person prohibits direct killing of the innocent because this killing imputes a moral identity of death. But when killing does not do this it is not immoral. Thus, killing an unjust attacker does not violate our created immortality or give us the identity of a killer.

Killing an innocent person violates not just their created condition of immortality, but justice as well, while the death of a guilty party violates immortality but not the requirements of justice. Precisely because justice is not violated, the deliberate killing of those guilty of serious offenses is not objectionable. Deliberately destroying one who was created for immortality can never be done when the one killed is innocent of any action meriting death. But when guilty deliberately killing them may not be unjust or a disproportionate punishment in some instances. Being created immortal means that God alone has the power to determine when our lives are to be ended, and we can only end the life of another when their actions against us personally or the common good are so grave that their death is demanded.[110]

In *The City of God,* Augustine argued that Christians do not commit suicide in any circumstance and that Christians have no authority to self-execute. Augustine's arguments here are quite clear: suicide is wrong because it is deliberate killing of the innocent.

> For it is clear that if no one has a private right to kill even a guilty man (and no law allows this), then certainly anyone who kills himself is a murderer, and is the more guilty in killing himself the more innocent he is of the charge on which he has condemned himself to death. We rightly abominate the act of Judas, and the judgment of the truth is that when he hanged himself he did not atone for the guilt of his detestable betrayal but rather increased it, since he despaired of God's mercy and in

> a fit of self-destructive remorse left himself no chance of a saving repentance. How much less right has anyone to indulge in self-slaughter when he can find in himself no fault to justify such a punishment! For when Judas killed himself, he killed a criminal, and yet he ended his life guilty not only of Christ's death, but also of his own; one crime led to another.[111]

He denied that it was legitimate to kill oneself for any reason, for the law against killing forbids destroying all innocent human beings, including oneself.[112]

> It is significant that in the sacred canonical books there can nowhere be found any injunction or permission to commit suicide either to ensure immortality or to escape any evil. In fact we must understand it to be forbidden by the law 'You shall not kill,' particularly as there is no addition of 'your neighbor' as in the prohibition of false witness, 'You shall not bear false witness *against your neighbor*.' But that does not mean that a man who gives false witness against himself is exempt from guilt, since the rule about loving one's neighbor begins with oneself, seeing that the Scripture says 'You shall love your neighbor as yourself.'[113]

He condemned suicide not only because it was culpable killing, but also because it was against the virtue of fortitude. The pagans held up Cato and Regulus as exemplary suicides, but Augustine points out that both of them were defeated and beaten men, Cato by Caesar and Regulus by the Carthagenians.[114] He denied categorically that suicide showed greatness of soul or virtue.[115] This virtue is not seen by self-assassination, which shows that one lacks the strength to endure hardships.[116] It is not permissible to kill oneself to avoid falling into the hands of one's enemies, for neither the Patriarchs, nor Jesus Christ, nor the Apostles did this.[117]

> What we are saying, asserting, and establishing by all means at our command is this: that no one ought deliberately to bring about his own death by way of escaping from temporal troubles, for fear that he may fall into eternal afflictions; it is wrong to commit suicide because of the sins of others, for this is to bring upon oneself a heavy burden of sin, whereas another's sin could not defile one or because of one's past sins, for one has more need of this life on their account, so that those sins may be healed by repentance; or through longing for a better life, hoped for after

> death, for those guilty of their death are not received after death into that better life.[118]

He believed that the Christians had a better example of coping with suffering and defeat in the figures of Job, the Apostles, and Jesus himself than in these other suicidal individuals.[119]

> There are however certain expressions to the law against killing, made by the authority of God himself. There are those whose killing God orders, either by a law, or by an express command to a particular person or at a particular time. In fact one who owes a duty of obedience to the giver of the command does not himself 'kill'– he is an instrument, a sword in its user's hand. For this reason the commandment forbidding killing was not broken by those who have waged wars on the authority of God, or those who have imposed the death-penalty on criminals when representing the authority of the state in accordance with the laws of the State, the justest and most reasonable source of power. When Abraham was ready to kill his son, so far from being blamed for cruelty he was praised for his devotion; it was not an act of crime, but of obedience. One is justified in asking whether Jeptha is to be regarded as obeying a command of God in killing his daughter, when he had vowed to sacrifice to God the first thing he met when returning victorious from battle. And when Samson destroyed himself, with his enemies, even by the demolition of the building, this can only be excused on the ground that the Spirit, which performed miracles through him, secretly ordered him to do so. With the exception of these killings prescribed generally by a just law, or specially commanded by God himself – the source of justice – anyone who kills a human being, whether himself or anyone else, is involved in a charge of murder.[120]

To avoid defilement, some women in Augustine's time committed suicide, and their acts were extolled by some Fathers while others were highly critical of them.[121] These sorts of suicide were very difficult to condemn, for the motives were exceptionally laudable even though the acts were reprehensible.[122] But Augustine would not countenance these acts even to protect virginity, for even though these women would be ravished, they could retain their innocence, and self-murder would be far worse than being molested.[123] Augustine and others thought that a virgin who suicided to prevent being raped committed a crime far worse than what the rapist would do and brought guilt on herself that she could have otherwise avoided:

> But how was it that she [Lucretia] who did not commit adultery received the heavier punishment? For the adulterer was driven from his country, with his father; his victim suffered the supreme penalty. . . . The highly praised Lucretia also did away with the innocent, chaste, outraged Lucretia. Give your sentence. Or if you cannot do this, because the culprit is not present to receive punishment, why do you extol with such praises the killer of the chaste and innocent. . . . Such is not the behavior of a Christian woman. When they were treated like this they did not take vengeance on themselves for another crime. They would not add crime to crime by committing murder on themselves in shame because the enemy had committed rape on them in lust.[124]

Even though this may sound cruel, Augustine thought it worse for a woman to commit self-murder than to suffer rape, but there is a persuasive consistency to his reasoning here. He admits that some early Christian virgins committed suicide to preserve their chastity, but he believes they were either acting under divine command or were simply mistaken.[125]

Augustine denied one could even commit suicide to avoid committing sin, for if that was permissible, confessors could urge penitents to kill themselves after being absolved of their sins to avoid falling into further sin.[126]

> There remains one situation in which it is supposed to be advantageous to commit suicide; I have already begun to discuss this question. It arises when the motive is to avoid falling into sin either through the allurements of pleasure or through the menaces of pain. If we agree to allow this motive we shall not be able to stop until we reach the point when people are to be encouraged to kill themselves for preference, immediately they have received forgiveness of all sins by washing in the waters of holy regeneration. For that would be the time to forestall all future sins – the moment when all past sins have been erased. If self-inflicted death is permitted, surely this is the best possible moment for it! When a person has been thus set free why should he expose himself again to all the perils of this life, when it is so easily allowed him to avoid them by doing away with himself? As the Bible says, 'A man who is fond of danger will fall into it'

(Eccles. 3. 26). Why are men so fond of all these great dangers, or at any rate are willing to accept them, by remaining in this life, when they are allowed to depart from it? If a man has a duty to kill himself to avoid succumbing to sin because he is at the mercy of one man, who holds him prisoner, does he suppose that he has to go on living so as to endure the pressures of the actual world, which is full of temptations of all times, temptations such as that which is dreaded under one master, and innumerable others, which are the necessary accompaniment of this life?[127]

Augustine argues that this would be the most persuasive argument for suicide possible, and yet he denies it is sound. He would not allow suicide to escape disgrace or avoid punishment, and he regards suicide to escape punishment as an illicit attempt to atone for guilt.[128] The guilt of one who kills himself to escape punishment increases in relationship to his innocence.

Battin suggests that the basis of the traditional Catholic teaching on suicide was Augustine's opposition to the practices of the Circumcellions and Donatists who either killed themselves, or had themselves killed, to gain salvation.[129] The implication here is that he would not have argued against the practice if these fanatics had not made the orthodox Christians look bad. But in claiming this as the basis of Augustine's views, Battin is reducing the Catholic moral objection to suicide to a political objection: the orthodox Christians were trying to protect the reputation of true and legitimate martyrs against the fanatical, suicidal Circumcellions. But, as we saw in chapter 2, Augustine was the first Christian author to write extensively about suicide, even though he was hardly the first to condemn it, and he did so for many reasons, not just because the Circumcellions and Donatists were practicing self-murder in the name of Christ. Had the Circumcellion extremists never arisen, orthodox Christians still would have condemned suicide quite vigorously because it was direct killing of the innocent and because it was so widespread in the empire. Augustine's condemnation was not merely an aspect of an overall anti-Donatist political strategy. It was endorsed in the Middle Ages, not because of Christian opposition to the Donatists or Circumcellions, but because of the perceived moral correctness of his teaching. Before and after the emergence of the Circumcellions and Donatists, there was such a clear and strong aversion to killing among the orthodox Christians that suicide was not a major problem for them. But the peculiar nature of the

Donatists, Circumcellions, and the Church in North Africa made suicide a problem that the Church had to resist aggressively.

Without doubt, there is some truth in the view that Augustine condemned suicide partly because of these fanatics and partly because they challenged and threatened Catholic integrity, orthodoxy, zeal, and ardor. But that is not the whole story because he also argued with pagans who presented their heroes like Cato and Seneca as so virtuous that they suicided to preserve their virtue. Battin misunderstands the threat of the Circumcellions and Donatists to the Church, and she overstates their threat because they were only strong in small areas of North Africa. Peter Brown correctly shows that the threat of the Donatists and Circumcellions was relatively insignificant because they were inordinately concerned with preserving the purity of the Christian faith against the new Christians admitted to the post-Constantinian church.[130] They had more of an effect on Catholic sacramental theology than on Catholic moral teaching, and Orthodox Christianity condemned Donatist and Circumcellion suicides as part of its overall attempt to stop the abuses of human life that were so common in the latter Roman Empire. If the Donatists and Circumcellions posed any threat to orthodox Christians, it was because they made the more moderate Christians appear lax, sinful, and tepid in comparison to those who were willing to kill themselves as a twisted symbol of their devotion to God, but this was not a great problem for the orthodox. Their lack of scruple about self-execution threatened to make the orthodox Christians who rejected suicide as a sign of faith appear uncommitted and morally lax. The orthodox Latin Christian resistance to suicide expressed itself in forgiveness of those who apostasized and sought penance and forgiveness; and this spirit of forgiveness angered the fanatic Donatists and Circumcellions, for they believed that handing over the sacred books to the Romans was intolerable, that salvation could be found only through martyrdom, and that any refusal of martyrdom was equal to apostasy. The Donatists' suicidal tendencies were too extreme for most Christians, and they posed less of a threat to the credibility of the Church than did their unfounded claim that the Christians suffered from loose morals.

Like Augustine, Aquinas condemned suicide and extolled martyrdom as a moral ideal precisely because martyrdom was a sign of devotion to God and was a virtuous act. The authentic martyr differed from the self-killer because the martyr did not aim at, intend, seek, choose, or physically cause his or her own death. The martyr accepted death out of love for God and others, as an act of selfless devotion to God and others. The martyr's death was an act of charity and self-sacrifice because he or she gave his or her life to God or to another not for their own benefit but for the other, and did not destroy it for worldly and self-serving reasons. Authentic Catholic martyrs had to be individuals of impeccable holiness, selflessness, and moral virtue who did not provoke their killing in any way, and their deaths could not be motivated by any selfish concern.

Martyrdom is less morally enigmatic than suicide because the martyr acted with greater freedom than did the suicidal person. The martyr's decision to accept death is not complicated by the fear, pain, or suffering that limits the suicidal person's range of options and makes the morality of suicide so complicated. The martyr has much greater freedom to either accept or reject death than does the suicidal person who is not as free to reject death because of the driving fear of suffering, loss of dignity, or pain. The martyr did not choose or decide for death, but decided not to abandon faith knowing this decision *might* cause another to inflict death. The martyr or self-sacrificing individual did not justify his or her action by appeals to compassion, sentiment, emotion, fear of death or suffering, but on the basis of what is the most charitable and selfless action possible. In an authentic martyrdom, unlike a suicide, the martyr did no harm to anyone and was the victim of the lethal acts of another.

The person who gave his or her life for another or for an altruistic or religious reason, and not from motives of self-interest, was not only more free, but was also more morally, spiritually, and psychologically mature than the suicidal person. A clear sign of this maturity was the ability to do what was good for others, particularly when done at one's expense. The martyr who gave his or her life shows a maturity and freedom for self-giving lacking in the suicidal person, and a mark of maturity is the capacity to shed concern for one's well-being and satisfaction in order to do what is of benefit for others.[131]

Devoting an entire question of his *Summa Theologica* to the question of suicide, Aquinas gave the Church's teachings on this issue their best expression:

> *Objection 1.* It would seem lawful for a man to kill himself. For murder is a sin in so far as it is contrary to justice. But no man can do an injustice to himself, as is proved in *Ethic.* v. 11. Therefore no man sins by killing himself.
>
> *Obj. 2.* Further, it is lawful, for one who exercises public authority, to kill evildoers. Now he who exercises public authority

is sometimes an evildoer. Therefore, he may lawfully kill himself.

Obj. 3. Further, it is lawful for a man to suffer spontaneously a lesser danger that he may avoid a greater: thus it is lawful for a man to cut off a decayed limb even from himself, that he may save his whole body. Now sometimes a man, by killing himself, avoids a greater evil, for example an unhappy life, or the shame of sin. Therefore, a man may kill himself.

Obj 4. Further, Samson killed himself, as related in Judges vcxxvi., and yet he is numbered among the saints (Heb. xi). Therefore it is lawful for a man to kill himself.

Obj.5. Further it is related (2 Mach. xiv. 42) that a certain Razis killed himself, *choosing to die nobly rather than to fall into the hands of the wicked, and to suffer abuses unbecoming his noble birth.* Now nothing that is done nobly and bravely is unlawful. Therefore suicide is not unlawful.

On the contrary: Augustine says (*De Civ. Dei* 1. 20) "Hence it follows that the words 'Thou shalt not kill' refer to the killing of a man;–not another man; therefore, not even thyself. For he who kills himself, kills nothing else than a man."

I answer that, It is altogether unlawful to kill oneself, for three reasons. First, because everything naturally loves itself, the result being that everything naturally keeps itself in being, and resists corruptions so far as it can. Wherefore suicide is contrary to the inclination of nature, and to charity whereby every man should love himself. Hence suicide is always a mortal sin, as being contrary to the natural law and to charity.

Secondly, because every part, as such, belongs to the whole. Now every man is part of the community, and so, as such, he belongs to the community. Hence by killing himself he injures the community, as the Philosopher declares (*Ethic,* v. 11.)

Thirdly, because life is God's gift to man, and is subject to His power, Who kills and makes to live. Hence whoever takes his own life, sins against God, even as he who kills another's slave, sins against that slave's master, and as he who usurps to himself judgment of a matter not entrusted to him. For it belongs to God alone to pronounce sentence of death and life, according to Deut. xxxii, 39, *I will kill and I will make to live.*

Reply Obj. 1. Murder is a sin, not only because it is contrary to justice, but also because it is opposed to charity which a man should have towards himself: in this respect suicide is a sin in relation to oneself. In relation to the community and to God, it is sinful, by reason also of its opposition to justice.

Reply Obj. 2. One who exercises public authority may lawfully put to death an evildoer, since he can pass judgment on him. But no man is judge of himself. Wherefore it is not lawful for one who exercises public authority to put himself to death for any sin whatever, although he may lawfully commit himself to the judgment of others.

Reply Obj. 3. Man is made master of himself through his free-will: wherefore he can lawfully dispose of himself as to those matters which pertain to this life as ruled by man's free-will. But the passage from this life to another and happier one is subject not to man's free-will but to the power of God. Hence it is not lawful for man to take his own life that he may pass to a happier life, nor that he may escape any unhappiness whatsoever of the present life, because the ultimate and most fearsome evil of this life is death, as the Philosopher states (*Ethic.* iii, 6). Therefore, to bring death upon oneself in order to escape the other afflictions of this life, is to adopt a greater evil in order to avoid a lesser. In like manner it is unlawful to take one's own life on account of one's having committed a sin, both because by so doing one does oneself a very great injury, by depriving oneself of the time needful for repentance, and because it is not lawful to slay an evildoer except by the sentence of the public authority. Again it is unlawful for a woman to kill herself lest she be violated, because she ought not to commit on herself the very great sin of suicide, to avoid the lesser sin of another. For she commits no sin in being violated by force, provided she does not consent, since *without consent of the mind there is no stain on the body,* as the Blessed Lucy declared. Now it is evident that fornication and adultery are less grievous sins than taking a man's life, especially one's own life: since the latter is most grievous, because one injures oneself, to whom one owes the greatest love. Moreover it is most dangerous since no time is left wherein to expiate it by repentance. Again it is not lawful to take his own life for fear he should consent to sin, because *evil must not be done that good may come* (Rom. iii, 8) or that evil may be avoided, especially if the evil be of small account and an uncertain event, for it is uncertain whether one will at some future time consent to a sin, since God is able to deliver man from sin under any temptation whatever.

Reply Obj. 4. As Augustine says (*De Civ. Dei* i, 21) *not even Samson is to be excused that he crushed himself together with his enemies under the ruins of the house, except the Holy Ghost, Who had wrought many wonders through him, had secretly commanded him to do this.* He assigns the same reason in the case of certain holy women, who at the time of persecution took their own lives, and who are commemorated by the Church.

Reply Obj. 5. It belongs to fortitude that a man does not shrink from being slain by another, for the sake of the good of virtue, and that he may avoid sin. But that a man take his own life in order to avoid penal evils has, indeed an appearance of fortitude (for which reason some, among whom was Razis, having killed themselves thinking to act from fortitude), yet it is not true fortitude, but rather a weakness of soul unable to bear penal evils as the Philosopher (*Ethic* iii, 7) and Augustine (*De Div. Dei*. 1.22-23).[132]

In contrast to Augustine, Aquinas argued against suicide because it was contrary to nature and the virtues. He did present some new arguments against suicide, and following Augustine, he held that it was not only against love, but also against fortitude, temperance, hope and faith, prudence, our obligations in justice to the community and God, and ultimately our natural inclination to life. Suicide is contrary to charity, proper self-love, justice, fortitude, the legitimate prerogatives of the common good, the demands of a proper relationship with God, and is an evil means to a good end when it is performed to escape suffering, shame, or an occasion of sin. Suicide is contrary not only to the moral but the theological virtues as well. According to Aquinas, the aim of Christian life was to grow in both the cardinal and theological virtues and develop our powers to act well and virtuously in all situations, and the virtues that bring this about are prudence, temperance, justice, fortitude, faith, hope, and charity. Prudence requires one to form one's actions in such a way that true good comes from them. Temperance enables us to restrain our drives and tastes for pleasure so that they do not do evil in their pursuit.[133] Justice enables one to give everyone what is their due, and it equips one to effect what is good in complicated situations.[134] Fortitude gives us the ability to do what is good in spite of trying and difficult circumstances.[135] Aquinas condemned suicide as contrary to fortitude because the suicidal person does what is evil when doing what is right and good is difficult. All have a responsibility to develop their ability to do what is right, not only when this is easy, but also when this involves some difficulty, and fortitude enables one to do what is good in spite of the pain, suffering, or loss that we might experience in seeking to do the good action. The demands of fortitude differ from case to case, but one who deliberately kills another innocent person because of fear violates the virtue of fortitude. Less proximately, suicide is contrary to the virtues of temperance and prudence. Often, individuals kill themselves by letting emotions of self-pity get the best of them, and they violate temperance, which requires us to not let disorderly emotional states lead us into sin. It violates prudence as well because it is not a morally good means (deliberately destroying innocent human life) to a morally legitimate end.

For Aquinas, suicide violated justice because deliberately destroying innocent human life is not an act that is properly due them. This life deserves to be protected, and justice demands that it only be indirectly and unintentionally destroyed if absolutely necessary for the sake of other proportionate goods or values. He also objected to suicide because it was against the virtue of hope that gave individuals the motivation to seek to do what was truly good, especially in difficult circumstances.[136] In a suicidal action, one reacts to stress, threats, and demands so violently that one destroys innocent life to escape, and this virtue prohibits allowing even desperation or despair to justify acts of self-destruction. For Aquinas, suicide also compromised the virtue of faith.[137] In the Catholic perspective, all evils have been placed under the power of Christ, and while this does not imply freedom from all temptation, it does mean that the grace and power of Christ will not allow us to be ultimately overwhelmed by evil. To self-execute in the face of evil is to implicitly deny that Christ has finally and definitively overcome evil and is contrary to faith because it implicitly denies that Christ succeeded in delivering us from death. Suicide implies that they ultimately triumph over him, and implies that Christ's victory over sin, despair, and death was incomplete or empty.

Suicide also violates charity, the virtue requiring one to do good to all, even to oneself.[138] One must always do good and never deliberately do harm; but in a suicidal act, one inflicts the greatest physical harm possible on oneself. This command means that destroying oneself to avoid pain, suffering, despair, or death is against authentic love of self. Just as taking mind-altering drugs that can seriously impair one's mental and emotional ability to exercise love and charity is against this form of love, so also is killing oneself.

Suicide, for Aquinas, is contrary to the requirements of the natural law, which holds that a number of ends or objects of human action bring us human fulfillment, and it is from these principles that Catholic moral teaching objects to suicide.[139] These fundamental human goods include life, justice, truth, the common good, and friendship and there are natural inclinations toward these values. When we act to directly support, promote, and protect these values, we not only perform morally good acts, but we achieve our natural human end. But when we deliberately destroy these goods, inhibit their realization, or undermine them, we not only perform immoral actions but also inhibit our own human growth and fulfillment. Aquinas also regarded suicide as against our natural inclinations, a claim related to Aristotle's and one that is not well-understood today. These natural inclinations are correlative to the ends of human existence, and while they do not determine the morality of actions, they guide us in our deliberations about the goodness or badness of actions. These inclinations point to what we rationally apprehend as good and lead us to self-preservation and human flourishing. They give a "feel" for what is good or bad, right or wrong, just or unjust, but they do not in themselves identify and define the morality of the actions. They give a "sense" of what was temperate, courageous, false, or unfair, but they do not transform this inarticulate sense or intuition into a moral reason why an action is good or bad. A good example of these inclinations is our basic drive to foster, promote, and protect our lives. This drive would manifest itself in our natural sense to flee from danger and seek out the basic necessities of life, such as food and water, and in our aversion to self-destruction through suicide. This basic inclination to preserve our lives is usually so strong that most people can only overcome it when their agony, misery, suffering, desperation, and pain become unendurable.

Aquinas's judgment was reaffirmed by numerous medieval and early modern Catholic moral writers, and even today it is endorsed by virtually all modern Catholic moralists. Henry Davis, for example, held that it was never morally permissible to directly kill oneself, even as a means to a good end.[140] Koch-Preuss held that euthanasia (and thus suicide) was the destruction of the temple of God, and "a violation of the property rights of Jesus Christ."[141] In 1975 Thomas O'Donnell said that

> [t]he Catholic Church has consistently taught that suicide is a totally undefensible and gravely sinful injection of disordered self-referenced determination into the providential plan of God's love. It is seen as the ultimate violation of the divine prerogative of the author of life. We might add that the divinely endowed rights which the Founding Fathers of American democracy held to be self-evident – carry with them certain corresponding fundamental responsibilities. The most profound of these responsibilities is drastically and definitively abandoned in the act of self-destruction, and, indeed, in this context euthanasia and suicide are very much of a piece, and present the same theological distortion of the right order.[142]

Modern Catholic teachings confirm this view. The *Declaration on Euthanasia,* issued by the Congregation for the Doctrine of the Faith in 1980 argued that:

> 1. No one can make an attempt on the life of an innocent person without opposing God's love for that person, without violating a fundamental right, and therefore without committing a crime of the utmost gravity.
>
> 2. Everyone has the duty to lead his or her life in accordance with God's plan. That life is entrusted to the individual as a good that must bear fruit already here on earth, but that finds its full perfection only in eternal life.
>
> 3. Intentionally causing one's own death, or suicide, is therefore equally as wrong as murder, such an action on the part of a person is to be considered as a rejection of God's sovereignty and loving plan. Furthermore, suicide is also often a refusal of love for self, the denial of the natural instinct to live, a flight from the duties of justice and charity owed to one's neighbor, to various communities or to the whole of society – although, as is generally recognized, at times there are psychological factors present that can diminish responsibility or even completely remove it.

> However, one must clearly distinguish suicide from that sacrifice of one's life whereby for a higher cause, such as God's glory, the salvation of souls or the service of one's brethren, a person offers his or her own life or puts it in danger. (cf. Jn 15:14)[143]

This passage is representative of contemporary official Catholic teachings on suicide, and it sums up well the reasons for the Catholic tradition's rejection of suicide. Some might contend that Catholic teaching is inconsistent in its rejection of suicide, but while the issue has been debated at length, traditional Catholic thought on this issue (as we saw in the last two chapters) clearly has strongly opposed it. Catholic opposition to suicide in this statement is based on its belief that innocent human life is to be immune to deliberate killing, and hence, it regards suicide as intrinsically evil. It denies that there are ever adequate reasons for deliberately destroying an innocent human life, just as there are never adequate reasons for deliberately raping or torturing others. In the classical Catholic perspective, actions have an intrinsic moral nature, and if an act is immoral it should not be done under any circumstance. Official Catholic teachings have held that suicide is intrinsically immoral when considered in and of itself because it involves a direct attack on innocent human life. Allowing direct and deliberate killing of the innocent would run counter to virtually everything in classical western Christian moral tradition which held that innocent human life should not be deliberately destroyed in any circumstance. This tradition sought to protect the innocent by proscribing abortion, infanticide, killing of noncombatants in war, suicide, killing of hostages, and terrorist killing; allowing deliberate self-killing would undermine arguments against all these other forms of killing.

The classical Catholic understanding of the doctrine of double effect also rejects suicide because it violates the criteria for morally legitimate indirect killing. For an action to be indirectly intended, the principle of the double effect requires that: (1) the action itself be morally good; (2) the intention of the agent be morally good; (3) the good effect not be brought about by the bad effect; and (4) the evils brought about be proportionate to the good effected. Suicide, but not martyrdom or self-sacrifice to protect another, is not indirect killing because the death of the individual is either an end in itself or a means to another end. And in an authentic suicide, only one of the conditions (proportionality) might be hypothetically present, but this is insufficient to constitute a true suicide as indirect. In a true suicide, neither the action itself (deliberately killing) is a good one, nor is the intention of the agent, for the agent intends death either as an object in itself or as a means to another object. And while the proportions between good and evil effects might be favorable in the minds of some, the good effect of a suicidal act is brought about by means of the evil effect, which is the death of the agent.

Margaret Battin argues that the principle of the double effect encourages suicide because it permits self-killing for the good of others.[144] She construes this principle to mean that morally evil actions can be permitted to bring about good effects, even though this interpretation has been explicitly rejected by its mainstream classical interpreters.[145] Battin misunderstands the meaning of this principle, for it only permits morally good acts that have an evil effect as a foreseen but unintended consequence, and it expressly prohibits intrinsically evil acts (such as suicide) undertaken as a means to promote good aims. She does not understand that such suicides are prohibited as immoral deeds performed for good ends. Authentic suicides, however, have death as their direct object and not merely as an unintended side effect, and they are thus prohibited by the principle of double effect.

If the principle of double effect prohibits anything, it forbids killing yourself either as an objective in itself or as a means to another objective. Because of its severe restrictions against intending death either as a means or as an end, and because it only allows death to be a foreseen but unintended consequence of a morally good act that is the last and only reasonably available means of protecting and promoting a basic good of human existence, it is impossible to believe that this principle encourages self-assassination. Rather than promoting suicide as Battin contends, this principle works to prevent it by eliminating confusion between laying down one's life for another and killing oneself to effect a good.

The Critique of the Catholic Teachings on Suicide

Professor Battin claims that the analogies invoked by the mainstream Catholic tradition to ban suicide do not persuasively and solidly support its prohibition of self-execution.[146] To show that this is the case, she makes a number of points to show their weakness. But contrary to her claims, I will show that these analogies do support the common Catholic prohibition of reflexive killing.

According to Battin, condemning suicide as an illegitimate destruction of the gift of life is a faulty analogy because we regularly destroy gifts, particularly when they have lost their value.[147] She believes that gifts (including the gift of human life) can be legitimately destroyed when they lose their value. It is wrong to destroy gifts when they retain their value, but when value is lost, no evil is done in destroying them.

But this principle does not apply from the central Catholic perspective, for the "gift" analogy retains its validity, and destroying a gift that retains its value offends the value of the gift.[148] In the classical Catholic outlook, human life, made in the image of God, never loses its value, and it can never be deliberately destroyed because it has *supposedly* lost its value.[149] This image is only destroyed at death, and life retains its value up to that point, thus making its deliberate destruction immoral. Battin believes that, whatever the value of a life, it can be overwhelmed by profound suffering, which would justify suicide. But by way of objection, this claim would imply that Christ's life would have lost its value when he was dying on the Cross because of his agony. In the Catholic perspective, life in such circumstances not only retains its value, but probably has even greater value because it is more like the life of Christ when he sacrificed himself on the Cross. If anyone would have been justified in suiciding because of suffering, it was Christ, and yet he declined to do this, and heeding this example, Catholic morality rejects suicide in such instances. Just as Christ accepted these sufferings as a means of manifesting fidelity to his saving mission, the Christian accepts these for that reason and to proclaim the Lordship of Christ and their desire to share in the salvation of the world. Catholic moral teachings did not accept the notion that such a life is worthless.

Battin argues that it would be legitimate to destroy images when they distort what they represent, and that human life can be deliberately destroyed when its character is radically distorted by suffering, pain, or illness. When a nation's flag is so tattered and worn out that unfurling it brings ridicule on the nation, it would be legitimate to destroy it. But from the common Catholic perspective, one who accepts terminal suffering with faith in God does not distort the image of Christ, who suffered so deeply in his crucifixion for us, but rather exemplifies Christian fidelity and love of God. Rather than distorting the image of God in the human person, one who accepts their terminal sufferings with faith in Christ is actually a fuller image of Christ than is one who suicides. The Christian who accepts suffering unto death to give witness to God's love and the sufferings of Christ, rather than distorting the image of Christ or God gives fuller reality to that image.

Battin argues that the early Church had no unified teaching against suicide, and implies that its teachings are defective because of this.[150] This is not true, however, for the episode of Paul and his jailer suggests that there were clear objections raised to suicide in even the earliest days of the Church. But even if this episode is not interpreted *primarily* as a lesson about suicide, it at least shows that the faith and practice of the early community was rather clearly and strongly against suicide.

There were few fully unified and systematic moral teachings in the early Church and most of the early moral teachings of the Church were unrefined at best. The teachings against abortion, infanticide, masturbation, fornication, homosexuality, and murder were immature, undeveloped, and rudimentary in the early Church, and they only came to full development in the Middle Ages, long after the fundamental moral character of the action had been determined. But their primitive character is not a conclusive argument against their validity, for it may well have been that few in the early Church believed that suicide complied adequately with the demands of Gospel life, just as few believed that abortion, adultery, fornication, or infanticide were in harmony with the moral teachings of Jesus. What is more important than the state of the primitive teachings of the Church was the character of the mature teachings of the Church in the Middle Ages. When these teachings reached their full development, they became remarkably consistent in their verdict against suicide. For by the time of Aquinas, not only did he explicitly write against suicide, but so did virtually all other orthodox Catholic moralists and theologians of his era.

Battin claims that classical Catholic teachings encourage suicide more than any other religion because they encourage Catholics to seek martyrdom for the faith.[151] This charge is like saying that a nation that encourages its soldiers to be willing to lay down their lives to defend against an unjust attack encourages suicide. There is a difference between suicide and martyrdom just as there is a difference between suicide and patriotic self-sacrifice. The Catholic church is no more guilty of encouraging suicide by teaching that giving up one's life for the faith is good than is the general of an army who expects the ultimate sacrifice from his soldiers. Her charge is also not fair because Islam has traditionally encouraged what is considered to be martyrdom more than Catholicism, and yet suicide is very rare in Moslem society. Faith, virtuous action, and self-sacrificing love for the good of others brings salvation just as certainly as does laying down one's life for another. Battin implies that it is the deaths of martyrs, rather than the underlying faith, that brings them salvation, but this is not true. Orthodox Catholicism welcomed the intense faith of the martyr, but that did not mean that it encouraged Christians to cause their deaths in testimony to their faith. To confuse this veneration of the faith of the martyrs with endorsement of suicide shows a serious misunderstanding of the teachings and practices of the Church.

Battin also believes that Catholicism promotes suicide by demeaning this life and unduly glorifying the life to come.[152] St. Paul said that he was torn between his desire to be one with Christ in heaven and being one with his brothers and sisters in Christ on this earth (Phil 1:18-26). But this statement by Paul does not mean that he was a Circumcellion and tried to provoke others to kill him, and he did not give any indication that he seriously considered slaying himself to achieve this union with Christ. He longed to be one with Christ, but only as a reward for a life of discipleship, faith, and charity. He sought this so deeply that he would even accept death, but would not bring it on himself to obtain the union. Catholicism traditionally considered the life of an eternal union with God superior to this mortal and troubled life, but it does not teach self-hatred, self-destruction, or rejection of the world through self-killing as legitimate ways of achieving this union.

If it was true that Christianity encouraged suicide because of its overvaluation of the life to come, then why does Luke tell us that Paul attempted to stop the jailer from committing suicide (Acts 16: 25-34)? St. Luke believed St. Paul stopped him because he thought suicide to be seriously sinful and would jeopardize his possible salvation and this is why he urged him to profess faith in Christ. Catholicism encouraged a love for others that imitated Christ's love for us, which is not the same as promoting self-slaying. Catholicism taught humility before God, but it does not promote the transformation of humility into self-hatred or hatred of the world as a way of obtaining salvation.

Battin challenges the oft-made Catholic claim that suicide is wrong because God has dominion over our lives, and she asserts that life is fundamentally our own, which apparently means that the person should be allowed freedom to dispose of life according to their own judgment.[153] Her view implies that we have full and complete control over our lives and that the morality of self-killing is primarily determined by our will and consent. This presumes that consent can convert a morally evil act into one that is morally good and that subjective motives can make acts objectively right or wrong. If this is true, then dueling and gunfighting, which involve consented killing by proxy, would be morally good.[154] From the Catholic perspective, her assertion that we should guide our lives by our own judgment alone is close to Pelagianism. Catholicism is suspicious of claims that we entirely control our lives and are accountable only to ourselves because it respects our human freedom and knows how deeply we need the grace of God to sustain our moral integrity.

Aquinas held that self-slaying was immoral because it was the one action from which one could not repent, for successful completion of suicide eliminates any future possibility of repenting.[155] Battin denies this and believes that there could be an instant for repentance *inter gladium et jugulum*.[156] But one can only repent of self-killing after one has died and not before death has actually been inflicted. Before a suicidal act causes death, one only harms oneself, and one can repent of this, but repentance for suicide can only come after death, which is impossible. One could feel contrition after the dagger entered, which might lessen one's moral guilt, but that would not make the action morally good. Aquinas's position retains its force, for it is not possible to repent of suicide after a suicidal act brings death.

Battin asserts that contemporary sociobiology shows that suicide is now more common in animals than was previously thought, and that one cannot argue anymore that suicide is against nature.[157] Her claim that animals commit acts of suicide that are morally similar to those committed by humans is rather difficult to accept because it implies that animals have free will, intelligence, and insight equal to ours, that their suffering is comparable to ours, and that their suicides can adequately mirror human suicides. If certain animals do commit true suicide (and this is highly debatable), it is in response to instincts and natural forces and not for the reasons that humans do. It is hard to believe that animals exterminate themselves because they believe their suffering or loss of dignity are too great to bear, or that their inability to benefit others has been so great that they feel they must self-execute.

To say that suicide is natural because animals supposedly exterminate themselves presumes that both human and animal natures are subject to the same imperatives of the natural law, the same experiences of suffering, and the same intelligence, insight, and freedom as us, but this has been rejected by the vast majority of natural law theorists.[158] She has unfortunately confused the "law of nature" of ancient and medieval philosophy, which governs natural and nonrational animal nature, with the "natural law," which rules intelligent persons. The natural law's moral norm is a rational law found only in humans and the law of nature governing animals is only analogous to the natural moral law in humans.

Battin denies that suicide is a cowardly act, and she holds that it can often be highly courageous because one is required to tolerate the pain and suffering involved in self-administered death.[159] This is a peculiar claim for it implies that the suicidal person should face severe pain and suffering of artificially induced death rather than face the pain and suffering of allowing death to come naturally. I thought suicide was supposed to bring release from pain and suffering, but here she seems to be saying that it can entail more suffering than not suiciding and is as virtuous as accepting pain and suffering without killing oneself. But if this is true, should not the compassionate person denounce suicide as causing suffering rather than relieving it and should not the morally serious person refrain from it because it risks moral guilt, which is not found in refraining from suicide?

Battin makes this assertion by equating the morality of suicide with that of martyrdom, even though doing this denies that causality makes any substantial difference in the morality of these two kinds of acts. She believes that the cause of a suicide is irrelevant to its moral character, even though it can be crucial to other aspects. Her view that suicide is morally courageous is inconsistent with some of her other opinions. She admits that it is wrong to escape evils if one has a duty not to flee them, and because of this a killer cannot take a hostage to prevent his capture. And she would probably agree that a member of a tank crew could not kill his commander in order to flee a battle. But she holds that one could suicide to escape suffering or loss of dignity and she does not see self-killing to escape suffering as more evil than either of the two above-mentioned actions. She holds that suicide is often legitimate, if not commendable, in order to avoid evils, but she contradicts this elsewhere and says that it would be legitimate to flee evils only if the flight would not involve doing evil in the process.[160]

Her view mistakes true courage, which confronts evils for the sake of good, with false courage, which prompts difficult and evil acts in order to do other evils. To say that suicide can be as virtuous as martyrdom is like saying that the heroin addict who regularly faces the torment of drug withdrawal is as courageous as the laborer who faces the pain, tedium, and monotony of his work to support his family. True courage is only seen when one faces evils for the sake of a valid and authentic good, and not to promote purely self-centered interests. If it is true that death is a greater evil than suffering, it is unreasonable to choose death over further suffering, but if it is less of an evil than continued suffering, the courageous action would be to not commit suicide and to persevere in one's suffering. Despite her assertions, suicide is an act contrary to the virtue of fortitude, which enables one to tolerate trials, suffering, pain, and adversity in order to do what is morally good. Suicide to escape suffering is self-murder, which is unethical and contrary to what the virtue of fortitude requires in the situation.

Battin argues that Catholic teaching against suicide is mistaken when it asserts that suiciding to escape suffering is morally wrong because there are some sorts of suffering that one should avoid and whose presence makes suicide morally good.[161] But this view directly attacks the traditional Catholic teachings about the Paschal Mystery because it entails that Christ's decision not to commit suicide to accept the Cross was morally wrong because his suffering was sufficient to warrant suicide. If ever there was suffering that warranted escape, it was Christ's, but one reason why mainstream Catholicism revered and venerated Christ was because of his refusal to flee it by suiciding. Classical Catholic spiritual theology regarded openness to suffering as a means of spiritual growth.[162] Contemporary developmental psychology sees the childish and immature person as one who seeks to control all aspects of reality, and to force reality to conform to their will.[163] Precisely because they want to escape suffering, immature people attempt to control reality and refuse to be shaped by its demands. And by comparison, the mature are flexible and responsive enough to allow their emotions, beliefs, and attitudes to be shaped and molded by the demands of reality and their relationships with others.

Suffering can bring self-transcendence by breaking down the rigid and introverted ego. In many instances, one is only open to self-transcendence through suffering and fleeing situations of suffering destroy the possibility of spiritual and moral growth. When the ego is rigidly closed in against the demands of reality, suffering shatters its inflexibility to make way for a new and more responsive, open, flexible, and adaptive ego.[164] And when the ego yields to the demands of reality by accepting self-transcending suffering, it develops a potential it previously lacked and becomes more dynamic. Suffering can cause the individual to create and resurrect a new self that is less selfish and egocentric and more dynamic and open to the demands of others. Suffering can serve our spiritual growth by detaching us from self-love so that we can love and obey the call of Christ, even to the point of laying down our life for our friends.[165] Many Christian spiritual writers, nonreligious philosophers, and psychologists have argued that spiritual growth and psychological maturity can only come when one does not flee suffering through self-execution, but only when accepting suffering causes one to strip away egotistical concerns and self-centeredness.[166] One must adopt a "spirit of poverty" to grow in Christ, and only by abandoning egocentricity and self-centeredness can one achieve this self-transcendence.[167] Self-centeredness causes us to shun the demands of charity, justice, discipleship, and Christian moral growth. For most, only by accepting suffering to achieve self-transcendence can we radically challenge and break down this egotism and self-centeredness and live in selflessness and charity.

Christian spiritual writers saw suffering as imposing a "spirit of poverty" that detaches us from our egocentric concerns and allows us to be more other-centered or more focused on Christ.[168] Suffering strips away from the self all of the finite loves that keep the person from making themselves a total self-gift of love to Christ. Death is the ultimate form of suffering because it forces the ego to completely "let go" of existence itself and acknowledge total impoverishment. Suffering to the point of death compels the ego to be totally open to the reality of our own mortality and to neither resist death when it comes nor to invite it before its time. By accepting death when it comes, one possesses a full "spirit of poverty" and "letting go" of existence shows the ultimate in maturity and freedom.

In Christian spirituality, seeking to control and to master death, by making it our servant, forcing it to serve our convenience, and subordinating it to our egotistical concerns is a failure to be open to reality and a failure to be mature spiritually. By being open to death and not trying to control it or make it an event where the person "lets go" life itself as a means of expressing love for Christ death becomes an occasion of spiritual growth. Accepting death and suffering on its own terms is a sign of full psychological integrity, spiritual maturity, and confidence in Christ because it shows an unlimited and unrestricted openness to not just reality, but also to the grace of Christ. Yielding to it and accepting it when so doing would be an act of self-giving and of faith in Christ makes it an occasion for full devotion, faith, and love of God. Battin's claim that suffering should be spurned fails to understand suffering's role in the spiritual life. The claim that Catholic theology promotes suicide as a means of escaping suffering is alien to the traditional Catholic understanding of suffering's prominent role in Christian life. Rather than endorsing self-killing to flee suffering and gain salvation, Catholic spirituality espouses acceptance of even terminal suffering as a means of furthering maturation, charity, love, and fuller union with the sufferings of Christ.[169]

Conclusion

Classical Catholic objections to suicide are cogent and solidly grounded on both Scriptural teachings and the orthodox Christian heritage. The Catholic critique of suicide is rooted in teachings of the Scriptures, even though these teachings are not always immediately evident to the casual reader. The Scriptural critique of suicide became more formal and explicit through time. The philosophical basis of this viewpoint is the classical natural law theory enhanced by the Catholic theory of action and is consistent with the principle that deliberately killing innocent persons is immoral. Traditional Catholicism rejected suicide because it takes seriously the moral principle that innocent human life is not to be willfully destroyed for any reasons whatsoever. It rejected self-killing because it believes close analysis of the reasons for suiciding reveals serious weaknesses and because there are better ways to solve problems than by suicide. Catholic teachings on the morality of suicide have been criticized for being archaic and outdated, but these criticisms have been deeply flawed and have not fully understood the teaching of the Church. Charges that the strong Catholic teachings against suicide actually promote it are not persuasive, as they would imply that condoning suicide is the best way of preventing it. The Catholic teachings against suicide provide significant protection for those who are vulnerable to self-assassination because of their circumstances, and the Church's teachings against suicide are actually works of love as they help to protect these people from themselves.

Notes

1. Battin, M., *Ethical Issues in Suicide*, (Englewood Cliffs, NJ: Prentice Hall Series in the Philosophy of Medicine, 1982).
2. For general studies, see Battin, M., and Mayo, D., Eds., *Suicide the Philosophical Issues* (New York: St. Martin's Press, 1980); Battin, *Ethical Issues in Suicide;* Wallace, S., E., and Eser, A., Eds., *Suicide and Euthanasia: The Rights of Personhood*, (Knoxville, TN: University of Tennessee Press, 1981). Also see the journal *Suicide and Life-Threatening Behavior*.
3. Mayo, D., "Irrational Suicide," in *Suicide: The Philosophical Issues,* 133-36. Mayo fears that acceptance of rational suicide might bring about serious abuses such as the use of suicide to escape difficult situations such as conscription into

the armed services. See his "Contemporary Philosophical Literature on Suicide: A Review," in *Suicide and Ethics*, (New York: Human Sciences Press, 1983), 340.
4. Sullivan, A., "A Constitutional Right to Suicide," in *Suicide, The Philosophical Issues,* 229-54. Sullivan claims that the foundation for this right to self-assassination is found in the penumbra of rights now generally called the right to privacy. These rights include not only the right to refuse medical treatments, but also the right to perform actions that bring no harm to others. But Sullivan discounts the claim that the state has an interest in preventing suicide, an interest that was articulated in *State v. Congdon:* "[T]he basis of the State's police power is the protection of its citizens. This protection must be granted irrespective of the fact that certain individuals may not wish to be saved or protected" (76 N.J. Super. 493, 185 A.2d. 21, 32 [1962]). See also *John F. Kennedy Memorial Hospital v. Heston,* 58 N.J. 576, 279 A.2d 672 (1971).

Herbert Tonne argues that "autoeuthanasia" should replace the term suicide as a way of underscoring it as a means of expressing autonomy, "Suicide: Is it Autoeuthanasia?" *Humanist*, 29 (July/August 1979), 44-45. I would suggest that suicide is more accurately described as self-execution, self-assassination, self-killing, reflexive killing, self-extermination, or getting rid of oneself.
5. Francis, L., P., "Assisting Suicide: A Problem for the Criminal Law," in *Suicide: The Philosophical Issues,* 254-66.
6. Barrington affirms that the desire for death is a legitimate desire and that it should not be suppressed. But if this is a legitimate desire, what sort of desire would not be a legitimate desire? The desire for pleasure is a legitimate desire, but most would hold that it is illegitimate to express it as a desire for crack cocaine. What of the masochist, who inflicts grave bodily harm on himself or herself? Individuals with desires such as these often impose grave burdens on our health care system and great stress on others. And we must ask if these are not desires that should be limited because of the burdens they impose on others. Mary Rose Barrington, "Apologia for Suicide," ibid., 90-103.
7. Ibid., 98-102.
8. Feinberg, J., "Suicide and the Inalienable Right to Life," in *Suicide: The Philosophical Issues,* 223-28.
9. Ibid., 226-27.
10. Ibid.
11. Williams, G., "The Right to Commit Suicide," *Medico-Legal Journal* 41 (1973): 26-29. Thomas Szasz, "The Ethics of Suicide," in *Suicide: The Philosophical Issues,* 195-97.
12. See Lebacqz K., and Engelhardt, T., "Suicide and Covenant," ibid., 84-88. "Thus, there is nothing in principle morally wrong with suicide," 85.
13. This is not an unprecedented situation, for a Colorado judge allowed Hector Rodas to starve himself to death despite the fact that he had two small children.
14. Lebacqz, K., and Engelhardt, T., "Suicide and Covenant," "Respect for persons as free moral agents should entail that they be allowed to choose that which endows their lives with meaning as long as such choice will not seriously affect the freedoms of others or violate prior agreements between persons," ibid., 84-85.
15. Ibid., 87:

> Viewed within the perspective of justice, therefore, there are at least three instances in which suicide may be right: Those in which *prima facie* obligations of covenant-fidelity cease to exist, those in which the suicide fulfills *prima facie* obligations of covenant-fidelity, and those in which

obligations of covenant-fidelity are superseded by demands of justice on a larger scale.

16. Slater, E., "Choosing the Time to Die," in *Suicide: The Philosophical Issues,* 204.

17. Ibid., 202.

18. Wood, D., "Suicide as an Instrument and Expression," in *Suicide: The Philosophical Issues,* 152-53.

19. Breger, M., "Law, Technology and Public Policy: Suicide and Euthanasia," in *Life Span: Values and Life-Extending Technologies,* Ed. by Veatch, R., (San Francisco: Harper and Row, 1979), 248-72. In light of the U. S. Supreme Court decision in *Cruzan v. Missouri,* it is less likely that laws against suicide will quickly be overturned in this country.

21. Weiss, R., "Developmental Biology: Dorian Gray Mice," *Nature* (1 April 1993): 411. In both the carp and in the Galapagos turtle, researchers have noted that these animals do not stop growing after they attain sexual maturity and they show less signs of aging than do other creatures.

22. Outka, G., "Social Justice and Equal Access to Health Care," *The Journal of Religious Ethics,* 2 (Spring 1974): 11-32.

23. Callahan, D., *Setting Limits: Medical Goals in an Aging Society,* (New York: Simon & Schuster, 1987). For a series of articles rebutting Callahan's claims, see Bradley, G., and Barry, R., Eds., *Set No Limits,* (Champaign-Urbana: University of Illinois Press, 1991).

24. See Boyle, J., "The Concept of Health and the Right to Health Care," *Social Thought* 3 (Summer 1977): 5-17.

24. Beauchamp T., and Childress, J., *Principles of Biomedical Ethics* (New York: Oxford University Press, 1979), 87-94. Fletcher, J., "In Defense of Suicide," in Wallace, S.E., and Eser, A., Eds., *Suicide and Euthanasia: The Rights of Personhood,* 39. Fletcher shares with Beauchamp and Childress the view that suicide is morally justifiable to the extent that it "maximizes human well-being," ibid.

25. Beauchamp, T., and Childress, J., *Principles,* 87-94.

26. See Mayo, D., and Battin, M., *Suicide: The Philosophical Issues,* 331.

27. Fletcher, J., "In Defense of Suicide."

28. Kohl, M., "Voluntary Death and Meaningless Existence," in Kohl, M., *Infanticide and the Value of Life,* (Buffalo: Prometheus Books, 1978), 208. Kohl differs from many other advocates of suicide because he does not hold suicide to be a fundamental human right, but only a *prima facie* right. "This *prima facie* right to life involves the right under the proper conditions to die how, when, and where we choose or would choose if we were capable of doing so," 209.

29. Ibid. Unlike Engelhardt and Lebacqz, Kohl denies that autonomy is the foundation of the right to suicide. He rejects this because it would permit suicide with inadequate knowledge and because it fails to distinguish between "experiment and preferable means of problem solving," 208. He argues that this right is to be based on utilitarian considerations alone.

30. See Mayo, D., "Contemporary Philosophical Literature on Suicide: A Review," in Battin, M., and Maris, R., *Suicide and Ethics,* (New York: Human Sciences Press, 1983), 332; Battin, M., "Manipulated Suicide," in *Suicide: The Philosophical Issues*. Battin accepts the morality and rationality of suicide, but she warns that "I think we must do so with a clear-sighted view of the moral quicksand into which this notion threatens to lead us: perhaps then we may discover a path around" (p. 179).

31. Battin, M., "Suicide: A Fundamental Human Right," in *Suicide: The Philosophical Issues,* 267-85.
32. Ibid.
33. Such a principle would also bias judgments about women who commit suicide, for they usually kill themselves by drug overdoses while men most often kill themselves by more violent actions such as shooting. If we hold that "nonviolent" methods of suicide are more permissible, we will inadvertently be condoning more suicides by women.
34. See Mayo, D., "Contemporary Philosophical Literature on Suicide: A Review," 332.
35. Ibid., 332. What she means by "nonviolent" is not entirely clear, for she holds that shooting oneself could be nonviolent. She implies that a suicide is nonviolent if it does not cause undue distress in others. But this is problematic, for this defines the violence of an action in terms of the reaction of third parties and not by the nature of the action. It is difficult for one to predict how others will react to one's suicide, and it also limits legitimate suicides to those about which others agree. If this is true, it would seem to call into question whether suicide is a "fundamental human right," as no other rights of this nature seem to be so limited. This qualification ignores claims of contemporary suicidologists that suicides are dyadic and aim at manipulating or coercing another into some action or forbearance. If this is true, virtually all suicides would be excluded because virtually all would be malicious in some form or other. A further problem is that there might well be nothing such as a "nonhateful" suicide. And if suicide is a fundamental human right, whether it is done out of love or hate should not make any difference. And if contemporary suicidologists are correct and all suicides are "dyadic" and attempts to modify another's behavior, all suicides might well fall into the class of "hateful" self-killings.
36. If self-killing were to be considered a fundamental human right, then selling oneself into slavery could be a fundamental human right, particularly if one could enhance one's dignity by saving one's family from destitution by doing this.
37. Battin, M., *Ethical Issues in Suicide,* 146-52.
38. For an account of his death, see Holland, F., "Suicide," in *Talk from God,* Royal Institute of Philosophy Lectures, 2, 1967-68 (London: Macmillan, 1969), reprinted in Rachels, J., *Moral Problems,* (New York: Harper and Row, 1971), 394.
39. See Battin, M., *Suicide: The Philosophical Issues,* 166-67.
40. Stell, L., "Dueling and the Right to Life," *Ethics,* 90 (October 1979): 7-26.
41. See Mayo, D., "Contemporary Philosophical Literature on Suicide: A Review," 340. This position, while generally on target, fundamentally understates the case, for it fails to see that suicide is inherently uncontrollable.
42. Mayo, D., "Irrational Suicide," in *Suicide: The Philosophical Issues,* 134.
43. Battin, M., "Manipulated Suicide," in *Suicide: The Philosophical Issues,* 177-78.
44. Ibid., 178. She argues that this should be done because it would be a greater abuse of these persons to force people who have good reason to die to continue living than to tolerate their deaths. But this is a highly debatable point. Who is to say that the irreparable damage done to a person manipulated into suicide might not be worse? If manipulated suicide was permitted, it would not be possible to repair the damage done, and this might be a greater injustice than prohibiting some from suiciding.

45. Baelz, P. R., "Suicide: Some Theological Reflections," in *Suicide: The Philosophical Issues,* 71-83.
46. Barrington, M. R., "Apologia for Suicide," in *Suicide: The Philosophical Issues,* 95.
47. Wood, D., "Suicide as an Instrument and Expression," in *Suicide: The Philosophical Issues,* 153.
48. See Mayo, D., "Irrational Suicide," 133-38; and Battin, M., "Manipulated Suicide," in *Suicide: The Philosophical Issues,* 169-83.
49. See Mayo, D., "Contemporary Philosophical Literature on Suicide: A Review," 338-41. Erwin Ringel argues in favor of the "slippery slope" by noting that "the slightest deviation from this principle–that *every* human life is important, and so every human life is to be saved–would not only undermine the entire idea of suicide prevention: it would be . . .'that first step from humanity to bestiality'". ("Suicide Prevention and the Value of Human Life," 208).
50. As a verification of this, see Tooley, M., "Abortion and Infanticide," in *The Rights and Wrongs of Abortion,* Ed. Thomson, J. J., (Princeton: Princeton University Press, 1974), 52-85. In this article, Tooley argues that the differences between a late-term unborn child and a newly born infant are so insignificant that principles allowing abortion would allow infanticide in some cases. He uses moral justifications of abortion to justify infanticide of some newborns.
51. Battin, M., "Manipulated Suicide," in Mayo, D., *Suicide: The Philosophical Issues,* 169-83.
52. Steele, W. W., and Hill, B. B., "A Plea for a Legal Right to Die," *Oklahoma Law Review,* 29 (Spring 1975): 328-48.
53. Wallace, S. E., "The Right to Live and the Right to Die," in Wallace, S. E., and Eser, E., *Suicide and Euthanasia: The Rights of Personhood,* 83.
54. Ringel, E., "Suicide Prevention and the Value of Human Life," in *Suicide: The Philosophical Issues,* 205-11.
55. Bogen, J., "Suicide and Virtue," in *Suicide: The Philosophical Issues,* 290.
56. Ibid., 290.
57. Probably more than any other virtue, fortitude, patience, and perseverance denote the moral character of a person. Virtues such as justice and temperance are rather common virtues, but fortitude and perseverance are shown to their fullest extent only in situations of grave danger, risk, or harm. One can only know if one has those virtues by facing situations of suffering and trial and by not fleeing them. To commit suicide in those situations would be to fail to test one's strength and the scope of one's virtues.
58. Peretz, D., "The Illusion of 'Rational Suicide'" (Book review of *Suicide: The Philosophical Issues*) *Hastings Center Report,* 11, December 1981: 40-42.
59. Hendin, R., *Suicide in America* (New York: W. W. Norton, 1982).
60. O'Donnell, T., *Medicine and Christian Morality,* (New York: Alba House, 1975), 26.
61. This view would be in accord with the classical Roman Catholic doctrines of the double effect and of indirectly intentional action. In the case of the soldier who jumps on a live hand grenade to save his friends, this principle would hold that the directly intended action was the smothering of the grenade and the good effects derived from that action. The unintended effect is the death of the soldier and this effect is neither intended nor is it an effect that enhances the morality of the act in Roman Catholic theory. See Haring, B., *The Law of Christ,* vol. 3 (Paramus, NJ: Newman, 1966), 36.

62. He criticizes the notion of rational suicide by arguing that it is irrational to decide for something of which no one has ever had any experience of whatsoever. See Devine, P., "On Choosing Death," *Suicide: The Philosophical Issues,* 138-44.

Approaching from the other side of the issue, Eliot Slater criticizes the notion of rationality and argues that it should not be used to deprive the mentally ill of opportunities to end their lives. See "Choosing the Time to Die," ibid., 199-205. And Margaret Battin notes that there are difficulties with asserting that suicide can be rational. But none of these authors assert that the notion of "rational" self-killing could be a culturally, historically, and sociologically conditioned concept, and the failure to recognize this diminishes the effectiveness of their arguments in behalf of suicide.

63. Ibid., 29.

64. Battin, M., *Suicide: The Philosophical Issues,* 38.

65. In primitive Israelite law, the avenger, or *go'el* was required to avenge injury, harm, or death upon the one who appointed him. This primitive law was instituted to protect whole groups who could be destroyed if anyone thought the revenge meted out to them was unjust. This primitive law permitted relatives to avenge an injury or harm done, and it forbade killing to gain revenge, and one who intentionally killed another was to be handed over to the avenger by the city fathers. It distinguished accidental killing from deliberate homicide, and it allowed accidental killers to flee to a city of refuge where they could be spared as long as they did not return.

66. Dt 19:1-13; Nm 35:10-34. Battin, M., *Ethical Issues in Suicide,* 39-49.

67. See McKenzie, J., *Dictionary of the Bible,* (Milwaukee: Bruce, 1965), 767. In He 11:32 Samson was listed among the great men and women of the Old Testament who, although they suffered grave moral faults, were saved by faith. Included in this list were Gideon, who slew his daughter and Rahab the harlot. They were heroes of the Old Testament and they showed that God could accomplish his purposes through them despite their sinfulness and lack of moral rectitude. McKenzie's view of Samson's death is unclear, for he may not have thought Samson committed suicide and thus did not see any moral problem in the death of this giant, or he may have seen it as a grave fault for which Samson should have been condemned. But it is difficult to believe that this author would have condoned his death if it was believed to be suicidal.

68. See McGowan, J., "Jonah," in *The Jerome Biblical Commentary,* (Englewood Cliffs, NJ: Prentice-Hall, 1968), 633-37.

70. Dumm, D., "Tobit," in *The Jerome Biblical Commentary,* 620.

70. McKenzie, J., *Dictionary of the Bible,* 777.

71. See Battin, M., *Ethical Issues in Suicide,* 30. Battin notes that Zimri and Abimilech also committed suicide and they did so in payment for their sins. She fails to see, however, that these Old Testament figures share a deeply rooted sinfulness in common that drives them to self-destruction.

72. There are different accounts of the death of Judas. Matthew claims Judas hanged himself (Mt 27:3-10), though this is the only account in the Gospels of his death. Acts of the Apostles suggests that he fell from a window, and there is no hint of suicide. Papias held that he swelled to such monstrous proportions that he could no longer pass where a horse and cart could easily drive through. See Lake, K., "The Twelve and the Apostles," in *The Beginnings of Christianity,* vol. 5 (London: 1933), 37-59.

73. Alvarez interprets the silence of Matthew over the suicide of Judas to mean that he approved of the suicide as an atonement for his sins. This is an eccentric opinion that would be quite out of character for the Evangelist and inconsistent with the views of such suicides expressed elsewhere in Scripture.
74. In Jn 13:27, John stated that Satan entered into Judas and Judas spoke in a manner that was similar to what was said in Mk 5:12 and Lk 8:30. Raymond Brown reminds us that in the Johannine perspective, Judas was one of those who "preferred darkness to light because their deeds were evil" and he notes that Satan formally entered the drama at the Last Supper in the person of Judas. See Brown, R. E., *The Gospel According to John,* vol. 2 (New York: Doubleday, 1970), 579.
75. The only group to venerate Judas was the Gnostic sect of the Cainites who regarded the God of the Old Testament as the cause of all evil in the world. See Cross, F., *The Oxford Dictionary of Church History,* (Oxford University Press: New York, 1970), "Cainites," 219.
76. McKenzie, J., *Dictionary,* 463.
77. Battin, M., "Ethical Issues in Suicide," 33. She speaks mostly of Christianity in general, but the assertions she disputes are predominately those of Catholicism, as these arguments have been articulated in their most complete form by the Catholic authors.
78. Maloney, G., *Man: The Divine Icon,* (Pecos, New Mexico: Dove, 1973), 164-65.
79. Lecky, W., *A History of European Morals,* vol. 1 (New York: Appleton, 1869), vol. 2, 47-48, 65.
80. Schweitzer, A., *Civilization and Ethics,* Tr. by Russell, L., and Campion, C. T., (London: Black, 1949),
81. Pius XI, *Acta Apostolici Sedis,* 22, (1930), 553-54.
82. Pius declared that the lives of both the mother and child "are equally sacred and no one, not even public authority, can ever have the right to destroy them." Pius would only attribute this sanctity to persons and not to all life as would Schweitzer.
83. Maloney, G., *Man: The Divine Icon,* 99-103.
84. See Sullivan, J., *The Image of God,* (Dubuque, IA: Priory Press, 1963), 44-46. Virtually all of the pre-Nicene and post-Nicene fathers located the image either in the mind or in some other noncorporeal aspect of the human being.
85. See Maloney, G., *Man: The Divine Icon,* 70; Ramsey, P., *Basic Christian Ethics,* (Chicago: University of Chicago Press), 258.
86. Ibid.
87. Gregory of Nyssa wrote the following:

> For He who made man for the participation of His own peculiar good and incorporated in him the instincts for all that was excellent, in order that his desire might be carried forward by a corresponding movement in each case to its own like, would never have deprived him of that most excellent and precious of all goods; I mean the gift implied in being his own master and having a free will. For if necessity in any way was the master of the life of man, the 'image' would have been falsified in that particular part by being estranged, owing to this unlikeness to its archetype.

(*De Oratione Catechetica Magna,* chap. 5, *LNPF,* 479, Tr. by Maloney, G., 139-40)

88. Maloney says the following:

> Gregory seems to imply that the mortal, material element of man, in which part the passions and sex are radicated, was an addition to the intended nature of man. 'The grace of the resurrection is the restoration of fallen man to his primitive state.' Yet in other places, as has been already suggested, Gregory considers the material body, distinguished by being of one or the other sex, as God's fully willed and created man, through his foreknowledge of man's sins:
>
> > But as He perceived in our created nature the bias towards evil, and the fact that after its voluntary fall from equality with the angels it would acquire a fellowship with the lower nature, He mingled, for this reason, with His own image, an element of the irrational.
>
> God's plan provided that man, with a mutable nature, would cooperate in his own liberation. But this process of 'return' to man's ideal situation of immortality and incorruptibility was not entirely within man's own power.

Maloney, G., *Man: The Divine Icon*, (p. 148)

89. Ibid., 140-41.

90. Ibid.,

> One who regards only the dissolution of the body is greatly disturbed and makes it a hardship that this life of ours should be dissolved by death; it is, he says, the extremity of evil that our being should be quenched by this condition of mortality. Let him, then, observe through this gloomy prospect the excess of divine benevolence. . . . Now since by a motion of our self-will we contracted a fellowship with evil . . . falling away from that blessedness which is involved in the thought of passionlessness, for we have been viciously transformed--for this reason, man, like some earthen potsherd is resolved again into the dust of the ground, in order to secure that he may part with the soul which he has now contracted, and that he may, through the resurrection, be reformed anew after the original pattern; at least if in this life he has preserved what belongs to that image. (*De Oratione Cathech. Magna,* 7, *LNPF,* 405)

91. Cyril of Alexandria, *Commentary on the Gospel of John*, 3 vols., Ed. by Pusey, P. E., (Oxford, 1872), III, 316,

> Our transformation will not be a transfer into some other nature . . . for we shall be what we are, that is, men—but we shall be incomparably better. The point is this, we shall be incorruptible and imperishable, and besides this we shall have been glorified.

92. Sullivan, J., *The Image of God*, 8.

93. Maloney, G., *Man: The Divine Icon*, P. 73.

94. *On the Incarnation*, Ed. Schaff, P., and Wade, H., in *A Select Library of Nicene and Post-Nicene Fathers of the Christian Church,* 2d series, vol. 4, 4. (Grand Rapids: Eerdmans, 1957). "For man is by nature mortal, inasmuch as he is made out of what is not; but by reason of His likeness to Him that is (and if he still preserved this likeness by keeping Him in his knowledge) he would stay his natural corruption and remain incorrupt"

95. Ibid.

96. Ibid., 98

97. *De Trinitate,* XV, 20, 39:

> We have done our best to admonish those who seek a reason for such things to perceive the invisible things of him as they are able through the things that are made, and especially through the rational or intellectual creature

which is made in the image of God; through which they may see, as in a mirror, if they can and as far as they can the Trinity of God in our memory, understanding and will.

98. Sullivan, J., *The Image of God*, 48.
99. Ibid., 48.
100. Augustine, *On the Trinity*, Ed. by Schaff, P., (Grand Rapids: Eerdmans, 1956), XII, 7, 12 (BAC 5:670)
101. *On the Trinity*, XV, 1, 1 (BAC 5:828):

[W]e have now arrived at the image of God in man, in that wherein he excels the other animals, that is by reason or understanding, and whatever else can be said of the rational or intellectual soul (*anima*) that pertains to what is called the mens or animus. For by this name some writers . . . distinguish that which excels in man, and is not in the beast, from the soul (*anima*) which is in the beast as well.

102. Ibid., XII, 7, 12 (BAC 5:670).
103. See Sullivan, J., *The Image of God*, 48.
104. Aquinas, T., *Commentarius in Libros Sententiarum,* Ed. by Mandonnet, P., (Paris: Cerf, 1929), Bk. II, d.16, a. 4.
105. *I Sent.*, d.28, q.2, a.1.
106. Aquinas, T., *Summa Theologica,* Tr. by English Dominican Province of the Order of Preachers, (New York: Benzinger, 1947), I, q. 93, a. 2.
107. Ibid., I, q. 93, a. 1. Also see *I, Sent.* d. 28, q. 2, a. 1.
108. Aquinas, T., *I, Sent.,* d. 16, a.1, a.3; *Summa Theologica.,* I, q. 93, a.3.
109. Original sin destroyed the immediate possibility of obtaining immortality, but it did not destroy the remote possibility of gaining it through the redemptive actions of Christ.
110. The theological foundation of the teachings against suicide is the doctrine that innocent human life is created in the image of God. Because the human person, in contrast to all other living beings in the material universe, is a spiritual creature possessing intelligence, freedom, the capacity for love, and the capacity for moral life, the person shares in, images, and mirrors the divine nature. This is the case because the human person is a personal being who is by nature intelligent, good, free, loving, spiritual, and the human person alone reflects these qualities in the material order. By reason of its free, spiritual, and intelligent nature, the human person participates in the life of God in a certain limited, but specific, fashion. There is a certain proximity and closeness between God and persons, which makes a lethal attack on a person a remote attack on God himself.

Made in the image of God, the human person participates in a limited way in the life and existence of God since we mirror his nature. Because of this enduring image of God's nature in our own human nature, the Catholic theological tradition has held that God could take on human nature and his grace can dwell in us, enabling us to share more fully in his life. The image of God was not destroyed by Original Sin, for it is intrinsic to our nature, and the loss of the use of some human powers does not destroy the sacredness and value of the human being. To destroy an innocent life is to indirectly and remotely attack the highest work of creation, the work that most perfectly represents God in creation, and is analogous to attacking a nation's flag, for both are images of a higher and greater reality. The Catholic tradition has considered suicide wrong because it is precisely such an attack.

111. Augustine, *The City of God,* Book 1, chap. 17, Tr. and ed. by Bettenson, H., and Knowles, D., (New York: Penguin, 1972), 27.
112. Augustine, Bk I, Ch. 20. "If this is so, it remains that we take the command 'You shall not kill' as applying to human beings, that is, other persons and oneself. For to kill oneself is to kill a human being."
113. Ibid., chap. 1, Book 20, 31.
114. Ibid., chap. 23.
115. Ibid., chap. 22.
116. Ibid., chap. 22. In Cato and other noble Romans who suicided to preserve honor and dignity, Augustine found "weakness in a mind which cannot bear physical oppression, or the stupid opinion of the mob."
117. Ibid., chap. 22.
118. Ibid., chap. 26. In this condemnation, Augustine is striking at two of the most common motives for suicide: desire for a better life, and guilt ostensibly over the wrongful actions of others, but more probably and realistically, over one's own guilt.
119. Ibid., chap. 24.
120. Ibid., chap. 21.
121. The most famous of these cases was that of Pelagia who was abducted by soldiers, but before they ravished her, she excused herself and went to her room where she threw herself from her window to escape being attacked. Augustine condemned this even though it was approved by Jerome. See *De Virg.*, 3, 7; *Ep.*, 37.
122. Alvarez attributes rejection of suicide to preserve one's virginity by the early Church to Augustine's authority. Augustine argued that if one killed oneself to atone for one's sins, one was usurping the authority of the Church and the state. And if one suicided while innocent and to avoid sin, one was putting blood on one's hands, which was wrong. And Augustine considered suicide worse than other sins because one could not repent of it. See Alvarez, A. "The Background," 27.
123. Augustine, *The City of God*, Bk. I, Chs. 18, 25, 26.
124. Ibid., chap. 19.
125. Ibid., chap. 26.
126. Ibid., chap. 27.
127. Ibid., chap. 27.
128. Ibid., chap. 17.
129. Ibid., chap. 27.
130. Brown, P., *Augustine of Hippo*, (Berkeley: California, 1969), 213-24.
131. The most interesting exception is the person reported by Fedden in the Roman empire who suicided to keep his family from going into debt, for this is a very peculiar and questionably ethical form of charitable suicide. The cancer patient who suicides to prevent his children from being driven into penury could properly be described as an altruistic suicide. These individuals are different from the martyr because they were the agents through whom death comes, unlike the martyr who allows death to brought on him to achieve an altruistic goal. These are true suicides and are not to be confused with one who refuses medical treatment to save their family from radical expense.
132. Aquinas, T., *Summa Theologica*, II-II, Q. 64, a. 5.
133. Ibid., II-II, Q. 141, Art. 4, Resp.
134. Ibid., II-II, Q. 58, Art. 1, Resp.
135. Ibid., II-II, Q. 58, Art. 1, Resp.

136. Ibid., II-II, Q. 20, Art. 4, Resp. An action is against hope if the person brings a greater evil on himself or herself than the evil they are seeking to avoid. Suicide is thus contrary to hope because in a suicidal act, the person commits a greater evil than what is feared and avoided, and for this reason the common morality would argue against it.
137. Aquinas holds that suicide is against the virtue of faith because it is against love. And as faith is a species of love (Ibid., II-II, Q. 4, art. 3), suicide would also be against faith. Charity is the "form" of faith, as it is of all the virtues, and an act against charity as suicide is would also be contrary to faith.
138. Ibid., II-II, Q. 64, Art. 5, Resp. Aquinas holds that every creature loves itself, and that suicide is contrary not only to this natural love of self but also to charity and the love with which a person is required to show to himself or herself.
139. Ibid., I-II, 94. Q. 2. For an excellent study of the development of natural theory from the ancients to contemporary times, see Crowe, M. B., *The Changing Profile of the Natural Law*, (The Hague: Martinus Nijhoff, 1977).
140. Davis, H., *Moral and Pastoral Theology,* vol. 2 (London: Sheed & Ward, 1956), 142.
141. Koch, A. and Preuss, A., *A Handbook of Moral Theology,* vol. 2 (St. Louis: B. Herder, 1921), 76.
142. O'Donnell, T., *Medicine and Morals*, 45.
143. Sacred Congregation for the Doctrine of the Faith, June 26, 1980 *Declaration on Euthanasia*, Para. 4, in McCarthy, D., and Moraczewski, A., *Moral Responsibility in Prolonging Life Decisions*, (St. Louis: Pope John Center, 1981), 290-297.
144. Battin, M., *Ethical Issues in Suicide,* 66-67.
145. Generally on this issue, see my "Stones and Streetcars: A Clarification of the Principle of the Double Effect," *Irish Theological Quarterly*, 48 (1981): 127-36.
146. Battin, M., *Ethical Issues in Suicide,* 33-48.
147. Ibid., 42-45.
148. Ibid., 46-47.
149. Catholic theology holds that the image of God was not destroyed by original sin. Even though the *similitudo Dei* was obliterated by this sin, it was restored by Christ. This position has been endorsed by most of the Fathers, and the only real discussion among them was where the *imago Dei* was to be found. Only in Protestant theology does one find original sin utterly destroying the *imago Dei,* which is a position strongly defended by Karl Barth and Emil Brunner. See Sullivan, J., *The Image of God;* and Cross, F., *The Oxford Dictionary of Church History,* "Imago Dei," 693.
150. Battin, M., *Ethical Issues in Suicide,* 33.
151. Ibid., 29, 71-75.
152. Battin, M., *Ethical Issues in Suicide,* 65. The more flamboyant forms of Christianity might put it this way:

> [I]n this carnal, corrupt world, the soul is shackled to the lusts of an insatiate body; in contrast, the next world promises luminous, clarified existence, in which the soul, cleansed and purified of its contaminating association with the body is finally free.

Battin's critique of this position is not fully persuasive, however, for she admits in the next sentence that "this view is not orthodox."
153. Battin, M., *Suicide: The Philosophical Issues,* 42.

154. Dueling is morally akin to suicide because the those aggrieved as a result of a duel were not granted any rights of restitution which implies they consented to being killed if they could not kill their opponent first.

155. Aquinas, T., *Summa Theologica*, II-II, Q. 64, A. 5.

156. Battin, M., *Suicide: The Philosophical Issues,* 52-53.

157. Battin, M., *Ethical Issues in Suicide,* 53-57. Battin, like David Hume, seems to presume that the natural law is the basis of Catholic teaching against suicide, while I have shown that the foundation of its objection is the moral teaching against the taking of innocent life, and the natural law argument is secondary to that teaching. Notice that she does not say that "animal suicide" justifies deliberate taking of innocent human life.

158. See May, W. E., "The Natural Law and Objective Morality: A Thomistic Perspective," in *Principles of Catholic Moral Life,* (Chicago: Franciscan Herald, 1980), 163. May deals with this confusion between the law of nature governing animals and the natural law determining human moral standards:

> It is very important to understand St. Thomas here, who is surely *not* saying that the natural law, properly and formally as law, is something infrarational, an instinct that humanity shares with other animals, brute animal facticity. For he has stressed in the body of the article that the natural law as such pertains only to human beings. In brutes there is no natural law, only a natural *aestimatio,* a power or force of nature impelling them to act in ways appropriate to achieve their ends.

159. Battin, M., *Suicide: The Philosophical Issues,* 58-59.

160. Ibid., 60.

161. Ibid., 57-62.

162. See Gammache, R., "Suffering Adult Development", (Ph.D. diss., Urbana, University of Illinois, 1985), 89-92. Gammache argues that, among other responses to crises and suffering, the person must be able to let go of life itself in order to mature and grow.

163. Delany, S., *Married Saints*, (Freeport, NY: Books for Libraries Press, 1969), 37.

164. See Gammache, R., "Suffering Adult Development," chaps. 1 and 2.

165. Peck, S., *The Road Less Travelled*, (New York: Simon and Schuster, 1979).

166. Egan, H. D., *Christian Mysticism: The Future of a Tradition* (New York: Pueblo, 1984), 10-11. Also see Cassell, E. J., "The Nature of Suffering and the Goals of Medicine," *New England Journal of Medicine*, No. 306, Vol. 11, 639-45.

167. For example, see Tanquery, A., *The Spiritual Life: A Treatise on Ascetical and Mystical Theology*, (Tournai, Belgium, 1930); Golan, N., *Passing Through Transitions: A Guide for Practitioners*, (New York: Free Press, 1980), 12.

168. Gammache, R., "Suffering Adult Development," 79.

169. Ibid., 28-30. Gammache illustrates this well in his discussion of Marsha Norman's play "Night Mother," which describes the development of the ego of a woman who is suffering from terminal illness, public humiliation, and loss of a loved one. The play relates how a young woman who is suffering from epilepsy tells her mother of her plans to commit suicide because her husband has abandoned her and her son who has become a thief, and perhaps worse. In his commentary on this play, John Kroll noted the following:

> This woman tells her mother that 'I'm tired, hurt, sad, I feel used, I'm not having a particularly good time,' says Jessie. 'And there's no reason to think it won't get worse.' It's not the state of the world that bothers her, its not being abandoned by her husband or the disaster of her son that has

driven her to her decision. 'It's my own self, someone I waited for who never came. *I'm* what I was waiting for. It's *me* that might have made a difference to me.' (J. Kroll, "Night Mother," *Newsweek* [3 January 1983]: 42)

In such a situation, it is the self that is facing destruction because it was "the lack of a future, the lack of a sense of self capable of facing any more hurt, and the lack of joy which suggested life has nothing to offer but suffering" (Gammache, "Suffering Adult Development," 21). Also see Pope John Paul II, *Salfivici Doloris: On the Christian Meaning of Human Suffering,* Apostolic Letter, 11 February 1984 (Washington, DC: U. S. Catholic Conference, 1984).

5

The Rationality of Suicide

Can the act of self-killing be a rational act? Is reflexive killing the most rational action in a given circumstance or situation? Are there circumstances in which various evils such as suffering are so great or the loss of dignity so profound that not killing oneself would be irrational? It has been a commonplace belief in much contemporary medical and ethical literature that suicide is not a rational act and that any attempt to inflict lethal harm on oneself is an irrational decision, probably immoral, and not to be condoned by either medicine or morality.[1] However, in recent years, a significant body of literature has developed which argues that suicide is not only rational and moral in some instances, but is also the most rational action that can be taken by some individuals and in some circumstances. More and more philosophers, ethicists, suicidologists, and physicians are now vigorously arguing that suicide is morally permissible in some cases, and that it is the recommended action in some difficult and trying instances. Because of these developments, it is necessary to review claims that suicide may not only be a rational action, but also the most rational action possible in some circumstances.

Suicide as a Rational Act

The Hemlock Society claims that suicide can be a rational action in some instances because it ends profound, needless suffering.[2] It asserts that suffering that ends only in death is without value, is an evil, and is to be escaped if possible, and when suffering reaches this point, suicide can be rational. For Hemlock, refraining from reflexively lethal measures to be freed from such suffering is irrational, and possibly immoral because of the unnecessary suffering that results.

But deciding what constitutes rationality in the context of suicide is quite complicated. Most philosophers have argued that rationality means efficiently and expeditiously achieving one's own goals and interests, whatever they might be.[3] Generally, proponents of suicide argue that persons are rational when they realistically consider alternatives and question how it will realize human goals or fundamental interests and then choose the means that will enable them to realize those goals or interests.[4] No matter how moral or immoral an action might be, suicide could be considered rational if it facilitated the attainment of goals and the fulfillment of one's interests, irrespective of their nature. The difficulty with such a view is that it makes it theoretically possible for virtually any action to be rational as long as it contributes to the realization of some subjectively defined goal regarded as being in one's interests.

David Daube claims that it is difficult to affirm the rationality of suicide because of our cultural bias against it, and the fact that other societies see it as a rational action causes Daube to urge further examination of our attitudes about suicide.[5] Japanese society, for example, traditionally allowed suicide and even admired it in some instances. But it has had a much longer history of permitting suicide than Western cultures. It traditionally regarded suicide as more of a self-punitive act required to maintain moral integrity and preserve honor than as an analgesic act undertaken to escape suffering or pain, and suicide acquired this character because it performed a much different social and religious function in Japan than elsewhere. To contend that we should endorse suicide as do the Japanese is naive because we would do so without endorsing the moral, social, cultural, and religious environment of Japan, which would severely distort the practice of suicide. Suicide is more of a social, religious, and moral necessity in traditional Japanese society than in the West because their concepts of honor are narrower and more brittle than ours, and Shinto concepts of reconciliation, mercy, and forgiveness are less developed than they are in Western society and religion. Even though suicide has acquired a moral and religious respectability in Japanese religion and society, this feature is generally absent in Western suicidal practices, and they have a great deal of difficulty preventing suicide partly because of this.[6] Suicide to escape shame or protect honor became a social necessity in Japanese culture because it lacked integrated notions of forgiveness and reconciliation similar to those found in Western cultures. For our culture to become more tolerant of suicide, it would have to adopt attitudes of duty, shame, forgiveness, mercy, and honor similar to those of the Japanese, and also give suicide the moral and religious quality and respectability necessary to control it. And doing this might well force us to reevaluate the role of many critical, long-standing Western values such as mercy, charity, forgiveness, and reconciliation in Western culture and religion.

Endorsing suicide practices similar to those of the Japanese could also require some compromises of Western notions of individual autonomy and rights that are not deeply imbedded in the Japanese social and religious traditions. While it is true that strictly self-sacrificial acts could confirm the honor and dignity of a person, it is not evident that acts of self-assassination necessarily preserve or enhance one's honor or dignity. Authentic acts of self-sacrifice can overcome the shame attached to cowardice, but it is not evident that reflexive killing can do this. And if suicide would not guarantee this, it would be irrational to attempt it for this purpose. Daube's contention that we should examine our "biases" is correct, and such an examination must be thorough and cautious. We must ask if the "prejudices" informing our approach to suicide are illegitimate "biases" or whether they are grounded on intelligent understanding of the difference between morally legitimate and illegitimate forms of killing. One must know if these biases against suicide promote fairness and protect the weak, depressed, despairing, and vulnerable, for if they do, they might then be morally and rationally defensible biases and presumptions. For example, much Catholic thought in recent years has emphasized the need to develop a "preferential option" for the poor, which means that we should develop a bias, prejudice, or presumption in favor of protecting and promoting their interests. Such a preferential option is "prejudicial," but it is a fair and charitable prejudice that should not be abolished. Such a bias promotes the security and well-being of the vulnerable and it deserves endorsement. Similarly, the "bias" against suicide stems from a moral conviction that this type of killing for any reason is a violation of justice, fairness, and the transcendent value of human life. It is a bias like the "preferential option" for the poor because its purpose is to protect the weak and vulnerable from exploitation and injustice.

Stephen Nathanson argues that self-killing can be rational when it is part of an individual's Rawlsian "plan of life."[7] Nathanson suggests that it is up to agents to appropriately value reality and develop a "plan of life" that gives it the highest value if they are to make suicide a rational act and a coherent part of one's plan of life. Nathanson is not merely arguing that one should plan for one's death when it appears to draw near, but that such a plan should be a central aspect of one's entire life. He claims that no one's life makes any difference when one considers reality broadly, even though our lives mean much to us personally.[8]

Nathanson's basic premise here is wrong, for suicide cannot fit into a coherent and emotionally healthy plan of life. While such a plan might appear to be rational in a purely speculative and theoretical sense, including it in one's practical plan of life would be irrational and emotionally unhealthy. Planning one's own demise would require an emotionally unhealthy fixation on death and suffering, and it would be more rational to exclude suicide from one's plans and to only seek to arrange positive, constructive, and productive experiences into one's life. Making positive, protective, and beneficial plans for others in the event of one's death would be quite rational, but planning one's own self-administered execution is not clearly of any positive benefit. His proposal presents further questions about what would be involved in making suicide a part of one's "plan of life." Would this mean that one would think about it at length and plot it out over a long period of time? Would it mean that one would dispassionately outline one's life and deliberately put a self-inflicted death at the end, and if so, would absence of passion or emotion make an action more rational? If this is a standard for rational suicide, then the plotting of the Gestapo against the Jews would have been rational because it was dispassionate. The absence of passion or conviction does not necessarily entail rationality, for people who defend themselves from unjust attacks often do so quite passionately, and yet their actions are not considered to be irrational.

Nathanson assumes that one's life could be so shaped and formed by suffering, pain, and illness that one can rationally, morally, and validly plan to end it at a given time or in a given situation. But this attitude is often absent in those who suffer these trials with a more mature openness to reality and is more common in immature personalities who seek to control and dominate life in order to shield themselves from forces and events compelling them to adjust their lives to the forces of reality. A morally good life plan should integrate one's life activities and promote maturity, selflessness, concern for others, and self-transcendence, which integrates positive actions and growth into life. A life plan should promote the development of the virtues and powers of the individual, and it is not clear if suicide could do this. If achieving psychological growth through suffering is a universally desirable human objective, and if we can grow spiritually, morally, and psychologically in all situations of suffering, then suicide in the face of suffering would be irrational and not in one's interests. Planning one's suicide would defeat that aim as it would commit a person to renouncing our human project of limiting suffering in generally unspecified circumstances.

What the incorporation of suicide into one's life plan would practically entail is unclear, but Nathanson claims a suicide would be rational if one simply incorporated it into one's life plan with no further stipulations or requirements. Such a criterion for rationality is too vague to be administered practically, as it would allow many incompetent and irrational people to easily justify suiciding because the suicidal usually create intricate plans for their suicides long in advance. A small number of suicides are responses to unexpected and undesired crises, and these are truly irrational. But to make the planning of a suicidal action a criterion for rationality is a serious error because it would not only make one unduly pessimistic, it would also work to undermine one's estimation of their ability to cope with challenges, threats, and crises. This criterion is incorrect because even the most irrational of suicides involve planning, and suicidologists would agree that a "plan" is not a sure indicator of rationality. Some cope well with crises while others do not, and it is often difficult to predict how a given individual will react to various sorts of crises.

Given the ambiguity of the concept of a "life plan" one would have to ask if those who conditionally opt for suicide would be acting in a fully informed and therefore rational manner. To make one's suicide plans comprehensively rational, one should plan for not just one future possible situation in which suicide could be considered as rational, but for a great variety of such situations, and one should lay out a wide variety of options for each of these future possibilities. Paradoxically, however, the cumulative effect of such a plan might be quite irrational because one would have to develop such an astonishing array of suicidal plans to cope with these contingencies. Just as we would question the rationality of someone who made comprehensive, minute, and detailed security plans for virtually all possible attacks and threats, so also would we question the rationality of one who made detailed plans for suicide in such a wide variety of situations. Making these sorts of plans would be irrational because suicide is such a monumental decision that it cannot be adequately and rationally prepared for in advance. It would be irrational to plan for this because it is such an absolute, irrevocable, final, and monumental decision that it requires far more information about the situation in which it is to occur than one can gain beforehand.

The claim that suicide would be rational when it would fit into a "plan of life" is not certain because of the difficulty of understanding what a rational "plan of life" would be that includes suicide. Nearly every suicidal person at one time or another incorporates suicide into their "plan of life," and according to Nathanson, this would make their suicide rational, which is most doubtful. If it is true that suicide becomes rational when incorporated into a "life plan," then virtually every suicide would be rational, for nearly all suicidal persons plot their deaths in some fashion. And if it is true that suicide attempts that fit into a "plan of life" are rational, then virtually all attempts at self-killing would be rational acts because nearly all who commit suicide mull over it for a great while.

Contrary to Nathanson's views, a truly rational plan of life includes a plan to seek out opportunities to flourish and develop unique and distinctive talents. One who evades opportunities to develop their abilities, exercise virtues, or grow in personal excellences is not living rationally, and if one chooses to end his or her life by suicide, one is abandoning opportunities to develop the virtue of fortitude and perseverance. This is not to say that it is immoral to decline opportunities for heroism or radical virtue, but when one is forced by circumstances to choose between extraordinary moral actions and acts such self-killing, they are not acting rationally.

Jerome Motto argues that suicide is rational when there are "personal experiences of pain exceeding a threshold that is unique to that individual."[9] The problem here, however, is that there are hardly any situations where pain cannot be controlled because of contemporary advances in pain control, as shall be shown in chapter 7. And even when one cannot suppress pain to a tolerable level, it is now possible to titrate analgesics so precisely that one can reduce a patient to semiconsciousness so that they would not have to suicide to escape pain. Pain can usually be limited or wholly overcome, and there are very few sorts of pain that are beyond some level of control. This view was supported by an international leader of the mercy killing movement, Dr. Pieter Admiraal, who claimed that pain is not a sufficient reason for giving euthanasia, and he believes that suiciding to relieve pain is not rational.[10]

Allowing suicide to escape pain and suffering cannot be supported in a responsible society that cares for its weaker and more vulnerable members. Allowing suicide for this reason provoked a famous response by Dr. I. Phillips Frohman, which was quoted by Professor Yale Kamisar in his famous article "Some Non-Religious Views Against Proposed 'Mercy-Killing' Legislation."[11] Frohman noted that this action would be rational "only if the victim is both sane and crazed by pain."[12] Motto's view is paradoxical because the suicidal person must be both calculating, reflective, probably dispassionate and reasonable, and near insanity from pain and suffering. And it is not clear why Motto does not include psychological suffering as a condition to justify suicide, for this kind of suffering can often be more trying than physical pain.

Motto believes that procedures for ending the life of a patient should be largely controlled by the patient, but it is not clear why others involved with a patient should be denied involvement in these decisions, particularly if they have some important interest in the patient's life or death.[13] Allowing patients to make this decision alone could free them from the responsibilities of their decision, and survivors would have to assume responsibility for the undesired consequences of the patient's death. Rather than giving the patient full and unrestricted control over a decision to end life, it would be more fair to distribute some of this control to those who will survive the patient, as they will have to live with the results of the suicidal choice.

Szasz and Kolber deny that suicidal behavior should be understood according to the "sickness" model, and Kolber argues that people kill themselves for a wide variety of reasons, some of which do not involve "sickness."[14] Kolber defends claims that suicide is rational and criticizes contemporary assertions that it is the result of "mental illness" for being simplistic.[15] It might well be that the mental illness model of suicide is in some ways inadequate, but it is sufficient to illustrate the impaired freedom and competence of many who attempt self-assassination. Kolber's view is quite controversial, for, as we shall see in the next chapter, classical suicidology has argued that there is strong evidence that the suicidal person acts under profoundly debilitating psychological forces and influences. While it is possible that the medical model of suicide is deficient in some ways, it does point out that virtually all who attempt suicide do so under mitigated freedom and voluntariness, and it argues rather persuasively that the majority of suicidal actions are not performed by the fully rational and competent with adequate full control of their lives. This model refers to the mental states of the suicidal only in an analogous fashion, but it captures the truth that suicidal decisions are critically impaired or handicapped in some manner because of these psychological forces. It would probably be more helpful to speak of the suicidal individual as functioning under mental impairments and burdens that need to be lifted than of mental illnesses, but the categories of mental illness do show that mental competence is an issue concerning suicide.

Robert M. Martin is not so much concerned with the rationality of suicide as with justifications for preventive interventions.[16] He objects that "paternalistic" antisuicide interventions cannot be morally justified, and claims that suicides done for good motives should generally be acceptable, while those done for selfish motives should not.[17] By this he seems to mean that suicides to save the lives of others, or to protect honor, dignity, or virtue should be acceptable, while those done to escape pain, embarrassment, or shame should be rejected. He implies that we should permit selfless, brave, and noble suicide, but condemn cowardly, selfish, and craven suicides; this, however, is not an accurate portrayal of the Catholic view of suicide. He misunderstands the distinction between self-sacrifice and suicide, and he believes the acceptability of self-sacrifice is based on subjective moral evaluations rather than on the nature of the action performed. Traditional Catholic moral teachings rejected acts or omissions aimed at death as either a means or end, regardless of whether the motives or consequences were egotistic or altruistic. It condemned suicide to escape pain as well as suicide to protect the life of another. As we saw with Augustine's teachings, even suicides to escape occasions of sin were condemned, and he would not allow maidens to kill themselves to avoid being ravaged. While some might extol the suicides of the ninety-three Jewish maidens trying to avoid being raped by Nazis, the traditional Catholic view of suicide would condemn these actions as well-intentioned but immoral acts employed to achieve good ends.[18] Other philosophies and theologies might accept suicide for virtuous ends, but Catholicism has traditionally not done so.

Martin believes that there are few persuasive reasons for intervening to stop a rational suicide.[19] He denies that one can intervene to prevent a suicide arising from "false desires" because a false desire for death is a desire, and therefore has a *prima facie* claim for satisfaction.[20] But the difficulty with claiming that virtually all interventions are immoral is that in suicide, a private individual deliberately destroys innocent life, and there is a general moral obligation incumbent on all to protect this kind of life. It is rather clear that one can justify killing unjust attackers, though it is less clear that one can justify killing another who unjustly attacks other innocent persons or who has committed some other serious offense as a punishment. And it is not at all clear that one can morally justify allowing innocent persons to kill themselves, particularly those who are in pain or ill health to "relieve" themselves of their condition. Justifying the destruction of the lives of those who are suffering, in despair, pain, or terminal illness is not as easy as justifying the deliberate killing of those who are aggressors or attackers. Prohibiting this intervention implies that there are some cases when innocent life could be willfully destroyed, which weakens further justifications for intervening when the innocent lives of others are in jeopardy and it is against Catholic teachings. Martin presents what is in fact a radical position in objecting to paternalistic interventions, for even the strongest proponents of rational suicide admit that most suicides are irrational and should be resisted whenever possible. If his views are taken seriously, it would be virtually impossible to offer substantial protection for the despairing, disturbed, immature, and incompetent who try to kill themselves because of the difficulty of determining the rationality of their actions. Martin favors few restraints on "rational suicides," but his zeal puts the irrational and immature in great danger of being made more vulnerable to themselves.

Glenn Graber argues that suicide is rational "when a reasonable appraisal of the situation reveals that one is really better off dead."[21] He holds that suicide could be a rational action if it was the best thing for the person to do in the situation.[22] This seems to mean that suicide would be justified if a person suffered a serious accident that would cause him to become "a different person after the accident."[23] He also wonders if suicide would be justified if it was the only way a spy could keep from divulging information, or if it was the only way one could prevent serious loss of honor. He does not explicitly conclude that suicide would be better, but he clearly believes it possible that self-assassination could be rational in these instances. He does not discuss at length what should be done if one would be a better person in some respects after the accident. He believes that a decision for suicide could be rational if it avoided the "pitfalls" involved in such a decision, and he seems to mean that the self-killer could only reach this judgment by a disinterested analysis of the situation.

One can doubt the rationality of the view that suicide would be permissible if one could be "better off dead," for one must clarify the meaning of being "better off." Usually one is better off possessing a good, escaping an evil, or, more accurately, being freed from an evil and coming into possession of a good. But in the case of suicide, one supposedly escapes evil, even though one might not come into possession of another good as a result, for this act abolishes existence and does not guarantee coming into possession of another good. It is incoherent to hold that an individual's existence and well-being would be improved by self-destruction. It is not evident that one can "be better off" by ceasing to exist, for in order to "be better off" one would have to "be," which would not be the case when one destroys oneself. One who was suffering greatly might be "better off" dead if they could be relieved of that suffering without ceasing to exist, but ceasing to exist without coming into possession of a another significant good seems to be a less than fully rational way of coping with evils. Catholic theology has confronted this issue by saying that one would be better off dying than committing sin or better off in heaven than in this life, but not that one would be better off committing suicide than being in pain.[24] Graber assumes that destroying a being's existence is better for that being than merely allowing it to continue at a diminished level, but this is contrary to common sense which holds that total loss of existence is a greater loss than deprivation of some functional capacities. Graber's view is worrisome because, if taken one step further, one could also view suicide as rational if others would be better off because of one's own death. This judgment can rest on a belief that there are no evils or disvalues after death because it is simple annihilation, but many of the great religions of the world have said that great evils may await those who suicide.

Graber argues that it is hypothetically possible that suicide would be the best action imaginable in a given situation, but when considered in a broader context, such a judgment becomes more doubtful. As we shall see in chapter 8, consideration of the ordinary and customary effects of suicide on society, the family, the health and legal professions, and those who are tempted to suicide leads one to believe that it is not rational. And even a rationalistic and individualistic perspective might not consider suicide as rational because that perspective itself might not be rational. Graber might be able to justify the rationality of suicide from a narrowly individualistic perspective, but that narrow individualism, divorced from social, familial, and public policy responsibilities is hardly credible today. Graber's perspective could only be adequately justified by showing why suiciding would be better than living with the aid of fuller personal, social, familial, and psychological support. When studied in that light, I do not think he could justify claiming that no existence is superior to a life with fuller support and aid.

His view that suicide would be rational in the situation when one would be better off dead is logically similar in its formal character to St. Anselm's argument for the existence of God, which held that God was the greatest being imaginable.[25] It is true that if there is such a being, it would be God, but it is not clear that such a being actually exists. Graber hopes for and presumes that there is a future possible condition in which individuals might be better off dead as a result of suicide, but like St. Anselm's God, it is not patently evident that such a condition in fact exists. Because we simply do not know what lies beyond death, the reasons for believing that such a condition exists are not stronger than the reasons for believing that such a condition does not exist; and it seems foolish to end one's life because of a hypothetical possibility.

Margaret Battin has set forth the most comprehensive criterion for determining the rationality of a suicide. She claims that an act of reflexive killing would be rational if the suiciding person had a realistic worldview, adequate information, avoided bringing harm to others, the ability to reason, and acted in accord with their fundamental interests.[26] But these standards are quite formal and ambiguous, and the most troubling condition is the last one. What does it mean concretely and in practice to say that someone is "acting in accord with fundamental interests"? If suicide can be rational when it is in the interests of the agent, then almost any action could be rational because nearly every action can be in the formally defined "interests" of an agent. Interests can be defined economically, hedonistically, intellectually, religiously, or socially, and because of this almost any action can be considered in one's interests.

There are further questions that can be raised about Battin's criteria. What precisely does it mean for a person to be able to "reason," for even the wholly mad and insane can reason, even though they do not do it well. Even further, what does it mean to have a "realistic" worldview?[27] From their perspective, the depressed and despairing might have a realistic worldview about the possibility of finding security, hope, and contentment, but does that mean they are rational? Why does Battin not require that those contemplating suicide prove their psychological health? This condition hardly ever appears among criteria for rational suicide, probably because it is so clear that those who contemplate self-destruction suffer from serious psychological conditions. Requiring proof of mental health and emotional stability would limit endorsements of suicide by the emotionally or mentally unstable and provide them the protection they need.

Battin also holds that suicide could be justified by the interest a person might have in protecting their dignity.[28] Besides the fact that the concept of "dignity" is ambiguous, it covers over some important differences. Allowing oneself to be killed for the good of another or for a worthy cause has been widely regarded as a way of preserving and promoting dignity. True martyrs promote their dignity, not by killing themselves, but by affirming their causes so strongly that they would rather lose their lives than betray them. But it is just not clear that direct self-execution protects dignity in the same way because many of these "dignity-protecting" suicides have been acts of miserable cowardice rather than ones promoting dignity.

Soll claims that all we know of death is that it is annihilation, which is all we need to know to judge suicide rational in some instances.[29] He argues that suicide can be rational even though we do not fully understand death, and suicide is not certainly irrational even if our beliefs about death are incorrect.[30] The view that suicide can be rational even if based on a false belief is difficult to understand, for false beliefs generate both rational and irrational acts. Believing the earth to be flat can cause absurd and false conclusions, but it can also give rise to the science of astronomy. True beliefs, in comparison, will cause rational actions, but false beliefs can cause either rational or irrational acts. Soll's assertions do not clearly defeat arguments for the irrationality of suicide, for he argues on behalf of its rationality because it permits escape from evils and leads us nowhere. He is not absolutely certain that death leads nowhere, but he holds that there is no acceptable evidence that anything follows death. This shows the weakness of his claims because they stand on an absence rather than the presence of positive evidence about what follows death. He justifies his view by claiming that we make many decisions without much knowledge and yet these decisions are not irrational. While this is true of many kinds of decisions, making serious or weighty decisions with a glaring lack of information, knowledge, or evidence is irrational. Soll refuses to acknowledge what others know well: suicide appears less rational when its broader social implications are considered, and it is not sufficient to contend that suicide is rational merely because one knows it would lead to annihilation. It looks less rational when one recognizes that allowing it can induce the unstable and despairing into it. It looks less rational when one sees that there are other less destructive ways of coping with suffering. It looks less rational when one takes into account the mental and emotional states of those who commit suicide. Would knowing that suicide destroys our existence and eliminates occasions of personal, psychological, and spiritual growth modify our beliefs about its rationality? Would knowing of a long-standing Western tradition that regards suicide as immoral, cowardly, and radically undermining personal integrity influence judgments about its rationality? Would knowing that one's suicide could induce others to self-execute change people's judgments of it? Would knowing that one's suicide could make it easier for the emotionally disturbed and unbalanced, despairing or hopeless to end their own lives influence judgments about its rationality? I think all of these questions should be answered affirmatively, but Soll apparently does not deem these worthy of consideration.

James Margolis argues that suicide could be rational if it would be instrumental in enabling persons to attain their goals.[31] He presumes there are rational human goals that self-killing can promote, but he neither defines these goals nor argues for their existence. Like other criteria for rationality, this one is also purely formal and is not based on the material content of human goals. Like Battin, Margolis does not stipulate that the agent has to be psychologically sound, or that the goal has to be rational itself, but only that the suicide be instrumentally efficient. This criterion also does not consider the incongruity of a suicide being a rational way of pursuing irrational goals. If a man thought he was the emperor of Rome, committing suicide to become a god would be theoretically rational because it might be instrumental in achieving his goal of acting like the emperors of old. Margolis's criterion also ignores the difficult problem of determining what to do when an individual's interests collide with those of others. This dilemma cannot be solved simply by saying that suicides would be rational if they enabled individuals to achieve their goals, as this could bring a great deal of harm to others. Suicide served Hector Rodas when he starved himself to death in 1986, but it is not clear that it served the interests of his two small children he left behind. Was this still a rational action, even though it served his interests but not those of his children? Fairness would seem to require that one examine the manner in which a suicide furthers the interests of not just the agent, but also of those influenced by the deed.

Margolis declares that suicide can be rational because it can promote "fundamental" interests.[32] But it is hard to see how self-killing can be in one's "fundamental" interests, if by this one means the basic interests of an individual such as life, truth, justice, and knowledge, for suicide prohibits the attainment of all these goals. And if these fundamental interests include such values as freedom, dignity, or self-determination, there would be far better ways to promote these interests. Suicide can no more promote these fundamental interests than can dueling, gunfighting, or selling oneself into slavery. Suicide could hypothetically enable one to escape suffering, but that is insufficient, for one would have to ask at what cost? There are many ways to escape suffering or attain one's fundamental interests and goals, but suicide is perhaps the most definitive and final of these methods.

Margolis believes that an authentic suicide only involves one who acts simply to end their life, and suicides to attain other goals are not fully authentic. He believes that a suicide can be rational when "life has ceased to have a sufficiently favorable significance or because taking one's life under the conditions does have a sufficiently favorable significance."[33] But if a suicidal action can be invested with enough significance to be ethically and rationally justified, could not other similar actions be invested with equal meaning? Margolis does not give serious consideration to the possibility of less drastic actions being taken to alleviate the terrible conditions of a patient. He presumes that there are types of pain that truly cannot be alleviated by aggressive analgesic, pastoral, or psychotherapeutic treatment, but this opinion is not shared by more advanced physicians, psychiatrists, and psychologists today.

For Margolis, suicide would be even more rational if one "decided that life was utterly meaningless" or "sincerely believed it to have no point at all."[34] This is paradoxical because suicide becomes more rational to the extent that life becomes more meaningless and vice versa. In this perspective, the rationality of suicide increases as life's meaningfulness decreases, and its appearance of rationality is inversely proportional to the meaningfulness of life. The rationality of suicide is thus grounded on the absurdity and meaninglessness of life and it loses its coherence to the extent that life gains its meaning. According to Margolis's criteria, all that is needed to make suicide irrational is to illuminate the meaninglessness of life or experience. But this approach begs the crucial question: in the objective order, can there be such a life, and if so, would this life be "utterly meaningless"? Classical Catholic theology would deny these and hold that life accompanied by suffering is not utterly meaningless and futile and suicide does not become more rational as life loses its meaning.[35] His view that life accompanied by suffering is meaningless can be vigorously contested as superficial, and unable to understand how our intelligent confrontation with suffering leads to a fuller grasp of the meaning and value of human existence.

Ronald Maris asserts that suicide is a rational act because it alone can solve the problem of life.[36] This is so because life is hard, painful, anxiety-producing, unfair, and short in the best of conditions. But he admits that suicide can be irrational in some instances because it can betray life itself and generally diminish "the life force"; suicide also reflects "bad faith."[37] David Mayo argues, however, that suicide does not resolve the problem of life that Maris defines so well, but merely repudiates it, and there is much truth in that view. Suicide abolishes the problems of life by abolishing life itself, which is not an intelligent solution to the problem at hand. The answer suicide gives to the riddle and mystery of life is to destroy life itself, which is not much of an answer. An authentic solution to the problems of life resolves the problems but permits life to continue, and opting for the solution that destroys life with all of its problems does not appear to be the pinnacle of rationality.

Benjamin Mijuskovic argues that suicide could be rational because loneliness can overwhelm the psyche and serve as an adequate ground for self-killing:

> Loneliness constitutes the most primary, universal, and necessary condition or structure of human consciousness hence of man's existence and consequently . . . each of us is terribly alone and lonely. . . .(Since) loneliness is the most pervasive force within awareness, it follows that when it overwhelms the individual psyche, it often does (and perhaps should) serve as an adequate ground for suicide.[38]

This is wrongheaded, however, for loneliness that can be overcome is not an adequate grounds for self-killing. Only irretrievable and hopeless loneliness might stand as an adequate reason for suicide, if there is such a thing. Loneliness, except when it results from profound psychological disorder, is relatively fleeting, harmless, and not terribly difficult to overcome in most instances and he does not give sufficient consideration to the possibility that his standard could permit suicide to run out of control. His proposal must be rejected because it would justify self-killing for just about any reason whatsoever, as almost everyone experiences loneliness at some time that "overwhelms their psyche." Not only does this justification fail, but it is also unfair because it can induce the emotionally unstable and those with inadequate personalities into suicide more than it would for others. This standard is unacceptably lax and nebulous, for if something as easy to overcome as loneliness can warrant deliberate self-killing, then far more grave and trying conditions could warrant it as well.

Mijuskovic believes that procedures are needed to permit voluntary cessation of life to occur at the time, place, and manner controlled by the patient. This would mean that those wishing suicide could override the decisions of physicians, counselors, and family members who might not only have an interest in their continued life, but who also might believe their suicidal decision to be utterly wrong. As the suiciding person would not have to "live" with the consequences of his or her decision, it would be rational to allow those who would have to live with its results to have some control over the decision. But Mijuskovic's standard would mean that those who were denied any involvement in the suicidal decision would have to suffer the consequences of it.

A problem with establishing these procedures is that criteria would have to be developed to distinguish between those who are "rational" in their desire for suicide from those who are marginally so, and this seems to be beyond the realm of practical possibility. These criteria and procedures would have to be quite complex and detailed in order to distinguish "rational" from "irrational" suicides, and their procedural enactment without these precautions could endanger those who were only incompetent, mildly depressed, or somewhat irrational. If determining the rationality of suicide was simple and straightforward, then only minimal safeguards would be required, but because the rationality of these actions is so obscure, the administrative procedures to permit suicide would have to be more complex than what Mijuskovic acknowledges.

Richard Brandt has argued that some suicides are clearly irrational and should be prohibited, but others are rational and there is a moral duty to assist them.[39] If this is so, then one must ask how far this obligation extends. Would this duty mean that one would have to assist Hitler in suiciding so he could escape punishment because this would appear rational from his perspective? Would one have to assist another if the act was rational in the agent's worldview, but irrational in one's own? If so, then Brandt is implicitly claiming that one's right of conscience can be overridden to assist suicide? Would this obligation to assist in rational suicides extend to dueling if such acts are rational in the minds of the duelers? Dueling, consented self-killing by proxy, is virtually identical to suicide in morally relevant terms, and both actions seek to promote dignity, even though dueling does this by a proxy. And if there is an obligation to assist "rational" self-slaying, there would seem to be an obligation to assist in rational self-slaying by proxy.

In essence, this argument is not formally different from considering suicide rational when the person would be better off dead than alive. Brandt's perspective presumes that relinquishing the possibility of any and all experiences, goods, and values in this life is better than experiencing one catastrophe. This presumption is unrealistic, for it assumes that there are experiences of pure and unadulterated evil, and it concludes that it is practically possible to experience only evil without any other compensating goods or benefits. But it is hardly ever the case that experiences can become so purely and wholly terrible that it is better to have no experiences at all. In the speculative order, this might be possible, but it is less than certain in the practical order. Brandt admits that depression can limit one's capacity to reason clearly and that it can render a suicidal desire irrational. Having admitted this, it is perplexing that he does not pursue it further and recognize that there are not just a few, but many conditions, that can radically limit freedom and voluntariness, thereby making suicide irrational. If he pursued this possibility, he would quickly see that these emotional and psychological impairments make practically all suicides irrational.

In conclusion, the arguments in behalf of the rationality of suicide show rather limited insight, are not above criticism, and are not without flaws. More popular but less well formed and articulate arguments in behalf of rational suicide have also been presented. For example, Elizabeth Bouvia argued that suicide was a rational action for her because she was hopelessly trapped in a "useless" body that was racked with multiple sclerosis.[40] But one cannot be entirely confident that she really believed this, for when she was given an opportunity by a court to commit suicide, she renounced her plans to do so.[41] Others have argued in the same vein that assisted suicide is rational for those who suffer from various conditions such as Alzheimer's or Parkinson's disease, but these arguments have not been well formulated. These less refined claims are not as powerful as those dealt with here, and they can be regarded less seriously.

Suicide as an Irrational Action

While many judge suicide as rational, there are some who do not agree. George Murphy opposes the view that suicide is rational and claims that most suicidal persons "are suffering from clinically recognizable psychiatric illnesses often carrying an excellent prognosis."[42] Murphy asserts that the clinical data about suicide undercuts claims that suicide can be rational because

> the desire to terminate one's life is usually transient. The "right" to suicide is a "right" desired only temporarily. Every physician should feel the obligation to support the desire for life, which will return even in a patient who cannot believe that such a change can occur. To cooperate in the patient's hopelessness violates an important responsibility of the physician.[43]

His concern has also been given limited support by David Mayo who agrees that most suicides are irrational and are motivated by clinical pathologies, even though some are free from these forces and are rational.[44]

The irrationality of suicide has been stressed by other authors as well. Devine claims that attempts to understand death are irretrievably futile because of its obscurity, and this makes any choice for it irrational. Arguing from this "opaqueness," he holds that

> if, as seems plausible, a precondition of a rational choice is that one knows *what* one is choosing, either by experience or by the testimony of others who have experienced it or by something very like it, then it is not possible to choose death rationally. Nor is any degree of what one desires to escape by death helpful, since rational choice between two alternatives requires knowledge of both.[45]

In a matter as serious as the ending of one's existence, he contends that there are insurmountable barriers to adequately understanding the nature of death, and because of this, choosing death can never be rational. One can choose death only as part of an overall intention to protect justice or innocent life, but to choose death solely for itself is irrational because it is shrouded in mystery and darkness.

Oates argues that suicide is an irrational act because the experience of death–if it can be called an experience at all–is not the creative kind of act that some suggest it is:

> But can one freely choose a condition, a state of being, that has never been experienced except in the imagination, and there *only in metaphor?* . . . Rationally one cannot "choose" death, because death is an unknown experience, and perhaps it isn't even an "experience" perhaps it is simply nothing; and one cannot imagine nothing. The brain simply cannot fathom it, however glibly its thought-clusters may verbalize non-existence, negation of being, death, and other non-referential items.[46]

This perspective seems to be more realistic and accurate than regarding suicide as either a release from suffering or an act done to promote the interests of the self-killer. As death cannot be experienced, choosing it can be no more rational than choosing other supposed goods that are beyond experience. Choosing death to escape suffering, promote dignity, or escape a useless body is analogous to choosing some sort of noumenal being that may or may not exist and whose existence we could not verify in any way.

Mirroring this viewpoint, Donnelly argues that suicide cannot be a rational act because it involves an illicit appeal to some future state of the person whose death would preclude any such state.[47] This argument has some force, for in choosing death, one chooses to experience a state that destroys all possibility of experience. There is a certain irrationality in choosing suicide because a person ends their existence in order to experience its goods and values more fully. Opting for death as a means of escaping suffering is analogous to choosing to marry after self-emasculation because one wants to experience the joys and pleasures of marriage and children! The former action precludes the latter just as ending one's existence by suicide precludes any experience of release from suffering. Donnelly asserts that we know death to be nothingness and there is no good reason to choose nothing rather than something. A life of suffering has negative aspects to it, but it also has a number of positive elements, and it is not irrational to seek to escape those negative aspects, but to do so by ending the possibility of all experience is doubtfully rational.

Colleen Clements disagrees with both of these authors and asserts that suicide is neither rational nor irrational:

> Suicidal judgments must be viewed as affect or attitudinal stances and . . . these are primary states having precedence over rational analysis. Before all valuation (ethical, cognitive, and aesthetic) human beings have an attitude concerning their existence in the world. . . . It is a yea-saying or a nay-saying attitude (or various mixtures of both) which cannot be evaluated in terms of cognitive (rational) values, since it is the precondition for all values.[48]

This approach has a certain attractiveness because it suggests that those who commit suicide are more subject to this nay-saying approach and can be dangerous to themselves because they are not readily deterred from self-killing. She urges care that one's prerational affective stance not make one wholly immune to reevaluation, for some of these affective orientations can be quite harmful or irrational. When that is so, one cannot say that suicide is either rational or irrational, and it can be subjected to scrutiny.

The fictional character Todd Andrews in John Barth's *The Floating Opera* asserts that suicide is rational because everything is ultimately meaningless. Stanley Hauerwas, however, challenges this and points out that this ultimate meaninglessness makes no difference either, because there is then no more reason to commit suicide than not to do it.[49] The claim that suicide is permissible because nothing makes final sense is ultimately contradictory, for not even rational suicide makes final sense and it too is ultimately irrational. Hauerwas notes that all values are at best relative, but even relative values are worth preserving, and the relativity of values does not make suicide rational in itself. We might not be able to find ultimate, final, and definitive value in this life, but we can find relative and limited values that can help us "muddle along."[50] This is an interesting claim, for it suggests that while self-execution might not be wholly rational, it could be just as rational as not killing oneself because neither attitude is fully rational in the larger picture.

Herbert Hendin takes issue with Richard Brandt's views that suicide can be rational when it is the best action in the situation:

> [M]ost (current philosophical) writing attempts to defuse the absolute nature of suicide by a process of intellectual assimilation. The issues of death and dying are rationalized into a language and style that at times seem more appropriate to descriptive economics. . . . Brandt's arguments are (not) convincing. The tendency to think that life can be measured on a balance scale is itself a characteristic of suicidal people.[51]

He concludes that suicide is not a rational action because it proceeds from an irrational balancing, measuring, and calculating of life. He rightly points out that constantly measuring and comparing life and its experiences to gain the greatest benefits and goods and minimize its harms and evils is irrational because it is ultimately fruitless. A more rational and realistic approach acknowledges that there is an unpredictable, immeasurable, and mysterious aspect to life that demands a constant openness to change and renewal in life.

H. A. Neilson rejects the argument that suicide is rational when life has lost its meaning and he claims a person might have no interest in living for either rational or irrational reasons. He therefore asserts that a statement that "my life no longer has meaning" begs the question of why it has lost meaning.[52] Neilson holds that a suicide is not rational simply because a life is judged meaningless, for one would be rationally obliged to show that there are good and sound reasons for it being meaningless. This is an important point and it makes note of Margolis's failure to see that our human condition is such that we must create the meaning of our lives in the existential moment. For Neilson, one of the distinctive features of human beings is that they confer meaning on their existence, and when one has decided that life no longer has meaning, one has essentially abandoned this uniquely human "meaning-bestowing" project of human life, which itself is irrational. Declaring life meaningless is essentially a declaration of despair, and it is more a sign of the person's impotence in the face of reality than of the rationality of the situation.

The view that suicide is rational is not simple and straightforward because it is not clear that there is such a thing as impartial rationality. The Protestant ethicist Allen Verhey expresses well the problems of impartial rationality with respect to neonatal euthanasia:

> [B]ut here impartial rationality begins to fail us, for it tends to reduce role relations--for example, the relation of the doctors to Infant Doe or his parents or the relation of the parents to Infant Doe--to *contractual* arrangements between independent individuals. That is a minimal account of such roles at best, and when its minimalism is not acknowledged, it is an account which distorts the moral life and the covenants of which it is woven. The stance of impartial rationality cannot nurture any moral wisdom about these roles or sustain any moral traditions concerning them. And it is our confusion about these roles, our diminishing sense of a tradition concerning them, that accounts for the failure of a competent physician, compassionate parents, and duly humble justices to make the morally right decision with respect to the care of Infant Doe.
>
> There are other inadequacies in the stance of impartial rationality which bore on the story of Infant Doe. The stance of impartial rationality tends to emphasize the procedural question, the question of who decides, rather than the substantive question of what should be decided. The first and final question in the care of Infant Doe was who should decide, and the answer was consistently that the parents should decide. I am not saying that question or that answer is wrong, but I am saying that it provides

> only a minimal account of the moral issues and that if its minimalism is forgotten or ignored, the moral life and particular moral issues can be distorted. I am saying that a fuller account of morality would focus as well on substantive questions--on the question of *what* should be decided--and on questions of character and virtue--on the question of *what the person who decides should be.*
>
> Let me call attention to one other weakness (or inadequacy) of the approach of impartial rationality. This approach requires alienation from ourselves, from our own moral interests and loyalties, from our own histories and communities in order to adopt the impartial point of view. We are asked, nay, obliged, by this approach to view our own projects and passions as though we were objective outside observers. The stories which we own as our own, which provide our lives a narrative and which develop our own character, we are asked by this approach to disown--and for the sake of morality. Now, to be asked to pause occasionally and for the sake of analysis and judgment to view things as impartially as we can is in certain contexts not only legitimate but salutary, but neither physicians nor parents nor any Christian can finally live their moral lives like that with any integrity.[53]

Echoing Verhey's complaints about the alienating and insufficient stance of impartial rationality, Stanley Hauerwas argues persuasively that suicide is rational only within a tradition, and that tradition implicitly holds that there are forms of suffering that have no value, which cannot disclose the meaning of life more fully. Suicide affirms that meaning in life is only found by escaping life as it is, and suicide only appears rational in that tradition. But in other traditions such a view is irrational, and these other traditions indict the community for a failure to care for and give comfort and hope to the individual. The classical Catholic perspective would agree with Hauerwas because this kind of suicide sees no positive value to suffering, while Catholicism believes there is a positive dimension to suffering in all of its forms.

The Rationality of Suicide from a Catholic Perspective

The previous sections sketched contemporary arguments for and against the rationality of suicide. This section will concern the issue of rationality of suicide from the viewpoint of traditional Catholic morality, theology, and philosophy.

Classical Catholic teaching has held that rationality is only one among many norms for determining the permissibility of actions. Aquinas taught that all virtuous actions were rational, but rationality was not the only standard for determining the ethical uprightness of actions as they had also to be in accord with other moral norms. Virtuous actions are rational, but simply because an action is rational does not mean that it is virtuous or morally good. Some forms of murder or violence meet criteria for rationality but are still not permissible because they violate other moral norms.

In a suicidal action, one seeks to control, manage, command, and manipulate death and make it come on one's own terms, and this whole approach to the nature of death is questionably rational. A suicidal person believes that bringing death at a preselected time can control it and make it submit to one's will. But from the mainstream Catholic perspective, this is not control over death, but only trivially "negotiating" the time, place, and means of it. To attempt to "control" death in this way may seem rational, but in a broader perspective it is ultimately futile because all one has done has been to name the time and place of death, which is not truly controlling it. While the suicidal person seeks to gain mastery over death, Catholic faith recognizes that death will ultimately prevail for only Christ can truly "control" it and bring victory over it.

From the classical Catholic perspective, a more rational approach to "death control" would be to live a healthy life and delay death as long as possible to share as much as one can in the grace of Christ, which delivers us from death. In the traditional Catholic perspective, death is only transcended by submitting to it in faith and hope in the power of the Christ to deliver us. Death is under God's control and not ours, and it is arrogant to believe we can control and manipulate it to our own advantage. From the vantage point of Catholic faith, submitting to death, accepting it when it comes, and allowing God to deliver from it is more rational than trying to control it with our trivial powers.

The view that death can be rationally managed to our own benefit badly misunderstands it, treats it foolishly, and fails to show a proper for it. Many Catholic thinkers hold that it is reasonable to fear death and both Catholic and Protestant theologians give good reasons for this. William F. May writes:

Death not only threatens a man with separation from the flesh; it also tears him away from his community. This threat has already been anticipated in the discussion of the revelatory power of the flesh. Death means the unraveling of the human community. It divides husband and wife, father and son, and lovers from one another. Not even the child is exempt from this threat. In demanding the reassurance of a voice, the touch of a hand at bedtime, he shows that he knows all the essential issues involved in a sleep that is early practice in dying. Death threatens all men with final separation, exclusion and oblivion. And again, this threat is operative beforehand, as the fear of oblivion can prompt men to force their way into the society of others in ways which are ultimately self-isolating.

But death also threatens men with separation from God. This is the terror of death that men have never fully faced because they have never wholly honored the presence of God. But it is the terror of which all others are but prologue and sign. Men fear separation from their flesh because they know life in and through their flesh. They fear separation from community because they know life in and through their community. But what are these compared with the separation from God, who is the source of life in the flesh and life in the community? This question remains partly rhetorically for all men inasmuch as they do not know fully what they ask. But it was the last question on the lips of the One whom Christians worship and adore in his cry of abandonment from the cross.[54]

Because death does this, we refute our fear of it, according to Paul Ramsey by "thing-ifying" our dying. This is the wrong sort of response, for it causes us to "thing-ify" other persons as well:

> "[T]hing-ifying" death reaches its highest pitch in the stated preference of many people in the present age for *sudden* death, for death from unanticipated internal collapse, from the abrupt intrusion of violent outside forces, from some chance occurrence due to the natural law governing the operation of automobiles. While for a comparative calculus of indignities suddenly *unknowing* death may be preferred to suffering knowingly or unknowingly the indignity of deterioration, abject dependence, and hopeless pain, how ought we to assess in human terms the present-day absolute (noncomparative) preference for sudden

> death? Nothing reveals more the meaning we assign to human dignity than the view that sudden death, death as an eruptive natural event, could be a prismatic case of death with dignity or at least one without indignity. Human society seems about to rise to the moral level of the "humane" societies in their treatment of animals. What is the principled difference between their view and ours about the meaning of dying "humanely"? By way of contrast, consider the prayer in the Anglican prayer book: "From perils by night and perils by day, perils by land and perils by sea, and from *sudden death,* Lord deliver us." Such a petition bespeaks an age in which dying with dignity was a gift and a task *(Gabe und Aufgabe),* a liberty to encompass dying as a final act among the actions of life, to enfold awareness of dying as an ingredient into awareness of oneself dying as the finale of the self's relationships in this life to God or to fellowman--in any case to everything that was worthy.[55]

What is lost in contemporary demands to permit rational suicide and death with dignity is a proper fear and concern for death, and the classical response of Catholicism to this tragedy has been to call for faith and hope in God because this leads to a properly human response to death.

Those who favor rational suicide usually weigh various goods against one another or against different kinds of evils and harms. Without claiming that these sorts of commensurations are impossible, a question remains as to whether one can validly weigh the value of human life against other values. The precise value of human life is somewhat obscure because this value derives from its image of the divine nature, which is unlike other values, and this obscurity makes it difficult or impossible to commensurate its value against others. Classical Catholic theology held that the human life is inherently different from the life of other beings, which can be disposed of when they no longer serve particular wishes and desires, because human life possesses sanctity. While other values are respected and esteemed, the sanctity of human life requires it to be revered as the living image of divine life itself and demands that it not be deliberately destroyed when innocent. Because of this, the evils of death and suicide cannot be directly and straightforwardly weighed against other goods and values.

Mainstream Catholic beliefs reject claims that ending a "degraded" or "undignified" existence through suicide is rational as these claims can often be dangerously thin veils for prejudices against various classes and groups. Such justifications can be profoundly discriminatory because they would not permit one prospering and in good health to commit suicide, but would easily allow the suffering, disabled, and handicapped to do so. Such claims are also questionable because ending one's existence on account of an experience of "degradation" or loss of dignity is irrational, as these states result more from subjective perceptions than from some objective conditions.

Traditional Catholic morality rejects such justifications for the rationality of suicide because they would have justified Christ committing suicide at the Crucifixion. Usually, a degraded existence is not simply one that is impoverished and filled with pain, but is covered with shame and disgrace. This was precisely the kind of existence Christ experienced in his passion and death, and rather than condemning it, Catholic faith has praised his life at that point as a powerful sign of God's love for us. To say that destroying the sort of life Christ experienced in his passion would be rational implies that Christ's most definitive miracle and saving act of offering himself on the Cross was ultimately absurd and irrational, an idea that is quite alien to classical Catholic thought. Such a doctrine implies that Christ was foolish in not suiciding as he drew closer and closer to the point of our salvation. But Catholic theology has held that the deeper Christ descended into this "degraded existence," the more fully he was able to show his love and the closer he came to fulfilling his Messianic mission and his victory over death and sin.[56] In classical Catholic belief, the most debased existence one could experience was not Christ's on the Cross, but that of Judas's utter loss of trust and sinful betrayal of Jesus in his suicide. Catholic faith did not condemn Christ as irrational for refusing to commit suicide, but rather it condemned Judas as "irrational" for having despaired ultimately in spite of the promise of forgiveness given by Christ. Catholicism's veneration of the crucified Christ gives substance to its claim that no condition is so degraded that it justifies suiciding.

Mainstream Catholic beliefs hold now that when a person declares their existence to be so degraded that suicide is rational, they are most often speaking from depression and fear than from a rational assessment of their condition. This sort of verdict is more frequently a result of their own subjective judgments than it is an analysis of their objective medical condition, for others are able to live with similar infirmities without making such claims. These judgments say more about their subjective ability to cope with threats, sufferings, and trials than about the objective conditions of their life. Only recently have Catholic thinkers begun to employ the term "dignity" as a moral category, for traditional Catholic faith has regarded the terms "dignity" and "degradation" as ambiguous, and these terms ordinarily referred more to moral failures than to one's physical condition and capabilities than to the moral quality of actions. We tend to think as those who capitulate to their base instincts as degraded and without dignity while those who suffer and endure grave physical afflictions and tragedy are more dignified and more deserving of respect and sympathy. Rather than being a means of enhancing dignity, traditional Catholic belief sees "analgesic" suicide more frequently as a capitulation to despair, self-hatred, tragedy, guilt, and suffering. A more traditional Catholic approach saw individuals enhancing their dignity, not by repudiating life and bringing death on themselves, but by performing charitable, courageous, or just deeds even when these involved pain and suffering. These two conditions should not be confused because we do not lose their dignity on account of pain and suffering.

Many people live in pain and poverty and yet preserve their dignity, while others who live in great comfort and luxury often lead quite shameful lives. "Dignity-enhancing" suicide aims more at modifying the subjective perceptions of either the patient or others than at rectifying some objectively existing state of affairs. Suicidal patients often manifest a great deal of guilt, and suicide is frequently a vain attempt to alleviate that guilt. In the traditional Catholic perspective, inflicting death on oneself in the midst of grave suffering is to yield to that suffering, while enduring suffering with pride, peace, and self-confidence masters it. To face suffering in these circumstances increases patience and courage and these virtues deepen one's dignity. In contrast, suiciding in the face of suffering is a failure to integrate these virtues, and rather than ending one's life, a more fully rational approach would be to adopt the attitude that one can gain benefits from all forms of suffering.

The mainstream Catholic perspective also objected that suicide to flee a "useless body" was a questionably rational action because of the debatable claim that physical disabilities render life meaningless and undignified. Many disability-rights activists are firm in asserting that there are few disabilities that utterly and completely strip life of meaning or value, and they wonder if escaping these disabilities through suicide is truly rational.[57] Many with disabilities are adamant in holding that the prejudices of the able-bodied create more difficulties for the disabled than do their disabilities. They press this point because they believe there are few handicaps that totally destroy a person's capacity for a productive and rewarding life, making it hard to affirm that life can be useless or futile. With advances in medicine, rehabilitation theory, technology, and institutions to aid the disabled, their plight is far better now than it was even quite recently, which gives substance to their objections about the necessity or rationality of suicide for the disabled.

The mainstream Catholic perspective on rational suicide raises similar objections to claims that it would be rational for those with severe mental disabilities to kill themselves. If having a mental or emotional disability means anything, it is that these individuals are not fully capable of making complex and difficult decisions about life and death. Asserting that such a suicide is rational is also objectionable because it would make the mentally and emotionally handicapped more vulnerable to the abuse and malice of others. These persons often have diminished rational abilities and can be more readily manipulated into believing that their ruminations about death and suicide are fully rational or coherent. The emotionally and mental disabled are fragile and vulnerable, and being a little overprotective of them may not only be more rational, but also more charitable too.

From the traditional Catholic perspective, the assertion that deliberate reflexive killing can be rational is questionable because such a view would make suicide morally obligatory in some instances. If suicide is a fundamental moral right, or if it would be the last and only available means in some instances of preserving some particular value, it is hard to see how it could not be obligatory in some situations or circumstances, and yet few if any proponents of rational suicide have argued that this should be the case. This can cause one to question its rationality, because if suicide were a fully rational act, it would inevitably have to be obligatory in some circumstances, a claim consistently rejected by the Catholic tradition.

At the root of human activity is our struggle with moral evil, for our human dignity and integrity derive from the way we confront evil. Serious human endeavors unavoidably involve suffering and sometimes even tragedy, but suiciding in the face of these suggests that welcoming death is a legitimate and fruitful way of confronting them. From the Catholic perspective, suicide is doubtfully rational when viewed in the context of the nature of the human enterprise of struggling against evil, suffering, tragedy, and misfortune. Endorsing the rationality of suicide authorizes abandoning the struggle against evil, suffering, indignity, and tragedy, which is questionably rational when viewed in a broader and deeper perspective. Coping with suffering, trying to understand it more fully, and not allowing it to drive one to self-destruction is probably more fully human, and more rational than is embracing death through self-slaying.

Catholic faith claims that suicide is irrational because it is ordinarily based more on a fleeting wish than on a set inclination or desire. Most suicidal wishes are precisely that--wishes, rather than results of serious reflection, contemplation, and rational analysis, and as merely wishes, they are questionably rational because they deal so superficially with such a serious issue. This is not to say that all wishes are irrational and should be avoided, but only that their rationality should not be presumed and that suicidal wishes should be carefully examined. This is paradoxical, for classical Catholic faith would see not only a temporary wish, but also an enduring desire for death as irrational. Most advocates of rational suicide presume a rational desire endures through time, but Catholic teachings would question this view as it doubts the suggestion that brief and fleeting wishes for death are rational.

Historically, Catholicism objected that suicide is irrational by pointing out that acts appearing to be rational within an individualistic context might be highly irrational in a broader, social, familial, and public policy framework. Most proponents of rational suicide implicitly assume that advanced societies allow as much individual freedom as possible, and their arguments in behalf of rational suicide stress neither the importance of society nor community, but the individual. Catholic social theory challenges that perspective and argues that fairness requires that suicide be viewed not just individualistic, but in social and communal contexts as well. Viewing suicide from a more social and communal perspective would challenge its rationality, for suicide often rather proximately involves society in the deliberate killing of many who might not want to be killed.

Even further, whether regarded as rational or not, suicide has devastating effects on nuclear and extended families, irrespective of the manner in which it is performed. Like other forms of violence, it is well known that suicide can become cyclical and repetitive in families, which gives further grounds for questioning its rationality. The cyclical character of suicide is seen both in the elderly and teenagers who suicide most frequently of all and who are more vulnerable to being made victims of epidemics of suicide than any others.

Conclusion

It is quite possible that the question about the rationality of suicide might be the wrong one, for the proper question might be whether suicide expresses a needed, proper, and fittingly hopeful response to the problems endemic to our life. The proper question might not be whether suicide is rational, but whether it is an authentic and truly human response to the human condition. Does permitting individuals to end their lives in times of suffering, burden, or trial foster a spirit of despair rather than hope, growth rather than capitulation? Does suicide promote what is best in us as responsible humans or allow us to betray our responsibilities? It seems that hope, rather than despair, should be promoted and endorsed when people face terminal illness, and endorsing the legitimacy of suicide is contrary to the spirit of hope that should prevail in our human lives.

Rather than arguing that suicide is not rational, it might be better to assert that it is wrong, not because it is irrational, but because it fails to properly and adequately understand human life. The libertinism that holds suicide to be rational demands that preserving human life be justified before its own court of narrow and superficial rationalism, and it fails to see that human life has a claim on us in and of itself. Life can be preserved by reason of its own merits, and it does not have to justify its existence by appealing to extrinsic values. Liberal approaches to suicide are obsessed with the question of rationality when they should be asking if it is intelligent, wise, and prudent. They should be asking whether suicide is fully rational, human, and wise.

Notes

1. This has been the official position of the American Psychiatric Association, which has recently come under sharp attack. "Changing Concepts of Suicide," *Journal of the American Medical Association*, Vol. 199, No. 10, (6 March 1967): 162. However, today there is widespread questioning of the view that suicide is irrational. See Motto, J., "The Rights of Suicide: A Psychiatrist's View," in *Suicide: The Philosophical Issues,* 212-19.
2. Humphry, D., *Compassionate Crimes, Broken Taboos*, (Los Angeles: Hemlock Society, 1986).
3. See Brandt, R., "The Rationality of Suicide," in *Suicide: The Philosophical Issues,* 117-32. Brandt argues that it is obviously true that suicide is rational in some cases because it is the most effective means of escaping painful terminal illness that holds out only useless suffering for the patient.

4. See Mayo, D., "Contemporary Philosophical Literature on Suicide: A Review," in *Suicide and Ethics:*

> Among philosophers addressing the issue of rational suicide, nearly all ascribe to a conception of rational decision making and action which may be characterized in broad strokes as follows: a person acts rationally to the extent that he realistically considers his alternatives with an eye to the extent to which they are likely to realize his goals or fundamental interests, and then opts for the alternative which he predicts will maximize the realization of them. (p. 319)

5. Daube, D., "Three Footnotes on Civil Disobedience in Antiquity," *Humanities in Society*, (Winter 1978): 69-92. This is a value judgment that is open to dispute. Daube has confused martyrdom, bravery in warfare, and acts of courage with morally objectionable suicides. Kamikaze pilots were grudgingly admired for their feats in World War II, not so much because of the success of their attacks, but because of their remarkable courage and unswerving devotion to their nation. The admiration mistakenly given to the "divine wind" and banzai soldiers was that accorded the martyr. Acts of such extraordinary bravery should not be confused with the suicides of Japanese businessmen who commit *seppuku* after having disgraced their companies to escape shame and dishonor. And they certainly should not be confused with suicides to escape criminal punishment, pain, or suffering.

6. See "Apparent Mass Suicide Stirs Japan," *The Washington Post,* 3 November 1986, A17, A18. On 2 November 1987, seven women followers of cult leader Seiji Miyamoto immolated themselves. These women, all members of the Friends of Truth church, left letters indicating they wished to follow their leader to death. Such mass self-executions stirred concern in Japan over the rise of suicide because it paralleled the medieval practice of *junshi* in which retainers would follow their lords to death in an act of supreme loyalty. Earlier in 1986 Japan was also rocked by a number of teen suicides by young people who followed the popular religious leader Yukiko Okada who killed herself by jumping from a hospital roof in Tokyo (ibid). Japanese have sometimes killed their children when and if the parents attempt suicide after being involved in a dishonorable episode. But if the parents survive the suicide attempt, they are often accorded leniency, for the killing of the children is seen as an act of mercy, sparing them shame and dishonor.

7. Nathanson, S., "Nihilism, Reason, and the Value of Life," in Kohl, M., Ed., *Infanticide and the Value of Life* (Buffalo: Prometheus Books: 1978), 192-203.

8. Ibid. Nathanson argues that rationality is not to be equated with stepping back and taking a broader view of things, for that ultimately leads to a "cosmic" perspective where nothing matters. He rightly points out that a rational decision takes into consideration the fundamental interests of an agent.

9. Motto, J., "Rational Suicide and Medical Ethics," in *Rights and Responsibilities in Modern Medicine: The Second Volume in a Series on Ethics, Humanism and Medicine,* Ed. Bassom, M., (New York: Alan R. Liss, Inc., 1981), 201-9.

10. He made this point in a debate with me on *Nightline,* ABC television, New York, 3 February 1987.

11. This article first appeared in the *Minnesota Law Review,* 42 6, May 1958, 969-1042, and was reprinted in Horan, D., and Mall, D., *Death, Dying and Euthanasia* (Frederick, MD; Alethia, 1980), 423.

12. Frohman, I. Phillips, "Vexing Problems in Forensic Medicine: A Physician's View," *New York University Law Review,* (1956): 1215, 1222.

13. This is not clear because the patient is often the least well-informed of all parties concerning a medical decision. Further, the patient's decision to end treatment could force health care providers to violate their professional codes of conduct. Allowing the patient full control over medical decisions would not necessarily guarantee that the best decision would be made. It would not guarantee that the patient would not be manipulated by others.

14. See Szasz, T., "The Ethics of Suicide," in *Suicide: The Philosophical Issues,* 195-98; and Kolber, A., "Suicide: Right and Reason," *Bioethics Quarterly,* 2 (Spring 1980): 46-55.

15. Kolber, "Suicide: Right and Reason":

> [M]y themes are that the concept 'suicide' is extremely complex, that the popular professional and public view of suicide is simplistic, and that among the consequences of this difference are serious and confused ethical issues and a limitation of our understanding of suicide. (p. 46)

16. Martin, R., "Suicide and False Desires," in *Suicide: The Philosophical Issues,* 144-49.

17. Martin, R., "Suicide and Self-Sacrifice," in *Suicide: The Philosophical Issues,* 63.

18. See Battin, M., *Ethical Issues in Suicide,* (Englewood Cliffs, NJ: Prentice Hall Series in the Philosophy of Medicine, 1982).166-67.

19. Martin, R., "Suicide and False Desires," in *Suicide: The Philosophical Issues,* 144-49.

20. Ibid., 149.

21. Graber, G., "The Rationality of Suicide," in *Suicide and Euthanasia: The Rights of Personhood,* (Knoxville, TN: University of Tennessee Press, 1981), 60.

22. Ibid.

23. Ibid.

24. Sacred Congregation for the Doctrine of the Faith, *Declaration on Euthanasia,* para. iii.

25. Anselm, "Proslogion", in *St. Anselm,* Tr. by Deane, S. N., (Chicago: Open Court, 1903), 3-10, 14-17.

26. Battin, M., *Ethical Issues in Suicide,* 132-53. Also see Mayo, D., "Contemporary Philosophical Literature on Suicide: A Review," 321.

27. The problems involved in determining what constitutes a "realistic" worldview and assessment of the world have been pointed out well by psychiatrist Jerome Motto who supports the idea that suicide can be rational in many instances. See "The Right to Suicide," in Battin, M., *Suicide: The Philosophical Issues,* 214-16.

28. Ibid., 274-77.

29. Ibid. Soll confidently asserts that death is simple annihilation, but one must ask how he came to that knowledge, for many religions would strongly affirm that there is some form of personal existence beyond death. He compares a judgment to annihilate oneself to eating oysters or getting drunk for the first time by claiming that we do not have knowledge of any of these. The judgment that death is simply annihilation is a religious belief that should be judged as all other religious beliefs are examined. It is not self-evident that death is annihilation and while highly probable, an existence after death cannot be entirely ruled out. Were the state after suicide simply and certainly annihilation, as he implies, then the dictates of religion concerning suicide would be irrelevant.

30. Soll, I., "Commentary on Joyce Carol Oates 'The Art of Suicide,'" in *The Reevaluation of Existing Values and the Search for Absolute Values,* vol. 1, *Proceedings of the Seventh International Conference of the Unity of the Sciences* (New York: The International Cultural Foundation Press, 1979), 191-93.

31. Margolis, J., *Negativities: The Limits of Life* (Columbus: Charles Merrill, 1975), 26.
32. Ibid., 26.
33. Ibid., 28.
34. Ibid., 24. Margolis claims that when the values, attitudes, beliefs, and knowledge under which a person operates bring about such frustration and failure that life loses its meaning, biological life should be ended because of this frustration. But would it not be more rational to interpret this phenomenon as a call for a radical shift in values, beliefs, moral principles, aims, ambitions, desires, and hopes? To justify suicide because of a loss of meaning is to punish biological life for failures in one's emotive, intellectual, and spiritual life. Rather than justifying suicide, this view would justify a radical alteration in one's views and attitudes toward our biological life.
35. Sacred Congregation for the Doctrine of the Faith, *Declaration on Euthanasia,* para. iii.
36. Maris, R., "Rational Suicide: An Impoverished Self-Transformation," in *Suicide: The Philosophical Issues,* 8.
37. Ibid., 11.
38. Mijuskovic, B., "Loneliness and Suicide," *Journal of Social Philosophy* 11 (January 1980): 11.
39. Brandt, R., "The Rationality of Suicide," in *Suicide: The Philosophical Issues,* 123.
40. See Longmore, P., "Elizabeth Bouvia, Assisted Suicide and Social Prejudice," *Issues in Law and Medicine* 3, 2 (2 November 1987): 157.
41. *Bouvia v. Superior Court,* 225 Cal. Rptr., 304-5.
42. Murphy, G., "Suicide and the Right to Die," *American Journal of Psychiatry* 130 (April 1973): 472-73.
43. Ibid., 472-73.
44. See Mayo, D., "Irrational Suicide," in Battin, M., *Suicide: The Philosophical Issues,* 132-38; and Mayo, D., "Contemporary Philosophical Literature on Suicide: A Review," 318.
45. Devine, P., "On Choosing Death," *Suicide: The Philosophical Issues,* 139.
46. Oates, J., "The Art of Suicide," ibid., 166-67.
47. Donnelly, J., "Suicide: Some Epistemological Considerations," in *Analysis and Metaphysics: Essays in Honor of R. M. Chisholm,* Ed. K. Lehrer, (Dordrecht, Holland: D. Reidel, 1975), 282-85.
48. Clements, C., "The Ethics of Not-Being: Individual Options for Suicide," in *Suicide: The Philosophical Issues,* 105.
49. Hauerwas, S., "Rational Suicide and Reasons for Living," in Verhey, A., and Lammers, S., *On Moral Medicine: Theological Perspectives in Medical Ethics,* (Grand Rapids: Eerdmans, 1987), 465.
50. Ibid.
51. Hendin, H., *Suicide in America,* (New York: W. W. Norton, 1982), 218-19.
52. Neilson, H. A., "Margolis on Rational Suicide: An Argument for Case Studies in Ethics," *Ethics,* 89 (1979): 396.
53. Verhey, A., "The Death of Infant Doe: Jesus and the Neonates," reprinted in Ed. Verhey, A. and Lammers, S., *On Moral Medicine,* 490-91.
54. May, W. F., "The Sacral Power of Death in Contemporary Experience," reprinted in Verhey and Lammers, adduce., *Morals in Medicine,* 179
55. Ramsey, P., "The Indignity of Death with Dignity," reprinted in Verhey and Lammers, adduce., *Morals in Medicine,* 190.

56. See Brown, R. E., *The Gospel According to John,* XII-XXI Vol. 29a of the Anchor Bible Series (New York: Doubleday, 1970), 912. Brown claims, and virtually all leading Johannine scholars concur, that the Crucifixion of Jesus is the moment of his glorification; the time of greatest shame is the time of greatest glory.
57. Longmore, P., "Elizabeth Bouvia, Assisted Suicide and Social Prejudice," 159.

6

The Voluntariness of Rational Suicide

Are "rational" suicides the result of voluntary decisions? In recent years, there has been much controversy about the rationality of reflexive killing, and numerous authors have argued that willful self-killing can sometimes be rational. Many philosophers have suggested that suicide can be rational in some instances, but not many have systematically and rigorously probed the prior question of whether suicidal acts are truly free and done with sufficient knowledge and consent to make them authentically voluntary. It is somewhat surprising that this question has not been raised more rigorously because it is difficult to declare an action rational unless it is rather clear that it is sufficiently voluntary. As a result, many seem to presume that suicide is morally acceptable once it is determined to be rational without first determining it to be authentically voluntary. Some now claim that there are situations in which a decision to end one's life would not be just a free, voluntary, and willful decision, but possibly the most free and deliberate action one can perform.[1] This issue is important because it raises questions of whether the action can be rational if it is not adequately voluntary.

In this chapter, I will argue that the suicide decision does not meet contemporary criteria for rationality because it does not meet generally accepted standards for voluntariness. To do this, I will first examine the psychological aspects of the suicide decision to show that the conditions of minimal voluntariness required to make it rational are not present in it. Then I will identify the criteria necessary to constitute a level of knowledge, consent, and freedom sufficient to make the action voluntary and argue that suicidal decisions do not meet these minimal criteria.

Classical Catholic teachings have held that authentic human choices require adequate knowledge, consent, and freedom to be voluntary, and these conditions are not found in "rational" suicides.[2] They argue that decisions made by individuals should not be taken to be rational merely because they appear voluntary.[3] To say this is not to imply that decisions to end one's life made with full knowledge, voluntariness, and freedom would be morally permissible and should therefore be permitted, but only that a decision to end one's life by suicide should not be presumed to have been done with sufficient voluntariness. A close study of the psychological forces underlying such decisions reveals their doubtfully voluntary character. Those who commit suicide do so for what they believe are "rational" reasons, but these reasons are not what drive them to self-execute, and what propels them to this decision are internal psychological forces that compromise their voluntariness and eliminate other possible responses to their crisis.

Judging whether an act of reflexive killing has been done with sufficient voluntariness is often difficult. For example, most presume that a soldier who jumps on a hand grenade to save his comrades is acting voluntarily. Yet, many believe that a man who throws himself off a cliff to escape attack or one who suicides in order to avoid a slow and painful death is probably deciding with deficient voluntariness due to pain, fear, and depression. There are many similarities between these actions, and it is not clear why one appears voluntary and free while the others do not.

Catholic teachings have not traditionally raised the question of the voluntariness of suicidal decisions in a serious way, but modern suicidology has shown rather clearly that these decisions are usually made under the influence of powerful psychological forces that compromise voluntariness. Psychological analysis categorizes actions as intentional, subintentional, or unintentional, and suicide is usually considered to be a subintentional decision. In an intentional act, the agent directly and consciously brings about the action. An unintentional act occurs when the agent does the act without choice or when one's choice plays no role in the action at all; the individual is not responsible for the act in this case. But in subintentional action, the agent shares the causality of the action with some other extrinsic or intrinsic cause; there is mitigated and limited responsibility for the act. This implies a limited degree of moral culpability for the decision, but it also implies a significant, but probably not total, loss of freedom and voluntariness.

This chapter will argue not so much that suicide is subintentional as it is subvoluntary and hence cannot be considered a controlled and rational performance of the agent. The subvoluntary character of suicide means not only that the person is not fully responsible for the action, but also that the agent is not adequately free to choose alternatives. In a suicidal act, the agent bears part of the moral responsibility for direct destruction of innocent life, even though this culpability is reduced by the radically restricted freedom of the person. The most important aspect of the subvoluntary character of suicide is that the agent's freedom is limited or qualified by intrinsic or extrinsic factors but not wholly abolished, as it is in an involuntary act. The suicidal person usually has other options available, but they cannot choose them because they are crippled by their shattered ego and internal psychic conflicts; as a result, their freedom to do so is radically limited. Because of this limited freedom, what might be options for others are not for them, and their decision is subvoluntary.

After showing the subvoluntary character of suicide, I will explain why the suicidal action is not sufficiently voluntary to be accepted as a rational and controlled act. And finally, in light of the complex psychology of the suicidal decision, specific kinds of self-killing will be examined to show that they are not done with sufficient freedom, consent, and voluntariness to be considered rational.

The Suicidal Decision: A Psychological Portrait

Proponents of rational suicide fail to understand the profoundly ambivalent character of a suicidal decision because they do not understand the psychological forces that drive it, and thus they conclude it to be a voluntary and rational decision. Suicide is a "subvoluntary" action because many environmental and psychological factors compromise and limit its voluntariness. From the perspective of suicidology, the traits and dynamics of a suicide described in what follows are common to all suicidal desires irrespective of their circumstances, condition, age, or motives.

From a psychological perspective, suicide is a "problem-solving" behavior of a most peculiar and unproductive sort, for it is an attempt to solve the problems of pain, despair, suffering, and dying by destroying the subject rather than eliminating the causes of the suffering or bringing the person to a different understanding of them. But as a problem-solving behavior, suicide is particularly brutal, inefficient, and unproductive. Everyone faces suffering and emotional problems, for all experience failure, loneliness, rejection, or the loss of health, love, or social status. At one time or another, all feel rejected, tense and unable to cope, and suicide is only one of many possible ways of dealing with these difficulties. Those contemplating suicide try alternatives but find no relief or improvement, which is why they become lethal and their exhaustion and fear become so pervasive that they strike at themselves. They become exhausted because of the fruitlessness of their struggle and they see suicide as a last resort solution. They contemplate suicide long and hard, rehearse it, and develop a plan to do it as other options gradually lose their power to relieve their suffering.

In this decision, environmental factors exacerbate the suicidal person's suffering and precipitate their ego crisis, raising this internal conflict to a lethal level. They justify their decision by claiming that their suffering, indignity, and loss of meaning are so profound that suicide is the only answer. But suicide is the final act of self-destruction to protest an inflexible ego, alienation, social isolation, obsessive-compulsiveness, and depression. That suicide is not rational crisis management is seen in the disproportionate violence of the suicidal person in relation to the extrinsic factors invoked to justify it. Commonly, the suicidal justify their decision by appeals to loneliness, pain, frustration, and rejection, but these conditions are not proportionate to the ultimate act of self-destructive violence. Advocates of rational suicide claim that such reflexive violence is rational, and ignore that it is more of an uncontrolled flight and escape from a threat or crisis than it is a rational management of a problem. The suicidal person is analogous to an army in flight, without control, restraint, or order, which is witnessed by their conflict, confusion, and ambivalence.

Flight from suffering, pain, threats, or challenges is the most notable feature of suicide and the suicidal are brought to flight in three distinct stages.[4] First, they find themselves in a highly distressed and perturbed condition because of various environmental or psychological factors, usually some traumatic loss. Inimicality is the second stage of their suicidal journey and at this stage the suicidal generate certain counterproductive behaviors and show a great deal of antipathy toward themselves and others. In this stage, because they have usually become more involved in drug or alcohol abuse, they have grown hostile, quarrelsome, and aggressive. But neither of these states makes the person reflexively lethal, for it is only at a later phase that the suicidal person becomes deadly to themselves. The best indicator that the stage of lethality has been reached is when the person starts using the language of despair. They usually become lethal when they conclude that all of the other problem-solving options are ineffective and that the only escape from their suffering is that offered by suicide. The suicidal person becomes exhausted and despairing because of their struggle to escape their pain, and they believe that suicide alone will provide them with their needed relief. From the psychological standpoint, the decision to suicide is a capitulation to these destructive psychic forces and tensions that exhaust and trap them, lead them to despair, crush their ego, and their will to survive. Why one ultimately despairs and becomes reflexively lethal is still shrouded in mystery, but in all likelihood, the suicidal believe that striking out at environmental factors will not relieve their sufferings and they attack themselves as the easiest way of making the pain vanish. In struggling against the psychic threats to their integrity, the suicidal exhaust themselves, capitulate to these forces, and become reflexively lethal.

Suicide is perhaps the most extreme form imaginable of acting out of one's internal conflicts.[5] It is an attention-getting device *par excellence* and the suicidal act out their ego conflicts in the bluntest and harshest manner possible. Suicide is a nonverbal translation of an unconscious conflict into conscious action, and is an attempt to call attention to the individual's problems in a violent, unfeeling, and brutal way. And it is this brutality that makes so many friends and relatives of the suicidal person suffer so deeply in its aftermath.[6]

Suicidologists are nearly unanimous in holding that suicides are "dyadic" in that they are undertaken not merely to rid the person of suffering and misery, but to compel some act or forbearance by another. Suicide is an act of manipulation because it aims at controlling another and forcing them to conform to the suicidal person's wishes. It is a punishment inflicted on others, or an act of revenge taken against another for perceived mistreatment or abuse. Suicide advocates are hard pressed to defend the appropriateness of suicide as a response to a loss of dignity or meaning in the face of other options. Their violence is simply not proportionate to a "meaningless" life or one "without dignity," but it is proportionate to a failing struggle against an inadequate ego.[7]

Suicide is more analogous to the violent self-mutilation of the schizophrenic than to the violence of the murderer; it is not so much an act of protest against loss of meaning or dignity as it is the ultimate act of self-mutilation. The schizophrenic self-mutilates because a given appendage seems offensive and seriously defective, and just as they attack this appendage, the suicidal person attacks the offending ego. Guilt plays a prominent role in most suicides, for self-mutilation is usually a radical means of purging one's guilt. Both the mutilating schizophrenic and the suicidal person come to a point in time when they lose their physical, emotional, or psychological will to continue their struggle, and they desperately strike back at the powers and forces, primarily within themselves, that cannot be contained with less violent means of control. In contrast, one who only has suicidal wishes, but does not become lethal, recovers their energy and reintegrates their ego to a certain extent.

Suicide is the ultimate act of self-criticism, self-rejection, and self-condemnation. It is the most definitive way of saying to oneself: "I do not forgive!" When measured against one's often unrealistic ideals, the suicidal person feels inadequate, and they demonstrate their inability to forgive themselves by acting with extreme reflexive violence.[8] Suicide is an inner-directed act that manifests a lack of moral scruple and restraint, for rather than adjusting to the sometimes harsh demands of reality, the suicidal bring utter devastation on themselves without concern for the rightness of the act or its impact on others.

Not only do powerful psychological forces drive the suicidal to despair, but socioeconomic factors also contribute to this as well. The reasons commonly invoked to justify suicide usually differ according to one's socioeconomic condition, and those of one socioeconomic group will appear utterly rational and convincing to them, while they will appear frivolous and irrational to those in other socioeconomic groups. The most advantaged tend to commit suicide because of a boredom with life, while those immediately beneath them usually give medical or financial reasons for suiciding, and romantic reasons are the most common among the moderately advantaged.[9] The less advantaged commit suicide from feelings of loneliness or isolation, and the least advantaged usually do not give moral reasons for suicide, but do so to protest the world and its cruelty as a whole.[10]

Suicide occurs at all stages of terminal diseases and will most probably occur if there is: (1) stress; (2) dejection, agitation, or overdependency; (3) low tolerance for pain or discomfort; (4) excessive complaining or demanding and attention-getting behavior; (5) severe depression, anxiety, exaggerated desire to control others; (6) relative alertness and orientation; (7) exhaustion of physical, economic, and emotional resources; and (8) prior suicide attempts.[11] Age and sexual differences have a bearing on suicidal practices as well, and two groups at highest risk of suicide are elderly men with cancer of the larynx and younger men with Hodgkin's disease or leukemia. Men are more lethal than women, but women make many more suicide attempts than men; men commonly use violent means such as shooting or hanging to kill themselves, while women usually self-destruct in less violent ways by taking drugs or slashing their wrists. In general, the wish to kill decreases with age, while the wish to die increases.[12] The elderly are more prone to suicide than the younger, and older men are the most lethal.[13] Younger males are more intensely antipathetic toward others, while chronic feelings of despair, depression, and discouragement are more common in older males.

In addition to these above-mentioned qualities, there are four common characteristics of suicidal persons. The first is a reflexive orientation of their violence in response to both environmental and egotistical causes. The suicidal suffer from divided intentionality, for while they justify their decision by blaming environmental factors, their lethality is directed at themselves rather than at their environment. Murderers usually blame extrinsic factors for their actions and they direct their lethality at those extrinsic and environmental causes. In a suicidal person, the environmental causes provoke the ego's self-destructive reaction, but the real sources of the suicidal wish are intrinsic to the person, and striking at the extrinsic causes would not eliminate the underlying causes of their self-destructive wishes. Their lethality is not pointed at another because the suicidal person sees the cause of their distress as the ego itself and not something extrinsic.

These intrinsic factors are the dominating factors in the suicidal decision, and almost always they are so strong that they reduce suicide to a subvoluntary act. Advocates of rational suicide argue that extrinsic factors alone cause and justify suicide, but suicide almost never occurs only in their presence alone and without these intrinsic psychological factors. Suicide advocates claim that some suicides do not result from intrinsic psychological forces and are therefore voluntary, but there is little support for this view in contemporary suicidology, and the burden of proof for this claim is on proponents of rational suicide. One commits suicide partly because of the force of environmental factors, but primarily because the ego is unable to maintain its integrity in the face of threats and challenges on account of its own inflexibility, weaknesses, and defects. The suicidal ego is so frail and impaired that it believes that self-destruction offers the only means of relief, but its crisis cannot be resolved by merely striking out at the extrinsic causes of suffering because they are only the secondary, but not the fundamental causes. While the environment might be somewhat provocative and threatening to the person, it is less so than the defective ego, and the only definitive solution to the suicidal person's crisis is self-destruction. In this perspective, suicidal lethality is not misdirected, but is properly aimed at the self because the source of the person's distress and pain is primarily the weak and shattered ego and only secondarily the environment.

The suicidal decision usually results from the ego's failure to cope, not so much with the environment, but with its own inability to understand or control its own dangerous wishes resulting from its defects and inadequacy. As the suicidal person's ego constricts, it creates a sense of hopelessness that can deteriorate to the point of a cognitive defect.[14] In some cases, the suicidal suffer from an overbearing superego that cannot accept assistance because of an all-or-nothing view of life, which suggests that they are losing life's struggles.[15] The suicidal attack themselves when they lose confidence in their ability to sustain themselves or protect themselves from anguish and suffering, and this crisis of confidence provokes their reflexive attack. Their ego usually collapses when its perceptions of impotence, isolation, alienation, and abandonment overwhelm it, and this is often best overcome by reintegrating the suicidal person into a supportive community.

The second most common trait of the suicidal persons is ambivalence and unresolved conflict about their suicidal desires. The prototypical suicidal person is one who cuts his throat and fantasizes about rescue--both at the same time![16] They make elaborate plans to die, but also entertain fantasies of rescue at precisely the point they are to die. The most significant single factor in precipitating their decision is a traumatic experience of rejection.[17] The suicidal are ambivalent and in conflict because they seek a number of different and conflicting objectives in the same action. In their death decision they usually have one or more of the following: (1) a wish for surcease, escape, or sleep; (2) a guilt-driven wish for sacrifice, punishment, or restitution; (3) a hostile wish for revenge, power, control, or murder; (4) an erotic wish for passionate surrender, ecstasy, or reunion with beloved dead; and (5) a hopeful wish for life, rescue, rebirth, or a new start.[18] This desire suggests that a suicidal decision is a sign of an unconscious fantasy for immortality.[19] This is probably true, as many suicidal persons subconsciously seek to be united with a deceased parent or loved one.

The suicidal individual's ambivalence is seen even further in the conflict between their justification for their action and the direction of their lethal attack. While they claim their suffering is caused partly by the environment, they contradict that claim by striking at themselves and not at their environment. At the conscious level, the suicidal see environmental factors as the cause of their distress, but at the subconscious level they see their ego as defective and the primary cause of their suffering, which is why they attack it and not some extrinsic cause. They frequently blame their plight on the meaninglessness of their life or their loss of dignity, but their lethal act is not directed at this indignity or meaninglessness, but at their own ego, which signifies their ambivalence. This ambivalence is also seen in the mix of conflicting emotions and feelings. On the one hand, they express feelings of inadequacy, inability to control their environment, weakness, and dependence on others, but on the other hand, they can be very aggressive and hostile, given to sarcasm, and refuse to accept the help or counsel of anyone.

If the suicidal person's thinking is primitive and undeveloped, vigorous arguments are ordinarily not needed to dissuade them from going through with it, for they are usually hoping more for an intervention and support from another than for death. But this does not always apply to one who suicides primarily to escape serious pain or deprivation, for ordinarily they can be brought through their stage of lethality by reducing their pain and restoring their psychological energy and confidence, which can be extremely difficult in some situations.

The third feature commonly found in suicides is that most of them happen after significant thought, planning, reflection, and struggle, and relatively few suicides occur on the spur of the moment. This takes place even in what appears to be the most irrational and impulsive kinds of suicide, for they usually ponder long and hard beforehand whether to carry it out. It is common for the suicidal action to be planned and rehearsed in the person's imagination as well as in preliminary or preparatory actions, and in almost every suicidal plan, there is evidence of ambivalence, conflict, and mixed motivations.[20] The suicidal person's death-dealing plans gain a force of their own, and once the decision has been made, the plan takes on a life of its own. As the plan develops, reality recedes in the person's mind and the power of the suicidal fantasy grows.[21] These fantasies reinforce one another and the suicidal person becomes more and more habituated to them, such that they cannot free themselves from their soothing effects and the plan itself ultimately drives them to choose death.

The fourth common feature is that the suicidal suffer from depression and is usually a dependent-dissatisfied personality who suffers from ego splitting.[22] The suicidal commonly show all of the symptoms of severe depression: (1) dejection; (2) mood swings; (3) loss of appetite; (4) sleep disorders; (5) despondency; (6) apathy; (7) withdrawal; (8) low tolerance for pain; (9) agitation; (10) severe feelings of hopelessness and helplessness; (11) excessive demands and complaining; (12) a strong need for attention; (13) controlling and manipulating activity; (14) exhaustion of physical and emotional resources; and (15) a feeling of lack of support from one's friends and family.[23]

The suicidal usually have rather weak family support and are more concerned with bodily functions than are the nonsuicidal. They are more likely to be manic-depressive, have parents with psychiatric difficulties, and be in more intense relationships with others than the nonsuicidal. A few suicidal individuals show no symptoms of a crisis or personality change and do not give voice to their conflicts, but most suicidal personalities give rather clear warning of their self-destructive inclinations. Emotionally dependent on others but dissatisfied with that dependency, the suicidal constantly demand support and special attention from others. They desperately want control, not only over their own life, but over the lives of others as well, and when that control begins to slip away they often descend into despair and lethality. They need the support of others more than do the nonsuicidal, have more difficulties with their relationships and have a strong need to please others. The suicidal suffer stress more severely than others and this is manifested in the deep depressions that they experience.

Terminal illness and cancer in particular increase depression and stress, which makes these patients more prone to suicide. In their recent book, David Thomasma and Edmund Pelligrino noted that

> even the briefest experience with illness shows that ill persons often can become so anxious, guilty, fearful or hostile that they make judgments that they would not make in calmer times. Patients become so preoccupied with their diseases and their bodies, and many see their bodies as objects that have failed them. Patients are forced to reassess their values and goals. These primary characteristics of illness alter their personal wholeness to a profound degree. They also change some of our assumptions about the operation of personal autonomy in the one who is.[24]

Relative to other patients, the terminally ill and those with cancer are more prone to suicide, are more anxious, hostile, disturbed, agitated, and they complain more often of controls imposed on them. Marked depression is expected of the seriously ill, and most terminal patients are more anxious and expressive of guilt and inadequacy than others.

With the elderly or sick, their suicides are often precipitated by some abrupt, unfeeling action or decision by another, they give fewer indications of their suicidal ruminations, and they show less acting out and fewer warnings.

Suicide is more common among alcoholics because their chronic depression fosters strong self-destructive tendencies. Alcohol weakens the self-preservative functions of the ego and allows latent suicidal urges to emerge.[25] In chronic alcoholics, suicidal fantasies dominate when their drinking gets out of control, and about 5 percent of all alcoholics commit suicide. Many do this because they never feel able to free themselves from their depression or a dependent relationship that finally falls apart, leaving them abandoned and open to suicide.[26] The psychotic are also far more susceptible to self-destruction than the nonpsychotic and their inability to clearly comprehend their world leaves them feeling of abandoned, helpless, and isolated, increasing their lethality.[27]

The feature most frequently associated with suicide is a failure of the ego to orient itself to the external world and an inability to control dangerous wishes.[28] The suicidal usually manifest serious ego splitting and perceive that the one being killed is not their real and true self, but another self, and under the burden of stress and guilt they believe that the self that is destroyed is separated from the one that is tormented. Because of this ego splitting, the suicidal often claim they feel weak and confused until they attack themselves, at which point they feel strong, purposeful, and avenging. They feel this way because suicide destroys the tormenting side of their fragmented ego. This ego splitting is seen in the significant changes that most of the suicidal manifest shortly before their deaths.[29]

The violence of the suicidal person is proportionate to their choice to end once and for all the torment of a weak, rigid, brittle, and defective ego, but it is not proportionate to the extrinsic causes that are blamed for their condition such as indignity or meaninglessness. Suicide is the product of a schizoid mind that fails to understand that the person's reflexive lethality is aimed at the true self rather than at an imaginary tormenting self. The suicidal have lost their ability to manage the events of their life and they strike out at the cause of their disorder, their very self. Suicide is the ultimate ego crisis and the suicidal person denies the ego because it is fractured, chaotic, empty, and impotent, and the decision to suicide affirms all of these in their minds. A frequently heard claim of those who attempt suicide is that "there was no other way out of the situation," which usually expresses more the chaos, powerlessness, and emptiness of their ego than the objective futility of the situation. The inescapable pain, suffering, and agony are more of a measure of the paralysis and emptiness of their egos than of the objective futility of their situation.

If this profile of the suicidal person is accurate and if suicide is really the result of these forces, it calls into serious question contemporary claims that the suicidal decision is a voluntary act. This profile suggests strongly that suicide is subvoluntary and that the suicidal person is not adequately free to make a rational decision because he or she is driven by these complex and subtle psychological forces. Rather than deciding with full voluntariness for suicide, as one among many options, this profile suggests that the suicidal person capitulates to the profound psychic forces of guilt, depression, despair, ambivalence, and fear and flees to it as the last and only perceived safe haven. In the following section, I will try to make this point clearer by showing that the suicidal decision lacks the elements of a truly free, voluntary, consented, and knowledgeable human action.

Suicide and Voluntariness

The Subvoluntary Character of Suicide

The previous examination of the psychological factors underlying the suicidal decision argues strongly that suicide is a capitulation to these forces and is an attack on a deficient ego more than it is a rational and intelligent way of coping with a serious environmental crisis. But this portrait of the suicidal personality does not definitively demonstrate that it is a subvoluntary decision, for such a judgment can only be properly made after a closer examination of the basic elements of voluntariness. The question of the voluntariness of an action is important because the absence of adequate voluntariness means that the agent lacks adequate control over the action, which in turn implies that the action may not be fully rational. Adequate voluntariness means that the agent truly possesses and controls the action and has responsibility for it.

This section will describe the basic elements of a controlled and voluntary action to show that suicide is subvoluntary and does not result from adequate control by the agent. To determine whether an action is truly under the control of the agent and is more than a subvoluntary act, the following conditions need to be met:

1. A voluntary act proceeds from true and adequate knowledge and presumptions about the act in which the agent knows the nature and moral quality of the decision. For a decision to be sufficiently

voluntary that it can be a controlled performance of the agent, the knowledge and presumptions governing the choice must be true and adequate, and the agent must know the nature of the act being done. A decision made from inadequate or false presumptions, or without adequate knowledge, consent, or freedom is either involuntary or subvoluntary because it is not fully under the agent's control.[30] Acts that are voluntary enough to be under the agent's control are not the products of ignorance, false or insufficiently grounded presumptions, are not caused by extrinsic forces or the decisions of others, and they follow from the knowledgeable, free, consented, and deliberate choice of the person.[31] This is not to claim that decisions supposedly made with full freedom, knowledge, and voluntariness are rational and moral, but that decisions made with insufficient freedom, presumptions, knowledge, or consent are not under the agent's control and are not sufficiently voluntary to be considered rational.[32]

An authentically voluntary act is a rationally planned and deliberately chosen act, and it is not fully voluntary if it derives from an irrational or absurd plan.[33] The end or objective of the decision must be included in the consciously formulated proposal for action.[34] This standard excludes coerced or extrinsically manipulated actions, and it also excludes some choices or actions done impulsively, in panic, or in extreme fear because they do not result from a deliberate plan or proposal of the agent.[35] In most suicidal decisions, it is not easy to know if the agent's decision and action is being manipulated and if their decision is truly voluntary, intended, and planned. And in most suicidal decisions, it is usually the case that their knowledge and presumptions about the act are seriously deficient.

2. For a suicide to be more than subvoluntary, the agent has to be both objectively and subjectively free to renounce the suicidal decision and choose another course of action. An act is voluntary when there is sufficient freedom for the agent to do either the action or an alternative in identical circumstances.[36] And if there is no other objectively available option, or if the agent is not able to subjectively choose another option, the act would be subvoluntary or involuntary. The freedom of the agent here must not only be an objective freedom, in which there are real and objective alternatives available to the agent, but also a subjective freedom in which the agent is psychologically capable of choosing a different course of action. This is an important requirement because many suicidal persons lack the subjective freedom to select options extrinsically available to them.

3. The agent must consent to and affirm the means to the end of the act, the act itself, and the foreseen effects of the action as both

desired and sought after for the act to be more than merely subvoluntary. There are probably few moral judgments that are harder to make than that concerning the level of consent given an action, for there are many actions that agents profess to reject and not consent to, and yet perform. In a voluntary act, the agent agrees with, affirms, and accepts the decision, the means to achieve the end, and the consequences of the act.[37]

If one dies from an unconsented causal series they did not initiate, the action is not voluntary, and one who wills to die but does not will and consent to the means to bring that about is not suiciding. One who dies accidentally on the way to a suicide attempt does not perform a fully voluntary and free suicide, even though they may have given consent to this death, because they do not control the means to bring about their death. The act would be voluntary or subvoluntary depending on the proximity of the agent in the causality of the action and the level of consent given to the means that brought about the effects.

In the following sections, I will discuss the specific requirements of knowledge, freedom, and consent that have to be present for a suicidal action to be considered more than subvoluntary in order to show that the suicidal act is not voluntary.

Adequate Knowledge, True Presumptions, and Voluntary Suicide

For an act to be legitimately voluntary, the agent has to act from adequate presumptions and knowledge about the nature and effects of the action, which means that the decision must be made with knowledge of the substance and moral character of the action.[38]

1. The requirement of adequate knowledge demands that the agent presume, or have reason to presume, that the action being chosen would result in self-annihilation.[39] This ordinarily requires the self-slaying person to presume, or have sound reason to presume, that the action being planned will certainly and in itself bring self-destruction rather than paradise, Nirvana, or some sort of heavenly state. It is doubtful that those who suicide fully comply with this requirement as they are usually concerned with compensation, rest, comfort, escape, revenge, or restitution and do not dwell on the fact that suicide truly brings death. While those who study suicide usually consider it to be either a self-destructive act of flight, panic, or revenge, or an act of atonement for guilt, most suicidal persons believe they will not actually suffer death, and because of this, one can wonder if they possess true and adequate knowledge and

presumptions about the consequences of their action. Because of the strength of contemporary suicide propaganda, it is very easy to believe that suicide simply ends one's problems swiftly and painlessly while ignoring the fact that it ends one's existence.[40] Many of the suicidal presume death is either akin to a dream state, or to an experience of utter human fulfillment, and they fail to see that it is the destruction of our human existence as we know it.[41] Most suicidal persons approach death from something of a Manichean perspective and regard it as a transcendent condition that frees the body from all of its pain, suffering, and misery. The suicidal usually regard their postmortality condition as full human existence but free from pain, suffering, and misery and not as total self-destruction. Suicidal individuals infrequently choose death as an end in itself and usually choose it as a means to another end, all the while paying pay scant attention to what suicide really is. Classical Catholic teaching has quite consistently rejected a choice for death for either purpose, and it is unlikely that those contemplating suicide fully grasp this because of their confusion and ambivalence. It held that death could be inflicted on an individual who had grievously harmed the common good, or to defend innocent life, but it rejected deliberately destroying the life of an innocent individual as an end or as a means.

The requirement of adequate knowledge demands that the person have a *realistic* concept of death in which they understand that death is self-destruction of their being and existence as they now know it and is not a certain escape to pure bliss. Most suicidal persons believe suicide brings about escape, alleviation of guilt, restitution, rest, passionate surrender, or revenge, but they ordinarily do not see it as self-extermination, which violates this criterion of adequate knowledge. They usually presume they will survive their self-execution in some fashion and achieve their subconsciously intended goals without truly being destroyed, and these questionable presumptions can reduce an action to the subvoluntary level. This presumption that suicide brings full life rather than destruction shows the presence of a form of ego splitting that is quite common with the suicidal and justifies wondering how clearly and completely they understand their suicidal act.[42] They believe they will exist after death in full and uncompromised human fulfillment and flourishing. But classical Catholic spiritual theology has held that suffering is alleviated not simply by death, but through union with God that comes from faith, hope, charity, and holiness. From the Catholic perspective, the suicidal viewpoint is theologically false because it attributes to death what is proper only to the life of grace.

For an action to be fully voluntary, it is essential that it be part of not only the person's plan of action but also the result of the means the person enacts. Thus, one who accidentally drops a banana peel on a staircase, slips on it and kills himself would not necessarily be suiciding because the lethal action would neither be part of the plan of the agent nor an element of a means deliberately chosen to bring about death. There is no solid reason to presume that banana peels are seriously lethal, and people do not ordinarily end their lives by stepping on them. But on the other hand, one who is going to throw himself in front of a train does not commit suicide if he is accidentally shot by a hunter on the way because he rightly presumes that walking through the woods is not a lethal act. He achieves his objectives and probably consents to them, but his death does not result from his plan and his death is not a suicide. But one who puts a loaded gun to his head and fires can reasonably presume death will result, and such an act is usually regarded as part of a suicidal plan and a reliable means of self-executing.

Virtually all suicidal persons experience some ambivalence, for on the one hand, most who suicide mull over it for a long period of time and minutely calculate their deaths, but on the other hand it is often an act of panic, desperation, and flight. If this sort of rescue-fantasy was less common in a suicidal plan, one could say with less reservation that a suicidal decision would possess adequate knowledge and presumptions. But given the fact that most suicidal plans include self-contradictory elements, it is difficult to say that they derive from a true and authentic plan.

2. When a choice involves a critical unavoidable error or suffers from certain crucial unintended errors, omissions, or ignorance it is subvoluntary or involuntary. Thus, suicides undertaken for the usual subconscious reasons, such as uniting oneself to a deceased love one or finding respite or rescue, would be ruled out as fully voluntary because they are done while mistaking crucial aspects of the action. If a woman shot and killed a man trying to get into her home at night believing him to be an intruder and not her husband, her action would not be entirely voluntary because she intended to kill a hostile intruder and not her husband. Similarly, one could mistake the quality of an act through forgetfulness or inadvertence, and this error would diminish the act's voluntariness. If someone was simply mistaken in judging a critical feature of an act, their decision would be voluntary in a qualified way, but it would not be entirely involuntary.[43] There is a serious presumptive error in a suicide that could compromise its voluntariness and reduce it to a subvoluntary

act because one strikes primarily and directly at the ego even though the act is understood as a counter to environmental factors. This is a serious misunderstanding for this sort of presumption sees an action that is gravely harmful as essentially beneficial.

3. The requirement that an act flow from true and adequate presumptions and knowledge also requires that acts not be performed under the burden of specific types of ignorance.[44] Unconsented and unwilled ignorance can limit or destroy an action's voluntariness and acts done under such ignorance would not be fully voluntary.[45] If a motorist struck a dog because he was too lazy to clean his windshield and could not see where he was going, this would be a peculiar form of voluntary killing. He could not plead that the death was involuntary because he freely and knowingly chose to drive with obstructed vision. Deliberate neglect of ordinary responsibilities does not make actions involuntary, and by neglecting to clean his windshield out of laziness, he deliberately made himself ignorant of what he was expected to know. This would be voluntary because one could reasonably presume that he would collide with something because of his impaired vision. But if a driver hit a dog he could not see on a dark, rainy night, it would probably not be voluntary because the death was not due to neglect or deliberate and defeatable ignorance.

Suicidal decisions made to provoke intervention and rescue as a means to gain passionate surrender, atone for one's misdeeds, begin a new life, obtain restitution or revenge, or inflict punishment on oneself are done under defeatable ignorance. They are undertaken under the influence of serious errors, and are voluntary in relation to the seriousness of the error and to the extent that the error can be overcome. But overcoming these errors is not simply a matter of conveying correct information to a suicidal person, for the profound psychological forces that drive them to suicide probably stand at the heart of these conceptual deficiencies. In some instances, this can be easily done, but in others, breaking through these barriers can be extraordinarily difficult.

4. For a decision to be truly voluntary, one has to have adequate or true presumptions concerning its moral character.[46] If one received a check in the mail and presumed it to be a gift while in fact it was meant for another of the same name, cashing it would not be an act of voluntary theft. Presuming that the check was meant for oneself would be wrong, but it would be a reasonable and adequate presumption in the situation. Taking the money would not be deliberate stealing, but would be taking what one presumed to be rightfully one's own, and because one had good reason to presume

that taking the money would be ethical, one's freedom to reject it would have been less than if one believed the taking of the money to be wrong.

There is an important reciprocal relationship between the moral judgments made about an action and one's freedom of decision, for one's freedom to decide is often qualified by the moral judgment one makes about an action. Concluding that an action is morally good disposes one to do it, while morally rejecting an act limits one's subjective freedom by inclining one against the act. This is important with respect to the suicide issue, for morally countenancing suicide disposes one toward it and limits one's freedom to renounce it. Sociopaths, for example, who do not believe violent acts that promote their personal interests are wrong, are more prone to use violence to solve their problems, and their freedom to reject even reflexive violence to solve their problems is usually limited. This sort of miscalculation can be most serious because the strongest inhibition to an action is usually a strong moral argument against it, and in its absence, many see little reason to refrain from suiciding. The suicidal decisions of those whose psychological states predispose them to endorse suicide are subvoluntary in the way that a sociopath's decision to act violently is subvoluntary.

Most who commit suicide ultimately disregard the morality of self-killing, not so much because they believe it is a morally good act as they consider its morality secondary to other issues such as finding relief from suffering or gaining revenge. They are less concerned with doing what is morally right than they are with serving their interests and escaping their plight. Some suicidal individuals do not believe self-interested reflexive killing has any substantial moral elements, and they see moral arguments against it as not so much false as irrelevant to the real issues of escaping suffering, alleviating guilt, or finding rest, for example. True moral judgments about the ethics of suicide can impede decisions in its favor, and mistaken judgments about the morality of suicide can assuage moral feelings against it. Many who are tempted to suicide find the voluntariness of their decisions limited because their psychological condition predisposes them to morally endorse the act.

This section has sought to lay out the various criteria for the presumptions, knowledge, and understanding of the suicidal decision and they lead to the conclusion that this decision is so obscure, ambivalent, confused, and incomplete that it is not voluntary, but subvoluntary, and done with false or inadequate knowledge and presumptions.

Subjective Freedom and Rational Suicide

Limitations on subjective freedom to choose, or the absence of this freedom due to disease or other psychological conditions encroach upon our voluntariness more than do limitations on our knowledge, and our voluntariness often is more restricted by restraints on our interior psychological freedom than by exterior physical restraints thrust upon our physical actions. Because our voluntariness is diminished more by restrictions on our freedom, it is necessary to examine the various extrinsic and intrinsic factors that can limit or destroy our freedom: violence, habits, pain, fear, pathological states, passions and emotions, and persuasion or manipulation. These forces can simply wrest control of the action from the agent.

1. Violence and physical pain can either radically limit, or even crush our freedom.[47] Depending on the magnitude of the violence or pain and one's subjective ability to tolerate it, classical Catholic moral theory has been virtually unanimous in holding that externally inflicted pain or violence can limit or destroy voluntariness. Violence from external forces can destroy our control and voluntariness over actions when it eliminates the physical possibility of physically performing acts, but these in lesser degrees may not always and everywhere destroy the agent's freedom.[48]

Classical Catholic thought has held that actions taken *because of* extreme pain are not fully voluntary.[49] Profound pain from illness or disease can be considered a form of violence, which can place some options beyond the scope of the agent and destroy control over the act.[50] At a minimum, physical pain can inhibit voluntariness because it can limit the options the agent subjectively feels are available.[51] For example, depending on the level of pain inflicted, espionage agents who betray state secrets under torture would presumably act either involuntarily or subvoluntarily because of the pain. When this torment becomes so great that escaping it dominates their consciousness and places any other course of action beyond choice, any decision for suicide would be at least subvoluntary. This is important, for pain can diminish or negate voluntariness in many ways. It can be the very subtle pain of inescapable guilt resulting from scrupulosity, compulsiveness or obsession, or it can be a severe sort pain that leads up to death. It can be the pain of unremitting long-term depression, or the pain of self-hatred that makes the ultimate act of self-mutilation seem like the only path of escape to the person. Radical pain can impair or cripple the agent and can wrest control of the action from him or her. The suicidal person can become so obsessed with their pain that they see self-assassination as the only means of escape and reject all other options. The suicidal can become so exhausted from their struggle with their pain or psychological conflicts that they become unable to entertain any other option to deal with the conflict than suicide, and this exhaustion further diminishes the voluntariness of their act.

2. Profound fear can compromise or destroy voluntariness when it causes a patient to lose or radically restrict their self-control.[52] If fear is so great that it skews or overcomes reason or judgment, and destroys control over the action, then actions flowing from it are involuntary or subvoluntary.[53] If a soldier became so overcome by fear that he lost control of his emotions, his flight from battle would be subvoluntary or involuntary.[54] If fear destroys the coherence of his thinking and leaves him so thoroughly muddled that he cannot exert any substantial control, his actions would be either subvoluntary or involuntary depending on the extent of the loss of control. But if fear only prevented one from thinking with full clarity, calmness, and deliberation, then an act would be only partly voluntary, and his flight could be an act of irresponsible cowardice.

Some distinctions must be made to determine whether voluntariness remains partly intact in a fearful suicidal patient. Fear can limit or abolish voluntariness for it can compel one to decide for something without giving that decision full consent.[55] Traditional Catholic thought held that actions done *with* but not *from* fear would be done with diminished voluntariness because this level of fear would not break the agent's control over the action.[56] And fear of suffering or extreme pain could destroy voluntariness, even though it would be possible for some actions chosen in the presence of fear to remain authentically voluntary if the fear was not the cause of action, but merely an accompanying factor of the act.

If an action, however, is truly caused by fear, it would be involuntary.[57] Thus, a suicide done from fear of further pain, torture, and torment would probably be involuntary because the agent would be acting merely to escape the pain and suffering. Actions resulting from indeliberate fear would be involuntary, but deliberate and willful fear would make an action fully voluntary. In this situation, one would put himself or herself into such an agitated condition that they could not adequately reflect or deliberate, but any attempted suicide would be voluntary in spite of this. The rationality of this action could be questionable, as one would wonder how rational it would be to deliberately put oneself into such an agitated state.

This condition would suggest that most suicides are subvoluntary because the suicidal are clearly in flight from something. Suicide is most commonly an act of flight or escape, which argues powerfully that it is caused and controlled by fear. If the fear was sufficiently weak to allow some freedom of decision and control over the action, the suicidal decision would be subvoluntary, but if the fear was so extensive that it actually caused and controlled the suicidal decision, the act would be involuntary. In most suicides, the person's fear is dominating, profound, and pervasive and it drives the person through the stages of perturbation and inimicality to lethality, but it usually does not render the action wholly involuntary. Its subvoluntary character is seen by the fact that even under this fear, the suicidal person can still plan his or her death, and often in great detail. This fear is not absolute and total, and is not sufficiently powerful to abolish all control and ability to plan; thus, the suicidal decision is subvoluntary. The controlling power of fear is also probably much deeper and pervasive in those disposed to suicide because of their ego's weaknesses and vulnerability. Their level of fear increases not only because of the environmental forces that can provoke fear in almost everyone, but also subjective threats they feel from their own psychic incapacities. The ego conflicts of many suicidal patients provoke much fear and drive them to extraordinarily violent acts. If their egos were stronger and more unified, their fear would be reduced, but their chaotic psychic state probably increases their fear and anxiety. The perfectionism, compulsiveness, self-hatred, ego splitting, and lack of confidence often join with other factors to radically increase their fear and limit their control of their actions.

3. Other factors such as habits or addictions may limit the control of an agent over their acts and it is quite likely that some addictions would be the primary cause of some acts.[58] Actions are often done in a habitual and inattentive manner, lacking full advertence and attention, and these actions can be either subvoluntary or involuntary.[59] Actions less final than suicide can be done with more restraints on freedom from habits, compulsions or addictions, but to be adequately voluntary, an act as conclusive as suicide demands more freedom from compulsions and addictions. Adequate voluntariness can only be ascribed to an action as serious as suicide if it is performed with full advertence and knowledge, and is free from the driving compulsions of habits or addictions, which seldom seems to be the case with the suicidal. For example, drug addicts can freely and voluntarily wash dishes and change clothes, but often more subtle and complex actions are doubtfully voluntary because of the limitations

their alcohol dependency can impose on their freedom and decision-making capabilities.

Drug or chemical addiction can also limit or destroy voluntariness by impairing judgment. In many instances, these substances act as depressants and exacerbate whatever tendencies an individual might have in this direction. They do this by destroying one's knowledge of what one is doing or creating such psychological conflict and turmoil that one's psychological energy is drained and one's options are limited.[60] Some drug or alcohol abusers, for example, do not act with full voluntariness because their actions are done with diminished advertence, and often their judgments are so skewed by the influence of these substances that they suffer from diminished control over their actions. And the effects of these addictions can extend over a long period of time as well, for chronic abusers of these substances can experience impeded voluntariness and decision-making ability for years.

Chronic and profound compulsiveness can also radically undermine voluntariness. This can make some individuals more prone to suicide, often masking severe ego conflicts and disturbances, and an extreme example of this is the "health addict" who becomes obsessively worried about their health and physical appearance. It is not uncommon for the entire identity of these personality types to become focused on their physical condition and appearance. In extreme situations they can react so strongly to the loss of health or beauty that they would prefer death to loss of health, strength, or beauty, and their suicidal decisions would be subvoluntary. They place such importance on physical well-being in their compulsiveness that its loss forces them to conclude that life has lost its meaning. Because reality cannot match up to their perfectionistic demands, they often go into near-despair, which makes their suicidal decisions subvoluntary. In the hospital, they frequently become the dependent-dissatisfied patients who move through the suicidal stages to lethality with a great deal of acting out and agitation. Drug addicts, alcoholics, and compulsives are all known to have higher than normal suicide rates, and with some extreme cases, these dependencies seem to actually cause their suicidal decision. And at a minimum, they probably limit the voluntariness of the suicidal decision if not totally destroy it.

4. Profound pathological states, such as epilepsy or severe neurological impairments can reduce an act to the subvoluntary or involuntary level.[61] One who suffers from profound neurological impairments, is wholly paralyzed, or has suffered major brain damage can act with restricted voluntariness. Besides altering the emotional

states of the individual by increasing their depression, these conditions can also create impairments of perception, reasoning, and understanding and can reduce voluntariness. These conditions do not make a suicidal decision entirely involuntary, but they can render it subvoluntary. This should be given consideration when confronting the demands of those with severe neurological impairments for assistance in suiciding, as these conditions can radically impair their voluntariness. This would imply that a suicidal decision of a victim of advanced Alzheimer's or Parkinson's disease might be subvoluntary because these neurological conditions could cause profound cognitive impairments.

5. More recently, some Catholic authors have argued that other conditions can reduce acts to the subvoluntary or involuntary level.[62] States of extreme passion or emotions such as profound depression, hysteria, or agitated states can also make an act subvoluntary or involuntary.[63] The severely depressed are often unable to give due consideration to reasonable options and this can further restrict their voluntariness. Similarly, those in profound grief are often less able to consider options for action than those not suffering in this way. A person who has suffered the trauma and grief of learning that they have a terminal illness and is expected to die soon could be so profoundly disturbed that any decisions they make might not be truly voluntary, for grief and shock could be controlling their decision.

In addition to this, constant and prolonged physical illness can cause neurotic tendencies that can limit voluntariness.[64] That some actions of the profoundly neurotic are subvoluntary is seen by the limited range of action open to many depressed persons. Their constricted emotional capabilities are a sign of their limited decision-making capacity and, by implication, their limited voluntariness. The dying, chronically ill, and terminal often suffer deep depression, which can force them to resort to extreme measures to find relief. And as a result, it is legitimate to question whether their voluntariness is fully intact in those situations, and to challenge suicidal desires and requests.

6. Finally, it has been suggested by Father Bernard Haring that the simple power of mass suggestion can limit the voluntariness of our acts, and in this he is quite correct.[65] The power of contemporary propaganda and advertising has grown so much that many of the less astute are unable to resist its blandishments. Contemporary opinion makers and the printed and electronic media create needs, invent crises, and legitimize dubious moral values to an extraordinary degree, and they can create a "need" in some for suicide. Not only

can the contemporary media "package" their message with astounding persuasiveness, but it can also censor opposing viewpoints in astonishingly subtle, sophisticated, and powerful ways. Their manipulative power is seen, for example, in its extraordinary ability to evoke images of grief, disaster, and suffering and maneuver young women into abortions when this is often the last thing they desire. Not only can our media present the consequences of actions they do not desire as utterly dreadful, but it can also effectively eliminate any undesired alternative by simple censorship. The power of modern mass media can also influence terminally ill persons into ending their lives, for many of these people could find such suggestions irresistible. One in such a situation who is often weak and ambivalent could find such criticism and rejection by their family and health care providers so intolerable that they could find their only realistic option to be suicide. For some, it might well be impossible for people to resist suicidal propaganda because of the power of this propaganda.

When a suicidal decision is made under the direct influence of the dictates of contemporary suicide propaganda, it is quite possible that it is subvoluntary. Alcoholics, or those in despair, grief, or depression are quite vulnerable to the blandishments of this propaganda and their voluntariness could well be significantly reduced by its seductive message. Individuals in these states, with little access to information other than that provided by prosuicide propagandists, could often be making a suicidal decision in the condition of "undefeatable ignorance" and subvoluntarily. One has much reason to suspect that many who decide to suicide are deeply swayed by this propaganda because one so often hears the exact same justifications for the actions from different mouths at different times.

This section has sought to show that the voluntariness of suicide is significantly reduced by various factors that can limit free and deliberate control over our acts. The conclusion that should be drawn is that these forces are present in such a substantial degree that not only is suicide ordinarily a subvoluntary action, but it may be fully involuntary in some cases.

Suicide, Voluntariness, and Consent

Catholic moral theology has traditionally held that an action lacking full and free consent is not voluntary, and an act given qualified, confused, or ambivalent consent would be either subvoluntary or involuntary. When one gives consent, one positively desires, affirms, or endorses the means and the end of the action in some way.[66]

One becomes affectively oriented toward it, endorsing and approving the good brought by the act and the means employed to realize this good.[67]

To give valid consent, one formulates a plan to achieve the desired and chosen object of the act.[68] Then, one reflects upon and deliberates about the nature, gravity, and circumstances of the act.[69] After that, a judgment is made to employ a specific means to achieve the given objective and the will elects a given means to accomplish the end.[70] Determining this, the person affirms, approves, endorses, and confirms the means to be used to achieve the end.[71] The agent then undertakes the necessary practical measures to accomplish the objectives sought,[72] and finally, the agent consents to the action, the agent "enjoys" what is being sought and shares in the fruits of the action.[73]

One can give qualified consent to actions in many instances, which can limit an act's voluntariness.[74] But even when one knows explicitly what is being sought and done in an action, one frequently does not give full and explicit consent. Giving clear but qualified consent to an action can reduce it from the voluntary to the subvoluntary. For example, a young woman who is raped might "tolerate" this in order to save her life, but if she does not give consent to it, it would not be voluntary on her part. Presumably, she would be intending to save her life by permitting the attack; she would be consenting to an act to save her life, and not to being raped. Similarly, a man who was caught in a burning building and chose to run one way rather than the other would not necessarily be consenting to death if he was to die as a result of his decision.

For a suicide to be fully voluntary, the person has to consent to the ending of their life and the means to bring this about. And a suicidal decision in the absence of this level of consent would be subvoluntary. Fully voluntary suicidal decisions flow from an intention to embrace death as a good for the individual, and this consent has to be given to death either as a means or an end in itself.[75] In such an action, consent is given to destroying life, and even though the motive behind a suicide might be the perception that human life itself has lost its value, death is seen as a good. Unlike the goods of justice and truth, which are universal and unconditional, the self-slayer ordinarily sees life as only a conditional value. They believe that life is a good only in relation to their projects and desires, and it can be destroyed when these cannot be fulfilled or accomplished. If one consents to taking an analgesic that would remove pain and "loss of dignity" without bringing death, their suicidal act should be presumed to be consented to because they had an option to serve their interests without bringing death on themselves, but declined it.

The difficulty with claiming that the suicidal person gives adequate consent to death is that it is not clear what the objects of their consent are, for the ambiguity of death itself makes it unclear what suicidal consent involves. Are they consenting to the escape from suffering? Death itself? The state to which they will be delivered in their fantasies? They might be consenting to what they see as a means of gaining bliss, escape, or respite, or they could be consenting to it as an act of simple self-destruction. At best, the consent given to a suicidal act is ambivalent, confused, incomplete, or nonexistent and not adequate to make the decision voluntary. Suicidal consent is subvoluntary because its possible objects are so contradictory, complex, and vague that the suicidal person is giving a qualified, confused, and contradictory consent at best. They do not simply consent to, affirm, and want death, for they want many other things as well, and if they consent to death, it is a limited, conditioned, restricted, and qualified consent. And as the suicidal decision aims primarily at escape when no other subjectively perceived alternatives are available, it is not clear that consent is given merely to escape or to death itself, which is why traditional Catholic moral thought has condemned suicide both as an end and as a means. If the suicidal person gives unequivocal consent to death, it is not evident by the rationalizations and justifications they give for their decision. The prototypical suicide is one who wants escape but does not want to die, which suggests that consent to death is hardly given with enthusiasm, but only bitterly and as a last resort, which qualifies the voluntariness of their decision. The usual reasons given for suicide are perceptions of meaninglessness, illness, financial burden, loneliness, or frustrated love, and the suicidal hardly ever say that they want death itself, which compromises the voluntariness of their decision. This argues rather forcefully that what they really want and consent to is relief from these conditions, and not death itself. They consent to death as a last resort because they see it as the only means of finding escape and respite. They feel driven to consent to it because without death, they see nothing but pain, suffering, and emptiness, and determining the scope and extent of suicidal consent is difficult because of the ambiguous nature of the consent, and it should be determined in relation to the psychological dynamics both underlying and driving the decision. It is difficult to believe that one who plans a suicide and also fantasizes about intervention and rescue is giving adequate consent to their death. In most instances, the person gives limited or conditional consent to the suicide, but it is difficult to see how their consent can be comprehensive and voluntary if they are wishing for rescue while taking lethal action against themselves.

When is Suicide a Voluntary Decision? The Hard Cases

In the previous sections, the conditions necessary for an act to be fully voluntary were examined, and in this section, two types of self-killings commonly perceived to be rational will be examined to see if they are truly voluntary: suicide to escape suffering and suicide to preserve one's honor and dignity. These are the "hard cases" for opponents of the view that suicide is a voluntary and rational decision, and if their voluntariness can be called into question, then suicides done in ostensibly less explicitly rational and voluntary ways can also be questioned.

Voluntariness and Suicide of Escape

Given the extremely complex psychological forces motivating the suicidal decision, it would seem that if a patient's suffering was profound, truly fear-provoking, and extraordinarily burdensome, there would not be adequate freedom, knowledge, and consent for such a decision to be voluntary. Suiciding in this case would be rational from a certain perspective because it would seem to bring escape from pain, but it would be questionably free and voluntary because the individual's perceived options would be so limited. In one respect it would be voluntary because it would be a straightforward choice to eliminate pain, but it would be voluntary only in a limited manner because of the pressure of events and a limited possibility of giving consent.

Suiciding to escape suffering would be at least subvoluntary, if not involuntary, because the knowledge, consent, and freedom of the person would be questionable. Usually, those who suicide for this reason are terminally ill, physically, psychologically, and emotionally exhausted, in difficult relationships with others, the victims of a recent traumatic episode, or burdened with severe ego conflicts. It is presumed that they suicide, not because of intense and intractable pain, but because of exhaustion, despair, loneliness, and distress, and given the frailty of their ego, the voluntariness of their decision would be questionable. This is the paradigmatic subvoluntary suicide because such a person is not merely acting to end suffering, but to escape it, draw attention to their misery, attack a defective ego, and strike out at a threatening environment. They descend into lethality because no other attempt to resolve their crisis has worked, and their perception of reality has narrowed, causing suicide to become the best possible means of resolving their conflicts and relieving their pain in their view. Suicide can be an unreflective and desperate grasp for power to gain some control over their tortured existence, and its voluntariness can be in serious doubt.

The voluntariness of those who suicide for this reason is also questionable because they are ambivalent about dying. They hope desperately for rescue, and consent to their deadly deed because they see no other option available to them. And as they usually suffer from serious neuroses, psychoses, alcoholism, depression, compulsiveness, or schizoid personality, their voluntariness and control over this act is even further in doubt. Their self-hatred and rejection often become so strong that self-reconciliation and harmonization become immensely more difficult and they cannot break free from their self-destructive habits. Their lethality often increases partly because of their social status, gender, and age, which makes their struggle to decide these issues even more difficult.

Voluntariness and Suicide to Protect Dignity

Is one who self-executes as the only perceived means of preserving his dignity or honor acting voluntarily? Even though this action might appear voluntary, a closer examination of the interaction of guilt, compulsion, and mass suggestion argues forcefully that such decisions are subvoluntary. The most common cases of suicide to preserve honor or dignity have occurred in the wake of personally tragic or disastrous situations for which the suiciding person either claimed or bore some responsibility for the disaster in his own eyes. The best examples were the suicides of Calanus, Jocasta, Lucretia, Cato, Marc Antony, Cleopatra, Cornelia, Arria, and Seneca. It was common in antiquity and the Renaissance to suicide in order to preserve dignity, but a closer look suggests suicide was chosen to escape feelings of guilt following upon some trauma, misfortune, or disaster for which they felt responsible.[76] Guilt plays a major role in most suicides done to preserve honor, and the power of feelings of guilt can often compromise voluntariness. A peculiar sort of honor is sometimes ascribed to the those who suicide for this reason, as it often takes an odd kind of courage to face the dagger. Sometimes a suicidal person displays the courage of a Socrates, but at other times, he or she shows the twisted courage of an SS concentration camp guard who kills himself to protect his "honor" after his guilt over executing so many innocent people overwhelms him.[77] Some admire honor suicides, while others condemn them as cowardly and undignified, but it is by no means clear that self-executing by itself enhances honor.[78]

The critical test case of suicide for honor was that of Socrates. His suicide was unusual, for he did it only after being unjustly accused to show that even in the face of death he would not betray his principles. But precisely because he suicided for these reasons, one must wonder if he was suiciding from a motive of guilt or whether it was purely to promote his honor and defend his moral integrity. His suicide is most unique, for he was condemned to death and could have saved his life by fleeing. More than suiciding to preserve his honor and dignity, he took the hemlock to show his fidelity and commitment to his principles, and it seems that his suicide was as much a martyrdom as it was a suicide, for death was to be unjustly imposed on him, and he killed himself to protest the injustice of the sentence. In the absence of this death sentence, it is highly unlikely that he would have suicided, and it is not entirely clear why he committed suicide, for he could have given as much of a witness to his integrity by submitting to the unjust sentence as he could have by suiciding. It is theoretically possible that his suicide was voluntary because he could have saved himself by fleeing, but it may have been a suicide to not only preserve honor, but also in despair to purge guilt over some of his past activities. This is difficult to say, however, because the account we have of his death is highly idealized, and the real-life historical circumstances may not have been as clear-cut or elegant as Plato suggests. Socrates is presented as the saint-martyr-philosopher, and we cannot be sure that his actual death was actually like this.

Most honor suicides are done under extreme social pressure, and in highly militarized suicides this can significantly reduce them to the subvoluntary. In World War II, thousands of Japanese soldiers committed suicide rather than be taken captive in order to avoid the guilt of having appeared cowardly by not fighting to the death for the emperor. These suicides show well the power of some societies and cultures to impose such profound guilt on their members such that they could sincerely believe there to be no options available to them except to commit suicide, and this is one reason why the voluntariness of suicides for the sake of honor can be questioned. Those who suicide for honor usually feel that they would be the objects of moral opprobrium if they did not self-execute, which is extremely difficult for them to tolerate because their compulsive personality creates a very critical, unforgiving, harsh, and hypercritical self-perception. This compulsiveness can drive the person to lethality and also reduce their decisions to the subvoluntary. The compulsive individual is responding to what he or she *perceives* to be extreme pressure to justify themselves and atone for perceived faults or failures.

The voluntariness of honor suicides, like other suicides, is even more questionable when one considers the fact that it is not clear what those who seek to kill themselves to preserve honor or dignity really want. There seems to be some truth that they are trying to preserve the integrity of a dyadic relationship with another who has great moral power over them. Japanese soldiers and kamikaze pilots apparently went to their deaths to preserve their honor before the emperor, and thousands of Japanese civilians who committed suicide at the fall of Saipan did so apparently to preserve the honor of their relationship to the emperor.[79] But, viewed in another way, they may have acted to preserve their moral reputation before friends, family, and society and to blunt social ostracism as much as they suicided to preserve their honor. And even further, those who suicide to preserve their honor may be grasping for some semblance of power or control in situations where they think they have lost this, which suggests even further that the voluntariness of their decision for death may be compromised. Given this different mix of motives in these suicides, it is simplistic to say that these suicides are voluntary and seek only dignity or honor.

Most suicides are a response to an acute crisis, and the period of lethality is usually brief and fleeting. The suicide decision to avoid dishonor or indignity can frequently be a panic-guilt response to such a crisis or trauma as in the case of the husband or father who commits suicide when his wife or children are killed. This sort of suicide can also be a desperate attempt to escape one's compulsiveness. With very compulsive persons, the fear of self-condemnation and consequent guilt can throw them into extreme depression or even despair, and suiciding can be a way of escaping these. These compulsions also make the person less capable of considering other options, and they are often cognitively capable of only a limited number of choices.[80] This compulsiveness can significantly reduce voluntariness by literally forcing the person to the action and effectively eliminating other options. This individual would be vulnerable to situations where they would lose control because they could easily lapse into depression or despair on account of its loss.

As mentioned above, Father Bernard Haring has protested that mass suggestion can limit the voluntariness of actions, and this seems to be quite true with those who suicide to preserve honor. There can be little doubt that at least some of these suicides are a response to the propaganda of some communities in which these individuals live. In almost every suicide done for honor, one can find a community having a potent influence on the individual to suicide and urging suicide in some instances to purge or atone for guilt. Because of the authority and persuasiveness of this propaganda, it is almost certain that those who suicide to preserve honor and dignity are acting subvoluntarily.

Conclusion

The aim of this chapter has been to show that it is exceedingly difficult to hold that the suicidal decision is not voluntary but subvoluntary and is therefore not fully rational because it is done with radically constricted subjective freedom. I have challenged the claim that rational suicide is voluntary by suggesting that even rational suicide is not sufficiently under the person's control to be considered as such, and that it flows from other forces that radically limit control and voluntariness. To baldly say that self-killing is voluntary ignores the complex psychological dynamics involved in such an act, and most who seriously contemplate self-slaying have such radically restricted freedom that consent and voluntariness are seriously in question.

Generally, the decision by a suicidal person to self-execute is less voluntary than a decision by a nonsuicidal person to terminate their treatments or to sacrifice their lives for another because the nonsuicidal individual is not deliberately and directly choosing death. Because of this, the nonsuicidal person has a more complete knowledge of what is being chosen, and greater psychological freedom to reject a death-dealing course of action. Our knowledge of the nature of death is uncertain, and the martyr or person who aims at something other than death is not aiming at an essentially unknowable reality, but a good that can be known, grasped, and understood. Because the good chosen by the nonsuicidal person is more easily known, the person who chooses it acts with greater knowledge and their choice is more voluntary. There is more ignorance involved in a suicidal choice of death because of the shroud of mystery that surrounds death.

Those who argue for the rationality of suicide fail to see that practically every person experiences a suicidal urge in their life and this urge appears entirely rational at the time it arises. The decision to self-execute is as much a response to that irrational urge as it is a free, knowing, consented, and voluntary act. These conditions severely restrict voluntariness, and to allow self-killing in such circumstances is to violate the canons of *free* choice and *free* informed consent. Without doubt, many suicide because of the extreme pain and despair of the persons, and this destroys or compromises the voluntariness of their actions. Our culture, which has become so tolerant of death and so intolerant of inconvenience, suffering, and pain, has exceptional powers of persuasion, and these powers can readily be employed to persuade the suffering and vulnerable that death is preferable to virtually any form of suffering.

Notes

1. See Williams, G., "The Right to Commit Suicide," *Medico-Legal Journal*, 41 (1973): 389-90.

> I hold with Thomas Szasz . . . that mental patients are people, who are entitled to their liberty and right of self-determination like anyone else. . . . I reject the argument that mental patients as a class are unable to form a competent decision to commit suicide. This may be the one rational decision that they are able to make.

2. O'Donnell, T., *Medicine and Christian Morality*, (New York: Alba House, 1975), 26.
3. This view is affirmed by a number of leading suicidologists such as Karl Menninger, *Man Against Himself*, (New York: Harcourt Brace, 1938); Durkheim, E., *Suicide* (Glencoe: Free Press, 1951); and Perlin, S., *A Handbook for the Study of Suicide*, (New York: Oxford, 1975).
4. Psychiatrically, suicide is best understood as an escape from what is perceived to be intolerable anguish. Psychiatric intervention aims at eliminating the internal and external pressures and compulsions that so terrorize the person that suicide seems to be the only option. See Ashley, B. and O'Rourke, K., *Health Care Ethics*, 375-76. Also see Menninger, K., *Man Against Himself*, and Perlin, S., *A Handbook for the Study of Suicide*.
5. Litman, R. E., "Suicide as Acting Out," in Shneidman, E., *The Psychology of Suicide*, (New York: Science House, 1970), 293-304.
6. Ibid., 294.
7. A study of suicide and euthanasia in Holland found that of the 3,000 assisted suicides annually, the vast majority were patients in their sixties who were fearful of "dependence, loss of dignity, humiliation, and pain." "Dutch Survey Casts New Light on Patients Who Choose to Die," *The New York Times*, 11 September 1991, B7. Men and women suicided at about the same rate, and those in their seventies and eighties killed themselves much less frequently than those in other age groups. There were few

cases of suicides in nursing homes, about twenty-five per year, and the demand for mercy killing was far greater than its application, for there were about 5,000 requests per year while only 3,000 were carried out.

In early 1992, the Dutch Ministry of Health informed doctors that "mental suffering" was not a sufficient reason for killing a patient, which could significantly reduce the number of mercy killings, as most doctors would admit that physical pain is not a sufficient reason for mercy killing (ibid).

8. See Freedman, A., Kaplan, H. and Sadock, B. J., *Modern Synopsis of Comprehensive Textbook of Psychiatry II,* 2d Ed. (Williams & Wilkins, Baltimore: 1976), 634.

9. Shneidman, E., "A Sociopsychological Investigation of Suicide," in Schneidman, *The Psychology of Suicide,* 240.

10. Ibid.

11. Farberow, N., Shneidman, E., and Leonard, C., "Suicide among Patients with Malignant Neoplasms," in Shneidman, E., *The Psychology of Suicide,* 343.

12. Farberow N. and Shneidman, E., "Suicide and Age," in Shneidman, E., *The Psychology of Suicide,* 169.

13. Farberow, N., Heilig, S. and Litman, R. E., "Evaluation and Management of Suicidal Persons," in Shneidman, *The Psychology of Suicide,* 278. However, other data suggests that the very old commit suicide less often than do the "young old."

14. Litman, R.,"Suicide as Acting Out," in Shneidman, E., *The Psychology of Suicide,* 298.

15. Ibid., 298. The suicidal often establish a pathological identification with hostile parents and with those who have died.

16. Freedman, A., Kaplan, H. and Sadock, B. J., *Modern Synopsis,* 451.

17. Ibid., 451.

18. Litman, R., "Suicide as Acting Out," in Shneidman, E., *The Psychology of Suicide,* 298.

19. Zilborg, G., "Differential Diagnostic Type of Suicide," *Archives of Neurology,* Vol. 92, (1936): 1347-69. It is also in the conflict of these plots and dreams that one also sees the ambivalence and subvoluntary character of the suicidal decision.

20. Litman, R., "Suicide as Acting Out," in Shneidman, E., *The Psychology of Suicide,* 303-4.

21. Shneidman, E., "Preventing Suicide," in Schneidman, E., *The Psychology of Suicide,* 433.

22. Litman, R., "Suicide as Acting Out," in Schneidman, E., *The Psychology of Suicide,* 303.

23. Ibid., 279.

24. Pelligrino E. and Thomasma, D., *For the Patient's Good: The Restoration of Beneficence in Health Care,* (New York: Oxford University Press, 1987), 15. Also see Cassell, E. J., "Disease as an 'It': Concepts of Disease Revealed by Presentation of Symptoms," *Social Science and Medicine,* 10, 3/4 (1976): 143-46; and Pelligrino, E., "Being Ill and Being Healed: Some Reflections on the Grounding of Medical Morality," *Bulletin of the New York Academy of Medicine,* 56, 1 (1981): 70-79.

25. Litman, R., "Suicide as Acting Out," in Shneidman, E., *The Psychology of Suicide,* 302.

26. In the opinion of one suicidologist, the person who is most dangerous to himself is not the most angry, but the one who has become involved in a transference relationship, placing all of their trust and hope in another individual, only to feel abandoned when they fail to fulfill that hope (ibid., 300).

27. Ibid., 279.

28. Ibid., 298.
29. Ibid., 301.
30. See O'Connell, T., *Principles for Catholic Morality*, (New York: Seabury, 1979), 46; Tanquery, A., *Theologica Moralis Fundamentalis*, (Paris: Desclee, 1955), 80-81; Prummer, D., *Manuale Theologiae Moralis*, (Freiburg: Herder, 1927), Tome 1, 31-33.
31. McHugh, J. and Callan, C., *Moral Theology: A Complete Course*, (New York: Wagner, 1930), Vol. 2, 10-11; Gury, J. P., *Compendium Theologiae Moralis,* annotated and amended by Ballerini, A. and Palmieri, G., (Rome: Prati, 1898), 3.
32. O'Donnell, T., *Medicine and Christian Morality*, 22.
33. See Grisez, G., *Abortion: Law, Choice and Morality,* (New York: Alba House, 1970), 309-20.
34. See Tanquery, A., *Theologica,* 80; This view is supported by Beauchamp, T., "What is Suicide," in *Ethical Issues in Death and Dying,* Ed. Perlin, S. and Beauchamp, T., (Englewood Cliffs, NJ: Prentice-Hall, 1978), 77.
35. See Battin, M., "Manipulated Suicide," in Battin, M. and Mayo, D., *Suicide: The Philosophical Issues,* 169-83. Battin holds that one may not object to a manipulated suicide if death is truly chosen by the agent (p. 178). To prohibit a person from escaping intolerable circumstances increases their misery and is ethically unwarranted for Battin. But she does not examine the freedom available to such a person to select an option other than suicide, and the freedom of a life-ending choice in that circumstance can be called into serious question.
36. McHugh J. and Callan, C., *Moral Theology,* 15; Gury, J. P., *Compendium,* 1, 11-13.
37. See Wouters, L., *Manuale Theologia Moralis*, (Bruges: Bayaert, 1932), 1, 9; Gury, J. P., *Compendium,* 1, 3-4; Tanquery, A., *Theologica,* 80-81; Prummer, D., *Manuale,* 31; McHugh, J. and Callan, C., *Moral Theology,* vol. 1, 10-35. While this is probably not the most insightful of all Catholic moral manuals, it is highly representative of Catholic moral teaching on these issues.
38. McHugh, J. and Callan, C., *Moral Theology,* 11; Gury, J. P., *Compendium,* 13-15; Prummer, D., *Manuale,* 32-34; Tanquery, A., *Theologica,* 94-95.
39. See Prummer, D., *Manuale,* 34. Classical moralists required *ratione objecti,* or knowledge of the act's object, which is doubtful in the case of suicides. Battin, M., *Ethical Issues in Suicide,* 137-38. Here Battin argues that a suicidal act lacking adequate information is not a rational suicide, and this point could be made even more forcefully: a reflexive death-dealing act is not a suicide if the agent does not know that it will bring death.
40. For example, see *The Euthanasia Review,* 1, 1 & 2. Also see Oates, J. C., "The Art of Suicide," in *Suicide: The Philosophical Issues,* Ed. Battin M., and Mayo, D., 161-68.
41. See Rachels, J., *The End of Life*, (New York: Oxford, 1986), 39-45.
42. No teachings concerning the nature of the soul dominated in the Catholic church until the Middle Ages, when Aquinas's doctrine gained widespread acceptance. Aquinas taught that the soul, upon death, possesses only a separated existence, but is reunited to the body at the resurrection of the body. In this classical expression, which has been accepted by virtually all Christian bodies with the exception of some orthodox Calvinist and Lutheran theologians, the soul's existence after death is distinct from that of the angels because it is destined for unity with the body. This, however, is a matter of religious belief, and the philosophical doctrines on this matter are in dispute.
43. See McHugh, J. and Callan, C., *Moral Theology,* vol. 1, 12; Prummer, D., *Manuale,* 34-36; L. 18-20. These classical moral theologians note that ignorance excuses only in morality and not before the law, which assumes that the law has been properly promulgated and understood by the subject.
44. Aquinas, T., *Summa Theologica*, I-II, Q. 6, Art. 8.

45. Ibid., I-II, Q. 6, Art. 8, Resp.
46. McHugh, J. and Callan, C., *Moral Theology,* 11. Also see Wouters, L., *Manuale.* The inability to know the moral character of the action was *ignorantia juris* by the classical moralists, which meant ignorance of the judgment that the moral law made of the action.
47. Aquinas, T., *Summa Theologica,* I-II, Q. 6, Art. 5.
48. Ibid. Thomas also argues that violence destroys voluntariness because it is contrary to that which is natural, but this is not fully persuasive in a world where a teleological physics does not prevail.
49. In these sorts of actions, the choice is made *because* of the fear caused by the pain and suffering, and this fear becomes the source of the action rather than the agent's choice.
50. Pain can diminish or destroy voluntariness because it can impede the commanded act of the will and commanded acts of the members of the body can be inhibited by external violence. Even further, Aquinas notes that pain weakens all activity, and who would usually strive after the good of life can have that drive weakened by constant pain and suffering. See Prummer, D., *Manuale,* 49-51. Aquinas claims that the will is weakened by pain and sorrow, but he asserts that pleasure acts in a contrary way and perfects and fulfills an action (*Summa Theologica,* I-II, 37, 3).
51. Wouters, L., *Manuale,* 18; Prummer, D., *Manuale,* 49-51; Tanquery, A., *Theologica,* 104-9; Gury, J. P., *Compendium,* 19-21. Prummer, Tanquery, and Gury all asserted that fear as well as extrinsic physical violence could restrict the voluntariness of an action.
52. Aquinas, T., *Summa Theologica,* I-II, Q. 6, A. 6.
53. Ibid. Aquinas taught that actions done with or through fear are of a mixed character, for that which is done through fear is involuntary, even though it becomes involuntary in the particular instance to avoid the evil. When one abstracts from the particular circumstances of the case, the action is involuntary, even though the action is voluntary in the situation.
54. Aquinas, T., *Summa Theologica,* I-II, Q. 45, A. 3. Moderate fear does not destroy voluntariness, even though strong fear can hinder actions by impeding one's reasoning.
55. Ibid., I-II, Q. 6, A. 8. Resp.
56. Ibid., Resp.
57. Ibid.
58. Ibid., I-II, Q. 49, A. 3. Habits predispose a person to act and to do so in a certain way. Acting contrary to that predisposition requires a countering of the force intrinsic to that disposition, and, as a result, a habit predisposing a person to suicide could limit the voluntariness of the choice for self-killing.
59. McHugh, J. and Callan, C., *Moral Theology,* vol. 1, 20; Prummer, D., *Manuale,* 32-33; Wouters, *Manuale,* 17. Willfully acquired habits increase the voluntariness of actions, but decrease the freedom of the effects of the action. People who habitually perform actions do so voluntarily, but their freedom to refrain from the actions is diminished by the actions.
60. Aquinas, T., *Summa Theologica,* I-II, Q. 10, A. 3.
61. Ibid., I-II, Q. 9, A. 2.
62. O'Donnell, T., *Medicine and Christian Morals,* 26-27; Prummer, D., *Manuale,* 62-67.
63. Aquinas, T., *Summa Theologica,* I-II, Q. 9. A. 2; Tanquery, A., *Theologica,* 99-104; Prummer, D., *Manuale,* 55-62; Gury, J. P., *Compendium,* 15-18.
64. Haring, B., *Law of Christ,* (Paramus, N. J: Newman, 1966), vol. 1, 112-14.

65. Ibid., 115. Haring probably has Nazi propaganda in mind, which stirred up violent and irrational hatred of foes and which could become so frantic that people would blindly follow the propagandists. Other forms of propaganda that use contemporary psychological mechanisms to manipulate followers, while less subtle, can be equally forceful in impeding the voluntariness of one's decisions.
66. Aquinas, T., *Summa Theologica,* I-II, Q. 74, A. 7.
67. Ibid., ad 1.
68. Ibid., I-II, Q. 15, A. 3.
69. Ibid., I-II, Q. 14.
70. Ibid., I-II, Q. 16.
71. Ibid., I-II, Q. 15, A. 3.
72. Ibid., I-II. Q. 16, A. 1.
73. Ibid., I-II, Q. 11, A. 3. This might seem to be a peculiar requirement for the granting of full consent, but it points to the fact that those who experience "enjoyment" from an action are oriented toward it affectively in a way that is different from those who do not seek, are repulsed by, and reject this sort of enjoyment. Some Nazi concentration camp guards who were gleeful at seeing Jews gassed gave a different kind of consent to their deaths than did those who reacted with horror, pity, and disgust to the murders.
74. McHugh, J. and Callan, C., *Moral Theology,* vol. 1, 17; Prummer, D., *Manuale,* 32-33.
75. See Sullivan, J. V., "The Immorality of Euthanasia," in Kohl, M., Ed., *Beneficient Euthanasia,* (Buffalo, N. Y: Prometheus, 1975), 13. Also see Merkelbach, B., *Summa Theologiae Moralis,* vol. 2, N. 349; Noldin-Schmitt, H., *Summa Theologiae Moralis,* vol. 2, N. 326; Aertnys-Damen, J., *Theologia Moralis,* N. 566; Davis, H., *Moral and Pastoral Theology,* vol. 2, 152.
76. Much the same can be said of many of the romantic suicides, for there is good reason to believe that many of these self-slayings were done to purge the guilt of a failed romance due to the self-slayer's misdeeds or omissions.
77. Many Nazi concentration camp guards and members of the SS *Einsatzgruppen* who followed Hitler's victorious armies into the newly conquered lands of the east to kill the *Untermenschen* could not cope with the massive killing they were assigned to do and committed suicide, developed alcoholism, or indulged in gratuitous violence. After witnessing some executions by *Einsatzcommandos,* SS chief Heinrich Himmler commented: "Look at the eyes of the men of this command, how deeply shaken they are. These men are finished for the rest of their lives." Commenting to a group of top SS officers that camp personnel were withstanding the pressures of their duties well, he said: "To have gone through this and--apart from a few exceptions caused by human weakness--to have remained decent, that has made us great." Even Adolf Eichmann commented on seeing a group of Jews go to the gas chamber: "I simply cannot look at any suffering without trembling myself." Herzstein, R. E., *The Nazis,* (Alexandria, VA: Time-Life Books, 1980), 140-48.
78. While it is not clear that self-slaying enhances one's dignity or honor, it seems that total commitment to the virtues or the promotion, protection, and preservation of fundamental human values such as truth, knowledge, life, justice, and the common good enhances the dignity of an individual in all instances and promotes dignity and honor. Dignity can be protected by fleeing from a grave moral evil, only if death is not deliberately sought as a means or end because doing this is a grave moral evil itself.
79. See Wheeler, K., *The Road to Tokyo,* in (Alexandria: VA, Time-Life Books, 1979), chap. 5.

80. The compulsive personality is characterized by ritualistic thinking, scrupulousness, action, and excessive concern for mistakes, danger, or evil thoughts. This heightened state of anxiety generally dampens the person's ability to investigate and act on different options. See Freedman, A., Kaplan, H., and Sadock, B. J., *Modern Synopsis,* 1209-10. For another example, see "Patient 'Cures' Obsessive Behavior by Shooting Self in Suicide Attempt," *The Daily Illini,* 24 February 1988, 11.

7

Indirectly Intended Analgesic Suicide: Clarifying the Principles

One of the most widely accepted and least criticized doctrines of medical ethics is that which allows painkillers to be taken by individuals in such doses that the recipient's life is unintentionally shortened. Because this doctrine is rather vague and ambiguous as it now stands and has not been studied closely, it could readily be subjected to abuse by patients with suicidal aims. In this chapter, I will examine the context of the development of this doctrine in classical Catholic moral teaching and determine what precise sorts of actions this doctrine was initially supposed to permit since this teaching is the classic statement of the condition under which toxic analgesia could be taken by a patient. This is necessary because, in its initial form, the teaching in fact was quite precise and restrictive, but that precision has never been made fully clear. I also wish to review the medical and clinical options now available to practitioners who might have to confront situations where they previously had to give potentially lethal doses of analgesia to patients in great pain.

On 24 February 1957, Pope Pius XII received an audience of physicians and surgeons on which occasion he gave answers to three questions concerning the alleviation of pain.[1] The three questions presented to him were: 1. May indirectly lethal doses of painkillers be given? 2. May patients in great pain be reduced to unconsciousness? 3. Is there a duty to accept pain and suffering?[2] In his answer to these questions, he denied that there was a general moral obligation to endure pain, referring to his statement of January 1956 on "Painless Childbirth" when he held that a woman was not morally required to endure the pain and anguish of childbirth.[3] He taught that pain and suffering were to be accepted to promote one's spiritual growth, but it was legitimate to take measures against them:

> We answered that there was no obligation of this kind. Man, even after the Fall, retains the right of control over the forces of

> Nature, of employing them for his own use, and consequently of deriving benefit from all the resources which it offers him either to suppress or to avoid physical pain. We added that, for the Christian, suffering is not something purely negative, but on the contrary, is linked with lofty religious and moral values, and hence can be desired and sought even if no moral obligation to do so exists in a particular case.
>
> In specific cases, which are the motives which allow avoidance of physical pain without involving any conflict with a serious obligation or with the ideal of the Christian life? One could list quite a number: but, in spite of their variety, they are finally summed up in the fact that, in the long run, the pain is preventing the obtaining of some good or advantage of higher worth.
>
> . . . Beyond doubt, suffering will never be completely banished from among men, but its harmful effects can be kept within narrower limits. And so, just as one masters a natural force to draw advantage from it, the Christian makes use of suffering as a spur to his effort to mount higher and purify himself in the spiritual life, in order to carry out his duties better and answer the call to higher perfection.[4]

He also declared that if a nonterminal patient was in great pain, an anesthesiologist could reduce the level of pain to an acceptable level or reduce the patient to unconsciousness:[5]

> It follows that one may not confuse consciousness, or suppress it, with the sole object of gaining pleasurable sensations, by indulging in drunkenness or injecting poisons to secure this state, even if one is only seeking a pleasant state of well-being. Beyond a certain dose, these poisons cause a disturbance, more or less pronounced, of consciousness and even its complete darkening.
>
> Is surgery, in practice, compelled to produce a lessening or even a complete suppression of consciousness by means of the state of insensibility (narcosis)? From a technical point of view, the answer to this question lies within your competence. From the moral point of view, the principles previously stated in answer to your first question apply substantially to the state of insensibility as much as to the suppression of pain. In fact, what matters to

the surgeon in the first place is the suppression of painful sense-perception, and not that of consciousness. When the latter remains fully awake, the violent and painful sense-experiences easily arouse reflexes and reactions which are quite involuntary, but capable of bringing undesirable complications in their train and even terminating in a fatal collapse of the heart. To preserve the psychical and organic balance, to prevent its being violently disturbed, is an important objective for both doctor and patient; and the state of insensibility alone allows for them to obtain it.[6]

In answer to the question of whether it was permissible to use analgesia even though it might result in the shortening of life, he answered:

> To declare that the dying have a greater moral obligation than others–whether from the Natural Law or from Christian teaching–to accept suffering or refuse its alleviation, is in keeping neither with the nature of things, nor with the sources of Revelation. Just as, in accord with the spirit of the Gospel, suffering helps towards the expiation of personal sins and the gaining of richer merit, those whose life is in danger have certainly a special motive for accepting it, for, with death quite near, this possibility of gaining new merits is likely soon to disappear. The motive, however, directly concerns the sick person, not the doctor who is engaged in relieving the pain--for We are supposing that the sick person is assenting to this relief, or has at least asked for it. It would clearly be unlawful to make use of anesthetics against the expressed will of the dying person (when he is *'sui juris'*).
>
> When, in spite of obligations still binding on him, the dying man asks for the state of insensibility for which there exists serious reasons, a conscientious doctor will not countenance it, especially if he is a Christian, without having invited the patient, either personally or, better still, through some others, first to carry out his obligations.
>
> But if the dying man has fulfilled all his duties and received the Last Sacrament, if medical reasons clearly suggest the use of anesthetics, if, in determining the dose, the permitted is not exceeded, if the intensity and duration of this treatment is

carefully reckoned and the patient consents to it, then there is no objection to the use of anesthetics and is morally permissible.

> If there exists no direct causal link, either through the will of the interested parties or by the nature of things, between the induced unconsciousness and the shortening of life--as would be the case if the suppression of the pain could be obtained only by the shortening of life; and if, on the other hand, the actual administration of drugs brings about two distinct effects, the only lawful relief of pain, the other the shortening of life, the action is lawful. It is necessary, however, to observe whether there is, between these two effects, a reasonable proportion, and if the advantages of one compensate for the disadvantages of the other. It is important also to ask oneself if the present state of science does not allow the same result to be obtained by other means. Finally, in the case of the use of the drug, one should not go beyond the limits which are actually necessary.[7]

It is clear that one could take potentially toxic analgesia because it was permitted by the principle of the double effect, but this would require that it be administered with the proper intention and that the pain be so grave as to make the relief from pain proportionate to the death of the patient. However, even if giving toxic analgesia would be in conformity with the requirements of this principle, the action would also have to meet other demands and would have to be prudent, respectful of the common good, and in harmony with principles governing other authentic types of indirect killing. Pius also warned of the possibility of taking potentially toxic analgesia, slipping over the edge, and becoming primarily lethal rather than therapeutic, which would make its use permissible.

This trilogy of statements implies that there is both a positive and negative aspect to pain and suffering and that benefits are involved in both permitting or alleviating pain and suffering. Pius did not hold that there is a moral right to live without pain, but only that it was not unjust to request indirectly intended life-shortening analgesia. While there was a value in suffering and pain, this value could be lost when it was so severe that one could not fulfill one's spiritual obligations.

At the time this teaching was proposed, Aidan Carr asserted that the allocution was issued to steer people away from total rejection of analgesia as well as from the indiscriminate use of it.[8] And John Lynch later said that the medication in question had to be truly analgesic in nature and could not be merely a lethal agent.[9] Also, he noted that the pain had to be serious enough to compensate for the incidental shortening of life, meaning that the pain had to be serious and beyond the control of any less harmful treatment.[10] Lynch believed that one might only take doses which increased the risk of death, but that is not entirely clear from the teaching.[11] He contended that there was nothing theologically novel about this doctrine, but I would differ with that judgment and hold that this teaching was quite innovative in some respects. In contrast to Lynch's view, I believe Pius's teaching was both original and somewhat difficult to grasp with clarity. I believe this teaching is in need of further clarification and explanation for a number of reasons.

First, since it was initially proposed, these principles received much support and little criticism, and many statements have been issued affirming them, but it is not clear that its full import has been grasped by those who give them virtually unqualified support.[12] Virtually all moralists have accepted these principles without qualification and apparently with little study.[13] For most authors appear to believe that these principles hold when one "lets oneself die" from the analgesia when a respirator or other morally ordinary life-sustaining medications are removed. But one can wonder if this is fully legitimately "letting die" if one is nonterminal and could live indefinitely as a result of the application of the respirator or some other readily available medications.

Second, in his book *Medicine and Christian Morals,* Thomas O'Donnell expressed concern that traditional distinctions between the use of extraordinary and ordinary means to preserve life might be construed to promote active and positive suicide as morally permissible.[14] He cautioned readers not to interpret this distinction to signify that unintended death by omission could be tolerated, but direct suicide by omission could probably be advanced more readily by misinterpretation of the ordinary/extraordinary distinction. But I believe misinterpretation of the principles of the legitimacy of indirect analgesic suicide could lead us to toleration of direct suicide more readily than could abuse of the ordinary/extraordinary distinction. This is so because advocates of deliberate analgesic suicide claim that there is no difference between indirect or analgesic suicide and active, deliberate, direct suicide. Even though this is by no means certain, it seems to also be widely believed that dosages of analgesia at any level can be given to a terminally ill patient in great pain. Further consideration of this doctrine is needed because an unexamined approach is more likely to promote euthanasia than is the ordinary/extraordinary distinction.

Third, this teaching should be clarified because there seems to be increasing tolerance of those who deliberately overdose on analgesics in order to escape painful or debilitating chronic or acute medical conditions. For example, Dr. Ronald Cranford persuaded two physicians in Winter Park, Florida to give lethal doses of analgesia to his mother-in-law, Betty Wright, who had been diagnosed with cancer six weeks earlier.[15] From what he said, it is not clear if a certainly lethal dose was administered to her, or if the painkillers given merely increased the risk of death.[16] Dr. Cranford asserted that he only wanted to end her pain, but given the size of the dose given her and his public espousal of other forms of euthanasia, this claim seems questionable.[17] And Dr. Peter Rosier attempted to end the life of his wife Patricia by giving her a massive dose of morphine, but this failed.[18] He was acquitted of all charges and there was little outcry against his acquittal.

Finally, Pius's teaching needs clarification because it is not evident what he meant by analgesic doses that "shortened life." Does that term mean that he permitted taking analgesic doses that could certainly *cause* death or if one may *only* take those that *increase* the risk or probability of death? If "shortening life" could include causing death, then one could directly provide certainly lethal doses of analgesia. But, if "shortening life" means only the latter, then some sorts of pain relief would be necessarily prohibited.

His teaching permitted indirect anesthetic suicide to relieve pain, but such a teaching had never been enunciated before and this doctrine of "indirect suicide" is in fact quite novel. I will refer to this practice of taking pain relievers in sufficient doses to unintentionally shorten life as "indirect suicide," a term suggested by Joseph Fletcher to describe the process of "letting a patient die by withholding life-sustaining treatment."[19] I believe this term describes this procedure quite well, for in indirect suicide, one directly aims at alleviating pain but accepts death as an unintended consequence. This action is strictly analogous to indirect abortion in which one aims directly at saving the life of the mother and indirectly causes the death of the unborn human life. Direct suicide involves directly intending one's death as a means of alleviating their pain. But indirect suicide involves alleviating pain despite the fact that the measures taken to relieve the painful condition will shorten life, or hasten or actually cause death. This sort of action can also be properly described as "suicide" in that it is allowing but supposedly not causing death for reasons of mercy. Toxic analgesia was *permitted* precisely in order to spare a patient pain and suffering, the very same motivation that undergirds direct suicide.

The state of medicine today is vastly different from what it was when Pius gave approval for this action. Analgesic medicine has changed so radically that The President's Commission for the Study of Ethical Problems in Medicine and Biomedical and Behavioral Research claimed that recent developments have allowed pain to be reduced to an acceptable level in virtually all cases.[20] In some areas where medicine is less advanced this might not be the case, but where more advanced medicine is being practiced, the reasons given for lethally overdosing being medically necessary are usually now considered to be invalid.

Analgesia was in its infancy when Pius gave permission for indirect analgesic suicide and there was little that could be done in his time to curb or control serious pain. Thirty years ago, it was easy for these patients to be inadvertently killed by being overdosed with pain killers because of the primitive state of pain relief and because the gap between the level of analgesia required to relieve pain and that which could kill was quite narrow. However, this gap has been so significantly widened today that the risk of lethally overdosing with analgesics has been eliminated in all but the most extreme and complicated situations. So much progress has been made in the past three decades in the development of opiate and nonopiate analgesia that we can now control virtually all kinds of pain. Whole new understandings of the psychology and psycho-kinetics of pain have been reached, and radical new surgical and psychological techniques of pain relief have been developed that have markedly increased the abilities of care givers to alleviate pain. But at the present time this is not the case and there are an extraordinary number of options available to health care providers to control pain. Because of this, there are few, if any, instances in which indirect life-shortening analgesia would be medically required. To demonstrate this, we will briefly summarize the capabilities of contemporary anesthesia.

Recent Developments in Analgesic Therapy

New Perspectives on Pain Control

Joseph Fletcher has written that the best possible news that advocates of suicide could hope to have would be that medical advances have made suicide no longer necessary.[21] With few exceptions, it can now be said that medicine has fulfilled this dream within the past ten years because developments in pharmacology, surgery, and medical practice have vastly improved physicians' ability of control pain:

> In the past thirty years, entirely new generations of pain relievers have been developed that are significantly safer and more effective than those available two or three decades ago. More than a few authors claim that now there is little reason to fear that proper administration of pain relievers would cause death, and because of this, there are very few if any situations in which the pain experienced by a terminally ill patient cannot be controlled.[22]

Despite this confidence, it seems that some terminal patients still experience profound pain when this is uncontrolled and persistent is one of the most feared side effects of cancer.[23] Recent studies have suggested that 60 to 90 percent of patients with advanced cancer receiving active therapy experienced moderate to severe pain.[24] Most patients (78 percent of the inpatient population and 62 percent of the outpatient population) experience pain associated with direct tumor involvement.[25] From 19 percent to 25 percent of patients experience pain from the cancer therapy, which is usually pain associated with chemotherapy, radiation therapy, and surgery.[26] From 3 to 10 percent of patients experience pain not resulting from the cancer or therapy.[27] And such noted researchers as Twycross have suggested that 25 percent of all cancer patients die either at home or in a hospital without relief from pain.[28] But it is now estimated by some authors that pain can be controlled in 90 to 99 percent of all cancer patients.[29]

> Families are often concerned that continued narcotics may hasten death. With appropriately titrated narcotics, this is simply not the case; continued narcotics simply assure that the death will be as peaceful and painless as possible. Similarly, inpatient nurses are often reluctant to give a scheduled injection when they find that the blood pressure is very low for fear that the injection may kill the patient. More often than not, such a patient does not have signs of excessive narcotics, such as myosis or respiratory depression, and the hypotension is merely the harbinger of their impending death. Withholding the appropriately prescribed narcotic will only result in the reemergence of pain and the

disruption of what otherwise would have been a satisfactory family vigil.[30]

And years of clinical experience has shown that effective pain control requires patience on the part of both physicians and patients. One author has claimed that

> there is no magic to successful pain control. Beyond a sound knowledge of the etiologies of cancer pain and the pharmacology of narcotic and non-narcotic analgesics, successful pain management requires a positive, patient, yet aggressive approach on the part of the practicing clinician. The patient and the family must be engaged as not only the focus of therapy but as integral participants of the palliative care team. Recent advancements in the research of the body's own opiates, endorphins and enkephalins may bring new understandings and new safer and more effective analgesic agents into our armamentarium for pain control.[31]

The aim of analgesic therapy is to raise patients to an analgesic level above the experience of pain and keep them in that condition throughout the course of their illness. Almost universally, the most efficacious therapeutic approach is a multifaceted one. Achieving this goal is more within the reach of the physician now because the pharmakinesis of analgesics is better understood than it was previously, and physicians can now determine with greater precision the extent of an analgesic's effectiveness. Analgesics can now be titrated more precisely against the patient's pain than was the case in previous times, thereby bringing the patient even more complete freedom from pain.[32]

Other principles have been learned in recent years as well. Proper pain control requires that physicians employ the most effective and expeditious route of drug administration. Regular administration of painkillers is absolutely necessary for their effectiveness, even though in many cases, this is not respected by clinicians.[33] To effectively deal with different types and levels of pain, it is now known that physicians must be familiar with what is called the "equianalgesic" character of pain relievers. This means that any switching or combining of drugs must be done with an awareness of the interactions of drugs and their potencies relative to one another.[34] When drugs are administered orally, adequate pain relief also requires that a regular administration of drugs be maintained, even if this means waking the patient at regular intervals at night to administer pain relievers.[35] It is also known that starting dosages at a lower level and gradually working one's way up to stronger doses is wise, for it lessens the danger of accidentally overdosing the patient. In addition, it enables continuous reassessment and obviates the need to reduce dosages later, which might result in increased pain for the patient.[36]

Many anesthesiologists and neurologists doubt that there is such a thing as "untreatable pain," and they note that the "pain threshold" can vary from patient to patient according to the individual mental states of the patients.[37] Some forms of terminal pain are extremely difficult to treat, but many pain specialists are confident that with close attention, even extreme pain can be relieved.[38] According to some specialists, there is no optimal or maximal dose of narcotics that can, or should, be given to terminally ill patients. Physicians should give dosages of pain relievers that control pain, for it is now within their power to adequately control adverse side effects. Most patients can have their pain controlled with four-hour doses of 30 milligrams of morphine.[39] However, in some cases, it is possible to give the equivalent of a four-hour dose of 400 milligrams of morphine orally to some without adverse side effects to patients.[40] Sometimes patients need narcotic analgesics over a long time, and if this is so, their administration should be tapered slowly to give precise and controlled pain relief.[41]

Intramuscular injections of analgesics often bring quick relief to profound and excruciating pain, but this method of delivery can lead to "peaks and valleys" where the patient experiences profound pain and is quickly brought out of it only to be plunged back into it again when the potency of the narcotics dissipates.[42] In order to achieve a more even and balanced level of pain relief with fewer peaks and valleys, regular oral administration of pain relievers, portable morphine pumps, or continuous intravenous morphine infusions should be used.[43] Morphine pumps permit patients to regulate their own delivery of pain killers, which usually results in better pain control, and they have been developed to enable patients to provide themselves with the level of pain relievers they feel they need.[44]

Precise and complete "pain evaluation" must be undertaken to fully protect the patient from pain, and sound procedures of pain relief require that there be constant reassessment of the patient's condition and new possible sources of pain.[45] Most patients experience multiple sorts of pain and all of the different sources of pain from which they suffer must be diagnosed and treated to bring complete pain relief.[46] When a patient continues to complain of pain, steps must often be taken to insure that all of the possible sources of pain have been diagnosed.[47] And if a patient requires higher levels of pain relief, reassessment should made to see if there are other sources of pain that have not been examined.[48]

Advanced Psychological and Surgical Approaches to Pain Relief

The psychological states of a patient can have a significant bearing on perception of and ability to tolerate pain.[49] Effective pain management requires the establishment of a trusting relationship with the patient.[50] The patient must be confident that the health care provider is earnestly striving to relieve pain and that the provider understands the unique psychological features of the patient's pain. For example, the suffering of a dying cancer patient is complicated by factors such as hopelessness, despair, and depression, and this sort of patient should be regarded as being different from the patient who has cancer pain but will not die from the disease. The former sort of patient will demand psychological and pastoral counseling different from that needed by the latter whose perceptions and emotional states will not color the pain experience in the same manner.[51] The health care provider must be aware of such conditions to be fully effective in relieving pain.

It has been estimated that 25 percent of all terminally ill cancer patients experience serious depression, which can aggravate their subjective experiences of pain.[52] Because of this, there has been much research into the purely psychological aspects of pain relief to enable patients to cope better with their pain. Various psychological approaches to pain relief, such as hypnosis, have been found to be effective in dealing with some types of pain.[53] While effective in many instances, they are limited by the attentiveness of the patient.[54] In addition, numerous cognitive and behavioral training techniques have been developed to deal with the anxiety and depression that are as much a part of the pain experience as the actual physical pain.[55] Relaxation training has been shown to be effective in giving the patient improved self-control over the experience and perception of pain.[56] It has also become more evident that if patients are tired, depressed, lonely, or anxious, their ability to tolerate pain often decreases, and if patients are more fearful of pain they may find themselves less able to cope with pain when it does come.[57]

Much more is known now of the physiology of pain than was the case thirty years ago and more can be done to relieve pain. When a person is in pain, various neurophysiological and neuropharmacological changes occur in the peripheral nervous system, producing changes in the central nervous system that shape the experience of pain. The greater knowledge we now have of the functioning of the central and peripheral nervous systems makes it possible to apply various surgical and nonsurgical methods to alleviate previously untreatable forms of pain. The different physiological mechanisms that account for the differences in responses to pain are also more fully understood than was previously the case.[58]

It is now even possible to locally freeze nerves to relieve pain, despite the fact that this procedure can bring about temporary loss of function.[59] "Trigger point" injections of either saline or local anesthesia can also be given to cope with some sorts of musculosketal pain.[60] And nitrous oxide can be effectively administered through a nonbreathing gas mask for short periods of time to improve alertness while alleviating pain and anxiety.[61] The dorsal rhizotomy procedure, which is quite effective in dealing with somatic pain in the chest or abdomen, involves cutting the sensory roots of nerves for pain relief, even though doing this almost always results in sensory loss.[62] In addition, the dorsal root entry zone (DREZ) procedure has been proven effective in coping with arm and leg pain of various kinds.[63] Peripheral, autonomic, epidural, and intrathecal nerve blocks to interrupt pain transmission are often able to relieve pain effectively for the short term or long term when other approaches are not successful.[64] And employing insights into the "gateway" theory of pain makes it possible to implant electrodes in individuals suffering from severe pain to inhibit certain neurological pathways that transmit pain.[65]

One of the most effective and durable neurosurgical techniques to alleviate pain is the cordotomy, which is often effective for thoracic or cervical pain,[66] and for the short term, this procedure appears to be quite effective in controlling some kinds of pain in terminal patients.[67] More than 90 percent of patients undergoing this procedure experience complete initial pain relief, but only 50 percent of these people have complete pain relief after six months.[68] In addition, the midline myelotomy procedure is effective for pain in the lower extremities, and it is usually not associated with severe side effects if done properly.[69]

These procedures have been developed in recent years and they have significantly enabled physicians to relieve pain in situations where this was not previously possible. And in addition to these new methods of pain relief, a whole new generation of nonopiate pain relievers has been developed that have given even greater power to alleviate pain and suffering.

New Developments in Nonopiate Analgesia

Many new types of nonopiate analgesics have been developed in recent years and they have proven to be quite effective. A new generation of drugs, non-steroid anti-inflammatory drugs (NSAIDS), have been found to be able to control severe pain by acting on the peripheral mechanisms of pain.[70] Some previously untreatable pain such as bone pain, which is commonly experienced by cancer patients, can now be treated effectively with these.[71] Effective against mild or moderate pain, these non-narcotic drugs do reach a peak potency, however, after which they tend to lose their effectiveness and thus they are not as effective against some sorts of severe pain as is morphine.[72] Drugs such as methadone can be used for patients with an allergy to morphine, and it can be used almost as effectively as morphine against severe pain.[73] Another new drug, Tramadol is an nonopiate pain reliever that is not associated with either respiratory depression or many of the other side effects commonly associated with morphine.[74] However, Tramadol is more likely to cause drowsiness than is morphine.[75] Nefopan is a nonmorphine derivative drug that does not cause respiratory depression like morphine.[76] It has a number of positive benefits, and not lead to sedation and in clinical does not bring about either respiratory or circulatory depression.[77]

The potent pain reliever Pentazocine does not cause either the tolerance or the spasmodic episodes sometimes found with morphine.[78] Another new drug, Methotrimeprazine, whose properties are still being discovered, provides pain relief from various types of cancer pain for patients who have a bowel obstruction.[79] It does not cause the respiratory depression often associated with morphine, and even though it does induce drowsiness, it represses vomiting and narcotic-induced nausea,[80] and antidepressants such as Elavil are successful in controlling neuralgia, migraine, and other chronic pain states, and there is a strong possibility that it could be effective with cancer pain.[81]

Corticosteroids can be effective analgesics for cancer patients, for even though they tend to produce weight gain, they also cause a sense of well-being in some instances.[82] They reduce metastic bone pain, and have been shown to give significant relief to patients with epidural cord compression and other types of pain.[83] The inflammatory responses of the body to cancer can often cause nerve-route compression pain, which was previously considered intractable, but corticosteroids can often be effective for this sort of pain.[84] Intracranial tumors can cause severe headaches, but high doses of corticosteroids are an effective treatment.[85] Soft tissues such as lymph nodes can be a source of severe pain, but these too can be effectively treated with corticosteroids.[86]

Various newly developed agonist drugs such as Tramadol and Nefopam can be employed in place of morphine if respiratory depression becomes a problem.[87] Combining various kinds of analgesics can enhance pain relief and also limit the harmful side effects of some individual pain relievers.[88] The use for example, of amphetamines with various opiate drugs can mutually limit their harmful side effects without limiting their analgesic potency.[89]

Finally, Nubain is a remarkable new synthetic nonopiate pain reliever that is equivalent to morphine in its pain-relieving properties, but at higher doses it does not increase respiratory depression as much as does morphine.[90] It acts within two or three minutes after administration by intravenous infusion or within fifteen minutes when introduced by injection.[91] The most frequent response of patients to this drug is sedation, but this is readily controllable as are some of its other minor side effects. And as this is a recently introduced medication, we may discover even more positive analgesic properties as time passes.

New Developments in Opiate Analgesia

It is the opinion of many pain relief specialists that modern opiate and nonopiate pain relievers, if properly administered, can bring relief to virtually any kind of pain.[92] With patients experiencing moderate pain, it is appropriate to begin with NSAIDS such as Ibuprofen or Naproxen or Dolobid.[93] Others patients with this sort of pain respond well to Indocin or Butazolidin, and if this level of pain cannot be eliminated, opiate analgesics can then be introduced. An adequate trial time, however, is required to determine if codeine will be effective, and if not, then opiate analgesics could be initiated.[94]

The most common and, in most instances, the most effective pain reliever is morphine,[95] and its capabilities are now better understood than they were in previous decades, and because of this practitioners are more able to control its harmful side effects than they were before.[96] For example, one study has suggested that the danger of respiratory depression is significantly reduced if the doses are titrated and if the painkillers are orally administered with increments increasing every forty-eight to seventy-two hours.[97] And even though it remains the most effective pain reliever for most sorts of cancer pain, serious side effects have been associated with it in the past.[98] In the past morphine has been known to induce respiratory depression, tolerance, vomiting, nausea, loss of consciousness, sedation, constipation, and physical dependence, but there are many drugs available now to limit or halt these undesirable side effects.

The most serious side effect of morphine is respiratory depression, which is found in about 14 percent of all cases.[99] But it is now possible to predict the onset of this side effect by attending to the combination of mental clouding, hallucination, and somnolence.[100] Unintentional overdosing, with resultant respiratory depression, has largely been overcome by the development of "antagonist" drugs that counteract these.[101] The recently developed drug Narcan, for example, has significantly reduced this danger, and if used carefully, it can significantly reduce the risks of overdose.[102] When this drug is used the pain previously experienced by the patient can reemerge in some instances, necessitating readministration of different levels of opiate or nonopiate analgesics.[103] The fear of seriously harmful or possibly toxic side effects of morphine has caused physicians to sometimes refrain from giving it in adequate amounts to relieve pain. If respiratory depression does occur when dosages of painkillers are stable, this is probably because there is either central nervous system damage or a metabolic imbalance.[104] But some researchers claim that dramatic increases of drug intake are associated with significant progression of the patient's disease and not with the development of tolerance of the morphine.[105] The key, however, to preventing toxic overdoses is careful titration of the analgesic for such patients.[106] Few patients slip from full consciousness immediately into respiratory depression, for they usually slide slowly from full alertness into a semiconsciousness, and then into complete unconsciousness. And when respiratory depression begins, there are signs that warn the physician that it is time to intervene with Narcan or to provide a respirator to aid or restore respiration. If a physician attends to these signs, there would be little risk of respiratory depression in most instances.

Many physicians and researchers are confident that the use of morphine, particularly by infusion route of delivery, is a safe and effective way of managing pain.[107] Also, around-the-clock narcotic administration and frequent reassessment of the patient should limit the possibility of respiratory depression and should not force limitations of dosages.[108] Many sound and innovative methods of administering drugs to overcome the harmful side effects of morphine have been developed in recent years. Where the oral administration of morphine cannot relieve pain, continuous intravenous infusion of morphine for terminal pain is often clinically effective.[109] Employing this route permits faster administration of the analgesic resulting in more prompt pain relief. And if it is necessary to give even more pain relief, morphine can also be administered in a wax-based controlled release system so that it is absorbed more slowly into the blood stream.[110] With this delivery system, pain relievers enter the system more evenly to keep a patient in a more constant pain-free status.

A less serious problem with morphine is that patients can develop toleration of it over time, and this often requires higher levels to be given,[111] which can increase the risk of accidental overdoses.[112] And toleration of the harmful side effects of morphine in some instances grows along with the patient's need for analgesics.[113] But development of tolerance for morphine should not cause a physician undue concern, for there have been reports of patients receiving hourly doses of 80 milligrams per hour of morphine by infusion without ill effect.[114] Nausea is a somewhat persistent problem for those using narcotic pain relievers, but a number of antinauseants have been developed to control this side effect in patients.[115]

Studies have shown that orally administered morphine is clinically effective in relieving the pain of cancer patients in approximately 95 percent of all cases.[116] After it has been determined that morphine is required, oral administration should be tried first, and if the patient remains in pain, parenteral administration of intravenous morphine infusion should then be adopted. Where severe pain is anticipated, there are a number of different options available such as continuous morphine injections, morphine pumps, and if rapid relief of pain is necessary, intramuscular injections.[117]

Cannabinoids have also been shown to be effective with various sorts of pain. These often produce euphoria and stimulate appetite to the benefit of the patient, even though there are a good number of undesirable side effects associated with their use.[118] Experiments in England have shown heroin to be an effective painkiller for patients with cancer if it is not possible to use morphine, and Twycross showed that regular administration of this drug can prevent addiction or tolerance.[119] However, other studies have shown that morphine is just as effective a pain reliever as is heroin alone or heroin mixed with cocaine in a Brompton's cocktail.[120]

This brief survey of recent developments in pain relief indicates that advances in technology and analgesia have eliminated the need of physicians in previous decades to risk overdosing terminally ill patients with morphine to bring release from pain. Today, if situations do arise where lethally overdosing with painkillers seems to be necessary, it is probably because the latest analgesics or pain relief techniques have not been attempted or properly administered. But, in hardly any clinical situations is there any need to lethally overdose a patient to eliminate pain. Because of this, the medical presumption should be that all pain can be relieved with astute assessment and proper utilization of what is available in our present day medical armamentarium.

Questions Concerning Indirectly Lethal Analgesia

Numerous questions emerge concerning the taking of indirectly toxic analgesia. Our culture has taken such a negative view of pain that it considers it a well-neigh absolute evil, and concomitantly, it has regarded pain relievers as ordinary and almost obligatory medication for virtually all conditions. An argument that analgesics would be futile and therefore morally extraordinary for dying patients in pain because they would only bring a short and temporary respite would be rejected without qualification in our culture.

Indirectly life-shortening analgesia is a unique form of indirect killing, for it is the only one permitted solely for the purpose of relieving pain. It is wrong to throw hand grenades into burning tanks to kill those trapped inside in order to relieve their pain, and indirect abortion was never permitted to alleviate the pain of the mother during delivery and childbirth. Only in the case of indirect analgesic euthanasia was pain considered to be proportionate to the life of an innocent individual. In virtually all instances where only indirect killing was permitted, it was allowed solely on the condition that it achieve a good that was proportional to life, and pain relief was never considered to be such a good. If relief from pain is considered a good proportiontate to life, this should be enunciated clearly and supported, because its proportionality is by no means evident.

1. What are the circumstances under which taking indirect life-shortening analgesia would be justified?

To answer this question, it is necessary to refer to other principles governing indirect killing in other circumstances, and most specifically those concerning abortion in order to relate them to the use of indirect life-shortening analgesia. It was in the Catholic debate concerning abortion throughout the centuries in which principles governing indirect killing were developed with exceptional sophistication and precision, and these principles are relevant to this issue. In this debate, direct killing, either as an end in itself or as a means to another end was regarded as inherently immoral. Directly intended abortion either to get rid of a child or as a means to save the life of the mother were not allowed, and while direct killing was prohibited, indirect killing that did not involve killing either as a means or as an end could be just and tolerable in some instances. But it was possible for indirect killing to be unjust if there was not a proportion between the goods and evils brought about by the indirect death, for example. Or if the means employed became morally evil for some reason, the indirectly intended action could be unjust and immoral.

To relate this to the teachings on toxic analgesia, it would not be permissible to take analgesics in certainly lethal doses to end one's life and thus relieve pain just as it would not be permissible to use a certainly lethal medicine against a viable fetus. Taking indirectly life-shortening analgesia would be in accord with the principle of double effect if the intention was only to relieve pain, if the analgesia was not *per se* lethal, and if the pain was so severe and intractable that it was proportionate to death itself.

2. Should it be required that one receiving toxic analgesia experience a significant therapeutic effect prior to or simultaneous with the lethal effect to justify giving toxic analgesia? Should it be permissible for one to succumb before the analgesic effect of the pain relievers is experienced?

It is possible in some circumstances that the therapeutic effect of the dose would be so minimal as to be almost nonexistent or that the toxic and therapeutic effects would occur simultaneously. Legitimate use of analgesia would make it necessary for one to experience some analgesic effect from the painkillers for the analgesia to be truly therapeutic. If a patient would experience no analgesic effect, it would be hard to validly claim that one was only intending to relieve pain and indirectly intending death because there would be no actual pain relief and death would be caused by the analgesics. In such a situation, the pain relievers would be predominately lethal and incidentally analgesic, which would make them direct causes of death.

If a person did not experience any of the therapeutic effects prior to death, it could not be said that the drugs were either primarily or equally therapeutic and indirectly lethal. If there was no pain relief prior to the onset of the lethal effect of the drug, but only the experience of the toxic effect, it could not be said that the pain relievers merely "shortened" life while eliminating the experience of pain, for they ended it before there was any relief from pain.

3. Is the difference between risking death, hastening death, shortening life, and causing death when taking toxic doses of analgesia of any moral importance?

These distinctions can be of importance when they distinguish between culpable and inculpable killing. Physically, intentionally, and deliberately causing death of an innocent person as a means or end is wrong and risking or hastening death could be immoral depending on the level of analgesic employed or the circumstances of its use.

Causing death. The level of analgesia taken by an individual can have a bearing upon the morality of its use. Probably the best guide for determining when the use of lethal analgesia would be direct killing would again be the principles developed in the centuries-long debate in the Catholic church concerning the morality of abortion. Most authors who rejected direct killing concluded that a medicine that was therapeutic for the mother and uncertainly lethal for the child could be used.[121] But physicians could not use medications that would be therapeutic for a mother if they would be certainly lethal to a fetus, though they could use those that were therapeutic for the mother and uncertainly lethal for the fetus.

In addition, the use of certainly lethal doses of analgesia would be wrong because they would be the means by which death would occur even if it were judged to be the only means available of relieving pain. If one gave a certainly lethal dose of painkillers to a patient, the hastening of death or shortening of life would be equivalent to causing death. But if the doses were not certainly lethal, hastening death or shortening life might not be the physical or moral cause of death, and death might be indirect and thus ethically permissible. To hasten death would involve using analgesics that were not as therapeutic as they were lethal, while causing death would involve the use of painkillers in a modality that would make it primarily lethal. The use of analgesics more lethal than therapeutic would make them the moral and physically direct cause of death.

This type of analgesia would be the fundamental and underlying cause of death, and it would not be merely a therapeutic measure that enhances the risk or probability of death: it would cause death and make it certain. Such an analgesic would be the proximate, material, direct, and immediate cause of death, and the classical tradition denied that such a cause could be true indirect killing. This is evidenced in the principle that saving the life of a mother from the threat of an ectopic pregnancy prohibited the removal of the mislocated embryo and required that only the pathological organ be removed. The reason for this subtle distinction was that removing the pathological tissue did not make the physical action immediately lethal to the conceptus.

Hastening death. In relation to the issue of taking pain relievers, if hastening death referred to acts that violated the requirements of the principle of double effect, it would then be culpable killing, but if the act described by this term did not violate these principles, it would not be direct killing. Hastening death would be direct killing if there were other means available of relieving pain, and if there was not sufficient pain to warrant the analgesics, the death would probably be direct as there would not be a good that would be proportionate to the evil of death.

This term could also mean that one would increase the probability of death by giving analgesics, and it would seem that this is what Pius meant when he referred to the shortening of life or hastening death. For if he did not mean this, it would be difficult to reconcile his teaching with his other teachings condemning the direct abortion of an ectopic pregnancy in which death was actually caused physically, or the case of direct euthanasia in which death was caused sooner than would naturally be expected precisely to eliminate suffering. If hastening entails the action becoming in some fashion the underlying and fundamental cause of death, it would not be permissible in his judgment.

But if hastening death only implies a relatively minor increase in the *probability* of death or a minor reduction of the defenses of the body when there are other highly lethal threats already present, then it would seem that use of this form of analgesia would be permissible, as the good of alleviating pain would compensate for the increased risk of death. This is a common occurrence in medicine, as many medications increase one's risk of death.

Risking death. There is a difference between causing and risking death. When one causes death, one initiates an independent, underlying, and fundamental chain of events that brings about death. But when one risks death, the agent chooses a course of action that may bring death under certain circumstances but will not certainly do so. The cause of death *may* be that chosen by the agent, but it might also be another cause that was not initiated by the agent. If the latter is the case, risking death might well not be culpable causing of death. For, in virtually all medical interventions, physicians indirectly intend to risk death and increase its probabilities through their use of medications and other therapies, and accepting or intending these risks indirectly does not make their actions immoral.

Another important difference between risking and causing death is that the risks of death may be brought about unintentionally by the agent. In some cases those who seek to heal often risk death as part of their striving for their therapeutic objectives, which is usually not present with those seeking to cause death. Similarly, intending to *risk* death indirectly as a side effect of a life-saving or life-sustaining action is not morally equivalent to intending to *cause* death deliberately by a given cause.

Taking analgesics that increase the risk of death is not morally equivalent to directly intending death. This principle should apply to taking indirectly lethal analgesia and it should prohibit one from taking a certainly lethal dose of painkillers in any circumstance. Such a dose would be the fundamental and underlying cause of death and its use would ordinarily entail a directly lethal intention. While such a medication might be given if it is equally lethal and therapeutic, the therapeutic effect would be so brief as to be disproportionate to the lethal effect of the drug.

Shortening life. Pius stated that it was permissible to give doses of analgesia sufficient to eliminate pain even if they would shorten life, but the meaning of shortening life is not entirely clear.[122] From what has been said earlier, shortening life could not mean asserting an independent causal chain that would end life in and of itself. It could not refer to the consequence of imposing a certain cause of death on a patient. If it is possible to make such a distinction, shortening life would have to mean that either the risks or probabilities of death occurring would be increased or an impediment to death would be removed because it is a cause of significant pain and suffering. The fundamental difference between shortening life and causing death has to be that a cause of death would be both necessary and sufficient to cause death while shortening life would involve a sufficient but not a necessary condition of death. In practice, one would cause death if one gave such a massive dose of analgesics that respiration would be suppressed, but shortening life would involve giving a dose insufficient to cause death independently, but which could bring it about in conjunction with other independently existing causes.

4. When indirect toxic analgesia is given, does one merely "let one die," or does one positively kill the one receiving the pain relievers?

To answer this question, consider the following scenario. A trolley loses its brakes on a mountain and comes to a fork in the tracks. On the left track is the president and on the right track is a homeless person. Does a driver who turns to the right merely let the street person die when the trolley runs over him, or does he directly kill him? Can it be argued that the physician "lets the patient die" when lethal analgesia is given in the way that he lets the street person die to save the president?

Ordinarily, from the point of view of morality, the object of an action is identified with the intentional object of the agent, for usually when a gun is fired at an individual, one presumes that the intention of the agent is to kill the victim. But there are certain instances when this is not the case. When it is clear that the one killed is engaging in an act of assault, the intention of the agent can be justifiably reconsidered. In a similar fashion, when the one who is killed was suffering greatly, the presumption is usually that the person was deliberately killed to end the suffering.

If one takes efforts to eliminate suffering, the measures taken must be fundamentally therapeutic, and essentially lethal measures cannot be allowed. To return to the Catholic debate on the morality of direct killing, after years of debate in the eighteenth and nineteenth centuries it was determined that a medicine could be used that was as therapeutic for the mother as it was lethal for the unborn child, and this principle should apply to the use of analgesia. This principle implies that pain relievers which are equally toxic and analgesic could be validly employed without a direct intention to kill. If the intention of the person is to take only pain relievers adequate to lower pain to a tolerable level without bringing death, and even though no lethal doses of pain relievers are taken, and the patient still succumbs, one would be "letting" the patient die, provided one took reasonable steps to save the life of the patient. If, after this kind of analgesia was taken, antagonists or a respirator could not preserve the patient's life, one would not be guilty of killing the patient, but only of letting the patient die. If, however, one did nothing whatsoever after giving the analgesic and refused to take even ordinary, customary, and nonburdensome life-saving measures, it could not be said that one "let the patient die." If the good of relief from the pain experienced by the patient is not proportionate to the evil of death, it would be hard to say that one "let" oneself die, for one would be ending one's life for a minor and morally disproportionate cause. And if one selected a level of analgesia that would certainly result in death for the particular patient under treatment, it would be hard to claim that one did not deliberately kill oneself but only "let" oneself die. This is rendered particularly difficult by reason of the fact that there is no issue of protecting another life or another similar value.

If the requirements of the principle of the double effect are carefully observed, one could persuasively contend that one who died after taking a dose of toxic painkillers would not be directly killing himself but merely allowing himself to die if denied the administration of extraordinary means such as a respirator. In situations where only a certainly toxic dose would entirely abolish pain, the physician would be obliged to only lower the level of pain of the patient to a tolerable level and not entirely eliminate it if so doing would kill the patient. Taking a certainly lethal dose would mean that one would not be "letting" oneself die, but would be certainly causing death. This would not be an instance of hastening death or shortening life, but of causing death.

5. May a pregnant woman take a certainly toxic dose of analgesia in order to alleviate severe, profound, and intractable pain?

This would not be a morally acceptable practice because the analgesia would be not only lethal to the victim of the pain, but also to an innocent who is presumably not suffering. Taking such a dose would be somewhat analogous to throwing a hand grenade into a burning tank where one crew member would be in great pain and would be killed by the grenade, but the other two trapped with him would not be in pain but would also be killed by the grenade. Most would say that you would have to get the men out who were not in pain before you could take measures to spare the other's suffering just as one could not give lethal analgesia to an automobile driver in great pain if he would lose control of the car and kill an innocent passenger.

Relating this question to the long and protracted discussion of indirect abortion among Catholic moral theologians between 1100 and 1600, it was generally concluded that a medicine could not be used to save the mother's life if it was primarily lethal to the unborn child and only incidentally therapeutic for the mother. And it was also generally agreed upon that a drug that was certainly lethal to the child could only be used if it was primarily and predominantly therapeutic for the mother.

This principle would imply that a dose of analgesia could only be used if it was primarily analgesic and only "incidentally" lethal. This would mean that taking certainly lethal doses of analgesia would be prohibited as they would be incidentally therapeutic and primarily lethal. Even further, in his other statement concerning the administration of anesthesia, Pius said that there was nothing immoral in rendering a patient unconscious to alleviate pain.[123] As the pains of childbirth can be quite intense and profound but temporary this statement would mean that the physician would have the option available of rendering the pregnant woman temporarily unconscious rather than risking her death and threatening the life of the child. It should be recalled that indirect toxic analgesia was only permitted if there was no other means available to alleviate the pain, and rendering the pregnant woman unconscious is obviously a means of temporarily reducing the pain. Thus, it would not be permissible to shorten the life of a pregnant woman in order to alleviate her pain.

6. May a patient refrain from taking clinically effective, inexpensive, and nonpainful measures after indirect life-shortening analgesia has been taken that would counteract the toxic effects of the painkillers?

To adequately respond to this question, we should recall that if a nonterminal, or in some cases, a terminal surgical patient accidentally went into respiratory depression as a result of analgesia, refusing to provide a readily available respirator or compensating medication would almost universally be considered to be malpractice or negligence. If a terminally ill patient not suffering from profound pain lapsed into respiratory depression, it would be common to give a respirator if so doing would not return the patient to a condition where he or she would need the respirator again. And similarly, a patient in severe pain should be given a respirator if they slipped into respiratory depression if so doing would not force the patient back into severe pain.

Would giving antagonists or a respirator to a patient who received life-shortening analgesia be extraordinary medical treatment or ordinary and required care? In recent years, the presumption has been that such life-saving measures should not be morally required if a terminally ill patient was in intractable pain. But this is subject to question, for if a surgical patient lapsed into respiratory depression from anesthesia during or after an operation, it would be gross malpractice to not provide a respirator or medicines such as Narcan to prevent death from this cause. A patient in a similar circumstance but in grave pain should be given a respirator and should not be denied it merely because they are in pain.

If a respirator would not be considered clinically futile for terminal patients not receiving analgesia, it should not be considered extraordinary for those who need it to counteract life-threatening analgesia. Where a respirator or antagonist would be clinically effective, nonburdensome, and only minimally painful, it should be given, for it is not certain that providing a respirator would inhibit the analgesic effect of the pain relievers. If these can be given in a way to enable one to remain free from pain, they should be given. If, however, using the respirator would return the patient to a condition of profound pain, then it would not be obligatory to employ it or other antagonists.

If this level of pain relief would be allowed only for the terminally ill in severe pain, is one not becoming involved in "quality of life" judgments? Would not this teaching create a double standard, allowing them to receive a higher level of pain relief than what was permitted for those who were in profound pain but not terminally ill or imminently dying? One must raise this question because the claim that only the terminally ill can receive indirectly intended life-shortening pain relief seems to condemn the nonterminal to a life of pain. But it is not clear that a different standard is being proposed here, for if those not terminally ill were allowed to receive indirect life-shortening analgesia, then the evil of pain would have to be proportionate to the evil of death, which is a difficult position to defend. The teaching on indirectly intended life-shortening pain relief appears to espouse a double standard *only* if it is viewed in isolation from the other questions. The principle that the nonterminally ill but gravely suffering cannot receive indirect euthanasia does not condemn the nonterminal such as those with Tay-Sachs and Lesch-Nyhan disease to a life of suffering for they can be given analgesia in doses sufficient to render them unconscious.

It is not the case that patients are condemned to a virtual life of agony because they are nonterminal but in great pain, for Pius permitted them to be rendered unconscious to escape severe pain.[124] His teaching on indirect analgesic euthanasia was issued in conjunction with two other statements precisely so that these people would not have to be condemned to such a life, but also so that they would not have to have their lives ended because of their pain. By allowing them to be rendered unconscious, Pius was not equating the value of relief from pain with the value of life itself.

Pius has not made a "quality of life" judgment holding that the lives of those who are near death do suffer from a reduction in value that makes the good of escape from pain proportionate to their deaths. This escape from pain is not of proportionate value to death when one is in good health, but only when one's health has so badly deteriorated that death is imminent. He was only saying that toward the end of life, the struggle against pain could become increasingly futile as death drew nearer.[125]

If this is not what he meant, then it would appear that he meant that pain would be simply proportionate to life at all points along the life-span. This would have been truly revolutionary, for it would have allowed toxic analgesia for all in severe pain, even for pregnant women, even when this would threaten the fetus, all of which he rather clearly rejected.

7. Is pain so great an evil as to be proportionate to death such that one can cause death to escape pain? Are there situations in which taking life-shortening analgesia would be disproportionate to death?

There is something quite unique about the principle that allows indirect killing to relieve pain, and this teaching is remarkable because Pius has in at least one circumstance elevated the relief of pain to a status equal to that of preserving life. Pius broke new ground by saying that, among the dying, great pain could be an evil proportionate to death. He apparently proposed this because he believed that there were issues of proportionality involved in profound terminal pain that are not there in terminal patients, for when a patient is expected to recover, the hope of an indefinite future without pain mitigates the gravity of the pain.

But when one's time is short and it would only be filled with pain, Pius permitted life-shortening analgesics to be employed because there would be nothing else available to mitigate the severity and harshness of the pain.[126] Pain and suffering can reach a point where bearing with or struggling against it becomes futile and one can gain no spiritual, moral, or psychological profit from continuing the struggle.[127] If there is little time left for the terminally ill, and if intense and intractable pain dominate that short time, these evils would be proportionate to the evil of indirectly intended death. Their lives do not lose their intrinsic value when in pain and close to death, but the short duration of expected life is disproportionate to the profound suffering experienced. When life is very short and one's resources for dealing with pain are exhausted, the struggle to preserve life becomes futile and if the patient is terminal or close to death, severe pain can become intolerable. This is not countenancing killing, but is permitting pain relief that shortens life indirectly.

8. Should a doctor only be allowed to reduce pain from an intolerable to a tolerable level if this is possible, or should the physician be required to eliminate all experiences of pain in the terminal, even if this implies the indirect death of the patient?

According to Pius's teaching, indirectly lethal analgesia should only be permitted when there are no other means available of relieving the profound and intractable pain experienced by the patient.[128] If analgesia could lower the patient's pain to a tolerable level, the proportionality between the pain and the evil of death would be lost, and justification for giving a lethal dose would be lost. If a physician gave a dose of painkillers that would either cause, hasten, or significantly increase the probability of death when giving a lesser dose would lower the experience of pain, the death of the patient would be directly intended.

9. Would a physician be morally permitted to give indirectly intended toxic analgesia if this was not requested by the patient?

Pius was rather clear that giving a life-shortening painkiller should only be given at the request of the patient so that the individual would be able to take care of any worldly or spiritual affairs that might remain outstanding.[129] This judgment objected to giving indirectly life-shortening analgesia by means of substituted judgment or proxy consent.[130] He did not state so explicitly, for he only countenanced giving analgesia when it was expressly requested by the patient under certain precise conditions.

The situation related to this question that presents serious problems is that of giving lethal analgesia to terminally ill neonates in profound pain such as Lesch-Nyhan children. Because they are infants, it is to be presumed that they have no pressing worldly or spiritual affairs requiring attention. Extrapolating from Pius's principles, it would probably be allowable for parents, in order to spare these children profound pain and suffering, to authorize indirectly toxic doses of painkillers if these were the last and only available means of alleviating profound and otherwise intractable pain, if such a situation should ever arise.

10. Would it be imprudent in some cases to take indirectly intended life-shortening analgesia?

It would seem quite evident from what we have said previously that taking indirectly lethal analgesia could be quite injudicious and contrary to the common welfare in some circumstances. This sort of act could be most imprudent when it would lead others to seek life-shortening analgesia for trivial or disproportionate reasons or in order to avoid serious duties and responsibilities. It would also be imprudent to allow this when it could create a social climate in which those with little justification would seek life-shortening analgesia to escape pain. The distinctions noted here are important because they distinguish between careful or cautious use of these treatments and those that would be quite harmful. They should not be abandoned or neglected for that would lead to inadvertent direct euthanasia. Permitting indirectly lethal analgesia in some cases could be quite unwise if so doing might appear to the simple-minded that the person was directly self-executing to escape pain. In such a situation, the proportions of good could be overcome by the evils of scandal and the leading of others into sin. The impact of such a practice on the common good should also be considered as it is quite possible that the well-being of a community could be jeopardized by permitting indirect analgesic suicide. It is very difficult to decide when analgesia only increases the risk of death and when it actually causes death, and these difficulties could lead to abuse. This abuse could put the elderly, disabled, incompetent, and dying in grave danger of being hastened from this life, and this sort of abuse could alter the proportionalities of the action.

11. What are the circumstances when morally permissible analgesia becomes toxic?

This is purely a medical question, but it is one of extreme moral importance, for giving a dose of analgesia that would be certainly lethal would be to cause death and not to merely hasten death or shorten life. To determine when analgesia is no longer life shortening but death causing, the physician must examine in detail the specific condition of the patient.

Conclusion

If indirectly life-shortening analgesia is to be allowed at all, it should only be permitted under the following conditions.

1. Doses of analgesia certainly known to be lethal should not be permitted, for it is not clear that one can only intend to relieve suffering and not cause death directly while using these. It is not morally permissible to take certainly toxic doses of other medications such as insulin for diabetics to relieve suffering, and so also, it should not be permitted to take certainly toxic overdoses of painkillers in order to relieve pain. Only analgesic doses that *might* accidentally and incidentally bring death, but which would not certainly do so, should be allowed to be given to patients. And analgesic doses that would be so immediately lethal that the patient would not experience any analgesic or therapeutic effect should also not be permitted because it could not be validly claimed that these were predominately analgesic and only incidentally lethal.

2. Rather than permitting potentially lethal analgesic doses if a patient is in unremitting pain, physicians should only be allowed to suppress their consciousness if doing more than this would endanger their lives. The development of new analgesic procedures and new generations of painkillers has made it possible to suppress consciousness more easily and to avoid threatening the life of a patient with pain relievers. If suppression of consciousness threatens death, a respirator should be supplied as a matter of course to offset the potential toxic effects of the morphine. Antagonists such as Narcan should only be withheld from patients manifesting signs of respiratory depression if it is medically certain that reversing the effects of the analgesia would bring a return of extreme, untreatable, and unbearable physical pain that could not be otherwise treated.

3. Because of the ambiguity of the classical doctrine on indirect euthanasia about "shortening" life, if indirect life-shortening analgesia must be permitted, it should only be allowed for those who are imminently dying. Indirect analgesic euthanasia should not be permitted for those who are medically stable and not terminally ill, for it may be killing rather than merely "shortening" the life of these other classes of patients.

4. So that indirectly toxic doses of painkillers to end suffering do not kill the innocent, they should not be allowed for pregnant women. To prevent abuse and involuntary killing of the unborn, they should only be given to adults competent to give free and fully informed consent, and not to the incompetent, or infants or minors who are not able to understand the complexities of their situations. The morality and clinical value of indirect analgesic suicide is doubtful because it is also not evident that giving toxic doses is good medicine.

5. Those who are not terminally ill but who are in great pain, should be allowed to be reduced to unconsciousness as their pain is not proportionate to the death that would be brought on by life-shortening analgesia.

6. Most important of all, if a patient suffers life-threatening consequences of analgesic medications, ordinary procedures to sustain life should be mandatory when potentially life-shortening doses of analgesia are taken. This would mean that life-sustaining treatments that would ordinarily be provided a terminal patient who was not in great pain should be given one who has received potentially toxic analgesia because of their serious pain. Pain should not be used as a factor to deny forms of treatment that would be life-saving, nonburdensome, and clinically beneficial. To allow pain to justify

withholding such treatments would be to make an illicit quality-of-life judgment about the lives of those experiencing a painful death.

To those who would claim that these refinements of the doctrine would impose radical pain and suffering on terminally ill patients, it can only be replied that the era of untreatable and intractable physical pain has passed. If health care providers are sufficiently astute and aggressive, virtually all pain can be relieved. If terminal patients do suffer profound and long-lasting pain it is most often because of some failure on the part of the health care providers. Rather than either killing these patients or forcing them to suffer profound pain, consciousness can be suppressed if *absolutely* all other pain relief measures fail.

We should recall that there is increasing evidence that the terminally ill, even when they are in great pain, do not actually wish to die, and if they had their choice, they would prefer to continue living without pain. A recent study by James Henderson Brown et al. noted that thirty-four out of forty-four terminally-ill persons wished to continue living, and the ten who did not wish to continue living all suffered from clinical depressive illnesses.[131] It should be presumed in the majority of cases that death as a result of the administration of pain relievers is not in accord with the wishes and desires of the patient.

The difficulty with administration of painkilling medication in the terminal or near-terminal state stems from a concern with the action of these drugs. The administration of certain painkilling drugs sufficient to alleviate pain may result in death, although not immediately, unless the drug is given in such a massive dose as to be obviously lethal. In circumstances where the medication is being taken as a part of an ongoing pain control regimen, the use of such "lethal" doses would be rare. In addition, the method of administration would likely be of a continuous variety (intravenous solution, implantable pump, patch, etc.), which would also limit the risk of a sudden toxic effect. Descent through levels of consciousness from analgesia, somnolence, coma, and death is a gradual process that can be monitored and modified. Should any other result be the case, physicians would avoid any administration of painkilling medications as the results would be too erratic to be useful. If the aim of the patient and physician is to alleviate pain, the physician could, if absolutely necessary, administer pain relievers to the point where the patient is sedated, and thus pain-free. To go beyond that and administer lethal doses would be unnecessary if the aim is simply pain relief.

Allowing indirect life-shortening analgesia without restriction is contrary to contemporary understandings of the patient-physician relationship in the healing process. It is paradoxical to advocate intensive interpersonal interaction between physicians and patients to promote healing and relieve pain as has been the case in recent therapeutic theory only to easily abandon interpersonal interactions by providing certainly lethal doses of medication. The greatest fear of many patients may well be that of unrelenting and uncontrollable pain, but an associated fear is that of isolation–being left alone in the face of disease or death. Administering a lethal dose of analgesia brings all patient-physician interaction to an end and isolates the patient from all future human interaction. Compassionate care for those in pain is inconsistent with taking certainly lethal treatments followed by abandonment of interaction. Truly compassionate pain relief encompasses attention to the individual's sense of desperation, despair, and isolation, the monitoring of these powerful analgesics and the person's response, and the administration of other medications needed to prevent a fatal event.

The principles governing the administration of indirectly intended life-shortening analgesia aim at enhancing patient care and protecting these vulnerable individuals not only from their own condition, but also from those who would exploit their suffering and pain. Given the advanced state of analgesia today, there should be few instances where giving indirect life-shortening analgesia should even be considered, but when such a practice does become a necessity, the above mentioned principles should be adhered to in the strictest manner possible.

Notes

1. Pope Pius XII, "Religious and Moral Aspects of Pain Prevention in Medical Practice," *The Irish Theological Record*, 87: 193-209.
2. Ibid., 198.
3. Ibid., 198-99.
4. Ibid., 198-99.
5. Ibid., 200-1.
6. Ibid., 204.
7. Ibid., 205-8.
8. "Roma Locuta," *Homiletic and Pastoral Review*, (December 1957): 829-34. This allocution also held that it was legitimate to suppress consciousness to alleviate pain despite the fact that this could bring about revelation of secrets if there was a true necessity for this.

9. Lynch, J., "Pain and Anesthesia: A Papal Allocution," *The Linacre Quarterly*, (November 1957): 129.
10. Ibid.
11. Ibid.
12. Sacred Congregation for the Doctrine of the Faith, *Declaration on Euthanasia*, 3 (1980); National Conference of Catholic Bishops of France, "Declaration des eveques anglasi sur l'euthanasie," *Documentation Catholique*, 72 (1975): 46; National Conference of Catholic Bishops of Germany, "Das Lebensrecht des Menschen und die Euthansie," *Herder Korrespondenz*, 29 (1975): 335-37.
13. For example, see Kelly, G., "The Duty of Using Artificial Means of Preserving Life," *Theological Studies*, 11 (1950): 203; Ashley, B. and O'Rourke, K., *Health Care Ethics,* 3d Ed., 386; "Prolonging Life Conscience Formation," in McCarthy, D. and Moraczewski, A., *Moral Responsibility in Life Prolonging Decisions*, (St. Louis: Pope John Center, 1981), 144.
14. O'Donnell, T., *Medicine and Christian Morals*, 55.
15. For a detailed account of his action see Cranford's "Going Out in Style, the American Way, 1987," *Law, Medicine and Health Care*, 17, 3 (Fall 1989): 209-11. Cranford claimed that he was merely executing the wishes of his mother-in-law, Betty Wright, but this is by no means evident from his account. It rather appears that he used his influence as a self-proclaimed "national expert" on this issue to persuade Mrs. White's physician to accede to his wishes. As can be seen through the course of this article, it is not clear that Cranford's action comports with the requirements of legitimate indirect analgesic euthanasia.
16. Ibid., 209.
17. Ibid., 210.
18. See "Dr. Rosier's Acquittal Both a Victory and a Warning," *The Hemlock Quarterly*, (January 1989): 1. It was not clear at his trial what the exact cause of her death was, for she had been given a dose of morphine sufficient to kill her, but testimony was given that her father suffocated her by placing a pillow over her head.
19. Fletcher, J., *Humanhood: Essays in Biomedical Ethics*, (Buffalo: Prometheus, 1979), 149.
20. President's Commission for the Study of Ethical Problems in Medicine and Biomedical and Behavioral Research, *Deciding to Forego Life-Sustaining Treatment*, (Washington, D.C.: U.S. Government Printing Office, 1983), 51.
21. Fletcher, J., *Medicine and Morals*, (Princeton: Princeton University Press, 1979), 203.
22. See Levy, M., "Pain Management in Advanced Cancer," *Seminars in Oncology*, 12, 4 (December 1985): 394-410; Stuart, G. J., Davey, E. B., Wight, S. E., "Narcotic Analgesics," in *The Continuing Care of Terminal Cancer Patients,* Ed. Twycross, R. G., and Ventafridda V., (Oxford: Pergamum, 1980), 79-116; Rigg, J. R. A., "Ventilatory Effects and Plasma Concentration of Morphine in Man," *British Journal of Anaesthesia*, 50 (1978): 759-64; Tywcross, R. G., "Overview of Analgesia," in *Advances in Pain Research and Therapy,* Ed. Bonica, J. J., and Ventafridda, V., (New York: Raven Press, 1979), 617-33.
23. Foley, K. M., and Sundaresan, N., "Management of Cancer Pain," in *Cancer Principles and Practice of Oncology,* 2d Ed. DeVita, V. T., (Philadelphia: Lippencourt, 1985), 1940.
24. Ibid., 1941. For further studies, see Foley, K. M.. "Pain Syndromes in Patients with Cancer," in Bonica, J. J., and Ventafridda, V., Eds., *Advances,* 2, 59-75; Molinari, R., "Therapy of Cancer Pain in the Head and Neck," in Bonica, J. J., and Ventafridda, V., *Advances,* 131-38.

25. Foley, K.M., and Sundaresan, N., "Management of Cancer Pain," 1943.
26. Ibid.
27. Ibid.
28. Tywcross, R. G., and Lack, S. A., *Symptom Control in Far Advanced Cancer: Pain Relief*, (London: Pitman Books: 1984), 8.
29. Melzack, R., Olfiesh, J. G., and Mount, B. M., "The Brompton Mixture: Effects on Pain in Cancer Patients," *Journal of the Canadian Medical Association*, 115 (1976): 122-26. Also see Mount, B. M., "Narcotic Analgesics," in Twycross, R. G., and Ventafridda, V., Eds., *Continuing Care*, 98.
30. Levy, M., "Pain Management," 398.
31. Ibid., 407.
32. Ettinger, D. S., Vitale, P. J., and Trump, D. C., "Important Clinical Pharmacologic Considerations in the Use of Methadone in Cancer Patients," *Cancer Treatment Report*, 63 (1979): 457-59; Inturrisi, C. E., "Narcotic Drugs," in *Medical Clinics of North America*, Ed. Reidenburg, M. M., (Philadelphia: Saunders, 1982), 1091-1104.
33. Foley, K. M., and Sundaresan, N., "Management of Cancer Pain," 1949.
34. See ibid.
35. Ibid.
36. See Levy, M., "Pain Management," 396; Stuart, G. J., Davey, E. B., and Wight, S. E., "Continuous Intravenous Morphine Infusions for Terminal Pain Control: A Retrospective Review," *Drug Intelligence and Clinical Pharmacy*, 20 (December 1986): 970.
37. Glynn, C. J., "Factors that Influence the Perception of Untractable Pain," *Medical Times*, 108 (1980): 11s-26s; Twycross, R. G., and Lack, S. A., *Symptom Control*, 3-4.
38. For example, bone pain is extremely difficult to deal with in many instances, but various nonpharmacological measures such as radiation therapy or orthopedic surgery can often be helpful. And if these prove ineffective, then morphine infusion or newly discovered flurbiprofen should be considered. See Levy, M., "Pain Management," 405.
39. Walsh, T. D., and Saunders, C. M., "Hospice Care: The Treatment of Pain in Advanced Cancer," *Recent Results in Cancer Research*, 89 (1984): 206-7.
40. Levy, M., "Pain Management," 397.
41. Foley, K. M., and Sundaresan, N., "Management of Cancer Pain," 1951.
42. Beaver, W. T., "Management of Cancer Pain with Parenteral Medication," *Journal of the American Medical Association*, 244 (1980): 2653-57.
43. See Foley, K. M., and Sundaresan, N., "Management of Cancer Pain," 1950; Stuart, G. J., Davey, E. B., Wight, S. E., "Narcotic Analgesics", 970.
44. See Foley, K. M., and Sundaresan, N., "Management of Cancer Pain," 1953; Stuart, Davey, and Wight, "Narcotic Analgesics", 970-71.
45. Foley, K. M., and Sundaresan, N., "Management of Cancer Pain," 1940-45.
46. For a comprehensive typology of cancer pain and the various types of pain experienced by cancer patients, see ibid., 1941-43.
47. Ibid.
48. Levy, M., "Pain Management," 396.
49. Foley, K. M., and Sundaresan, N., "Management of Cancer Pain," 1944.
50. Ibid.
51. Ibid., 1942, 1943. This apparently common phenomenon raises the question of whether or not the real purpose for giving painkillers in lethal doses is to relieve physical pain to alleviate these psychological states.
52. Holland, J., "Advances in Psychologic Support," in *Cancer Achievements: Changes and Prospects for the 1980's*, vol. 2, Ed. Burchenal, J. H., and Oettgen, H. F., (New York: Grune & Stratton, 1980), 723-32.

53. Ibid., 731.
54. Barber, T. X., "The Effects of 'Hypnosis' on Pain," *Psychosomatic Medicine* 25 (1963): 303-33.
55. Rybstein-Blinchik, E., "Effects of Different Cognitive Strategies on Chronic Pain Experience," *Journal of Behavioral Medicine* 2 (1979): 93-98.
56. Turk, D. C., Meichenbaum, D. H., and Berman, W. H., "Application of Biofeedback for the Regulation of Pain: A Critical Review," *Psychology Bulletin*, 86 (1979): 1322-41.
57. Glynn, C. J., "Factors that Influence the Perception of Untractable Pain," *Medical Times*, 11s-26s.
58. Foley, K. M., and Sundaresan, N., "Management of Cancer Pain," 1943.
59. Katz, M., and Joseph, R., "Neuropathology of Neurolytic and Semidestructive Agents," in *Neural Blockade in Clinical Anesthesia and Management of Pain*, Ed. Cousins M., and Briedenbaugh, P., (Philadelphia: Lippencourt, 1980): 122, 126-27.
60. Foley K. M., and Sundaresan, N., "Management of Cancer Pain," 1955.
61. Fosburg, S., "Nitrous Oxide Analgesia for Refractory Pain in the Terminally Ill," *Journal of the American Medical Association*, 250 (1975): 511-13.
62. See Loeser, J. D., "Dorsal Rhizotomy," in *Neurological Surgery*, Ed. Youmans, J. R., (Philadelphia: Saunders, 1982), 3664-70.
63. See Nashold, B. S., and Ostdahl, R. H., "Dorsal Root Entry Zone Lesions for Pain Relief," *Journal of Neurosurgery*, 51 (1979): 59-69.
64. Moore, D. C., "Role of Nerve Blocks with Neurolytic Solutions in Visceral and Perineal Pain," in Bonica, J. J., and Ventafridda, V., Eds., *Advances*, 2, 593-606.
65. See Melzack, R., and Wall, P. D., "Pain Mechanisms: A New Theory," *Science*, 150 (1965): 971-74. The implantation of these electrodes stimulates large-diameter nerves and closes the "gate" to central pain perception.
66. See Foley, K. M., and Sundaresan, N., "Management of Cancer Pain," 1957-58.
67. Ibid.
68. Ibid., 1957.
69. Cook, A. W., and Kawakami, Y., "Commissural Myelotomy," *Journal of Neurosurgery*, 47 (1977): 1-6; Fink, R. A., "Neurosurgical Treatment of Non-Malignant Intractable Rectal Pain: Microsurgical Commissural Rhizotomy with the Larkin Dioxide Laser," *Neurosurgery*, 14 (1984): 664-65.
70. Kantor, T. G., "Ibuprofen," *Annals of Internal Medicine*, 91 (1979): 877-82; Miller, R. R., "Evaluation of Analgesic Efficacy of Ibuprofen," *Pharmacotherapy*, 1 (1981): 21-27.
71. See Brogden, R. N.,, Heel, R. C., Spught, T. M., et al., "Naproxen Up to Date: A Review of Its Pharmacological Properties and Therapeutic Efficacy and Use in Rheumatic Diseases and Pain," *Drugs*, 18 (1979): 241-77; Backhouse, C. I., Engler, C., and English, J. R., "Naproxen Sodium and Indomethacin in Acute Musculoskeletal Disorders," *Rheumatology Rehabilitation*, 19 (1980): 113-19.
72. See Foley, K. M., and Sundaresan, N., "Management of Cancer Pain," 1946.
73. Hansen, J., Ginman, C., and Hartvig, L., "Clinical Evaluation of Oral Methadone in Treatment of Cancer Pain," *Acta Anesthesia Scandinavia*, 76 (1982): 124-27.
74. See Flohe, L., Ahrend, J., Cogal, A., Richter, W., and Simon, W., "Klinische Prufungen der Langzeit Applikation von Tramadol," *Arzneim Forschung*, (1978): 213-17.
75. Worz, R., "Control of Cancer Pain with Analgesics Acting in the Central Nervous System," *Recent Results in Cancer Research*, 89 (1985): 102. Tramadol does not cause respiratory depression in clinical doses, nor is it as strongly associated with constipation or harm to the cardiovascular system. It does cause sedation and sleepiness in many patients, and in a small number of patients, it does cause euphoria.

76. Ibid. Also see Zimmerman, M., "Neurophysiologische Untersuchungen Uber Einen Spinalen Wirkungsort Von Nefopam," in Gerbershagen, H. U., and Cronheim, G., *Nefopam: Ein Neuartiges Analgetikum*, (New York: Fischer, 1979), 18-26.
77. Worz, R., "Control of Cancer Pain," 102.
78. Beaver, W. T., Wallenstein, S. L., Houde, R. W., and Rogers, A., "A Comparison of the Analgesic Effects of Pentazocine and Morphine in Patients with Cancer," *Clinical Pharmacological Therapy*, 7 (1966): 740-51; Cabanne, F., Guerrin, J., and Wilkening, M., "Die Behandlung von Tumorschmerzen mit Pentazokin," in Janzen, R., Keidel, W. D., Herz, A., and Steichle, C., Eds. *Pain*, (Stuttgart: Theime, 1979), 444-46; De Thibault de Boesnighe, L., "Double Blind Study of the Analgesic Effect of Nefopam Hydrochloride (Acupan) and Pentazocine (Fortral) in Cancer Patients with Pain," *Current Therapy Research*, 24 (1978): 646-55. Pentazocine is associated with sedation and drowsiness more than is the case with morphine and it lowers the hallucination threshold.
79. Beaver, W. T., Wallenstein, S. L., Houde, R. W., and Rogers, A., "A Comparison of the Analgesic Effect of Methotrimeprazine and Morphine in Patients with Cancer," *Clinical Pharmacological Therapy*, 7 (1966): 436-46.
80. Foley, K. M., and Sundaresan, N., "Management of Cancer Pain," 1952.
81. Weiss, O., Sriwantanakul, K., and Weintraub, M., "Treatment of Post-Herpetic Neuralgia and Acute Herpetic Pain with Amitriptyline and Perphenazine," *South African Medical Journal*, 72 (1982): 274-75; Raftery, H., "The Management of Postherapeutic Pain Using Sodium Valproate and Amitriptyline," *Irish Medical Journal*, 72 (1979): 399-401.
82. Foley, K. M., and Sundaresan, N., "Management of Cancer Pain," 1953.
83. Gilbert, R. W., Kim, J. H., and Posner, J. B., "Epidural Spinal Cord Compression from Metastic Tumor: Diagnosis and Treatment," *Annals of Neurology*, 3 (1978): 40-51.
84. Hanks, G. W., Trueman, T., and Twycross, R., "Corticosteroids in Terminal Cancer —a Prospective Analysis of Current Practice," *Journal of Postgraduate Medicine*, 59 (1983): 28-32.
85. Black, P., "Brain Metastasis: Current Status and Recommended Guidelines for Management," *Neurosurgery*, 5 (1979): 617-31; Wilson, C. B., Yorke, C. H., and Levin, A. V., "Intracranial Malignant Growth, Primary and Metastic," *Current Problems in Cancer*, 1 (1977): 1-46.
86. See Twycross, R. G., and Lack, S. A., *Symptom Control*, 270.
87. Worz, R., "Control of Cancer Pain," 102.
88. Foley, K. M., and Sundaresan, N., "Management of Cancer Pain," 1950.
89. Beaver, V. T. "Comparison of Analgesic Effects of Morphine Sulfate Hydroxyzine and Other Combinations in Patients with Postoperative Pain," in Bonica, J. J., and Ventafridda, V., Eds., *Advances*, 553-57; Forrest, R., et al., "Dextroamphetamine with Morphine for the Treatment of Postoperative Pain," *New England Journal of Medicine*, 296 (1977): 712-15.
90. Barnhart, E. R., *Physicians Desk Reference 1987*, 41st Ed. (Oradell, NJ: Medical Economics Co., 1987), 904. Also see *Physicians Desk Reference*, 44th Ed. (1990), 925.
91. Ibid.
92. Twycross, R., "Clinical Experience with Diamorphine in Advanced Malignant Disease," *International Journal of Clinical Pharmacology Therapeutic Toxocology*, 9 (1974): 184-98; Porter, J., and Hick, H., "Addiction Rare in Patients Treated with Narcotics," *New England Journal of Medicine*, 302 (1980): 123.
93. Levy, M., "Pain Management," 405.
94. Ibid., 401.
95. Ibid., 399.

96. Ibid., 398-99, 403-5.
97. Walsh, T. D., "Opiates and Respiratory Function in Advanced Cancer," *Recent Results in Cancer Research*, 89 (1985): 116-17. Roxanol is a liquid preparation carried in a dropper bottle that permits ambulatory patients to find the level of pain relief equal to that of morphine without its inconvenience. MS Contin uses a wax-based release system that permits it to be given on a twelve-hour basis rather than a four-hour basis.
98. See Levy, M., "Pain Management," 399. Also see Walsh, T. D., "Opiates," 115-17. R. Worz points out that there are frequent undesired side effects of morphine usage. He discusses at length the methods of controlling these side effects and the other drugs now available that are just as effective as morphine, but do not bring the side effects it does. Another recently introduced drug that is very effective in dealing with severe or excruciating cancer pain is Dilaudid, but less is known about its management than is known about morphine.
99. Foley, K. M., and Sundaresan, N., "Management of Cancer Pain," 1950. Also see Stuart, G. J., Davey, E. B., Wight, S. E., "Narcotic Analgesics", 971.
100. Stuart, G. J., Davey, E. B., Wight, "Narcotic Analgesics," 971.
101. Foley, K. M., and Sundaresan, N., "Management of Cancer Pain," 1950.
102. Ibid.
103. Ibid.
104. Worz, R., "Control of Cancer Pain," 101.
105. Foley, K. M., "Patterns of Narcotic Drug Use in a Cancer Pain Clinic," in *Annals of the New York Academy of Science*, 362 (1980): 161, 167-68.
106. See Walsh, T. D., "Opiates," 116-17.
107. See Worz, R., "Control of Cancer Pain" and Walsh, "Opiates." Stuart, Davey, and Wight claim that the use of continuous intravenous infusion of morphine is successful in controlling cancer pain that cannot be controlled by more conventional therapies, and they urged use of this technique with close monitoring and assessment of patient needs. See Stuart, G. J., Davey, E. B., Wight, S. E., "Narcotic Analgesics", 970-71.
108. Foley, K. M., and Sundaresan, N., "Management of Cancer Pain," 1949-50.
109. See Boyer, M. W., "Continuous Drip Morphine: Titrating IV Morphine," *American Journal of Nursing*, 82 (1982) 602-4; Burnakis, T., "Treatment of Severe Chronic Pain by Continuous Parenteral Infusion of Morphine," *Hospital Pharmacology*, 18 (1983): 18-24; Citron, M. L., et al., "Safety and Efficacy of Continuous Intravenous Morphine for Severe Cancer Pain," *American Journal of Medicine*, 77 (1984): 199-204.
110. Levy, M., "Pain Management," 399.
111. Foley, K. M., and Sundaresan, N., "Management of Cancer Pain," 1951; Worz, R., "Control of Cancer Pain," 101.
112. Fraser, D. G., Letter to the editor, *Annals of Internal Medicine*, (1980), 781, 782.
113. Foley, K. M., and Sundaresan, N., "Management of Cancer Pain," 1951.
114. See DeChristoforo, R., Carden, B. J., and Hood, J. C., "High Dose Morphine Infusion Complicated by Chlorobutanol-induced Somnolence," *Annals of Internal Medicine*, 98 (1983): 335-36; and Miser, A. W., Miser, J. S., and Clark, B. S., "Continuous Intravenous Infusion of Morphine Sulfate for Control of Severe Pain in Children with Terminal Malignancy," *Journal of Pediatrics*, 96 (1980): 930-32.
115. See Levy, M., "Pain Management," 403-4. Approximately 40 percent of patients on narcotic pain relief experience nausea. Depending on the severity of the nausea, drugs such as Compazine, Haldol, Thorazine, or Reglan can be used to control these symptoms.
116. Mount, B. M., "Narcotic Analgesics", 102.

117. See Wenger, B., "Continuous Drip Morphine," *American Journal of Nursing*, 82 (1982) 602-4; Holmes, H., Letter to the Editor, *Drug Intelligence Clinical Pharmacology*, 12 (1978): 556-57.
118. Harris, L. S., "Cannabinoids as Analgesics," in *Mechanisms of Pain and Analgesic Compounds*, Ed. Beers, R. F., and Baset, E. G., (New York: Raven, 1979), 467-68.
119. Twycross, R., "The Measurement of Pain in Terminal Carcinoma," *Journal of Internal Medical Research*, 4 (1975): 58-67.
120. Melzack, R., Mount, B. M., and Gordon, J. M., "The Brompton Mixture versus Morphine Solution Given Orally: Effects on Pain," *Journal of the Canadian Medical Association*, 120 (1979): 435-38.
121. See Connery, J., *Abortion: The Roman Catholic Perspective*, (Chicago: Loyola University Press, 1979), 124-27, 141.
122. Pius XII, "Religious and Moral Aspects," 208.
123. Ibid., 206-8.
124. Ibid., 200-4.
125. Ibid., 207-8.
126. Ibid., 208.
127. Ibid., 205-8.
128. Ibid., 209.
129. Ibid., 207-8.
130. Ibid., 207.
131. Brown, J. H., Henteloff, P., Barakat, S., and Rowe, C. J., "Is it Normal for Terminally Ill Persons to Desire Death?" *American Journal of Psychiatry*, 143, 2 (February 1986): 208-11.

8

The Social Dynamics of Rational Suicide

The mainstream Catholic moral tradition has affirmed that certain sorts of actions can be prohibited because they harm society and the common welfare of all. The Second Vatican Council, in its *Pastoral Constitution on the Church in the Modern World,* held that promotion of the common good, the sum total of social conditions that allowed people as a community, as well as individual citizens, to reach their fulfillment, was deepening and broadening as we came to understand more fully what this involved.[1] In order to achieve a stable and well-ordered society, the Council taught that there had to be not only justice and security for all, but also the physical, moral, and legal conditions that enable a community to flourish, and these demands raised the question of whether a liberal suicide policy could fit into such a society. Like other monotheistic religious traditions, Catholicism has condemned suicide because it regards life as a gift of God to be used in faithful stewardship; however, Catholic moral teachings not only objected to suicide for moral reasons, but for social reasons as well.[2] Recently some consequentialist or proportionalist Catholic moral theologians such as Daniel Maguire have argued that suicide can be morally licit in some instances

> [H]aving said all this, however, I must concede, 'in a mournful mood,' to use Augustine's phrase, that suicide may at times be moral. Even then, like war, it will be tragic; but it can be moral. Generally, I judge, persons perform suicide because they have been stripped of the essential ingredients of human life – hope and love. It would be naive to think that human perfidy is not capable of depriving some of its members of these ingredients so that they can do no more and must depart. There may indeed be cases where all of the disvalues of suicide can be outweighed by ineffable pain and aloneness. In those cases, it is the survivors who are to be morally indicted, not the victim, who seizes the only remaining relief.[3]

However, other moralists have not gone as far in endorsing the morality of suicide, and with these few notable exceptions, a strong consensus exists among Catholic moralists against the morality of suicide. Many suicide proponents argue that it can be of positive value to society and should therefore be permitted. But mainstream Catholic views held that legal endorsement of rational suicide to benefit society would bring it serious harm. A liberal suicide policy would greatly harm society because: (1) it is uncontrollable and facilitates irrational and thoughtless self-killing; (2) it undermines common law tradition against killing the innocent and denies the vulnerable protection from themselves; and (3) it undermines the integrity and trustworthiness of the healing professions. The arguments that suicide is of benefit to society will also be explained and critically examined, and then arguments will be presented that suicide should not be socially or legally endorsed because it does serious social harm to society.

Killing to Control Suffering: An Uncontrollable Practice

Advocates of rational suicide argue that it should be legalized to allow competent people to end their lives when their suffering or loss of dignity become intolerable. Few of them would agree that legalized analgesic self-assassination or assisted self-killing would be uncontrollable in practice, and most are quite confident that unwanted and irrational suicides can be readily and effectively prohibited, even though the history of suicide suggests that the contrary is true. The uncontrollability of suicide and assisted suicide is seen most clearly in contemporary Holland. For years, advocates of assisted suicide in Holland vigorously denounced those who charged that involuntary suicide was being performed there. But, in April 1993, a Dutch court acquitted a physician who helped a nonterminal, but depressed woman commit suicide. Dutch courts have long held that suicide for patients whose suffering was "perpetual, unbearable and hopeless" was permissible, but this was the first case in which suicide was allowed for mental illness alone. "What the cause of her suffering was – illness or otherwise – is not important."[4] In light of this endorsement of assisted suicide for the nonterminal but depressed, claims that suicide can be adequately controlled ring hollow.

In recent years suicide has ranked as the sixth leading cause of death in Holland, claiming more lives than traffic accidents.[5] For men between the ages of fifteen and forty, and women between fifteen and sixty it is the third most common cause of death.[6] And for women between twenty and twenty-nine, it is the leading cause of death.[7] Official estimates in Holland are that 6,000 persons a year request assistance in suicide, but some reports have emerged claiming that 15,000 to 18,000 have either suicided or been helped to commit suicide.[8] It has also been noted that health care professionals tend to avoid suicidal people with the excuse that little is done to actively help them, and this aversion seems to stem from the belief that the medical profession has lost its interest in helping the suicidal.[9] Most recently the Dutch Parliament enacted laws that prohibited assisted suicides that did not require prosecution of physicians of those who assisted in suicides, but even this did not satisfy, and there have been more initiatives proposed to allow assisting in the suicides of incompetent patients who do not consent to assisted suicide, but who would if given the opportunity.[10]

Carlos Gomez, in his recent book *Regulating Death,* explained why Dutch attempts to regulate assisted suicide have failed, and he showed the extraordinary difficulties involved in any attempt to formulate a policy permitting rational suicide.[11] Gomez points out that there have been numerous attempts to establish precise, concrete, and specific laws to control and regulate voluntary self-killing in Holland over the past decade but all have failed because of the impossibility of satisfying the demands of physicians, the terminal or dying, the judicial system, pro-life groups, and the churches. The result has been judicial paralysis, an absence of policy, and legislative deadlock resulting in no effective controls on the practice.

This inability to formulate a policy to control suicide is not simply political in nature or the result of ill will. Suicide to abolish suffering and pain is uncontrollable in principle because there are no objective criteria to identify those forms of suffering that warrant self-execution and those that do not. "Analgesic" or "therapeutic" suicide cannot be controlled because there are no clear and evident differences between the various kinds of mental and physical suffering that would enable law or morality to differentiate those that should justify self-execution from those that should not. Suicide is uncontrollable in practice because as soon as one grants that a person has suffered sufficiently to warrant self-killing, others with similar but less serious kinds of suffering will come forward claiming the right to kill themselves on the grounds that their suffering is either equal to or worse than that of another given permission to self-execute. This is born out by the recent history of the Dutch experiments on euthanasia.

It is not just that there are no clear differences between different kinds of suffering, but it is also not clear what level of suffering is sufficient to justify self-killing. Ultimately, determining these would have to be left to the individual, for neither the law nor society could judge according to an objective standard when suffering became intolerable, and this would make it impossible to impose any sort of meaningful controls on it. Courts would not be able to appeal to objective standards of evidence and would have to rely solely on the subjective judgments of the individuals, which has not been allowed before in American common law. And the same would apply to those who would want to end their lives because of loss of dignity. A liberal suicide policy is unworkable in practice because there are no objective criteria by which one could determine if a person's suffering or loss of dignity would be sufficient to warrant self-killing.

A liberal suicide policy would require courts to differentiate the forms of suffering that would warrant suicide from those that would not, something that is not possible to do in a fair and objective manner. On what grounds could a court declare that the suffering of a handicapped person warranted suicide while that of a terminally ill cancer patient did not? How could courts seriously and persuasively object that the suffering of a man who failed to repair his brakes, totally paralyzed himself and killed his whole family warranted suicide, while the suffering of a young victim of multiple sclerosis would not? How could a court say that the suffering of a severely depressed but competent person would not justify suicide and was not worse than the suffering of the cancer patient, which would justify suicide? The most commonly asserted justifications for legalized suicide are virtually immune to objective identification and specification, which would make it well-neigh impossible to establish any solid limits against self-extermination. Because these criteria are so subjective, they are also quite susceptible to manipulation by others which could create very serious dangers for the vulnerable and naive.

A liberal suicide policy would pose a grave threat to the mentally and emotionally unstable in particular. For most people whose lives are going well, suicide is not a threat, but for the unstable, immature, weak, grieving, troubled, despairing, and depressed, suicide is a very serious threat. The law presently does nothing to romanticize suicide or make it attractive to the vulnerable, unstable, or disabled, but even with this very hostile attitude, suicide remains a serious threat to the weaker in our society. Suicide can be very tempting to the desperate, unstable, immature, or distraught, and it would be socially irresponsible to give them greater freedom to harm themselves as a result of their despair. Laws against suicide are not primarily for the happy, secure, and successful, but for the despairing, confused, troubled, weak, and failing. They aim at protecting these people from themselves, and abolishing them would radically increase the threat they pose to themselves. Should suicide be allowed in order to relieve suffering, it would inevitably acquire an air of moral respectability and would be touted by many as the primary solution to the grave suffering many of these people experience. Endorsing suicide would then cause many to see it as a positive good, and not as even morally neutral, because it would "enhance their dignity" by abolishing their suffering. Allowing suicide to become so romanticized could increase dangers for the immature, despairing, and depressed by making it irresistible to them.[12] This could persuade many to see that the blade, noose, or bullet as a sign of heroism and virtue because the mature and respectable would do the same.

One option suggested by suicide advocates is to permit purely voluntary suicide only for the "rational and competent," but even this is filled with problems. If suicide was permitted only for those who were "intelligent, rational, competent and mature," many of the incompetent and immature would see self-execution as a sign of intelligence, sophistication, maturity, and courage. The emotionally unstable would mimic the suicides of the emotionally stable, ignore the careful and precise limits that the mature would impose on self-killing, and would simply kill themselves when they thought it suited their interests, however irrational those might be. The immature and emotionally unstable frequently project their own failures and problems onto others, and they often see themselves as creating more trials, problems, and burdens for others than they really do. In addition, they often believe acts to be mature, intelligent, and reasonable that the mature and competent understand to be grossly destructive, callow, and irrational. Morally endorsing suicide to eliminate suffering would bring the weak, immature, and emotionally unstable to see death as the easy deliverer from all of their troubles, disappointments, and failures. If suicide came to be accepted as not just morally tolerable for the mature, competent, and intelligent to deal with trials and sufferings, but as something good for them, then many of the immature and unstable would come to regard their own deaths as morally good and justified because of the burdens they believe their lives impose on others, a misjudgment that could have tragic consequences. Stopping this would be extraordinarily hard because of the problem of proving the irrationality or incompetence of these adolescents. A further problem with permitting suicide to escape suffering for the rational and competent is that the unstable and immature do not perceive reality as do the mature and competent.[13] They often radically overestimate their own sufferings while underestimating their abilities to cope with them, which only increases their vulnerability to suicide. Because of this vulnerability they are even more tempted than others to inflict death on themselves to escape what they consider to be intolerable sufferings.

Those who would allow suicide on request do not adequately confront the serious problem of determining what should be done with those who would probably want to end their lives if they had the opportunity to do so, but cannot because they are incompetent. There is much in American common law tradition that affirms the fundamental equality of the incompetent with the competent, and because of this, some would argue that the incompetent have the same rights and freedoms as those who are competent. With the collapse of strict barriers against suicide, there would be strong pressures to legalize it for the incompetent in order to assure them of full equality with the competent.

Suicide advocates do not give sufficient consideration to the problems of protecting the incompetent from suiciding, and they have not offered persuasive and comprehensive programs for protecting them. This is an especially critical problem in light of the recent revelations about emerging practices of assisted suicide in Holland. At a recent conference, American Civil Liberties Union legal director John Powell, J.D., argued that the right to privacy and the principle of personal autonomy should be interpreted to mean that the incompetent enjoy the same rights as do the competent.[14] Just as minors have a right to abortion, so also would the depressed but healthy have a fundamental right to be killed at their request.[15] As an example of how bad the protection offered by courts to the incompetent can be at times, a judge recently heard only fifteen minutes of arguments before ordering the removal of a feeding tube from an incompetent patient.[16] This sort of casual and superficial approach could very well become the norm of protection for medically vulnerable persons, and it suggests that voiceless and incompetent people could easily be victimized by those who would benefit from their deaths. It would be naive to believe that these sorts of abuses would not occur, and only in an ideal world they would be fully protected.

Legalized suicide would enable the powerful, persuasive, and influential to protect their interests even more by inducing the oppressed and exploited into suicide. Among the first to be pressured to self-execute would be the handicapped, poor, elderly, dispossessed, underprivileged, exploited, and oppressed. Loosening restraints on suicide would increase, rather than lessen, risks to victims of prejudice, oppression, bias, and exploitation.

Protecting the Common Law Tradition on Suicide

A liberal suicide policy would also have harmful effects on society because it would undermine the common law tradition on homicide. Helga Kuhse argues in behalf of legalized suicide by claiming that good law should permit individuals to commit suicide to alleviate suffering resulting from natural causes.[17] Kuhse presumes that the law has a positive obligation to curb or limit suffering and it should be courageous enough to permit killing to bring this about. But the common law tradition has objected to allowing analgesic suicide because such a policy would logically commit it to allowing suicide for a whole range of other "higher" moral values as well. To be logically consistent, allowing analgesic suicide would require permitting suicides to protest political or social injustices because eliminating these social ills would be of greater moral value to society than is the alleviation of the sufferings of an individual citizen. And one would wonder if the law should also not permit some ritualistic or religious suicide if this would be required by religious beliefs to relieve sufferings and attain salvation? For these suicides would promote a higher moral objective than would escaping from suffering, and for that reason suicide could justified.

Alan Sullivan has argued that the state has no interest in banning suicide, and he believes that the state has sought to prevent suicide in the past mostly because of unjustifiable religious reasons.[18] But this is an eccentric opinion and most legal scholars believe that the common law tradition has held that the state has a clear interest in protecting innocent life and preventing its deliberate destruction, irrespective of any religious beliefs that might be involved. Besides seeking to preserve innocent human life from deliberate attack of any kind, the state has an interest in preserving the integrity of families and protecting children, the incompetent, disabled, and handicapped, and preserving the gifts and talents of the community. All of these interests bolster the state's concern for preventing suicide. The law has many interests to protect, and its barriers against suicide facilitate promoting this.[19] The common law tradition has imposed different levels of punishment on suicidal acts at different times in history, not because it has considered suicide right at some times and wrong at others, but rather because in some times and places stronger punishments and measures were required to show the seriousness of suicide. These also indicate that at some times, societies were more blind to its evils than they were at others. It has often been the case that when societies did not penalize suicide, it was because it was not widely practiced and there was little need for laws against it. But when suicides became more common, penalties were imposed to strengthen preventative programs. Some societies have adopted a rather cavalier attitude toward suicide, but almost inevitably, these policies had to be reversed because suicides rose to an intolerable level. Chapters 2 and 3 recounted these attempts and it should be recalled that many societies resorted to extreme and desperate measures to curb these practices.

Legalization of voluntary and assisted suicide would undermine the integrity of the common law principle that innocent human life should not be taken by private persons. The common law has held that the state alone could deliberately execute the guilty in very narrowly defined circumstances, but even this power was to be used cautiously. Even though this long-standing tradition has been repeatedly challenged, it has been consistently upheld in common law. It has only permitted deliberate killing by private citizens when this was necessary to protect innocent human life, but it has not allowed private citizens to destroy innocent human life in any circumstance. Legalized suicide would shatter this tradition and call into question all claims that innocent life should be protected.

Liberalizing suicide laws would run contrary to many trends in contemporary common law, which have condemned killing as an unjustifiably cruel punishment.[20] In the twentieth century, many have come to view any execution for even the worst crimes as inhumane, and yet suicide advocates see self-killing as an acceptable, compassionate, and moral choice for those who have committed no crime whatsoever. If advanced thinkers are coming to challenge even the morality of killing the guilty, how could one maintain logical consistency by allowing the killing of the innocent? Legalization of suicide would be ironic, for it would give legal protection to those who wished to use lethal force against the innocent, but it would deny the protection of the law to those who sought to use nonlethal force to protect innocent human life from being destroyed. In an era when many in both society and religion are trying to limit the killing of those who are certainly guilty of serious crimes, permitting suicide is simply paradoxical and logically inconsistent.

Legalization of suicide for the rational and competent to escape physical, spiritual, or emotional suffering would require that courts, law enforcement officers, and health care professionals not only determine competency, but also adjudicate the merit of petitions for suicide. Courts have traditionally been reluctant to allow this because it would demand examination and evaluation of the moral worthiness of motives as well as the mental and emotional capabilities of citizens to tolerate suffering. Traditionally, they have limited their competence to the examination of extrinsic actions and have refrained from judging actions on the basis of the moral values motivating them. But legalizing suicide would require courts to judge motive, intention, and capacity to endure suffering of the suicidal. It would also mean that law enforcement officers no longer would be able to intervene automatically and without reservation to prevent potential suicides, for they would have to evaluate the moral worthiness and competence of the suicidal.

If health care professionals were to be called upon to make these judgments, they would become the primary gatekeepers of life and death, and would have to decide which patients should be saved and which ones should be allowed to self-destruct, a judgment for which traditionally they have not been well prepared. The sorts of judgment would be very different from their usual medical judgments, for they would not be determining what methods were to be used to combat disease and death, but when they were to give death to their patients. Not only are medical professionals not adequately trained to make these decisions, but it is also not clear that law enforcement officers could legitimately intervene to prevent what they perceived to be suicide. They might be required to determine on the spot if a suicidal attempt was competent, well-motivated, informed, rational, and free or be charged with violating the individual's right to privacy, judgments they often feel inadequate to make. And if legalized as a fundamental constitutional right, no legal authority could intervene to regulate suicidal actions. Because legalization of suicide might radically compromise the power of society to protect people from self-slaying, it would seem to be a major threat to those who would be vulnerable to suicide, and this is a further reason for rejecting it.

The common law has been slow to permit suicide because it is such a final, complete, and definitive action, and if any mistakes are made in allowing a suicide, they could not be rectified. The common law demanded that there be moral certainty before any judgment of death be imposed. Attaining this degree of certainty would not be possible if courts were forced to judge motives and intentions to know if suicide should be allowed. If the law permitted suicide to eliminate suffering or promote dignity, it would abandon its strict criterion of legal certainty in these matters, which could mean looser standards elsewhere in the law resulting in yet unforeseen harm. If suicide were to become a fundamental legal right as Margaret Battin suggests, we would have to ask what other rights could also be considered as fundamental.[21] If the right to kill ourselves to escape suffering is fundamental, despite all of the problems that suicide causes others, why shouldn't consented killing by a proxy in dueling or gunfighting also be fundamental? Recreational drug use is very harmful and creates serious social problems, but these problems are arguably no less severe than what would result from widespread suicide. If suicide was permitted as a fundamental right, it is likely that logical consistency would require us to consider other equally socially harmful actions as fundamental rights also.

Suicide has been prohibited by the common law tradition because legalizing suicide would loosen restraints on our prejudices and would make it quite easy to manipulate the victims of our prejudices to end their lives. John Finnis noted that the biases of individuals or groups can deflect authoritative institutions from achieving justice in society, and a sound jurisprudence institutes measures to deal with this.[22] These institutions should not permit the law to abandon equitable systems of law enforcement, and a just legal system should not permit suicide because this would foster a very lethal form of discrimination against the vulnerable.[23] Also, legalized suicide would undermine the liberal tradition of expanding protections for minorities, the vulnerable, and victims of prejudice, for they would be the ones most strongly encouraged to commit suicide.

Legalization of voluntary suicide for those judged competent would imply that the consent of the agent is the fundamental right-making characteristic of a suicidal act. But if that were true, then why wouldn't dueling or gunfighting also be legally permissible because they are consented killing by proxy? It has only been within the last century that dueling and gunfighting have stopped, and if the law were to permit suicide, the legal ban on this form of consented self-killing by proxy would be weakened. Legalization of suicide would be questionable because it would canonize the principle that consent alone can justify some acts of killing of the innocent.

Legalized suicide undermines the common law tradition because the state has a responsibility to protect not only the rational and intelligent but also the weak and obtuse from harming themselves through error or misjudgment.[24] The state is not to simply prevent crime, fraud, and felony, but is also to protect all citizens from unwittingly inflicting harm upon themselves, and it is concerned with protecting the lives of the vulnerable, not only from others, but also from themselves. The rights of individual autonomy and personal liberty are not absolute and they can be legitimately restricted or restrained by the state to protect the rights of the incompetent, insane, and immature. To achieve this, the law can require motorists to proceed with extra caution in school zones to prevent children from being harmed, for example. Even the most intelligent and competent sometimes need the guiding hand of the law, and allowing suicide might be withdrawing protection from them when they need it most of all.

Allowing suicide for the incompetent would create problems for our judicial system as it would be difficult to determine if the suicidal consented to the death because the best witness to the action and the intentions of the victim would be dead. For example, in early 1989, Marty James announced on the ABC television program "Nightline" that he had "helped" in the death of his friend Ron Weigard who suffered from AIDS. He claims he first spoon-fed him barbiturates after which he put a plastic bag over his head and secured it with a belt. But whether this is what James actually did can never be known because the best witness to what James actually did (Ron Weigard) is dead.[25] We do not know in fact if Weigard consented to this, and if he did not, Marty James would be the last to tell us, for that would make him guilty of homicide. Similarly, Betty Rollin claimed she only assisted her mother Ida Rollin to commit suicide and Betty also asserted that Ida consented to it. In her book, *Last Wish,* Betty said that she sat at her mother's bedside saying: "You're doing it, mother. You're doing it. You're doing great!" as she took a lethal dose of pills.[26] But how do we know that her mother was so willing? What testimony do we have from her mother that this is exactly how things were? How do we know that Betty didn't simply kill her and then concoct a story to protect herself, or that Ida didn't commit suicide to expiate her guilt over the trouble and burden she caused Betty and her husband? How do we know that Ida Rollin was not being coerced and manipulated into her death by Betty? The only evidence we have concerning Ida's death is Betty's testimony, and it is in her best interest to claim that Ida was only carrying out the "competent" and "rational" wishes of her mother. There is no way of verifying Betty's claims because the only one who could do this is dead, and Betty's testimony is tainted because of her clear interest in proving Ida's competence. Her case illustrates well the difficulties of determining the facts in an assisted suicide.

Legalizing suicide would give a new and lethal twist to some of our culture's sexist biases. A review of the recent history of right-to-die cases involving suicide and withdrawal of food and water from patients suggests that the vast majority of those who died were women, which suggests a not so subtle misogyny in those advocating assisted suicide. Claire Conroy died shortly before the New Jersey Supreme Court granted an appeal that was presented by her nephew to remove a feeding tube that would have brought her to death from starvation or dehydration.[27] Ella Bathurst's daughter ordered her mother's physician to refrain from feeding her, and Ella lay immobilized on her bed for three days vainly begging the staff for food and water before she died.[28] Nancy Ellen Jobes died from dehydration after the New Jersey Supreme Court granted her husband's request to have her feeding tube withdrawn, and had the tube not been withdrawn, she would have lived indefinitely.[29] Marcia Gray died from the same cause, for her husband made a similar appeal and won the support of the Roman Catholic bishop of Providence, Rhode Island. Mildred Rasmussen died from starvation and dehydration after an Arizona court determined that this was in her best interests.[30] Sharon Seibert almost died after her physician-husband declared her to be persistently vegetative with no hope of recovery and petitioned to have food and water withdrawn.[31] Many years after this attempt, Sharon is now living safely and comfortably in a Minneapolis nursing home.

Beverly Requenna purportedly said while competent and unimpaired that she would not wish to live in a severely impaired condition, and she died after her husband ordered removal of food and water.[32] Hilda Peter was brought to death after her feeding tube was removed at the request of her surrogate-decision maker Eberhard Johanning.[33] The nephew of elderly mental patient Mary Heir petitioned a court to order the removal of her feeding tube but was not successful.[34] Four years after this episode, Ms. Heir was still alive. Elizabeth Visbeck's guardian objected to the removal of her gastrostomy feeding because she had never given any indication that she wanted it withdrawn. Yet a court ordered it removed, bringing about her death.[35] A North Dakota court argued that the feeding tube of elderly Iona Bayer, who suffered from permanent loss of consciousness after a heart attack, could have been removed because she had said to her family that she did not wish to have her life prolonged by artificial means.[36]

In the case of Nancy Milton, the court argued that this woman could refuse simple and successful medical treatments on religious grounds even though her physician believed she was suffering from delusions.[37] In Seattle, the male medical director and executive director of the Crista nursing home ordered removal of the feeding tubes of two elderly women at their families' requests. These men then threatened two nurses with reduction in status or dismissal if they did not remove the feeding tube from the two women. But the nurses continued to resist and were able to retain their positions despite the fact that the tubes were removed by others causing the woman's death.[38] Emily Gilbert was shot to death by her husband Roswell who believed this was merciful, even though she never asked him to do this.[39] Jean Humphry supposedly poisoned herself with the assistance of her husband Derek Humphry.[40] Humphry's second wife, Ann Wickett, was divorced by Derek after she learned that she had cancer, and she then committed suicide also.[41] Patricia Rosier, wife of Dr. Peter Rosier, was given a lethal injection by her husband when she was suffering from cancer, but it is not clear that she explicitly wanted to die in that way.[42] And only in the cases of Nancy Cruzan and Mary O'Connor did courts refuse to withhold food and water at the request of families, but the Cruzan case was heard again with supposedly new evidence, and her feeding tube was then removed.[43] And, most intriguing, only about four of the twenty or so people Dr. Jack Kevorkian assisted in suiciding were male.

In the past five years, we have seen only two notable cases where courts have allowed a woman to bring a man to death by removal of feeding tubes. Paul Brophy made it quite clear that he did not wish to live with severe neurological impairments, which enabled his wife to order removal of food and water.[44] And the wife of Daniel Delio was initially unable to obtain removal of his feeding tube from her husband, but this decision was later reversed, and the tube was withdrawn.[45]

On the other hand, women in other situations have been unable to gain court approval for similar actions taken against men, and we have seen no cases where a woman has been dealt with leniently for using violent means to kill a man out of compassion in the way that Roswell Gilbert did to his wife Emily. In the case of infant Lance Steinhaus, a Minnesota court argued that a feeding tube had to be provided him despite arguments to the contrary made by some.[46] A court ordered an enterostomy to be given to Mr. George Clark, despite the pleas of his family that his low quality of life justified denial of the procedure.[47] And the wife of George Vogel was unable to persuade a court to remove a feeding tube even though he was chronically unconscious.[48]

Many more women have been brought to death in right-to-die cases than have men, and this can be best explained by the influence of sexist bias against them. What explains this best is the predominance of the belief that a man should not be burdened by a woman who cannot fulfill her proper "feminine" responsibilities, but if a man would be unable to fulfill his proper masculine duties, it would generally be considered inappropriate for a woman to bring him to death. Ordinarily only if a man explicitly wishes this to be done to him is it to be allowed, even if his death would impose great burdens on the woman. This is what seemed to have happened with Hector Rodas, for he explicitly asked to be dehydrated to death despite the fact that his death would leave a wife and two small children behind.[49] Women, on the other hand, are expected to not to kill their men but are to bear their sufferings patiently. For, example, Clarence Herbert was dehydrated to death at the instigation of his physicians, and his wife Patti permitted this only because his physicians misled her about his treatment.[50] When she discovered this, she filed a multimillion dollar lawsuit against the doctors and hospital, for she never intended to kill him but only to tolerate removal of his medical treatments because she believed him to already be dead.

At the present time, the great majority of nursing home residents and chronically ill are women, and a liberal suicide policy tinged with sexist bias could bring them great harm. These right-to-die cases point to a disturbing trend that could significantly undermine the security and well-being of disabled, elderly, and incompetent women. Some might say that the larger number of women involved in right-to-die cases can be explained merely by the fact that there are more women who are elderly, chronically ill, and dying. But this explanation fails to see that just as great a percentage of the male population fall chronically ill and die as do women, and yet they are not made candidates for assisted suicide or withdrawal of treatment in the way that women are. The best explanation for this phenomenon is the presence of a bias against women that is more willing to deny the care that is given to men and bring them to death when they become burdensome more than they are with men.

Protecting the Integrity of the Healing Professions

A further reason for not legalizing suicide is that society has a responsibility to protect not only individuals, but also those institutions necessary for the well-being of all. Society and the state have clear duties to protect the integrity of public institutions, like police forces, as well as private institutions that promote the public welfare, such as the legal and medical professions.[51]

Legalizing suicide would seriously compromise the doctor-patient healing covenant, which is unique and deserves special protection from the law. In this covenant, the physician and patient mutually commit themselves to the goal of healing, and both of them can find their specific fulfillment by performing the duties required by their part of the covenant. Patients have a moral responsibility to promote their health and well-being, and filing to take reasonable and moderate measures to do this violates the physician-patient covenant. Physicians have a moral obligation to assist patients in doing this by offering their skill and expertise within reasonable limits. The well-being of both the patient and physician also requires that both of them do nothing to harm or compromise health or life.

A decision of a patient to reject healing measures because the cost or burdens would be too great or because there would be little chance that continued efforts to heal would be successful does not abolish the duty of the healer to give aid, comfort, and healing when needed. If patients should not only stop the healing process, but require physicians to act in direct contradiction to the covenant and become killers, that would change the very nature of the healing covenant. Allowing this raises the troubling question of what the obligations of physicians would be if patients were permitted to suicide. If a patient could unilaterally abandon the healing covenant by self-executing at the moment of their choice, doctors could justifiably ask why they should be bound to the healing covenant if they found it burdensome and abandonment of it beneficial. Or even further, why should a physician not be able to abandon healing labor for an incompetent patient and bring death to them if the patient would probably abandon the covenant if free and competent to do so? To be logically consistent, allowing patients to violate the healing covenant and commit suicide should require permitting physicians to abandon this covenant when they see little reason to continue.

Suicide should not be legalized because so doing would seriously and dangerously complicate the medical decision-making process. If suicide were to be legalized, it would probably only be allowed if placed under the control of medical professionals, and its legalization would force physicians to decide when to stop opposing death and when to actively bring it upon patients. Legalization of suicide would require physicians to determine when there would be valid medical reasons for suiciding and when a patient's sufferings are intolerable. But most physicians would regard doing this as a betrayal of their professional objectives; they would not believe themselves to be professionally capable of making these judgments and would be in great fear of the potential abuse that would come with the power.

Legalizing suicide would also require authorizing physicians to judge the suitability of patients for suicide and to determine who should be able to kill themselves and who should not, which would create serious problems for physician-patient relations. Some patients would fear that physicians would use their authority to manipulate and coax them into suiciding, just as physicians sometimes use their authority and power to cajole them into receiving treatments. This could seriously threaten the trustworthiness and integrity of physicians, and for patients in bad health, a visit from a physician could be viewed as being a visit from the executioner.

Physicians need the trust of patients to be effective healers because they often have to perform procedures and require activities of patients that cause pain and suffering, and it is easy for patients to refuse to comply with their demands and justify their decision by claiming that they believe that their doctors are trying to harm them. If patients, and particularly those who suffer from even mild paranoia, should have any objective reason to doubt or mistrust their doctors, they would resist the healing regimen the doctor would impose, not comply with medical orders, and frustrate their doctor's efforts. Those whose well-being would probably suffer most from legalized suicide would be the most paranoid and those whom physicians least like to treat such as the chronically and irreversibly ill elderly. Many of these patients are so fearful and mistrustful of doctors that they need little reason to avoid them, and if physicians acquired a reputation for being involved in or approving of suicide those who might need them the most might be the most reluctant to seek their help. Legalized suicide could impede access to health care of many who would badly need it, and if justice in health care means anything, it would mean that healing professionals should reject policies that would hamper access to it. To confirm that these are not just empty charges, the Dutch Patient's Association warned Dutch citizens in 1987 to avoid hospital admission if they thought their families might have interests opposed to their well-being because suicide and mercy killing have become so prevalent there.[52] They also warned patients to seek second opinions if they did not trust the judgment of their physicians.

Legalizing suicide would attract individuals to medical practice who would take pleasure in killing and relish assisting patients in their suicides. It is not uncommon for these sorts of people to appear occasionally in the allied health professions, but their appearance among physicians would be a vastly different matter because it is so difficult for the law to restrain and control medical misconduct. There are some people who would fancy this sort of activity, and placing suicide under medical control would make the practice of medicine quite attractive to them. Medicine would be the only profession where private citizens could pass legally protected to a "judgment of death" against innocent persons. Under a liberal suicide regime, medicine would be a dream come true for the sophisticated but perverse who love to kill, for they could inflict death on other innocents with full legal protection. It would be quite difficult for the medical profession to exclude these individuals from its ranks, and this could seriously harm its authority, prestige, and trustworthiness.

Finally, if suicide were given legal protection, physicians would become actively, directly, and proximately involved in the suicides of patients because they would have to decide which patients would be medically qualified for suicide. This could seriously harm their authority because the professional aim of physicians is to give healing aid whenever and wherever this is needed, irrespective of its circumstances. If physicians cease to aid the dying, despairing, or terminally ill, but advance their deaths, the moral and symbolic position and authority of the physician in society would be diminished or destroyed. By willing to give healing aid whenever and wherever it is needed, physicians stand as the model and ideal of how we are to relate to one another in society and achieve harmony by being willing to help one another in times of need. After abandoning and killing patients, physicians could no longer stand as a symbol of what is best in society: the willingness to give authentic aid whenever and wherever it is needed.

The Social Benefits of Suicide: Claims and Counterclaims

Margaret Battin believes suicide should be allowed if it would eliminate social burdens.[53] Alcoholics, those suffering from birth defects, the mentally ill, and invalids often impose serious burdens on families, which are not compensated for by any clear or outstanding benefits. Institutionalizing them can relieve the burdens others experience on their account, but in some cases this cannot come about and Battin believes that allowing suicide would be appropriate in those instances. Also, in other situations, there might be no other acceptable alternative to self-killing and she believes it should be allowed then.[54]

The argument that suicide benefits families is shallow and shortsighted, for it fails to see how profoundly disturbing the suicide of even a troublesome member can be to a family. At the purely speculative level, suicide could solve some problems, but in practice it causes far more problems than it solves. When a family member is deeply troubled, the entire family usually feels desperate and frustrated because of their inability to change the distressing conditions that precipitate the suicidal act. Suicide does nothing to alleviate the fear, anxiety, and frustration family members ordinarily feel about the difficulties a suicidal person confronts, and self-killing only adds guilt to their suffering, frustration, and anxiety. Suicide can eliminate some rather trivial burdens, but these are usually replaced by terrible burdens of guilt, self-doubt and self-recrimination. Many families of those who suicide often spend years wondering if anything could have been done to prevent their relative from self-destruction. Espousing suicide for alcoholics, the disabled, or elderly to relieve burdens on their families fails to see that the suicide eliminates problems at deeper levels for the family left behind. Family members usually want a "cure" for them, and not their extermination, and suicide usually exacerbates rather than relieves the family's sufferings.

Suicide also relieves some of the burdens of society as a whole, according to some of its proponents. The case of Captain Oates, who walked away from his exploration party so that they could survive their trek to the South Pole is often regarded as the paradigmatic example of how a suicide can benefit society at large. The chronically ill are cited most often as a persistent burden to society, and Nietzsche claimed that it would be courageous and morally good to allow these individuals to commit suicide:

> [T]he sick man is a parasite of society. In certain cases it is indecent to go on living. To continue to vegetate in a state of cowardly dependence upon doctors and special treatments, once the meaning of life, the right to life has been lost, ought to be regarded with the greatest contempt by society.[55]

Other contemporary suicide proponents, including Battin, argue that eliminating the severely brain-damaged is not merely morally tolerable but morally obligatory.[56]

Allowing those with birth defects to commit suicide because of the benefits their deaths would bring to others is also a false solution because it is unfair and discriminatory to the victims of these conditions. In a just and unbiased society where principles of fairness and equal treatment prevail, allowing those who suffer misfortune to self-exterminate in order to benefit the more fortunate is profoundly unfair and discriminatory and has no place in a society committed to eliminating prejudice and discrimination. The real problem is not with handicapped individuals coping with their conditions, but usually with others adjusting to their disabilities. A CBS "60 Minutes" program on Thalidomide babies illustrated this point very well, showing that many of these children were able to cope with their disabilities quite well and those who suffered the most were the families of Thalidomide children and not the children themselves.[57] The problem of the disabled in society will not be resolved by allowing them to kill themselves, but by changing the attitudes of others toward them and helping them cope with the handicapped. And the argument that the handicapped should be allowed to commit suicide to benefit others discriminates against them as is seen by the fact that those who want the disabled to kill themselves to benefit others would not allow the able-bodied to kill themselves to aid the handicapped. Battin also believes that suicide would have the beneficial effect of limiting overpopulation.[58] But if this were to be allowed, one would have to ask how this program would be fairly and justly administered. Should only the least productive be allowed to carry out demographic suicide, or should the most productive be allowed to participate in this program also?

A similar point can be made against the proposal to allow suicide for the mentally disabled because of the benefits that would come to society. Allowing them to suicide is as prejudicial as permitting the physically handicapped to suicide in order to benefit the able-bodied. The bias of this proposal can be seen by standing it on its head and asking if we should allow the emotionally stable and mature to suicide for the benefit of the emotionally disturbed, since it is the emotionally stable who cause distress to the disturbed. Few would permit this, however, which shows the prejudice against the emotionally unstable. While the least productive generate little wealth, they also consume far less of our world's resources than do the more productive, and even though the most industrious might create more, they also consume more and are a greater burden to others because of their elevated consumption levels. If we permit the most productive to commit suicide, the poor might be worse off, but allowing the less productive to self-assassinate would be discriminatory and would allow those who consume the most to reap the greatest benefits. This sort of policy would be unfair to many and it might be perceived as a program to exterminate the poor.

To argue that those with genetic handicaps or physical disabilities should be allowed to commit suicide would cause a great deal of harm to society. Margaret Battin denies that this view endorses Nazi racial views and she believes that such programs could be compassionate, just, and loving: "Such views need not be associated with Nazism or other extermination schemes, and they may be coupled with considerable charity and sympathy for the individuals involved."[59] But this is probably the most threatening suggestion one could possibly make to the disabled as it would impose extraordinary moral pressure on them to kill themselves, particularly if others perceived disproportionate hardships because of this. Many disabled persons already struggle with guilt because of the burdens they impose on others, and telling them their suicides would be of benefit to society would provide even stronger inducements to many of them to suicide when they are already suffering from feelings of guilt and inadequacy. The disabled who would self-exterminate for the sake of others and would be touted as martyrs while those who would not suicide would be condemned as cowardly, inconsiderate, egotistical, or self-centered.

Furthermore, we continue to see new measures being introduced to cure, palliate, and remedy their conditions, or to alleviate their suffering. These discoveries do not take place on a regular and planned basis, but usually emerge erratically and spontaneously, and it is unreasonable to hold that all hope is lost because of their unpredictability. Many disabled people do not hope for a total, complete and absolute relief from their condition, but only for a lessening of their pain and suffering, and new means of doing this are discovered every day. Allowing these people to suicide could undermine efforts to develop new measures to improve their condition. A major motivating factor for continuing research would be abolished, which could have a profoundly negative impact on the disabled over the long-run.

Permitting suicides because they would supposedly provide some benefits for society would be dangerous because this would create incentives for some to manipulate others into suiciding. For example, if Captain Oates's fellow explorers believed it would be morally permissible for others to suicide for the benefit of the entire group, what would have been wrong with them trying to persuade others in their party to wander away from the camp to save their own lives? Allowing suicide for the benefit of others would lead to disputes over who should commit suicide and who should be allowed to benefit from the self-execution. What truly benefits society is not suicide but acts of self-sacrifice or martyrdom. These can be of authentic benefit to others because of their witness to selflessness and moral integrity.

Plato believed that temple robbers and others guilty of serious crimes should be permitted to commit suicide to alleviate burdens they impose on society.[60] In a proposal similar to this, Battin has suggested that sociopaths should also be allowed to kill themselves, precisely because of the burdens they inflict on others.[61] She claimed that allowing them to suicide would permit society to rid itself of undesirables and the less fit, and while some might find this morally reprehensible social Darwinism, she sees no ethical difficulty with this kind of policy.[62] For her, "social Darwinism simply holds that suicide–chosen and performed by the individual–is to be welcomed as a natural self-cleansing mechanism on the part of the species."[63] She argues against involuntary killing of the seriously handicapped, but feels that it is more desirable ethically and easier to allow voluntary self-execution of the incurable, invalids, and others.[64] But, as we saw in chapter 6, the voluntariness of those who make a suicidal decision is usually quite doubtful.

Suicide proponents argue that it should be permitted because it would have a beneficial impact on overpopulation. But there would have to be hundreds of millions of suicides among the elderly, disabled, and handicapped to have any noticeable impact on world population, and such large numbers of suicides would cause massive changes in families, societies, and the world order. These large numbers of "demographic suicide" would have profoundly negative social, political, and psychological effects that would dwarf whatever demographic "benefits" would come from their deaths, for horrendous political struggles would revolve around the question of who should suicide. If enough people killed themselves to have any significant demographic impact, the grief, suffering, and social chaos suffered by those left behind would overwhelm any benefits that would come from their self-killing. Already there are more than 500,000 completed suicides worldwide annually, and even if these increased a hundredfold, there would be little impact on world population.[65]

The claim that sociopaths should be allowed to commit suicide because their death would benefit society is discriminatory and cruel.

It has been part of common law jurisprudence that individuals who knowingly and deliberately violate the law against homicide should be punished or deprived of their freedom after exercise of due process of the law. But allowing them to self-exterminate *because* of the harm they bring violates their rights to due process of the law and freedom from cruel and unusual punishments. This policy is objectionable because it would not benefit them but would inflict on them the gravest of punishments for actions for which they might not have been fully responsible.

A fairer and more humane policy would protect others from sociopaths and support measures that might be available to rehabilitate them. These troubled individuals are quite vulnerable to this sort of persuasion, for being already prone to violence, they would probably have few scruples about killing themselves if told this would be in their best interest. And if sociopaths, who are presumably not fully responsible for their actions, could be allowed to commit suicide to benefit society, what rational basis could there be for intervening to prohibit not only other "irrational" suicides, but other supposedly "rational" suicides as well?

According to some suicide advocates, self-assassination for the sake of social protest can also be of direct benefit to society, and these suicides could bid us to reject values that demand condemnation.[66]

Arguing that suicide should be permitted to advance social or political causes is weak because it is not clear that these suicides are effective means to these objectives and there are better ways to protest and reform society than by such violent measures. It would be more effective to speak out against the skewed priorities of society and then initiate positive measures, programs, and policies to bring reform than to kill oneself out of protest. Suicide for social reasons appears to be more of an immature overreaction to a frustrating event than a reasoned response to a crisis. Most political or social suicides fail politically because popular and common opinion intuits a difference between political suicides, like Bobby Sands, and martyrs, like Martin Luther King. Neither IRA protesters, such as Sands, who starved himself to death, nor Buddhist monks who immolated themselves to protest the Vietnam War, had much measurable impact on their opponents because neither were true martyrs. But Martin Luther King ignited the black civil rights movement precisely because of the moral power of his preaching. Achieving martyrdom requires a certain level of virtue and selflessness that is lacking in suicides. A more effective way of promoting a social agenda would be to argue effectively for the morality of one's own proposals and abstain from suiciding because of the strong moral objections many have to it. Coupled with the more common forms of promoting social or political change through the routine political and legislative processes, this is usually a more effective and efficient means of bringing about social and political change than is the radical and morally dubious method of suicide.

What ultimately breaks the back of arguments for "socially beneficial" suicides is the near-impossibility of stopping irrational suicides that imitate "rational" or "beneficial" suicides. Allowing "socially beneficial suicides" would increase irrational suicides because they would make it easier for the irrational to justify their own self-killing. Even though curbing irrational suicide is difficult and radical measures have often been taken by societies to stop it, advocates of social suicide persist in believing it can be controlled. They ignore the fact that it is quite easy for societies to destroy themselves, and many societies that have adopted liberal suicide policies have vanished from history, while those such as the Moslem, Catholic, and Jewish communities have rejected these policies and have survived for hundreds of years.

In summary, if one were to take each of the social arguments against suicide individually, they might not appear that persuasive, but when considered together they argue rather powerfully that suicide for social reasons is extremely dangerous and should not be allowed. Permitting suicide for some members of society would create very sharp social divisions and would aggravate class divisions, for societies would be divided into those for whom it is permitted and those for whom it is prohibited. It is probably for this reason that almost no society has ever positively *encouraged* suicide, a few have grudgingly tolerated it, and most have strenuously sought to limit it.

The Harm Suicide Does to Society

Margaret Battin claims that arguments against social suicide are not solid, and she therefore concludes that suicide should be permitted.[67] But it is not wise to discount these arguments, for they do raise some telling points against a liberal suicide policy. Here I wish to reiterate and evaluate some of the traditional arguments that have been made against suicide for social reasons to suggest that they retain their force and validity.

The first argument she rejects as insufficient holds that suicide can have ruinous psychological effects on families, causing long-term profound grief and severe guilt.[68] Advocates of suicide argue that grief after suicide is not found in all societies, but only in those where suicide is viewed as wrong and immoral, which should make suicide permissible in some cases.[69] Where suicides do no harm to families or friends, these advocates argue that there is no reason for prohibiting it.[70] But contrary to their views, numerous studies have been done on suicide's impact on children and spouses, and the weight of evidence shows that it inflicts much harm, grief, and misery on survivors. The popular author Kurt Vonnegut reinforced this very simply: "Sons of suicide seldom do well."[71] If there are families unharmed by suicide, they are not great enough in number to warrant a liberal policy.

But there is little to support the claim that suicide does not cause much grief and guilt in others, even where societies tolerate it. In spite of the fact that some forms of suicide were tolerated in Japan and India, survivors there still experienced much grief and guilt.[72] While a few might welcome some suicides, most suffer from much grief despite their praise for a noble or honorable self-execution. Even the suicides of Seneca, Cato, Antony, Lucretia, and Socrates caused much grief to their friends, families, and associates, and these survivors would probably say that their grief, guilt, and loss far outweighed any social benefits that might have accrued from the suicides. There are few instances of suicide not causing grief among survivors and when there is little grief it is because the suiciding person has acted so atrociously that survivors cannot grieve.

Some of the oldest arguments against suicide claimed that it deprived society of needed gifts, talents, and contributions. Beccaria asserted that one who suicided harmed his nation by abandoning it, even though this was not the greatest evil one could do to one's community.[73] St. Thomas Aquinas also held that suicide was harmful to society because

> every part belongs to the whole in virtue of what it is. But every man is part of the community, so that he belongs to the community in virtue of what he is. Suicide therefore involves damaging the community, as Aristotle makes clear.[74]

There is much truth in this view and the harm suicide does to society is best seen in teenage suicide, for in these self-killings, the future talents, gifts, strength, and hope of the community are destroyed. Others have rejected this, but their rejection implies that the suicides of some socially "useless" people should be permitted because they make no significant contribution to society. John Donne, for example, argued that monks and hermits are not condemned for fleeing the state, which implies that suicides should be allowed for the socially useless.[75] This rejection, however, not only has eugenic overtones, but also it is only tolerable if one considers societal contributions in the most narrow and materialistic terms possible. Permitting the unproductive (however they are classified) to self-execute would increase societal competition and interclass hatred and violence. This perspective on suicide would make a rather inhospitable environment for social critics whose contribution might be more negative than positive in many respects.

Rejecting this criticism is unjustified because of its radically constricted notion of what constitutes the human good and because it presumes that the only real values in human life derive from individual acts and choices. It is closer to the truth to say that basic human goods derive not only from human choice, art, endeavor, and technology, but also from our very beings. The bonds between parents and children are not based solely on what they do with or to one another, but also on what they *are* to each other. Many family members who mourn suicides grieve because of what those who have suicided have *been* to them and not just because of what they did *for* them. To justify suicide for those who fail to meet criteria for being beneficial to society is contrary to much twentieth-century liberal ethos that has criticized its superficiality.

John Donne rightly noted that legalization of suicide would bring down the social and moral barriers against most forms of suicide and would result in widespread self-killing:

> [Y]et the number of wretched men on earth exceeds the happy (for every laborer is miserable and beastlike, in respect of the idle, abounding men). It was therefore thought necessary, by laws and opinion of religion . . . . to take from these weary and macerated wretches their ordinary and open escape and ease, voluntary death.[76]

Suicide proponents frequently dismiss arguments that legalizing suicide would induce others to suicide, but it is true that opening the door to suicide does lead others to consider it. Margaret Battin, for example, believes that even widespread suicide would not necessarily be a great harm to society.[77] This is not what many people feel who consider themselves threatened by suicide. Legalizing suicide would create a culture in which self-killing would become commonplace, as recent trends show. Suicide is becoming more popular among AIDS patients, and their suicide rate is now sixty-six times the national average. The threat of widespread suicide is seen most clearly in the waves of suicides that have recently swept communities of Native Americans. At the Warm Springs Reservation 1 percent of the tribe attempted suicide between January and March 1988, which is an annual suicide rate of 4 percent.[78] Nationwide, young Indian men are killing themselves at a rate that is twice that of the national average for their age group.[79] At the Wind River Reservation in central Wyoming, there were nine suicide attempts in five weeks.[80] At the Alakanuk reservation in Alaska, which has a population of only 550 people, eight Eskimos killed themselves.[81] Suicide waves begin when an atmosphere of despair develops in a community that is difficult or impossible to abolish. When people feel themselves to be condemned and rejected by society, they kill themselves in reaction to it. This atmosphere of despair sweeps away the voiceless, despairing, weak, and troubled in our society and it is a real threat to them. Ray Calica of the Warm Springs reservation summed it up perfectly when he said that "within the reservation some of these kids feel like fourth-rate citizens. They're told, 'Your ancestor was no good, and you're no good either.'"[82]

Some suicide advocates argue that society has no obligation to protect those who are not able to reciprocate on account of physical or psychological impairments. Communities exist because individuals are selflessly willing to act for the good of others, and to allow some to destroy themselves because they cannot reciprocate eviscerates community. Endorsement of a liberal suicide policy shows how thinly some people view community and how willing they are to allow people to be destroyed to protect pure contentless individual autonomy.

Charlotte Gilman made the argument that people should not kill themselves when they still have an opportunity to do good or to perform morally good acts.[83] But, in her later years, she was diagnosed with cancer and decided to commit suicide. She justified her suicidal wishes at that time by claiming that she could no longer do much good for anyone.[84] This might sound like a justifiable reason for suiciding, but a closer analysis reveals its flaws. First, no matter how dismal a person's future might appear, one cannot say that no good can come from their being alive. Second, even if one is utterly incapable of actually doing good to others, one may still be able to do good to oneself. Helen Keller was able to do little good for herself or directly for others, but in response to her needs and very existence, great good came about. Third, one should not equate an inability to do good with doing evil, for small children cannot do much good, but that does not mean that they should self-execute.

A classical argument against suicide for the disabled has been that allowing this would brutalize the population at large. Against this traditional argument, Margaret Battin wonders if society can force these people to continue living:

> But to claim that those persons have an *obligation* to live (and suffer) in order to make normal individuals more humane and courageous is ethically questionable at best. One might also see it as a barbaric holdover of earlier European practices, according to which caged lunatics were placed on public display, criminals in public stocks, and physically anomalous persons were displayed in circuses, presumably for the moral edification as well as entertainment of individuals not so afflicted.[85]

She rightly argues that it is cruel and inhumane to subject the insane to mockery and ridicule, but she does not defeat the argument that allowing their suicides brutalizes others. This principle allows the insane to suicide, abandons them in their plight and brutalizes all in society. To legally permit the disabled to suicide is unfair to them and it would not build bonds of unity between the able-bodied and disabled. Arguing that the disabled who cannot reciprocate the good done for them should be allowed to suicide bites back because it would logically commit one to allowing the ungrateful to suicide.

There is a long tradition that rejects suicide because it would enable the guilty to escape just punishments. John Adams argued that permitting suicide would undermine the force of human laws because people could break them and then escape punishment by painlessly killing themselves.[86] Immanuel Kant argued that legalized suicide would promote crime because criminals would be able to escape punishment by self-execution:

> Nothing more terrible [than suicide] can be imagined; for if man were on every occasion master of his own life, he would be master of the lives of others; and being ready to sacrifice his life at any and every time rather than be captured, he could perpetrate every conceivable crime and vice.[87]

Aquinas taught that only public officials could punish crimes, and if suicide was permitted, suicides could punish themselves by ending their own lives on their terms, which would be unjust:

> A representative of the public authority may legitimately kill a malefactor in virtue of his power to adjudge the case. But nobody is a judge in his own cause. Therefore, no representative public authority may kill himself in respect of any sin, though he may, of course, hand himself over to the judgment of others.[88]

But advocates of legalized suicide dismiss arguments that lawlessness would result from legalizing suicide and permitting it might well promote respect for the law. In opposition to the view that most who suicide after crimes are thugs, Battin asserts that most who kill themselves after a crime are first offenders.[89] She argues that the person who suicides after a crime is usually not a "criminal type of man" and echoes a statement of a 1959 study of suicides by the Church of England.[90] But this argument supports laws against suicide because these individuals inflict punishments on themselves that are probably far worse than what they deserve. Even with laws against suicide, these novice criminals still kill themselves in great numbers and would do so in even greater numbers if this legal barrier were abolished, which would be quite unfair to them. And if legalized, many criminals would probably opt for quick and painless suicide as an option preferable to life-long incarceration. In most instances this would be unfortunate for them because it would permit them to punish themselves in ways that would be grossly disproportionate to the crimes they commit. The suicides of many accused or convicted criminals are done in moments of panic, and death by suicide would be far worse a punishment than what many a jury would impose. Allowing criminals to suicide would permit them to suffer far harsher penalties than the law would require or even allow in most instances.

Suicide proponents approach this issue with a naively confident spirit that there would be no harmful side effects from its legalization, that few people will be harmed, that it can be readily controlled, and that no one who does not wish to commit suicide will be brought to death. The arguments of suicide proponents that it should be permitted because of its benefit to society are unpersuasive because they do not grasp the serious threat that the harmful effects of suicide can pose to families, to the immature, to the emotionally and mentally unstable, or to society at large.

Conclusion

It has been argued that legalization of abortion has put our society on a slippery slope to legalized infanticide, suicide, and mercy killing, and recent attempts to legalize voluntary suicide have certainly given credibility to this prediction. But would legally endorsing voluntary suicide put us on a slippery slope toward something even far worse? There is good reason to believe it would lead us to mandatory nonvoluntary killing of the mentally and physically disabled and handicapped as is now happening in Holland. Our legal system is more permissive in many ways than Holland's and if they cannot prevent this, it is hard to see how we could. If the legal rights of the incompetent are equal to those of the competent, then it is hard to see why there would not be a legal duty to cooperate with their demands for assistance in suiciding. A duty would then devolve on those who give mercy killing to the incompetent, a duty based on the obligation to respect the right of the incompetent person to choose to die if they were competent to make such a decision. Legalization of suicide would bring us closer to legalized nonvoluntary mercy killing because the principles that would justify legalized mercy killing would be so confused that anything could happen. Suicide for social reasons should not be legalized in order to protect society, the common good, the professions, or the vulnerable. While legalized suicide might bring benefits to some individuals, the grave problems it imposes on relatives and families, the vulnerable, emotionally unstable, immature, despairing, the common law tradition, and the healing professions make legalization of self-extermination dangerous and unwise. Suicide should not be legally permitted in any circumstance because this attitude can become pervasive and unstoppable. As is always the case, destroying the lives of innocent persons never solves the real problems of human existence.

Notes

1. See Flannery, A., *The Documents of Vatican II: The Conciliar and Post Conciliar Documents*, (Grand Rapids: Eerdmans, 1984), 927.
2. Ashley, B., and O'Rourke, K., *Health Care Ethics: A Theological Analysis*, (St. Louis: Catholic Health Association, 1982), 376.
3. Maguire, D., *Death by Choice*, (Garden City: Doubleday, 1974), 186. This position is also affirmed by Charles Curran in his *Medicine and Morals*, (Washington, D.C.: Corpus Books, 1970) and John Dedek, *Contemporary Medical Ethics*, (New York: Sheed and Ward, 1975).

4. National Conference of Catholic Bishops, Secretariat for Pro-Life Activities, "Assisted Suicide: Any Limits?" *Life at Risk*, 3, (April 1993): 1.
5. Newsletter of the Netherlands Universities Foundation for International Cooperation, 1987, 4.
6. Ibid., 4.
7. Ibid., 3.
8. Schepens, P., "Euthanasia Our Own Future," in *Euthanasia in Holland*, (Ostend, Holland: News Exchange of the World Federation of Doctors Who Respect Human Life, 1987), 6. If Americans were to commit suicide at this rate, by extrapolation at least 400,000 Americans a year would end their lives by their own hands.
9. Ibid., 4. This point was made by a Leiden psychiatrist who noted that part of the problem of treating suicidal persons was the aversion that health care professionals have of them.
10. "Dutch May Broaden Guidelines," *New York Times,* 13 February 1993, A13.
11. Gomez, C., *Regulating Death*, (New York: Free Press, 1991).
12. Richard Momeyer believes that a decent society would allow some suicides, but only a limited number. It would do this without romanticizing them and would strictly control them. This, however, is impossible, for those with conditions very much like those allowed to suicide would protest that they were being treated unfairly. And those who were permitted to suicide would ultimately morally justify their deed by romanticizing the act. See Momeyer, R., *Confronting Death*, (Bloomington: Indiana University Press, 1988), 120-21.
13. Francine Klagsburn describes well how teenagers will often overreact to stressful situations such as divorces, school failures, or failures in relationships in ways that are extreme by adult standards. See *Too Young to Die*, (Boston: Houghton-Mifflin, 1976), chap. 3, 31-47.
14. Ibid., 1.
15. Ibid.
16. "Gesell Dies After Seven Weeks without Food," *NRL News,* 17 December 1987, 6. This case involved a petition to remove a feeding tube from an incompetent elderly man. The hearing only took fifteen minutes because there was no opposition expressed to removing the feeding tube from the facility, family, or physicians.
17. The critical question is what she means by suffering from "natural causes." This could be construed to mean not only cancer, but also genetic diseases, mental and physical handicap, or emotional breakdown, and if construed this broadly, this proposal would seem to validate suicide for virtually any reason.
18. Sullivan, A., "A Constitutional Right to Suicide," in Battin, M., *Suicide: The Philosophical Issues,* (New York: St. Martin's, 1980), 229-54.
19. See LaFave, W. R. and Scott, A. W., *Handbook on Criminal Law*. (St. Paul: West, 1972), 568-69; 83 C.J.S. 781-82; Byrn, R. M., "Compulsory Lifesaving Treatment for the Competent Adult," *Fordham Law Review*, 44 (1975): 16. American law was not as severe as was the British, but it nonetheless considered suicide a public wrong and unlawful. LaFave, W. R., and Scott, A. W., 569; 83 C.J.S. 783. Many states have allowed persons to use nondeadly force to prevent suicide: Ark. Stat. Ann. 41-505(4)(1977); Haw. Rev. Stat. 703-308(1)(1985); Mo. Ann. Stat. 563.061(5)(Vernon 1979); Neb. Rev. Stat. 28-1414(7)(1985); N.H.Rev. Stat. Ann 627:6-vi(1986); N.J. Stat. Ann. 2C:3-7(e)(West); N.Y. Penal Law 35.10(4)(1975); 18 PA. Cons. Stat. Ann. 508(d)(Purdon 1983); Wis. Stat. Ann 939(5)(West 1982).

20. See Grisez, G. and Boyle, J., *Life and Death with Liberty and Justice for All,* (Notre Dame, Ind: University of Notre Dame Press, 1979), 400. "Capital punishment is a bad means to a good end: just punishment." Also see Bedeau, H., *The Case Against the Death Penalty,* (New York: The American Civil Liberties Union, 1973), 2.
21. Battin, M., "Suicide: A Fundamental Human Right," in Mayo D. and Battin, M., *Suicide: The Philosophical Issues,* 267-86.
22. Finnis, J., *Natural Law and Natural Rights,* (New York: Oxford University Press, 1980), 265.
23. Ibid., 265.
24. Finnis argues that there are thirteen "second-order maxims" or general principles of law that require particular rules and determinations that promote stability, attainment of justice in society. One of these principles holds that in assessing the effects of legal acts, the weak should be protected from their weakness (ibid., 288).
25. Marker, R., "'Kill and Tell': The New Euthanasia Business," *Our Sunday Visitor,* 21 May 1989, 5.
26. Rollin, B., *Last Wish,* (New York: Simon and Schuster), 234.
27. *In re Conroy*, 98, N.J. 321, 486, A.2d 1209 (1985).
28. Investigative report #V85-299 filed by the Office of Health Facility Complaints, Department of Health, State of Minnesota, 12 July 1985. The investigation was conducted by Mr. Arnold Rosenthal and the case was called the "Loving Arms" case because of a television advertisement run by Abbott-Northwestern Hospital that claimed that its loving arms extended throughout Minnesota.
29. This case was the third in a trilogy consisting of "*In re* Farrell," No. A-76 (N.J. 24 June 1987); "*In re* Peter," No. A-78 (N.J. 24 June 1987); and "In re *Jobes*," (N.J. 24 June 1987) (Garibaldi, J.).
30. See Paulus, S., "Rasmussen v. Fleming," *Issues in Law and Medicine*, 2, no. 3 (November 1986): 211-17.
31. See Hoyt, J., "Chronology of Discrimination," *National Women's Health Network*, (March/April 1984): 75.
32. Kirkpatrick, G., "In the Matter of Beverly Requenna," *Issues in Law and Medicine*, 3, 1 (Summer 1987): 75. St. Clare's/Riverside Hospital bitterly opposed this decision but was forced to participate in what it perceived to be her suicide.
33. Kirkpatrick, G., "*In re* Peter," *Issues in Law and Medicine*, 3, 2 (Fall 1987): 175-82. After Ms. Peters died, it was learned that two previous companions of Johanning died in similar circumstances, and Mr. Johanning is now under investigation.
34. "*In re* Heir" 18 Mass. App. Ct. 200, 464, N.E.2d. 959 (1984).
35. Nimz, M., "In the Matter of Elizabeth Visbeck: An Alleged Incompetent Patient," *Issues in Law and Medicine*, 2, 5 (March 1987): 405.
36. "*In re* Bayer," No. 4131, slip op. (Burleigh Co. N.D. 5 February 1987).
37. "*In re* Milton," 29 Ohio St. 3d. (1987).
38. See "Two Families' Decision Letting Loved Ones Starve," *The Seattle Post/Intelligencer,* 14 April 1985, A6, col. 4.
39. See Humphry, D., "Gilbert Case Jury Failed to See Couple's Suffering" in Humphry, D., *Compassionate Crimes, Broken Taboos*, (Los Angeles: The Hemlock Society, 1986), 58-59.
40. See Humphry, D., *Jean's Way*, (Los Angeles: Hemlock Society, 1983).
41. Bole, W., "Ann Humphry's Final Exit," *Our Sunday Visitor,* 17 November 1991, 12. As we saw in the introduction, Ann Wickett believed that Jean was killed by Derek and that she did not die voluntarily.
42. See Humphry, D., "Dr. Rosier's Acquittal Both a Victory and a Warning," *The Hemlock Quarterly*, (January 1989): 1.

43. *Cruzan v. Harmon,* S.W. 2d. (S. Ct. Mo. No. 70813, 11/16/88.) *In re Westchester County Medical Center,* NY 2d (Ct. App., No. 312, 10/14/88.)
44. *Brophy v. New England Sinai Hospital,* 398 Mass. 417, 497 N.E.2d. 626 (1986).
45. *Delio v. Westchester County Medical Center,* 510 N.Y.S.2d 415 (Sup.Ct. 1986).
46. "Order in the *Steinhaus* Case," No. J. 86-92. (Juvenile, Div. Redwood Co. Minnesota).
47. Nimz, M., "In the Matter of George Clark," in *Issues in Law and Medicine,* 2, 5 (March 1987): 409-12.
48. *Vogel v. Forman,* Index No. 1741/86, slip. op. (N.Y. Sup. Ct. Nassau County, 27 October 1986).
49. *In re* Rodas, No. 86PR139, slip, op. (Dist. Ct. Mesa County, Colo. 22 January 1987).
50. *Barber v. People,* 147 Cal. App. 3d 1006 Cal. Rptr. 484 (1983).
51. Finnis asserts that law is to protect and promote justice, even by the use of coercive force, in the complete community, and for him this community even includes what he terms the "business" community and the "play" community. These communities exist to "secure the whole ensemble of material and other conditions, including forms of collaboration, that tend to favor, facilitate, and foster the realization by each individual of his or her personal development," 147.
52. Fenigsen, R., "Involuntary Euthanasia in Holland," *The Wall Street Journal,* 29 September 1987.
53. See Battin, M., *Ethical Issues in Suicide,* (Englewood Cliffs: Prentice-Hall, 1982), 97-99.
54. Ibid., 98.
55. See Nietzsche, F., "Twilight of the Gods," in *The Complete Works of Friedreich Nietzsche,* Ed. Levy, O. and Tr. by Ludovici, A., (London: Unwin & Alwin), 88.
56. Battin, M., *Ethical Issues in Suicide,* 99.
57. "60 Minutes," CBS Television, 28 February 1988.
58. Ibid., 100.
59. Battin, M., *Ethical Issues in Suicide,* 102.
60. Plato, *Laws,* Tr. by Bury, R. B., (Cambridge: Harvard University Press, 1967), vol. 2, 201-3, IX, 854B-C.
61. By way of example, Stephen Judy was convicted of murder and pleaded for the death penalty so that he would not do any more harm. See Battin, M., *Ethical Issues in Suicide,* 100.
62. Ibid., 101-2
63. Ibid., 101. Professor Battin notes that social Darwinism allows those whose genetic stock harms the human species to *select themselves* for elimination.
64. Ibid.

> But although social-darwinist views led to large-scale atrocities involving massive violations of human freedom, the social-darwinist view of *suicide,* as distinct from involuntary "euthanasia," may be less easy to defeat on moral grounds. It involves no apparent violation of human freedom, since suicide is conceived of as a voluntary act. (102)

65. Ibid., 1. Worldwide, suicide rates are 13 per 100,000 or 520,000 per year, which is equivalent to the population of Jacksonville, Florida.
66. Battin, M., *Ethical Issues n Suicide,* 105. This view was rejected by Immanuel Kant who believed that suicide was an affront to society. Kant, I., *Lectures on Ethics,* Tr. by Infeld, L., (New York: Harper Torchbooks, 1963), 151. Also see Fedden, H., *Suicide: A Social and Historical Study,* (New York: Benjamin Blom, 1972), 42.
67. Battin, M., *Ethical Issues in Suicide,* 95.

68. Lebacqz, K. and Engelhardt, T., "Suicide" in *Death, Dying and Euthanasia,* Ed. Horan, D. and Mall, D., (Washington: University Press of America, 1977), 695-96, 699.
69. Battin, M., *Ethical Issues in Suicide,* 81.
70. See Landsberg, P. L., "The Moral Problem of Suicide," in *The Experience of Death and the Moral Problem of Suicide,* Tr. Rowland, C., (New York: The Philosophical Library, 1953), 85.
71. See Cain, A., *Survivors of Suicide,* (Boston: Houghton Mifflin, 1976). Also see Klagsburn, F., *Too Young to Die,* 113-16. Klagsburn claimed that the children of suicides have a higher than average suicide rate because they grow up in a heritage of guilt, anger, and sense of worthlessness (p. 112).
72. See "Apparent Mass Suicide Stirs Japan," *The Washington Post,* 3 November 1986, A17, A18.
73. Beccaria, C., *An Essay on Crimes and Punishment,* (Albany: W. C. Little, 1872), 121-22: "He who kills himself does a less injury to society, than he who quits his country for ever; for the other leaves his property behind him and this carries with him at least a part of his substance."
74. Aquinas, T., *Summa Theologica,* (New York: Benzinger, 1947), II-II, Q. 64, 5. When speaking of the effects that suicide can have on society, Aristotle argued that suicide should not be legally permitted in a society because

> he who through anger voluntarily stabs himself does this contrary to the right rule of life, and this the law does not allow; therefore he is acting unjustly. But towards whom? Surely towards the state, not towards himself. For he suffers voluntarily, but no one is voluntarily treated unjustly. This is also the reason why the state punishes; a certain loss of civil rights attaches to the man who destroys himself, on the ground that he is treating the state unjustly.

Aristotle, "Nicomachean Ethics", Tr. by Ross, W. D., *The Basic Works of Aristotle,* Tr. by McKeon, R., (New York: Random House, 1941), 1138a.
75. See Donne, J., *Biathanatos,* (New York: Arno, 1977) Vol. II, Sect. V, 1:3143-49.
76. Ibid., 2723-29.
77. Battin, M., *Ethical Issues in Suicide,* 89. This opinion seems rather eccentric, for ancient Rome experienced widespread suicide and it was praised by very few for this.
78. See "Despairing Indians Looking to Tradition to Combat Suicides," *The New York Times,* 19 March 1988, A1, A8.
79. Ibid.
80. Ibid.
81. Ibid.
82. Ibid.
83. Gilman, C., "Taking Life Legally". These remarks were left in a suicide letter that was recorded by Howard, R., in *Magazine Digest* 90 (1947): 33.
84. Ibid.
85. Battin, M., *Ethical Issues in Suicide,* 86-87. She objects to David Novak's claim that the presence of the disabled can be an occasion for those without disabilities to exercise charity toward them. See Novak, D., *Suicide and Morality. The Theories of Plato, Aquinas and Kant and their Relevance for Suicidology,* (New York: Scholars Studies Press, 1975), 66.
86. Adams, J., *Essay Concerning Self-Murder,* chap. 3, para. 2 (Boston: Published for Thom. Bennet, 1700), 26.
87. Kant, I., *Lectures on Ethics,* 151.
88. Aquinas, T., *Summa Theologica,* II-II, Q. 64, A. 5.
89. Battin, M., *Ethical Issues in Suicide,* 92.

90. See Church Assembly Board for Social Responsibility, Church of England, *Ought Suicide to be a Crime? A Discussion of Suicide, Attempted Suicide and the Law*, (Westminster: Church Information Office, 1959), 7.

9

Proclaiming Hope and New Life to the Dying: Suicide and Pastoral Care

In February 1985, a task force commissioned by a synod of the Dutch Reformed church issued a set of guidelines entitled "Euthanasia and Pastoral Care" to advise pastoral ministers who care for those contemplating suicide or assisted suicide when in a state of intolerable and unrelievable physical or psychological suffering.[1] While it deals specifically with euthanasia, this document is important because it can be readily applied to suicide and it contains the fundamental elements of a theology of pastoral care that promotes and encourages suicide for the suffering and dying. It is a striking example of the theological, spiritual, and pastoral approach of many today who espouse suicide in some instances, and it merits close examination.

This chapter will consider the nature of pastoral ministry to the suffering and dying by first reviewing the guidelines proposed in "Euthanasia and Pastoral Care." There has been a growing trend in pastoral theology to tolerate self-execution by those in despair or grave suffering. These guidelines will be reviewed and examined because they express very well the theological views and perspectives of many who support rational suicide, and also because its arguments and principles will soon enter into the American churches as the suicide debate develops in the United States. Then I will present what I believe to be a more fully authentic Christian approach to providing pastoral care for those contemplating suicide than that proposed by this task force.

The Doctrines of "Euthanasia and Pastoral Care"

1. "Euthanasia and Pastoral Care" defines euthanasia as "the act that aims at intentionally terminating or shortening the life of

another, either actively or passively, at that person's request or in his interest."[2] Thus, the document does not limit itself to discussing merely voluntary assisted suicide, but also involuntary suicide, killing done that is in the purported interest of the one who will die.

2. The fundamental teaching of "Euthanasia and Pastoral Care" is that the pastoral minister's primary moral responsibility is to enable the dying or suffering person "to die in the joy of comfort of the Gospel"[3] and all other objectives are to be subordinated to that goal:

> The first thing to be noted is the attitude of the pastor. That attitude is determined by the idea of 'helping,' 'assisting.' A person about to die is being assisted.[4]

> For most of us in such a situation the comforting presence of others is of vital significance. The comfort is that there is someone who stands by you in your need, someone on whom you can depend, on whom you can fall back, who does not abandon you, who gives you a feeling of security. . . . Is not the essence of being a pastor, being comfortingly present?[5]

The pastoral minister should be careful and discrete about the sort of life that is supported, for it "is not our task to maintain a hell."[6] Because God is the Lord of life and opposes sickness and death, the pastoral minister is not to simply opt for life, but only for "a life that is worth living."[7] Christ himself did not opt simply and solely for life itself, but for the life of supreme quality, life in unity with the Triune God. He did not settle for life dominated and overwhelmed by sin, but rather chose a life worth living, a life in obedience to the Father that brought his grace, Redemption, and Spirit to the world. This is a life that is truly worth living, but even more than that, a life the God-man found worth dying for in or to Redeem us.

In the mind of the task force, the power and evil of death have been relativized by Christ's victory, and the Christian is freed from a tense idolization of life because Christ shattered its destructive and tyrannizing power over us. The evil of death is relativized and the Christian can embrace death as a relative evil to be overcome by Christ. This means that the Christian need not stand in absolute fear and terror of death and can even make death a friend. For the pastoral minister, suicide is not a betrayal or abandonment of life, but it can mean that a person has said farewell to life and has confidently put their life and future in God's hands.[8]

3. "Euthanasia and Pastoral Care" claims that the forces of nature are not to be identified with the will of God and our fates are not determined by impersonal and irrational human or animal nature:

> In the light of the Bible it is impossible to regard the natural course of things (for instance an illness) as simply the will of God. That kind of *natural* theology lacks all grounds. If one thing is clear through the whole Bible it is that nature and fate are not 'god.'[9]

Also, the natural course of events of one's dying is not necessarily identical to the course of events willed by God, which means that one can alter this course to suit oneself.[10] Christ suffered and died so that we could have the fullness of life, which means we are allowed to alter the natural course of events to draw close to God. Dying from natural causes should not be viewed as more ethically legitimate than causing one's own death, and a decision to take one's life should not necessarily be rejected or viewed with suspicion.[11]

We are free and rational agents who achieve our human fulfillment by exercising freedom and power over nature and are not subject to its blind forces. To be free is to not be bound by the bondage of slavery, natural forces, or religious idols, and authentic freedom means that one is liberated from all of the powers that hold one's life in their grip, including death, in order to exert rational control over them. Nature is constrained by these forces, and because Christians are free, nature simply cannot rule over us or be an unrestrained and unrestricted guide for our actions.

One who is seriously ill, near death, or who lies imprisoned in their body possesses less freedom than one who is healthy in mind and body, and such a person should be permitted to escape such radical limitations on their freedom:

> One who lies deathly ill in bed or someone who is in prison has less freedom (of movement) than someone who is healthy in body and mind, able to go wherever he or she wants to.[12]

To permit or encourage such a person to bring on death as the last expression of freedom is not unethical in the mind of "Euthanasia and Pastoral Care." This is not a betrayal of life, but an assertion of the power given us by Christ's victory over fate and nature. Assisting in their dying endorses and supports their limited and diminished freedom by not allowing nature to utterly and totally dominate.

4. "Euthanasia and Pastoral Care" denies any importance to the distinction between active and passive euthanasia, and it asserts that neither of these are always and everywhere wrong:

> We also like to say a word or two about the difference between active and passive euthanasia. It happens not infrequently that church members think that the first is always wrong, the second allowed in certain circumstances. However, in our judgment, ethically there is no difference whatever. Whether there is active intervention (for example by giving the patient something at his request) or (*passively*) stopping (further) life-prolonging measures –improper care; that may never be done!–in both cases, there is responsibility for hastening the arrival of death.[13]

The fact that there is no morally relevant difference between these ways of bringing death implies that actively performing an act of mercy killing can be as ethically acceptable as omitting some forms of care. The authors find that there are only emotional differences between these that should not be allowed to control the moral judgments we make of them. As it is morally acceptable to withhold medical care, it should also be permissible to give lethal injections to relieve pain and suffering because there is no morally relevant difference between them. In both cases, the result of the choice is freedom from pain, suffering, and the tyranny of natural forces, and the means by which this is brought about are of no moral importance. What is critical is that the person be freed from pain and suffering and find their dignity preserved through their decision to either actively bring death or be allowed to die.

5. When discussing the nature of pastoral care, this document argues that our model for caring for the suffering and dying should be Christ the Shepherd:

> Behind the term 'pastoral care' looms the image of a shepherd. Nowadays that picture may not mean all that much to us. But one aspect of it is illuminating: the shepherd looks for a way with his flock. Against that background, 'pastoral' or 'pastoral care' could be described as: 'to help find a way (out) in questions that deal with faith and life.'[14]

In accord with this model, the pastoral minister should help the patient to escape suffering and experience the joy of the comfort of the Gospel in their dying.[15] The authors discuss what it means to give a patient the joy of dying in comfort, and they essentially reduce the problem of providing this for a patient to the question of whether it is permissible to give, facilitate, or promote euthanasia. In reply, the authors state: "*we believe that in the light of faith under certain conditions the decision to (have) put an end to one's own life need not be irresponsible*."[16] They assert that the pastoral minister should give comfort to the dying and not abandon, but rather help them in whatever way possible.[17]

The minister should avoid moralizing about a suicidal person's actions or decisions. The pastor should not impose his or her own value patterns on the person, but should allow the person's own values to operate freely, thereby bringing them to reflect on the ramifications of their suicidal decision.[18] The minister should leave the question of suicide open to discussion by not directly denouncing it, but by being open to it as a legitimate option. The pastoral minister is to accept the suicidal person as a unique and responsible individual, and assist the person in deciding for suicide in a responsible, well-informed, and confident manner.[19]

The pastoral minister can bring the joy and comfort of the Gospel to the dying person by calming their fears, anxieties, and guilt about dying and not moralizing about self-deliverance. The pastoral minister should affirm their dignity and freedom from the irrational forces of nature by aiding and comforting them in their dying. The pastor should communicate by preaching, teaching, and counseling that suicide is not taboo, and is a morally acceptable option. Guilt and anguish over such choices are some of the leading causes of suffering and distress for the suicidal person, and the minister can be of great aid by showing tolerance and compassion to them. Charity demands that pastors relieve, and not increase, the guilt of a suicidal person by condemning them. Christ showed that he was the Good Shepherd by offering mercy and compassion to all who placed their faith and trust in him, no matter how sinful they might have been. As the Good Shepherd, he did not reject or abuse his flock but led it to the fields of eternal life through love, compassion, mercy, and forgiveness. The pastoral minister should imitate the Good Shepherd by not imposing guilt and indignities on the suffering or dying by making moralistic judgments about the choice of death made by the dying person.

The authors of "Euthanasia and Pastoral Care" hold that pastors should not try to answer all questions, even if answers are to be found in the Bible, but should allow the suicidal person to form appropriate responses from their own experience. The pastor is not an "answer book," ready to quote the Bible in response to each and every question, but should recognize that there are true mysteries and obscurities in life that not even the Bible can clarify or resolve. Christian ministry means that one should counsel the suicidal about the meaning of life in the context of Christian faith and not moralize about it or become arrogant and pretend omniscience in spiritual and moral matters. The pastoral minister should avoid making dogmatic pronouncements about death and morality and recognize that both are fundamentally mysterious and that each person approaches these from their own unique and individual perspective.

"Euthanasia and Pastoral Care" calls on ministers to be aware of defense mechanisms that can inhibit one from empathizing fully with the situation of one contemplating suicide:

> A pastor should also be aware of and learn to handle his own defense mechanisms, lest he shut himself off from people whose ideas are different from his or from people he does not particularly care for. Pastoral help presupposes the willingness to empathize with the other in his concrete situation.[20]

The pastor can easily use the suffering person's vulnerability to impose his or her moral standards and beliefs, but this would violate the autonomy and freedom of the dying person. To prevent this, the minister should be aware of his or her own moral preferences and not allow these to interfere with their primary pastoral responsibility, which is to aid the dying person in finding the joy and comfort of the Gospel in dying.

"Euthanasia and Pastoral Care" urges the pastoral minister to show solidarity with the patient if "medical power" manifests itself at the patient's expense, and its authors argue that suicide should be permitted as a means of protest against this abuse of power.[21] If health care providers impose useless, painful, or unwanted treatments on suffering or dying patients, the pastoral minister should promote the joy of comfort of the Gospel for them by protecting them from aggressive treatments. The desire to experience the joy of comfort in the Gospel and promote the maturity of the patient is to be protected by the minister, lest the patient become "lost in the system." This means that the minister should work in behalf of patients to prevent them from being treated impersonally or disrespectfully. The preferences and wishes of the patient concerning his or her care should not be subordinated to the imperatives of the health care system.

6. According to "Euthanasia and Pastoral Care," the minister should recognize that taking one's life is not always and everywhere immoral. They should bring the patient to recognize that not all biological life must be sustained, but only "life that is worth living":

> For us who are created in God's image, this means that we may live not only from the expectation that our life has a future, but also concretely that we must fight, with determination and creativity, against suffering, sickness, deterioration and death. We must fight *against* death and *for* a life that is worth living, a humane existence. It is not our task to maintain a hell.[22]

Life is a gift of God, but it is a gift that can be shattered or deformed by unendurable suffering or pain, and when this happens, putting an end to it is morally responsible. This sort of life does not "drop out of God's hand," but should be allowed to be brought to God with the aid of the pastoral minister in the joy and comfort of the Gospel.[23] When life reaches this stage, "Euthanasia and Pastoral Care" teaches that professing one's faith that life is a gift from God sounds absurd because death becomes preferable to life in such a condition.[24] The pastoral minister should aid in bringing the person to death rather than impose unworthy life:

> On the contrary, it [faith] gives central stage to freedom and responsibility. That is made very clear by Jesus in the parable of the talents. (Matt. 25:14-30) And the moment we speak of responsibility, we are not all that far removed anymore from such terms as 'maturity' and 'autonomy,' and 'self-determination.'[25]

Christ's victory over death means that life in such a condition is not to be idolized, but should be brought to an end and pastoral ministers should be tolerant of those seeking suicide in some situations. There is no absolute obligation to live as long as possible, but rather to live in such a way that life is not idolized. "Euthanasia and Pastoral Care" even goes so far as to say that refusing to end a worthless life is implicitly unethical and anti-Christian. The only obligation incumbent on individuals is to live with an acceptable quality of life, and there is no duty to continue living when the quality of the person's life is no longer acceptable to the patient.

According to "Euthanasia and Pastoral Care," hastening death in such a circumstance is a violation of the commandment against deliberate killing, but is a legitimate response to the higher command to love others as one would wish to be loved. Not all direct killing of the innocent is wrong, for this commandment may be broken in order to achieve some higher value or to fulfill the commandment of love, which occurs when one assists the suicide of a suffering person who has lost their freedom. Taking life in this instance is morally identical to a pregnant woman indirectly killing an unborn fetus to save her own life, or to soldiers indirectly killing civilians in the process of destroying a legitimate military target. Because of this, it would be morally legitimate to hasten death to achieve the higher value of experiencing a death in the joy of the comfort of the Gospel.

7. "Euthanasia and Pastoral Care" claims that one can self-execute when one's life has lost its worth in order to experience the "joy of the comfort of the Gospel," and the command against reflexive killing should be considered as binding except when it keeps one from ending a life not worth living. The reason for this is that the

> commands [of the Decalogue] delineate the area within which an inhumane life can happen. Therefore they are indispensable and beneficial. But if they are being used to maintain inhumane situations they turn into their opposite.[26]

This was because the Son of Man relativized all of the commandments of the Old Law and subordinated them to the existential needs of the person. Jesus warns not to worry about our lives, but to be concerned with God's righteousness (Mt 6:25ff), which the authors interpret to mean that we should only avoid killing individuals whose lives are no longer worth living. This applies as well to the commandment against killing, which is only valid if its observance eliminates inhumane conditions. "Euthanasia and Pastoral Care" teaches that ministers should impose no burdensome obligations on the dying or suffering, and their only duty is to refrain from imposing hardships or increasing the sufferings of others. The commandment against killing only applies to those who have lost a life worth living, and prolonging life that does not have this value is contrary to the aim of the commandment against killing.

8. "Euthanasia and Pastoral Care" allows assistance in suicide when suffering is unbearable, but it frankly admits that there are no objective criteria to measure when suffering or life become unbearable.[27] However, it does not prohibit giving assistance when the dying claim unbearable sufferings, and it asserts that these declarations require compliance.[28] It does not believe that the only condition that makes assisting in suicide morally permissible is

physical suffering associated with a terminal disease, for psychological suffering can be as terrible as physical suffering.[29] This type of suffering is highly complex because it often involves loneliness, guilt, emotional disturbance, and cognitive disorders, which can be as disturbing as physical sufferings. But if a person who wishes to die is suspected of not being fully earnest and sincere, it would be legitimate to not heed their requests.[30] Often patients are grateful for not taking such requests seriously, but if they still wish assistance with suicide, the pastoral minister should not deny them.[31]

9. The authors of this document believe that pastors should not be required to act against their conscience to assist in suicide, but if someone asks for assistance in dying, pastors who do not wish to give this assistance should find someone who will help them.[32] "Euthanasia and Pastoral Care" demands truthfulness at the bedside,[33] and it recognizes that many of the sick and dying cannot accept the full and brutal truth about their condition, which requires the truth be presented with tact, discretion, and gentleness.[34] But it insists that the truth not be covered over and that it be given as objectively as possible so that the patient's treatment decisions not be manipulated.[35]

10. "Euthanasia and Pastoral Care" holds that pastors should be cautious about preaching the Gospel to the sick and dying if this would be interpreted as mere empty piety and an obstacle to communication.[36] The Gospel is a liberating power, but many do not see it as such and they find its proclamation an abuse of "religious power" analogous to abuses of "medical power." Priority should be given to aiding and comforting them, and if the proclamation of a religious message would disturb or disrupt them, preaching and proclamation to the sick and dying should be avoided. Religious or moral teachings should not be used to dissuade a person from a suicidal choice as this could be offensive and an abuse of "religious power."

11. Finally, if patients request assistance in suiciding, "Euthanasia and Pastoral Care" holds that they should not be abandoned by the pastoral minister unless they should want to die alone.[37] The document also suggests that a liturgy of dying be provided for the suicidal if appropriate and possible, but it should be omitted if inappropriate.[38] They should be allowed to die at home, or if this would not be possible or desirable, the circumstances of the patient's death should approximate their home as much as possible. This principle is in accord with this document's overriding theme that the pastor is to provide comfort to the suffering and dying patient.

Christian Suicide: Problems and Paradoxes

In essence, "Euthanasia and Pastoral Care" is promoting Christian suicide, self-killing endorsed and blessed by Christian teaching. In this section, I would like to point out the paradoxes and problems with this approach.

1. "Euthanasia and Pastoral Care" implies that those contemplating suicide have very limited responsibilities to their families, friends, and society, and their freedom to end their lives is virtually unfettered. But this is an unacceptably narrow and superficial view of familial and social relationships, and endorsing this document would radically weaken family and social bonds because it would permit individuals to neglect their legitimate familial and social responsibilities. No matter what one's physical condition might be, there is an obligation to act in charity and love toward all, but "Euthanasia and Pastoral Care" appears to exempt the suicidal person from these requirements. Suiciding violates the love one should have for friends, family, and neighbors, and those who depend in various ways on the suicidal person. In spite of what "Euthanasia and Pastoral Care" claims about the freedom of the suicidal to do this, pastors should be willing to advise against suicides that might be irresponsible to one's family.

2. "Euthanasia and Pastoral Care" accepts suicide as a morally legitimate form of protest against medical abuse, but it does not understand the paradoxes and problems involved in such a policy. To their credit, the authors admit that petitions for death are usually pleas for help in coping with the problems of life, which implies that the pastoral minister should not accede to suicidal wishes in at least some instances. The pastoral minister should not be deaf, but should respond charitably and attentively to them. But the authors do not adequately understand the complications that can arise from teaching that suicide should be allowed for the person whose life is judged to not be worth living.

By way of example, if one had a "low quality of life," but ambivalently declared that they wanted to die, the pastoral minister would confront serious dilemmas because of the clash of the two principles that substandard life should not be continued and that uncertain requests for suicide should not be granted. The authors of "Euthanasia and Pastoral Care" would have to decide in behalf of one of these two conflicting principles and would probably endorse the former rather than the latter. But if they did this, they would violate the second principle and could not escape the dilemma of violating one of their two basic principles.

Like other forms of suicide for political purposes, suicide to protest medical abuse is irrational because it prohibits the victim from enjoying the results of their act of protest. This form of suicide is an inefficient political strategy because it can alienate many conscientious supporters who would otherwise endorse the protest but not the means employed. This form of protest could place an extraordinary burden of guilt on innocent health care providers who are not involved in the abuse of medical power but who might feel indirectly condemned by the suicide. Many health care providers strive conscientiously to sustain the lives of the suffering and dying, and they would resist being compelled to override these judgments to accede to a suicidal patient's wishes.

As we saw in the previous chapter, suicide to gain political objectives usually wins few new converts, and it often alienates those who object to the use of reflexive lethal violence for explicitly political goals. Suicide as a means of political protest is often tactically ineffective because opponents who accede to a suicidal person's demands do so more often because of the guilt they would experience in the aftermath of the death than on account of their agreement with the policy or the means employed to promote it. And those driven to tolerate the policy because of the gruesomeness of the suicidal threat will often resist acceding to further demands because they feel they have already been intimidated enough by such threats. A more thoughtful and charitable pastor would urge a suicidal patient to consider carefully the effects of such a decision, and would justifiably assert that the suicide might in fact achieve quite the opposite effect of that desired by the person. The requirements of Christian charity would demand that the suicidal individual take concerns such as these into consideration. A much more effective way to protest abuse of medical power would be to publicize the abuses of medical practitioners who profit unjustly from the misuse of their authority. Such an action would gain sympathy and support for reforms unobtainable by political suicide and would not give general support to curb medical abuse. Many are sympathetic to charges that medical power is being abused, but they would feel suiciding to protest it would be an even greater abuse.

Taking positive measures to improve health care would be a much more effective means of negotiating new power relationships with wielders of "medical power," and it would not offend those who would be sympathetic to these goals. Physicians know that patients have substantial power to control medical interventions, and violent measures such as suicide are not necessary to expand their control over care and treatment. If patients wish to reject medical treatment, all they need to do is make this known by signing an advance medical directive or investing durable power of attorney in another with the explicit instructions to refuse all medical care. It is also more effective for victims of medical abuse to continue to live, rather than to suicide, so that they can aid and assist future "oppressed" patients.

3. Another problem with "Euthanasia and Pastoral Care" is its view that the pastor should suppress his or her conscientious judgments and cooperate with a patient's suicide. The pastoral minister who objects in conscience to suicide would not be allowed by "Euthanasia and Pastoral Care" to either express that view or act on it, which is more restrictive than what is demanded of health care professionals. The authors want pastors to be faithful to their own moral views, but not dispute the judgments of suicidal patients, and be tolerant of views contrary to their own. But even though this document imposes these restrictions on opponents of suicide, it does not demand that suicide advocates be so open-minded and tolerant.

"Euthanasia and Pastoral Care" prohibits pastors from carrying their personal, religious, and professional judgments to the bedside, and in doing so, it requires them to be deceptive in their relationships with patients. It does not suggest that health care providers leave their professional, personal, or moral judgments at the door of the patient's room and abide by the wishes of the patient in all cases, but in the name of compassion, it requires this of pastoral ministers. A double standard prevails in administering the teachings of "Euthanasia and Pastoral Care" because it enables suicidal patients to impose their moral beliefs and judgments on pastoral ministers, but prohibits ministers from arguing in defense of their own. Health care professionals are permitted by their professional codes of ethics to refuse to comply with some demands of patients, but "Euthanasia and Pastoral Care" does not grant this liberty to pastoral ministers who confront suicidal patients. The authors of "Euthanasia and Pastoral Care" have created a serious ethical dilemma for pastoral ministers, and it is not clear they are even aware that they have done this.

For the authors of this document, patients do not have to produce objective evidence to prove their lives are no longer worth living (the authors even admit that this is not possible), and all they need do is make such a declaration to win the right to override the conscientious judgments of pastors. There is such a thing as abuse of medical power, but there is also abuse of patient power, and using one's subordinate, dependent, and suffering condition to manipulate others to act against their conscientious judgments is such an abuse. The pastor should not only be ready to protect the patient from abuses of medical power, but should also protect health care professionals from abuses of patient power, yet "Euthanasia and Pastoral Care" does not give this serious consideration.

4. "Euthanasia and Pastoral Care" contends that death by choice is not necessarily worse than "natural death" because it results from a "free decision." This is an unacceptable, vague distinction, for there are situations when death from natural causes is far better than "freely chosen" death. The death of one who does not deserve to die by the knowing, willful, free, and deliberate act of another results from a "free decision" and it has an aspect of immorality that is absent when death occurs from natural causes. It is inaccurate to say that there are no differences between the two, for only when death by decision does not involve any violations of fairness or the sanctity of life is it morally equivalent to natural death. This document fails to see that form of death is the greatest of all physical evils, and when an innocent person's death results from a free act, moral malice is added to the physical evil of death.

5. "Euthanasia and Pastoral Care" holds that active euthanasia is not substantially different from passive euthanasia, and this claim is a cornerstone of the doctrine that cooperation in "rational" suicide is not immoral. It rejects the classical doctrine that passive euthanasia is only morally permissible when medical treatments are judged excessively costly, futile, or excessively burdensome and holds that all forms of passive euthanasia are morally valid. This is so because omitting or foregoing safe, inexpensive, and nonburdensome life-sustaining measures introduces fundamental and underlying lethal causes, and is identical in its moral malice to a positive act of killing. But to omit futile, burdensome, risky, or expensive measures does not institute a fundamental cause of death because such a cause is already present, as the nature of the life-sustaining measures needed to preserve life confirms.

If it is true that "letting die" is not morally different from positive killing, then one who does not jump into shark-infested waters to save another who has fallen overboard and lets that person die is as much the cause of death as are the sharks who devour him. This is peculiar because the sharks do in fact seem to bear more responsibility for the death of the unfortunate person than the bystander. If there is no difference between these two kinds of choices, what would be the difference between omitting cardiac bypass surgery for a dying man because it would be futile or too expensive, and giving the same person a lethal injection to end their life?

The relationship between active and passive allowing-to-die is complex but important because in both cases an individual dies as a result of a choice, but in some instances, the choice for active killing is more responsible for the death than is a choice for passive allowing-to-die.

6. "Euthanasia and Pastoral Care" presents a rather narrow view of the needs of the dying or suffering patient. It presumes that these patients want to die almost more than anything else, even though recent studies have shown that this is not necessarily so.[39] It also assumes that the dying want total freedom from pain and suffering and will use any means to gain this, but this is not always and everywhere true either, for many see their suffering and dying as a time to bring their life to a close and reassert integrity and freedom through their dying. It fails to see that in many instances, killing a suffering or dying patient could be wrong because it would prohibit one from achieving self-transcendence through their sufferings.

For many Christians, the sufferings that precede death can be an occasion to achieve their complete and total union with Christ by sharing fully in his sufferings and death. Rather than wanting to die in a way that was utterly foreign to the suffering and death of Christ, some may want to not merely live, but also die as he did, to drink of his cup and share in his dying by not fleeing the sufferings that precede death. By permitting them to self-assassinate to experience "the joy of dying in the comfort of the Gospel," the Christian pastoral minister might be foregoing an experience of fuller union with Christ in his suffering. Thus, the pastoral minister should not simply presume that all patients want a painless death in any and all circumstances.

7. According to "Euthanasia and Pastoral Care," one is guilty of idolizing life by refusing to allow another to commit suicide to escape suffering. This is false, however, for one would be idolizing life if one demanded that everything conceivable must be done to save it without regard for cost, burden, or pain. But when one does not bring death on oneself and only takes common and ordinary means to sustain life and does not demand futile, radically painful, or burdensome forms of care or treatment, one is not making life an idol.

8. "Euthanasia and Pastoral Care" argues that those who minister to the suffering and dying should strive to alleviate the guilt they might feel by suiciding so that they can feel morally free to make this

decision. But asserting that all guilt associated with self-killing should be ignored might not be wise, as this guilt could serve the good purpose of justifiably deterring from this sort of action. There are some kinds of guilt that are right, good, and valuable, such as the guilt one might incur after rape, killing hostages in warfare, or abusing a child. The guilt often associated with suicide might well be beneficial, as it can serve to deter individuals from harming themselves; hence, a pastor should not try to alleviate such guilt and claim that such actions are legitimate and loving deeds.

The proclamation of the Gospel according to "Euthanasia and Pastoral Care" comforts the suffering and dying, assures that guilt is forgiven, and deepens understanding. But from the Catholic perspective, guilt is alleviated through the sacraments, repentance, and conversion. Suicide is a mortal sin in the Catholic view, and cannot be forgiven because one cannot repent after completing the action. This document is peculiar because it implies that the pastoral minister can almost drive out guilt *ex opere operato* by merely speaking words of forgiveness. Traditionally, Catholicism has taught that the sacrament of reconciliation functions *ex opere operato,* but that does not imply that we have no responsibility to strive to abolish the causes of the guilt and can neglect the demands of conversion. The pastoral minister does not have the power to remove guilt, for only Christ has this power, and it cannot operate freely if we do not confess, repent, and do penance for the sins that cause the guilt.

9. "Euthanasia and Pastoral Care" does not have a clear and adequate understanding of the concept of nature as it is used in moral discourse. This document argues that nature should not be a moral guide for action, but it paradoxically asserts that meeting the physical and natural needs for comfort and freedom from physical pain is the ultimate goal of pastoral ministry and this objective trumps all other issues. The ultimate objective of pastoral ministry to the suicidal is to bring them not only spiritual but also physical comfort, and justifying suicide in the absence of this judgment would be exceedingly difficult. Its attempt to radically undermine the role of nature in moral decisions fails to see that deliberate killing of the innocent is objectionable because it violates not only justice and other virtues, but also our physical and bodily inclinations toward the fundamental goods of human existence, which express our natural drives and orientations. It is not clear that the role of "nature" can be so easily reduced to insignificance in moral analysis, for most moralists have based the rights to such values as liberty, autonomy, and self-determination on some understanding of "nature." Nature

is not the only determinant of morality, but it is not clear that it should be so substantially disregarded as "Euthanasia and Pastoral Care" suggests. To make brute nature a moral guide is insufficient, but understanding it as conditioned by the dictates and exigencies of human reason and virtue aids us in grasping the moral truth.

"Euthanasia and Pastoral Care" strongly favors assisted suicide and believes pastoral ministers should do everything possible to promote it. In the next section, I will maintain that the model of Christian pastoral ministry for the dying presented in "Euthanasia and Pastoral Care" is inadequate and flatly contrary to biblical norms and apostolic practice and I will offer alternative viewpoints.

The Theology of "Euthanasia and Pastoral Care"

1. The Christology of this document is quite deficient because it only considers one aspect of Christ's life and ministry. "Euthanasia and Pastoral Care" holds that the primary model of ministry to the suicidal is that of Christ as the Shepherd, but if the image of the Good Shepherd implies anything, it suggests that he "lays down his life for his sheep" and does not stand by passively and allow his sheep to suffer death. Yet, one who follows the counsel of "Euthanasia and Pastoral Care" is not a "Good Shepherd" but is more like the treacherous hireling who abandons the flock. The pastoral minister should empathize with the dying person, but in the tenth chapter of the Gospel of John, the Good Shepherd will even die for his sheep and will take upon himself all suffering and burdens for their sake. Pastoral ministers should not be deterred from advising against suicide because it is the deliberate self-destruction of innocent human life and alienates one from Christ.

"Euthanasia and Pastoral Care" considers Christ only in his role as Shepherd but it ignores some other images from Scripture used to describe him: (1) Messiah; (2) Suffering Servant; (3) King; (4) Priest; (5) Teacher; (6) Redeemer; (7) Life; and (8) Savior. Had the authors considered these other aspects of his person, nature, and ministry, they might have seen that self-killing is quite opposed to Christian moral norms. Claims such as this demand a deeper study of the nature of Christ's ministry and person.

i. In fulfilling his mission as Messiah, Jesus is the Promised One who leads the new Chosen People to their promised land and to union with Father, Son, and Spirit. He is the one who goes forth before God's people from their old land of sin and slavery to a new land of eternal life (1 Cor 15:21; Rom 8:11; Gal 5:1-12). He gave hope to a people filled with despair, and while all before him were caught in slavery and death, he liberated all who followed him and gave them new life. The life he offered was vastly superior to our fragile and troubled life, and was utterly different from that wounded by sin. In the Old Covenant, Israel fell into infidelity and disobedience, but Jesus the Messiah lived in complete fidelity to God's commands and gave new life to his Chosen People through his fidelity (Mt 4:1-11; Heb 3:2).

ii. Jesus showed he was the Messiah by purifying the Temple and driving out the money changers whose greediness symbolized the sins of Israel that impeded the nations from coming to the Temple and giving worship (Mt 21:12f; Mk 11:15-17; Lk 19:45f; Jn 2:14-17). His action was a symbol of the divine fire and wrath that purified the world of sin and death.[40] Christ's anger at the money changers was not a character defect, but a sign of the fire of divine love that burned within him and that drove out sin and death. His anger was a sign of the fiery wrath that God directs against sin and death, and just as he did not tolerate sin at the portals of the Temple, so also was he intolerant of death in the rest of his life and ministry.[41] He definitively and absolutely purified the Temple because he was utterly free of the taint of sin, and alone he was able again to open the Temple to the Gentiles. Their sinful practices were a sign of the sins of Israel that alienated the nations from Yahweh by inhibiting them from coming to the Temple to worship. Being unable to worship the true God, they fell into the ways of sin and death.

iii. As the Suffering Servant, he was chosen by the Father to take upon himself the sin and evil of the world and expiate them.[42] He was the Innocent Lamb who was led to slaughter for the sake of the guilty. Rather than bringing death to the guilty, the Innocent One gave his pure and undefiled life for the sake of the guilty.[43] The Suffering Servant did not inflict death on others, but sacrificed his life to free them from it. He bore all of the evils of the world on himself, and the greatest of these was death itself.[44] He did not destroy suffering, but took it on himself and made it an offering to the Father, who responded to this act of love by sending the Holy Spirit.

iv. As the new King, he came to proclaim a new Kingdom of life for all of God's children that was brought about by his fidelity and obedience to God (Mt 2:2; Mk 9:47;1 Cor 15:24ff). His domain was one of justice, peace, love, holiness, and fidelity to the will of the Father, and was to create a domain free from sin and death. He definitively vanquished the forces hostile to his Kingdom of New Life, including death in all of its forms. As the new King, he did not compromise with the powers of sin and death that besieged and enslaved his people, but decisively broke their power. The new King accomplished this by total fidelity and obedience to the will of the Father, and the life of this new Reign is given to those who imitate his ways.

v. As the new High Priest, Christ was the one who offered a perfect sacrifice to the Father for the sins of his people (Heb. 5:3). He atoned for our sins and wiped them away, and because he is the priest who is utterly without sin, his sacrifice to the Father atoned for all sin and evil (Heb 3:1-3). Unlike the priests of the Old Covenant who suffered defilement because of their sins and who used the power of death to uphold the Law, Christ declined to do this because he was totally free from involvement with sin and death (Heb 7:26-7). They used the death penalty to enforce their commands about adultery, for example, but Christ refused to employ death for such purposes, as in the case of the woman caught committing adultery (Jn 8:1ff). While they inflicted death on those who violated their law, Christ refused to do this to those who would not accept his new Law of Love, but he sought to bring them to it by self-sacrificing love.

vi. As Teacher, Christ clarified and manifested the full truth of the Scriptures and showed himself to be the Messiah. He showed how the Scriptures were fulfilled in himself and how the Kingdom of God was in him (Mt 22:16; Mk 12:14; Mt 7:29; Jn 7:16). Christ is the New Moses who went to the desert, but unlike Moses, he did not succumb to temptation there, but led the new chosen people into the promised land (Mt 4:1ff). The Old Law employed death in many cases to punish sins. Jesus, however, refused to tolerate inflicting death as a punishment for sins in any circumstance (Dt 21, 22; Jn 8:3-12). He forbade not only murder, but even anger, so profoundly did he disassociate himself from death (Mt 5:22). As the true Teacher, he raised the prophetic and canonical teachings of Israel to perfection and eliminated the inconsistencies, the compromises that were necessary because the fullness of grace had not yet been given (Mt 5:17-20, 22:34-40). The Law of the Old Covenant allowed the use of death and permitted such actions as stoning for adultery. But as the story of the woman caught committing adultery shows, Jesus did not allow that, but rather called for repentance and offered forgiveness in place of death. In doing so, he eliminated compromises and any form of association with sin and death on his part.

vii. In his role as Redeemer, Christ was the one sent by the Father to ransom his people from the powers of sin and death and to save them for the Kingdom of new life (Mt 20:28; Mk 10:45; 1 Tm 2:6). As Redeemer, he was also the liberator who brought the resurrection of the body (Lk 21:28; Rom 8:23). Before his entrance into the world, death had complete freedom, but he gave it no latitude after his saving victory. Death was the great power he opposed as Redeemer and his Resurrection made his victory over death complete. Because of this victory over death, Christ assumed full authority over it, and shattered its power over his people.

viii. John identifies Christ as the source of life itself and as having no involvement or association with the ways of death (Jn 5:26). Jesus did not struggle or negotiate a compromise with the powers of death, but wholly destroyed them. The Evangelists repeatedly noted that many people did not understand Christ or his mission because he was so foreign and alien to them and part of the mystery of his character was his profound commitment to life. His ways were so different that many thought him to be some well-cloaked Satanic agent, but they repeatedly argued in the Gospels that he was purely divine, good, and life-giving.

ix. As Savior, Christ bestowed healing in a far greater way than could ever be given by merely mortal healers. He drove out sickness and death, and only he had the power to do this (Mt 9:22; Mk 3:4; Lk 6:9; Mk 15:30; Lk 23:35-39). If he had negotiated and worked out a compromise with sin and death, he would not be any different from us. He is Savior precisely because he utterly devastates sin and death and does not allow it to reign in our lives. As Savior, Christ saved us from death, not by making us utterly immune to it, but by drawing us from its grip.

2. I am not sure that the model of Christ as the Good Shepherd offers the best model for ministering to the suicidal, for the New Testament presents us with four excellent examples of ministering to the suffering and dying: (1) Jesus' own life; (2) the parable of the Good Samaritan; (3) the example of Jesus' Mother, Mary; and (4) Paul and the jailer.

i. If anyone had a right to bring a halt to his own suffering through suicide, it was Jesus. But rather than either killing himself or enlisting the aid of others to effect his death, he accepted his sufferings as a means of showing perfect love and obedience to the Father. He transformed suffering from an occasion that threatened fidelity to God and invited death as a means to save life and deepen one's unity with God. As the son of God, he had every means available to him to escape his suffering and pain, was free to commit suicide, and may well have been tempted to it at the Mount of Olives, but he decided against it. His death did not mean there was no obligation in faith to curb suffering, but that one is not to commit self-murder to avoid these sufferings.

Contrary to our Lord's example of accepting suffering and dying, swift and painless suicide often takes away the Cross that Christ calls us to bear in order to grow in his image and likeness. Christ destroyed the power of death by subjecting himself entirely to its power and then shattering that power. He did this to show that he had truly confronted death itself and broke its grip over us. Just as he allowed himself to fall under its sway, he allows us to fall into its grip, but he also calls us to place our faith in him and trust in him so that he can lead us through it to a new life. The orthodox Christian tradition held that it is only by accepting the Cross of Christ in all of its reality that we can fully imitate him in his living and dying. Even though his mission eventually led him to the agony of the Cross and death, Jesus accepted even these, and at the Mount of Olives he freely and deliberately accepted the Cross in obedience to the will of the Father (Mt 26:30-35; Mk 14: 26-31; Lk 22: 31-34). This does not mean that Christians must necessarily seek suffering or death, but that we should accept them when this is necessary to show our devotion to God.

ii. A further example of a more authentic Christian witness to Christian suffering and dying is seen in the story of the Good Samaritan (Lk 10:33ff). When the main character of this parable encountered the victim of robbers, the Samaritan did not ask whether the highwaymen's victim had a "life worth living," even though the man was near death, but provided him with basic care and did not abandon him. This parable symbolizes the sort of love Christ has for the suffering and dying, but it also shows the spontaneous and unquestioning love of neighbors that Christians should have for not just family and friends, but for everyone. The Samaritan could have helped the man die, or persuaded him to commit suicide, but instead of doing this, he did whatever was within his power to give life, hope, and comfort to the unfortunate man. He did not count the cost or burden to himself, but did what was within his means to comfort and sustain the man. The central point of this parable is that we are to show healing, care, comfort, and empathy for those suffering or near death, and not speed their way into death. The actions of the Good Samaritan are not just a model of Christian love in general, but of Christian care for the sick and dying.

iii. Another excellent example of an authentically Christian pastoral approach to the suffering and dying is seen in the life of Jesus' Mother. Mary is our model of faith because she was the first to say "yes" in faith to the call of God to serve the Savior (Lk 1:38). Her actions in the face of suffering and death are exemplary for all Christians because her response of faith was complete, tested, and perfect. She served him throughout his life, fled to Egypt to protect him (Mt 2), purified him in the Temple, (Lk 2:22-39), led him to his first miracle at Cana, (Jn 2:12) and when all of the Apostles fled in fear at the time of his death, she remained faithful to him (Jn 19:25-27). Orthodoxy and Roman Catholicism have taught that she was freed from Original Sin because she agreed to become the Mother of the Savior, and was the first to live fully in the grace of Christ's Kingdom. Because of this special grace, rather than protesting or rebelling against her Son's death and abandoning him, she remained faithful to him, allowed him to fulfill his mission, and encouraged, supported, and prayed for him. She serves as our model for caring for the dying and suffering because when her Son was being cruelly and mercilessly killed, she prayed for him and did not abandon him. She did not kill or assist in killing him to bring "comfort and joy" in dying, but tolerated his suffering and death to remain faithful to him. Her example shows powerfully how Christians should minister to the suffering and dying through charity, prayer, and faith, and not by calling for or assisting in their deaths.

iv. In the episode of Paul and the jailer, (Acts 16: 25-34) the Apostle reacted to a situation where an individual was tempted to suicide by calling him to show faith in Christ; he did not abandon this man to his despair. Paul's episode with the jailer is instructive because it shows that the apostolic church believed it had to proclaim the life and power of Christ even in the face of suffering and despair. Paul was bold about proclaiming Jesus' name as the one to be invoked in times of loss, suffering, and despair, but "Euthanasia and Pastoral Care" lacks that confidence and urges suicide in times of despair. Authentic Christian ministering to the dying requires teaching them to show fidelity and obedience to Christ, even during suffering, and letting oneself pass through death in faith in Christ.

3. From the theological perspective, the most serious deficiency in the theology of "Euthanasia and Pastoral Care" is its claim that "life not worth living" can be deliberately destroyed. It teaches that the commandment against killing is only to be observed when higher values are promoted and when "life worth living" is spared. But this interpretation lacks a secure foundation in Scripture and mainstream

Catholic moral thought and it is more in harmony with the principles of modern eugenics, utilitarianism, and consequentialism. The classical Catholic tradition was unanimous in condemning the killing of those who would be the most likely candidates for having a "life not worth living": the sick, weak, despised, and powerless. Christ came to destroy death, not life, and in the Christian perspective, the ultimate struggle of Christ was his confrontation with the powers of death.

There is nothing in Jesus' ministry to suggest that he came merely to save life that was "worth living," for he came to save all humanity not only from sin, evil and suffering, but also from death itself. He valued all human life, without respect for its condition, and by his healing power, he restored the most miserable to health or gave it back to those who had lost it. Not only did Christ seek to protect those who were suffering, as in his cure of the ten lepers (Mt 8:1-4; Mk 1:40-45; Lk 5:12-16; Lk 17:11-19), but he also gave life to those who had died, as in his raising to life of Lazarus and the daughter of the Centurion (Jn 11-12; Mt 8:5; Lk 7:2). He judged all human life worthy of his care, love, and sacrifice, and he especially valued the lives of those who were, in the minds of some, repulsive and who deserved to die: lepers, the blind, deaf, crippled, diseased, adulterers, prostitutes, and rebels. And if he did not give life to those who were dying, he called them to faith and promised them the gift of eternal life as he did with the good thief who was crucified with him (Lk 23:39-43). To say that Christ came only to save "life worth living" is to deny the universality of his saving mission as well as the fact that he came to save all people from sin and death, not just a few who met certain standards. This implies that he condoned consigning some to death because their "quality-of-life" supposedly did not meet Christ's high standards.

Destroying "life not worth living" was contrary to the practice of the apostolic and early Christian community because they, like Christ, were not repelled by the "unworthiness" of the lives of some, but embraced and healed those lives. As did Christ himself, the early community opposed sin and death itself, and not diseased, debilitated, or suffering human life.

In spite of what "Euthanasia and Pastoral Care" claims about the Decalogue, it taught some moral absolutes. It prohibited deliberate killing of the innocent and said nothing about the worth of the lives to be spared. Without exception, it forbade adultery even to save innocent life and it anathematized idolatry in all forms, even for the "good reason" of saving one's life (Ex 20:3-4; Dt 5: 7-8). It demanded honor for one's parents in all cases, and it even prohibited dishonor if it would bring about the realization of "higher" values. Throughout the history of orthodox Christianity, commentators were able to determine if an action was killing, theft, adultery, or idolatry or not. But having made this distinction, it never admitted that authentic acts of lying or adultery could be performed for any reason, even to achieve "higher ends." It allowed life or material possessions to be taken in order to protect the order of justice, but it is simply wrong to argue as does "Euthanasia and Pastoral Care" that the Decalogue permitted killing, theft, or adultery to promote "higher" values.

4. The claim of "Euthanasia and Pastoral Care" that the minister should protect people from discomfort and suffering is true, but this does not mean that the pastor should tolerate deliberate killing of the innocent to achieve this goal. More than giving physical comfort to the patient and easing their conscience, the pastor should strive to promote the faith, hope, and charity of the dying and suffering person at a time when this can be exceedingly difficult. As we shall see in the next section, the pastor's role is not so much to relieve pain, but to bring hope, offer Christ's forgiveness for sin through the sacraments, calm fear and anxiety, and recount the richness of Christ's love for the suffering and dying person. Rather than counseling in behalf of suicide, the pastor should deepen the person's hope by urging repentance, confession of sin, and renewal of faith and love in Christ.

5. "Euthanasia and Pastoral Care" claims that the pastor should facilitate suicide and enable patients to die in the joy and comfort of the Gospel, but traditional Catholic moral teachings hold that there are some things that cannot be done to find comfort and joy, and aiding in direct self-killing is one of them. In the classical Catholic view, suffering is a relative evil while mortal sin is an absolute evil that is always to be avoided. This view is in harmony with the fact that neither the teachings of Christ nor those of the apostolic community ever held that the suffering were to deliberately end their lives to experience the "joy of dying in comfort." The first concern of the pastoral minister should not be to alleviate the suffering and pain of the patient, but to preserve the moral integrity of the person and their relationship to God when they are being sorely tempted to despair. The minister should not purchase this joy at the expense of the person's relationship with God, but should give strength to them so that they do not sin to escape suffering. The joy that Christians seek should be that of imitating Christ's obedience to the Father, and maintaining fidelity and loyalty to him in threatening times. Catholic

theology has held that we can only share fully in Christ's victory and life if we first share in his sufferings, and the most perfect way we can do this is to accept our own sufferings and death in faith in Christ and love of God.

6. "Euthanasia and Pastoral Care" believes that its proposals foster the freedom and liberty of the dying patient, but its understanding of human freedom is superficial and insubstantial. The great twentieth-century German theologian Karl Rahner gives a much more complete view of the nature of our freedom, for he sees the person as the free being created by God to hear his word of revelation.[45] We are not simply "thrown" into an absurd and meaningless existence, but are created to encounter and serve God in our lives. This freedom entails a fundamental openness to God's revelation and allows us to be shaped and formed by our response to that revelation. Freedom is abused by refusing to hear God's Word and by not allowing ourselves to be shaped by it, according to Rahner, but for "Euthanasia and Pastoral Care," freedom is only abused when it is used to bring harm to others. The authors see freedom in purely horizontal and human terms while Rahner sees it in its theological, ontological, and existential aspects as it touches the very depths of our being and our relation to God.

In his understanding of freedom, death is not merely something that befalls us, as is the case with the beasts, but is an action we perform in the exercise of our distinctive, divinely bestowed liberty that draws us close to God.[46] Rahner perceives a link between freedom and death that implies that we have the freedom to make our act of dying one that draws us closer to God.[47] For Rahner, the pastor should guide the person to hear the call to faith, hope, love, trust, and obedience to God in their dying and make it an act of faith in and obedience to Christ.[48] Freedom is abused when used to take death upon oneself, but is legitimately employed to accept death and suffering in faith, hope, and obedience to the Father. The properly Christian act of dying is one of obedience and discipleship, and the dying person should break from egotistical concerns and show fidelity to God as their first priority.

7. Perhaps the most glaring theological deficiency of the perspective of "Euthanasia and Pastoral Care" is its failure to take the doctrine of the Paschal Mystery seriously. In the mainstream Catholic tradition, this doctrine has suggested that true Christian freedom results from such an attachment to Christ in faith, hope, and love that not even the threat of suffering and death can alienate the person from Christ or cause the person to betray Christ. This central

mystery of Christian faith asserts that faith in the power of God to deliver one from death brings life, which requires one to accept suffering and death in faith in God. The Christian is not to flee the suffering and death entailed by a life of faith and charity, but accept them as the Father's will, as did Christ. Christian freedom does not mean that one is freed from all suffering unto death, but that one can pass through these by faith and trust in Christ.

The teachings of "Euthanasia and Pastoral Care" demand that one look more closely into the question of how one leads the suicidal person from the portals of death and restores hope, self-esteem, and self-confidence in the face of their suffering. To be effective with them, one cannot solely proclaim the doctrines of the faith, for pastors must also seek to heal, give life and hope to the suicidal person, and the pastor should employ the doctrines of the Christian faith to lift the suicidal person from the despair that leads them to suicide.

Pastoral Ministry to the Suicidal: Shepherding to Hope

"Euthanasia and Pastoral Care" believes it is proper for the pastoral minister to endorse the states and conditions that lead to suicide, but the pastor should strive to heal and free them from the forces that lead to this choice. In what follows, I would like to briefly propose, from the Catholic perspective, a program for responding to the suicidal person.

The pastor should regard all suicide talk seriously, and should try to determine if the person is seriously suicidal or merely calling out for help. The primary function of the pastoral minister is neither to promote suicide nor even to provide psychotherapy, but to restore hope in the suicidal person who usually believes that their decision is justified because of external crises and threats. The single most important person who might intervene to prevent suicide is the pastor because he or she is best equipped to bring the hope of the Gospel to the person. Ordinarily, a person is in imminent danger of suicide if they speak in despairing tones of there being no hope and no options except death, and when someone reaches this point, the pastor is of more value than anyone else, because their message of hope is precisely what they need most of all at that moment.

Usually, the suicidal have thought long and hard about ending their life and have moved deeply into the spirit of despair and death. Because of this the primary responsibility of the pastor is to identify the psychological and social forces that have drawn the person down to this level. These psychological forces were discussed in chapter 6, and my concern here is not to reiterate them, but to show how the pastoral minister can dissipate them to renew the person's hope and turn them away from the suicidal decision. These forces of despair cloud the suicidal person's perceptions, reasoning, and judgments, radically constrict their freedom, and drive them to death, which is why the pastor should take pains to identify them and free the person from their grip. Pastors can frequently raise their hope by not only hearing their needs, but also by helping to resolve conflicts and problems they might be having with others.

The pastoral minister can fulfill his or her proper role of giving hope to the suicidal by countering the multiple causes of suicidal despair through the sacraments, the ministering of charity, and the preaching of the Gospel, and in what follows, I would like to show how this can be done.

Guilt. Guilt is perhaps the leading source of suicidal despair and is probably the strongest of all forces driving the desire for suicide. Suicide can be understood as striking at oneself out of guilt, to punish oneself for failures and misdeeds. It offers only an illusory escape from the threat and burden of guilt by promising to end everything, for the suicidal person's obsessions about self-killing often torment the person and deepen their sense of guilt. Suicide is a particularly violent way of purging one's guilt, and the pastor should make this clear to the suicidal person and explain to him or her better ways of doing this.

The suicidal react to what they see as an intolerable burden of guilt, and the pastor can strengthen their hope by showing that this does not have to be the case. To uncover this guilt, the minister should probe the suicidal person to disclose areas of their lives that are objects of self-recrimination, for these can often produce very profound, mysterious, and turbulent pain that can drive them to despair. Because of this guilt, the suicidal often react in panicked and despairing flight, and the pastor can stop this and give them hope by encouraging change and growth, accompanying them and showing them new ways of coping with their crises and problems. The suicidal should be brought to see that they are reacting to guilt, are being driven to the decision by their depression and despair, and are not acting with full or adequate freedom.

It is often the case that merely bringing them to light and showing the falseness of their self-directed accusations can relieve much of the pressure to self-execute. The minister should try to identify the forms of guilt the suicidal person experiences and bring them God's forgiveness for whatever causes this. Where there is good reason to be guilty, the pastoral minister should either join the person to pray for forgiveness, or offer them the sacrament of reconciliation. If a relationship with another is the cause of guilt, the pastor should encourage reconciliation and forgiveness with that person to expel this pain and burden. Much of the psychological pressure for suicide can be dissipated by bringing the person to seek divine forgiveness for their sins and misdeeds and also seek the forgiveness and mercy of others as well.

Self-hatred. The suicidal strike at their ego to punish themselves for its failings, chaos, and inability to thrive, and this reflexive violence derives from a deep self-hatred that can end in deadly despair. Suicide is the ultimate ego crisis and the suicidal person strikes at the ego because it is seen as empty and powerless. The suicidal have lost the ability to manage their lives and they strike out not at the causes of this disorder, but at the objects of the chaos in their lives, their own self. It is the ultimate act of self-mutilation, an act of self-hatred in which the person seeks to destroy the offending ego. It is not the act of a strong personality but of one who is weak and deeply disturbed. A frequently heard claim of the suicidal is that "there was no other way out of the situation," which expresses the emptiness of their ego more than the supposed futility of their situation. The suicidal find it impossible to love and respect themselves because of what they perceive to be their glaring failures, defects, and weaknesses, but this drives them into despair and ultimately reflexive attacks.

The pastor should point out that this self-hatred is unconscionable and opposed to Christ's love for us. There is a good and legitimate self-love that preserves and protects us, but self-hatred destroys this and ultimately leads to death. The pastor can help to overcome this self-loathing by urging the suicidal person to forgive the failings and offenses of not only others, but also their own as well. Doing this should enhance their self-esteem and dissipate their reflexive antagonism. This self-hatred derives from their compulsiveness and perfectionism and they need to learn better how to love not only others but themselves with all their weaknesses and deficiencies. They can only love that which is perfect and flawless, but that sort of love has no power to renew, give life or hope, or create. In loving what is faulty, defective, and weak, the suicidal person can give life through their love.

Inability to forgive and reconcile. The suicidal commonly burn with anger and resentment against others because of insults, hurts, and offenses, and this anger frequently increases their alienation, paranoia, suspicion, loneliness, hatred, and ultimately their despair. Much of the angry despair that drives them to lethality stems from their inability to forgive the failings, offenses, or hurts of others, and bringing the suicidal to accept and tolerate these offenses can often dissipate the anger that can culminate in despair. Suicide is the most perfect refusal of self-forgiveness imaginable, and it is contrary to the extraordinary mercy and forgiveness of Christ. The pastor can lead the suicidal person to forgive others' faults so that they can grow spiritually and morally, because failing to do this can lead ultimately into despair. By calling them to forgive others, accept and suffer under their sins and offenses, the pastor can restore their esteem and counter their despair.

Paranoia. Suicidal despair is often partly the product of a paranoid and schizoid mind that fails to understand that their lethal anger is aimed at their real self rather than at an imaginary and tormenting self. Much of their paranoia stems from their unresolved conflicts with others that are exacerbated by their unforgiving attitudes toward others. Because of their conflicts with and suspicions of others, they flee from relationships and they are never at rest or peace. They believe others do not love them and because of this, they feel they cannot love others. The suicidal often struggle desperately against the feeling that they are despised and rejected by others, which causes much self-hatred and recrimination that results in despair.

The pastor can counter this by helping to dissolve the despairing feelings of the suicidal person by urging them to forgive and be reconciled. The pastor can help this person by assuaging their paranoid fears about others and urging generous and forgiving treatment of those about whom they are fearful or mistrusting. If there are lingering conflicts and difficulties, the minister should do whatever is possible to help them resolve them and that would further relieve their paranoia. The pastor can best achieve this by urging the suicidal person to approach others in charity and love.

Compulsiveness. The suicidal person is usually an obsessive-compulsive individual who insists that reality be ordered entirely in accord with his or her wishes, aims, and desires, and this compulsiveness often contributes to their despair. They often have little confidence in their abilities to manage crises, and they reflect this by showing little confidence in the abilities of others to help them in their struggles. They commonly have little tolerance for newness, diversity, or openness to change, which they perceive as a lack of order and as contrary to what they support and endorse. Because of this, they reject people who do not meet their high standard for harmony, order, and precision. And when the order they value and desire begins to collapse in situations of suffering, death, or trauma, they react with panic and seek to destroy whatever remains rather than create a new and different order again. This compulsiveness often derives from a deep-seated anxiety and an unwillingness to trust others. They are unwilling to trust people who will provide for and take care of them; they feel they must handle all crises and difficulties themselves, which makes them anxious and suspicious of others.

The pastor can be of great help in dealing with this compulsiveness by urging the suicidal person to be more open to new relationships and situations. Calming their anxieties and urging them to be more trusting and dependent on others can also be of help. He or she can also urge them to be more open to the grace of God intervening in their life to support, sustain, and aid them. The pastor should urge them to let go of the collapsing order that leads to death and be open to another leading to life and hope.

Confused and constricted thought. Almost always, the suicidal are ambivalent about their decision for death, and this is not simply from the confused nature of the action, but also because they are prone to confused, chaotic, and irrational thinking. Because they frequently cannot think clearly, they lapse into despair and conclude there are no practical and possible solutions to their problems. They misunderstand their internal conflicts and the threats posed to them and believe they are in more danger from external threats than from themselves. There is a certain schizoid character to their thinking because they believe this act of extraordinary brutality and violence will bring them the rescue, peace, and security they desire. Because of this confusion, they suffer from severe ego-splitting and perceive that the one being killed is not their real and true self, but another self; they believe they must kill that other self in order to save their true self from the suffering, guilt, torment, and anxiety that they are experiencing. Reality has receded into the background, and their own fantasies have come to dominate. Their action is one of flight rather than of confrontation.

The suicidal person's confusion and ambivalence compromises their freedom and masks the subtle and controlling power of the forces that drive them into despair. The pastor can restore hope in the suicidal person by pointing out that their ambivalence about ending their life shows that they are not certain that death is the only option available and will bring what they desire. The subvoluntary character of their suicidal decision should be brought to light and should make it clear that they are being driven to their decision by subtle and powerful forces that confuse them and destroy their freedom. The pastor should lead them from this confusion and ambivalence by giving them options to suicide and showing them clearly the wrongfulness and destructiveness of self-killing.

The pastor can offer hope and life to the suicidal by bringing these dark and threatening forces to light, and enabling the suicidal person to assert their mastery over them. The minister can aid the suicidal by leading them to clearer thinking about suicide. The pastor should emphasize that their suicidal action shows they want help, attention, or escape from their problems, and should use this ambivalence to deepen their hope and diminish their desire for self-killing. The suicidal person's sense of their ability to cope with crises is usually very weak and they need to have their confidence and self-esteem revived. In their crises and conflicts, the pastor can remind them of Christ's love and grace for the suffering, despairing, alienated and weak, and assure them of the closeness and strength of Christ.

Self-centeredness and failed relationships. Most suicidal persons have experienced profoundly disappointing interpersonal relationships and have been unsuccessful in preserving enduring relationships, which is a primary source of despair for them. The suicidal have difficulties in relationships, are psychologically very brittle and can be quite demanding of others. The failure of these relationships has left them bitter, lonely, and disappointed to the point of despair. They tend to be impatient, self-centered, and have an exaggerated desire to control others. They use suicide as a way to strike back at those who have disappointed them; it is an act of revenge and hostility as much as it is an act of despair. The suicidal usually experience much spiritual pain because they feel lonely, neglected, or rejected by one whom they love deeply, and the pastor can give real hope by working to overcome this loneliness and rejection. The spiritual pain, anxiety, loneliness, guilt, and grief of the suicidal person can often be overcome by merely listening to them. They frequently make suicidal threats because of a sense of loneliness and abandonment, and helping to resolve these problems can often stop the threat. The suicidal person often feels much guilt because of their selfishness and lack of charity to others, for rather than giving themselves in service to others, they have used others or abandoned others in need, which causes them to lapse into despair at times. They feel guilty for having mistreated others, and the suicidal decision is often a flight from the guilt they feel from their past deeds. It is an act of egotism and flight from one's challenges that is uncharitable and inconsiderate of their interests. Suicide is the most extreme self-centered and attention-getting behavior imaginable, and the pastor should remind the suicidal person that charity is a better way of gaining attention.

The pastoral minister should focus on the cause of their difficulties in interpersonal relationships: their selfishness, unforgiving attitude, perfectionism, compulsiveness, and lack of charity. The pastor should urge the suicidal to regard others with greater charity, seek forgiveness for any wrongs they have done, and strive to treat others charitably. Insofar as suicide is an act of revenge, the minister should call the suicidal person to Christian love of enemy and forgiveness for any wrongs suffered. And as it is an act of despair flowing from disappointment and loneliness, the pastor can give hope by showing the suicidal person that they need to find God's forgiveness through the sacraments. The pastoral minister can be quite effective in helping the suicidal by reminding them how egotistical the suicidal act can be. It is the ultimate act of selfishness, and it leaves a welter of problems behind.

Alienation from conscience. The suicidal person is usually one who has suppressed the voice of conscience and has accepted suicide as a morally valid and legitimate response to their crises and sufferings. But conscience is a guide and beacon, and when its voice has been suppressed, those prone to suicide lose their moral direction and lapse into despair. Conscience does not deprive one of hope, but promotes and protects it, and by not listening to it, they are unable to find any direction or guidance at critical moments in their lives. Although they suffer a great deal from self-recrimination and guilt, they are often obstinate and unscrupulous. Suppressing their conscience not only allows them to justify suiciding, but also causes them to mistreat others. This in turn makes them feel isolated and abandoned. Silencing this voice, they can no longer protect themselves from despair since it cannot guide them in their difficulties.

The pastor can give hope to the suicidal by becoming their consciences for them and urging them to listen to the objections raised to self-killing. To suppress its voice is to ignore the best guide they have to protect and preserve themselves, and the pastor can give effective guidance by urging them to not strike unscrupulously at themselves in a suicidal act.

Depression. The suicidal commonly suffer from severe depression and they show many of its signs of dejection, anorexia, mood swings, sleep disorder, despondency, apathy, withdrawal, low tolerance for pain, agitation, severe feelings of hopelessness and helplessness, excessive demands and complaining, a strong need for attention, controlling and manipulating activity, exhaustion of physical and emotional resources, and a sense of a lack of support from one's friends and family. They are more likely to be involved with alcohol, or some other substance dependency, and will probably have more psychotic tendencies than others.

One can gain much insight into suicidal ruminations by seeing these as acts of desperate flight from pain, grief, and suffering from one who is exhausted and dispirited. Their depression creates in them mixed and conflicting emotions. They feel weak, and yet become exceptionally hostile. They can be exceedingly demanding of others, but are incapable of responding to the demands of others. They are highly stressed and feel deeply dejected, which causes them much confusion and excessive complaining. They are intensely antipathetic toward others, but demand the utmost sympathy for themselves, and when this does not come they have chronic feelings of despair, depression, and discouragement.

The suicidal feel intimidated by these forces of depression and despair, and the pastoral minister should firmly assert that Christ's grace, love, and forgiveness are more powerful than the forces that dampen their hope, spirit, and enthusiasm. This depression can often be countered by stressing that charity is a means to build bonds of unity and love with others. The pastor should also point out that the crisis of their depression can also be a result of a lack of faith in God's providence, for the depressed often do not seriously believe that God's grace and love are found through prayer and faith. The pastor should call these people to revitalize their lives of prayer, as their prayer lives have frequently deterioriated badly.

Conclusion

Dr. Pieter Admiraal noted in a television interview that in Holland lethal injections are often given by doctors while Catholic priests stand by watching and blessing the action, and he also noted, rather cynically, that he regarded these priests as little more than social workers.[49] This remark strongly suggests that the credibility and authenticity of the Christian ministry can be compromised by too eager an endorsement of suicide and too intimate an involvement in the suicides of patients. How pastoral ministers relate to those contemplating suicide is crucial, for the attitude they take could well determine whether or not these patients die by their own decision and whether or not they find compassion, encouragement, hope, and true peace in their decision to die.

Ordinarily bystanders are tempted to flee the suffering of the dying person because their condition and impending death reminds them of and draws them closer to their own suffering and dying. But Bradley Hanson has pointed out that suffering isolates one from others, and it is common for a dying person to want help coping with their sufferings and to receive encouragement; moreover, they do not usually desire to raise the topic of suicide.[50] What they seem to want is for another to suffer with them, enter into their suffering, anxiety, loss of control, fear, and darkness to accompany and guide them successfully through it. What gives comfort and hope to the dying and suffering is not just another showing sympathy or empathy, but their entering into the suffering of the other person and truly participating in it.

In Hanson's perspective, one who encourages or permits suicide is not a true friend of the suffering, but is merely another individual who refuses to truly share in the suffering of the person, and is another one who ultimately abandons the dying person. Hanson urges pastoral ministers to remain faithful to the suffering and dying of the person and not abandon them by urging or cooperating with their suicides. This is not to say that others must take on physical afflictions identical to those experienced by the person, but that they ought take their sufferings onto themselves in a personal and experiential manner.

While this is good, a better way of drawing the suicidal person out of their isolation is to urge them to draw closer to Christ and through faith, hope, and service, enter into a deeper union with others. This is what Christ did for us, taking our sufferings on himself, and is what we should do for others. The isolation of the suffering and dying person is best overcome by drawing them more fully into the Body of Christ through service, faith, and obedience. The suffering and dying person feels deeply isolated and cut off because of their illness, pain, or impending death. But relating through faith to Christ and the Christian community, one can overcome that deep-seated sense of isolation more fully than by merely listening to the words of a pastoral minister.

Those who advocate rational suicide propose a view of death that is not shared by most in Western society. While virtually all in our society view death as an evil to be avoided and the inflicting of death as solving nothing, advocates of suicide envision it as an act that saves us from the most devastating and trying personal problems and situations we can confront. Pastoral responsibility would demand that this romantic and illusory view of death be challenged by pastoral ministers. It requires ministers to recall the person to Christ's view of death, which is that it is an evil, and therefore is to be opposed and not embraced. The suicidal person might assert that their decision is actually a virtuous act of freedom and autonomy, but the pastor should gently and tactfully counter this by pointing out that suicide is submission to the forces of despair, depression, and fear.

It is to be hoped that the theological perspectives proposed in "Euthanasia and Pastoral Care" will not gain widespread acceptance, not only because they are contrary to the Gospel vision of love, but also because they pose a serious threat to the vulnerable and medically dependent. Approaching the causes of suicidal despair in the manner briefly described here is a more appropriately Christian response than that suggested by "Euthanasia and Pastoral Care," and more in accord with classical practice.

Notes

1. Dutch Reformed church, "Euthanasia and Pastoral Care" (Unpublished manuscript, February 1985).
2. Ibid., 4.
3. Ibid., 5.
4. Ibid., 6.
5. Ibid., 8.
6. Ibid., 12.
7. Ibid. "Death is being conquered. The narratives about Jesus show that God opposes sickness and death and chooses for a life that is worth living" (p. 12).
8. Ibid., 12. "It [suicide] can also be an indication that someone has consciously said farewell to life and confidently puts it [life] into the hands of God."
9. Ibid.
10. Ibid. "In the light of the Bible it is possible to regard the natural course of things (for instance an illness) as simply the will of God."
11. Ibid., 11.
12. Ibid., 12.
13. Ibid., 4.
14. Ibid., 5.
15. Ibid., 5.
16. Ibid., 9.
17. Ibid., 6.
18. Ibid., 17.
19. Ibid., 21-22.
20. Ibid., 6.

21. Ibid., 6. Also see p. 17. "The helper must make sure that he does not assume a moralistic attitude in the sense that he begins to project his own value pattern on the person asking for help."
22. Ibid., 12.
23. Ibid., 10.
24. Ibid.
25. Ibid., 9.
26. Ibid., 11.
27. Ibid., 21-22.
28. Ibid.
29. Ibid.
30. Ibid., 22.
31. Ibid.
32. Ibid., 22.
33. Ibid., 20-21.
34. Ibid.
35. Ibid., 21.
36. Ibid., 22.
37. Ibid., 22.
38. Ibid., 23.
39. Brown, J. H., Henteloff, P., Barakat, S., and Rowe, C. J., "Is it Normal for Terminally Ill Persons to Desire Death?" *American Journal of Psychiatry*, 143, 2 (February 1986): 208-11.
40. Fitzmeyer, J., *The Gospel According to Luke,* vol. 2 (New York: Doubleday, 1985), 1260-69.
41. Ibid.
42. Fitzmeyer, J., *The Gospel According to Luke,* vol. 1, 485-86.
43. Brown, R., *The Gospel According to John,* vol. 2 (New York: Doubleday, 1970), 953.
44. Ibid., vol. 1, 60-62.
45. Rahner, K., *Hearers of the Word,* Tr. Richards M., (New York: Herder & Herder, 1969), 155. Also see his other works: *Hearers of the Word,* (New York, Herder & Herder, 1968); "The Eucharist and Suffering," *Theological Investigations,* vol. 1 (New York: Herder & Herder, 1967), 161-71; "The Scandal of Death," *Theological Investigations,* vol. 7, 141-45; "On Christian Dying," *Theological Investigations,* vol. 7, 285-93; "Theological Considerations for the Moment of Death," *Theological Investigations,* vol. 11, 309-27; "Ideas for a Theology of Death," *Theological Investigations,* vol. 13, 169-89.
46. Rahner, K., "The Scandal of Death," *Theological Investigations,* vol. 7, 141-45; Rahner, K., "On Christian Dying," *Theological Investigations,* vol. 7, 285-393; Rahner, K., "Theological Considerations for the Moment of Death," *Theological Investigations,* vol. 11, 309-27; Rahner, K., "Ideas for a Theology of Death," *Theological Investigations,* vol. 13, 169-89.
47. Rahner, K., "Ideas for a Theology of Death," *Theological Investigations,* vol. 13, 181-82; Rahner, K., "On Christian Dying," *Theological Investigations,* vol. 7, 287.
48. Rahner, K., "On Christian Dying," *Theological Investigations,* vol. 7, 285-93.
49. "Nightline," ABC television, New York, 3 February 1987.
50. Hanson, B., "School of Suffering," *Dialogue*, 20 (Winter 1981): 39-45.

Index

B

C

D

E

F

M

N

O

P

Q

R

S

T

V

W

Y

Z